MYTHS AND LEGENDS
OF ANCIENT GREECE

MYTHS AND LEGENDS OF ANCIENT GREECE

Originally titled *Classic Myth and Legend*

A. R. HOPE MONCRIEFF

ILLUSTRATED

GRAMERCY BOOKS
NEW YORK • AVENEL

Originally published under the title
Classic Myth and Legend.

Publisher's Note: The text has been slightly altered for this edition,
but has not been abridged.

Foreword copyright © 1995 by Random House Value Publishing, Inc.
All rights reserved.

This edition is published by Gramercy Books,
distributed by Random House Value Publishing, Inc.,
40 Engelhard Avenue, Avenel, New Jersey 07001.

Printed and bound in the United States of America

Library of Congress Cataloging-in-Publication Data
Moncrieff, A. R. Hope (Ascott Robert Hope), 1846–1927.
[Classical myth and legend]
Myths and legends of ancient Greece / A. R. Hope Moncrieff.
p. cm.
Originally published: New York: W. H. Wise & Co., 1934.
Includes index.
ISBN 0–517–11861–0
1. Mythology, Classical. I. Title
BL721.M6 1995
292.1'3—dc20   94–39818
                                                                CIP

8 7 6 5 4 3 2 1

CONTENTS

v

CONTENTS

LIST OF COLOR ILLUSTRATIONS

FOREWORD

Although they were sacred to a culture that flourished about twenty-five hundred years ago, the myths of ancient Greece were created around themes of universal significance. They have much to say about the relationship between the human and the divine, the purpose of life, and the awesome, inevitable power of fate. These legends have such power that through the ages they have strongly influenced and inspired artists and writers. As a result, it is impossible to fully appreciate many of the great works of Western culture without a knowledge of the mythology of the classical world.

In the myths of ancient Greece, the gods frequently choose sides in earthly disputes and personal relationships; they may aid or punish mortals, and the results are often considered explanations of the natural world or of human behavior. The story of Persephone and Demeter, for instance, explains the passage of the seasons by relating how a young girl, Persephone, is abducted by the god of death. Her mother, Demeter, grieves until she finds a way to retrieve her daughter from the Underworld for part of the year, and the earth itself suffers death and rebirth in sympathy with her. In the legend of Echo and Narcissus, the goddess Hera punishes the nymph Echo for talking too much by making it impossible for her to speak first or to be silent when anyone else is speaking. The handsome youth Narcissus rejects Echo's affection. As punishment Aphrodite, the goddess of love, fills him with a passion for his own reflection. The image in the water is, of course, ever elusive, and Narcissus pines away until all that is left is the flower that bears his name. Echo, too, wastes away from grief, until only her voice remains.

To the ancient Greeks, hubris—the desire to be too much like the gods—was a great vice, and many of these stories warn of the danger of excessive pride. Although Bellerophon, for example, is a mighty warrior who destroys the fire-breathing monster Chimaera and conquers the Amazons, when he tries to fly his winged horse Pegasus to heaven, Zeus, the principal god, sends a gadfly to disorient the horse, and Bellerophon falls to his doom. In another legend, Niobe, the wife of Amphion of Thebes, compares herself to Leto, the mistress of Zeus, by boasting of her twelve children. In retaliation, Leto's two children, Apollo and Artemis, slay all of Niobe's sons and daughters.

The ancient Greek myths and legends in this collection are all good yarns. In these timeless tales of high melodrama, fantastic adventure, and stark tragedy you will meet such characters as the avaricious King Midas, the courageous Jason, the treacherous Circe, and the murderous Medea. And there is enough of romantic love, loyalty, betrayal, vengeance, heroism, murder, lust, and greed in these stories to satisfy even the most avid devotee of television or movies.

Throughout the centuries and into our own time, the Greek legends have inspired endless variations on their themes and characters. Interest in the ancient myths blossomed during the Renaissance: Botticelli's painting *The Birth of Venus* pictures the birth from the sea of the goddess—the Greek Aphrodite— to symbolize the spiritual values of fifteenth-century Florence. The play-within-a-play in Shakespeare's *A Midsummer Night's Dream* takes place at the court of the legendary Athenian king Theseus and retells the fable of Pyramus and Thisbe—whose frustrated love and double suicide prefigure those in *Romeo and*

Juliet. In the nineteenth century, the great English poet Alfred, Lord Tennyson wrote three important poems based on classical myths, "Tithonus," "The Lotos-Eaters," and "Ulysses."

In modern times, George Bernard Shaw based his play *Pygmalion* on the Greek myth of the sculptor who created his own beloved; that now-familiar tale of a cockney flower girl transformed into a lady by a middle-aged linguistics professor later became the famous Lerner and Loewe musical *My Fair Lady.* James Joyce, when he created his novel *Ulysses,* about one man's day in Dublin, drew on the *Odyssey,* Homer's epic poem that chronicles the adventures of the Greek hero Odysseus. French directors Jean Cocteau and Marcel Camus each made haunting films based on the Greek myth of Orpheus and Eurydice, retelling the legend of a young man who journeys to the Underworld to bring his beloved back to life. And psychoanalysis pioneer Sigmund Freud named his theory of the Oedipus complex—the unconscious possessive feelings of a boy for his mother—after the Greek legend of Oedipus, the king of Thebes who, unaware of their identities, kills his father and marries his mother.

Whether they are used as the basis for new artistic works, or are read in their original forms, these ancient stories continue to enchant, inspire, and instruct. In *Myths and Legends of Ancient Greece,* A. R. Hope Moncrieff has not only superbly retold the tales, but has also provided a lengthy and informative Introduction to these wise and wonderful stories.

GEORGE PALMER BLAKE

New York
1995

PREFACE TO THE FIRST EDITION

This volume deals with the famous legendary fictions of Ancient Greece, that have furnished so many themes and allusions to modern authors. The origin of those stories and the nature of their mythological or dubiously historical personages are dealt with in an Introduction which, it is hoped, will not too much try the reader's patience. The stories themselves are presented in simple outline, illustrated here and there by purple passages from our own poets; and, at the end, it has seemed best to give a few legends in the shape of the noble verse that has embalmed them for us.

One difficulty requires to be got over by way of compromise. In our time the tendency is to return to the Greek names of gods and heroes who came to be better known under a Latinized disguise during the dark ages that copied the literature of Rome while neglecting that of Greece. As a rule, then, transliterated Greek names have been used; yet in some cases those characters are so familiar in another spelling, that it seems pedantry to call Hercules *Heracles*, and Pollux *Polydeuces*, or wholly to proscribe such current names as *Bacchus* and *Cupid*. If it comes to that, we must remember that the *Hellenes* knew themselves as *Greeks* no more than the Germans accept our *alias* for their *Deutsch* nationality. Not a few classic names, indeed, have become so well naturalized among us that we talk glibly enough of *tantalizing*, of a *rhadamanthine* judgment, of *bacchanalian* revels, of *herculean* labours, as of sons of Mars and smiles of Venus. Yet classic names and attributes are sometimes handled with more confidence than discrimination: it is not unusual, for instance, to catch hasty journalists pouring scorn upon the "Cassandras" of the opposite party, in manifest ignorance how poor Cassandra's prophecies came too true, to the undoing of those who would not mind them.

"Naught so tedious as a twice-told tale", remarked one eminent hero of ancient fiction; but these stories, though so often told, in such varied forms, may still bear retelling for readers unacquainted with the original versions.

MYTHS AND LEGENDS
OF ANCIENT GREECE

INTRODUCTION

The Growth of Myths

In the childhood of our world the myth-making faculty seems so much matter of course that the Greek word μῦθος, primarily meaning a word or speech, took on its special sense as work of fancy. Ignorant minds are moved by fear and wonder to interpret their experience in parables, the personages of which will be shadowy or misty images of their own nature, distorted beyond mere humanity and released from the limitations of earthly life. At the early stage of mental development passed through by each man, as by his kind, religion, law, and poetry go hand in hand, sanctioning a love of personification expressed for our children by such ideas as "Father Christmas", the "Man in the Moon", or the "Land of Nod". These playful myths are modified to edification by considerate elders; but from what tales will be hailed as satisfactory in the best-regulated nurseries we can guess how wild imaginations, without probability or proportion, may commend themselves to savage peoples whose growing perceptions can elaborate so rude sketches into a mythology.

In an age of comparative enlightenment such imaginations too long lay despised for nursery fables, to be forgotten in the schoolroom; but the new science of

folklore has put them in their true place as important
lessons in the history of the human mind. The first
thing that strikes a student of them is the resemblances
and coincidences found in "old wives' tales" all over
the world, obscured but not hidden under the differences
of colouring thrown upon them by diversity of custom
and environment. Two explanations of such marks of
identity have been put forward. It may be that these
stories took their outline in one cradle of races, which
were afterwards so widely separated as to have lost trace
of their origin. Or, can it be in the nature of man that,
under varying climes and conditions, he is apt to hit
upon similar explanations of the phenomena everywhere
threatening and upholding his life?

"The same heart beats in every human breast."

The question between these theories is complicated
by the consideration of migrations and conquests that all
along have gone to mix blood and thought. At one time
a Persian child may have learned its first notions from
a Mongol slave-nurse; and thousands of years ago the
rape of a Helen or the selling of a Joseph into Egypt
were everyday experiences all over the world. It is easy
to see how the races round the Mediterranean came to
share one another's legends and superstitions. But it
seems much more of a puzzle when we find hints of
like imaginations rooted in Australia, that through all
historic time has been cut off from other homes of man,
and in America, where for ages the human mind seems
to have had its own independent development from
savagery.

Non nostrum tantas componere lites, when ethnologists
are not yet at one on such questions. Nor need we
here go into controversies that have divided rival schools

of folklore students, the deepest of them still a matter of enquiry. "I have changed my views repeatedly, and I have resolved to change them again with every change of the evidence", says Dr. J. G. Frazer, confessing how the candid enquirer must play the chameleon upon the shifting colours of this freshly-turned-up ground. He is here speaking of totemism, meaning a special relation people believe themselves to bear to some fetish object or ancestral beast. The word *totem* is little more than a century old in our language, and it was only in our time that, from its being taken as the crest of an Indian clan, it has been promoted to rank as an index of primitive customs over the world, specially significant in connection with the law of exogamy that forbade marriage between sons and daughters of the same totem. Scholars have now had their eyes opened to once-neglected hints of totemism in ancient records; and Dr. Frazer has lately published four weighty volumes on a subject which to writers like Fenimore Cooper supplied picturesque features for fiction, till L. H. Morgan in his *League of the Iroquois* and J. F. M'Lennan in his *Primitive Marriage* began to point out the important bearings of what had seemed a mere primitive heraldry.

Some commentators on folklore are suspected of making too much of totemism as a key of interpretation. Similarly, in the last generation the theory was pushed too far that found a comprehensive formula for myths in the visible changes of the sky and the seasons. The blood-red giant whose strength declines after midday might well be the sun; the hero who sets out so briskly in the fresh dawn of life may find his career clouded by the mists of evening; the moon and the stars too had stories of their own, embroidered by fancy upon the background of night. This way of accounting for myths,

helped out by dubious etymologies, was boldly extended
till the four-and-twenty blackbirds baked in a pie were
like to become in grave eyes the hours of day and
night, and the maid hanging out clothes in the garden
was dealing with clouds when the frost bit her nose.
The sun-myth school, taught in Britain by Max Müller
and the Rev. Sir G. W. Cox, has now suffered eclipse.[1]
But there can, of course, be no doubt that the sun
and moon, the changes of weather and seasons, the
havoc of storms, floods, and droughts, played a great
part in suggesting the personages and scenery of nascent
imagination.

Some students, flying from the Scylla of universal
sun-worship, appear drawn to the Charybdis of looking
on the growth of vegetable life as a main source of
mythology, one indeed fruitful in hints for marvel.
Such superstitions as the "corn baby", still lingering
among our peasantry in half-jocular respect, such rites
as those of our nearly obsolete "Jack in the Green",
are survivals of fancies once taken very seriously, as
they still are in many parts of the world.   From its
most distant corners, missionaries, explorers, traders,
renegade white men, and other not always competent
witnesses, go on adding to the list of traditions, taboos,
sacrifices, charms, divinations, and other savage notions
and customs ; thus we have a growing heap of evidence
to be sifted, tested, and compared by scholars seeking
some consistent theory, a question that would not greatly
trouble the original shapers of myth and legend.

So much has been hinted to show how folklorists
are still at work on their foundations.   Enough for us

---

[1] The Dublin University publication *Kottabos* had a famous skit on this school,
adapting his own arguments to prove Max Müller himself a mere sun-myth!

to know primitive man as prone to wonder, to be moved by desires and fears "as old at once and new as nature's self", to look on all he does not understand as mystery, then to express his fears, aspirations, and amazement in rude fables, which, shaped by priests and poets with more or less conscious purpose, soon grew to be at once phases of faith and essays in science. Dim-sighted fancies they were, misled by refractions and shadows, yet gropings after truth, that, when lit by the dawn of knowledge and culture, might lose much of their original grossness, and be refined to inspiring systems of religion. The day is gone by when we could complacently look down on all paganism as a dead-level of ignorant idolatry and deceitful priestcraft.

> " Each form of worship that hath swayed
> The life of man, and given it to grasp
> The master-key of knowledge, reverence,
> Enfolds some germ of goodness and of right ;
> Else never had the eager soul which loathes
> The slothful down of pampered ignorance
> Found in it even a moment's fitful rest."

It is not difficult to see how ancient Greece gave a soil for the rich crop of religious imaginations that, embalmed by genius and artistic skill, have passed into the literature of the world, while kindred beliefs of other lands wither in oblivion or are preserved only as curious specimens in the collections of ethnology. That sea-broken peninsula, set about with islands which made stepping-stones to the mainland shores of the eastern Mediterranean, was from very early times a meeting-place of different races that here blended their stock of ideas as well as their blood. The autochthonous inhabitants, Pelasgians, or whoever they were, could not fail to be touched by hostile and commercial relations with the seaboard states of Asia and Africa, far before them in culture. Since the beginning of this century, it has been made clear that Crete was from about B.C. 3000 a strong sea-power of comparative civilization. The horizon of Greek history has been widened by the digging up of the Mycenæan treasures in the north-east of the Peloponnesus, where a new kingdom rose to greatness as that of Crete fell into decay. Then this horizon becomes clouded by swarms of Aryan invaders or immigrants pushing from the north, as their kinsmen descended upon Hindustan through the Himalayan passes, and as the Goths afterwards overran the other peninsulas of Europe. Thus divers influences from north and south met within the narrow bounds of Greece, whence they soon flowed back upon Asia in the prosperous Ionian and other colonies that kept their motherland in touch with the dreamy East, whose own developed superstitions, in turn, kept infiltrating into the minds of a race all along ready to absorb a variety of religious ideas.

There were repeated waves of Aryan immigration, the strongest of them the Achæan and the Dorian that fixed their main settlements respectively in the northern and southern part of this almost sundered land. The conquered and displaced tribes would not be exterminated, but to a large extent became absorbed among the invaders, if they were unable to preserve their independence penned up in rugged mountain fastnesses, as appears to have been the case in Arcadia, as was certainly the case with Dravidian stocks in India, and with the much-mixed Celts of our own Highlands. So here was a Medea's cauldron of flesh and blood, a hodge-podge which would boil briskly on the fires of time till there emerged a new national consciousness that by what seems accident took for itself the general names of

Hellas and Hellenes, then had to use its faculty for story-telling by inventing a fabulous Hellen as ancestor.

Myth-making had naturally thriven among this jumble of clashing races and blending superstitions. Nor was the Grecian mind thus evolved to be shut up within itself. The new seaboard states, like the old ones, had relations of commerce with other shores, that soon became relations of conquest. Pressed for room in their narrow and not over-fertile bounds, the enterprising Greeks swarmed out into colonies upon the Black Sea, and round half the Mediterranean. The south of Italy came to be known as *Magna Grecia*, where the chance of a tribe of *Graii* coming in contact with the Romans fixed on the whole race the Latinized name of Greeks, by which they have been best known to the modern world, as in some parts of Asia all Christians came to be "Franks", and among some American Indian tribes the colonists in general were "Boston men". Into Italy these intruders brought their religious notions to be grafted on often kindred roots already fixed in the soil by common ancestors, strayed from far and wide. Thus the Latin mythology readily adopted variants of the Hellenic forms, more clearly shaped by the influence of Greek literature upon conquering Rome. And in Asia the Greek mind not only lent but borrowed new inspirations that went to make its religion singularly rich in ideas to be shaped afresh by a love of personification and a sense for the beauty of life. Later on was to come a more fruitful union between the clear-eyed genius of Hellenism and the sterner Hebraic conscience. The myths of Greek paganism themselves had been cross-bred from mingling stocks, which might belong to sundered families of human thought and speech.

It is, of course, not to be supposed that any such mythology sprang into the world full-grown, as Minerva from the head of Jove. Its embryo forms are hidden from us in a remote past, unless we can catch them reflected in the fables of others at a stage of development passed through by forgotten ancestors of Homer and Pindar. The theophany of Olympus was an obscure and slow accretion; and to the end the materials of Greek faith remained imperfectly fused. Even in the Christian era time-honoured "stocks and stones" were worshipped with more fervour than the statues of famous deities. The "sweetness and light" supposed to characterize Greek conceptions came slowly to days of art and study, perhaps tinged mainly by the cultured life of cities, while rude Arcadians and the like clung to their old bogeydom. The earliest objects of adoration, of propitiation rather, appear everywhere to have been shapes of dread and horror, begetting imaginary monsters, "Gorgons and Hydras and Chimæras dire". It is a world-wide experience that such old superstitions persist through ages of higher faith, long after their origin has been forgotten. At this day there are peasants in Britain who profess to have advanced beyond the faith of Rome or of Anglicanism, yet unwittingly practise pagan rites of sun-worship, and with maimed observance keep the feasts of banished idols, themselves lingering unsuspected here and there, as in the shape of ugly obelisks approved among believers zealous to proscribe the sign of the Cross.

The serpent, the owl, and other animals represented as attendant on the Olympian gods were no doubt older than themselves, hallowed as totems long before Zeus took shape, still to pursue his earthly amours in such suggestive forms as a bull's or a swan's. An uncanny creature like the snake makes a very early object of reverence or abhorrence which it is long in losing. Even in Scotland, where more deadly snakes than adders are unknown, people will not eat an eel; and there is a lingering prejudice against pork, perhaps coming down from days when the pig was in such honour here as to name mountains and islands. In Greece, serpents were revered by the ignorant later than Lucian's day, whose exposure of the false prophet Alexander shows us a tame snake as chief " property " of that impostor's hocus-pocus.

Superstition would not so readily try her " prentice hand on man ". Early deities, after growing out of the totem stage, are apt to take female forms, as conceived in a matriarchal state of society, while rude morals exalt the certain mother above the dubious father of her children. Later, when the male has assumed his place as head or tyrant of the family, with woman for his drudge, he makes a god rather in the image of his own sex. The Cretan state seen flourishing from about B.C. 3000 appears to have had a female fertilizing spirit for its chief divinity, along with a special regard for the bulls that made a valuable asset to tribal wealth. Similar conceptions prevailed on the Eastern shores whence Greece drew the first seeds of culture. The Aryan invaders from the north must have brought with them the notion of a father in heaven, the shining *Dyaus*, whose name has passed into so many tongues. The marriage of this sky-god with the earth-spirit begot that brood of deities, for whom dominions could be found in the air, the earth, the sea, and the dark underworld, and who were fabled to mix their immortal blood with that of the national or local heroes making a link between god and man.

The Greek Pantheon was fortunate in finding more than one *vates sacer*, for want of whom so many gods as well as heroes have been buried in oblivion. Homer and Hesiod fixed for us the religious ideas obtaining nearly a thousand years before our era; and both of them mention bards who must have been handling the same theme for generations. The theogony of Hesiod, as Mr. Andrew Lang says, was for Greek youth what the catechisms of our own Churches are for us, presenting a formal view of Greek articles of faith. The title of "Greek Bible" has been given to the poems of Homer, which, whoever wrote them, appear to be earlier than Hesiod in their first form; yet it is remarkable that they put the gods in a loftier light, ignoring much of the grossness found in later stories; and this though the poet seems to be consciously archaizing, as when he sets his heroes in the age of bronze weapons, but here and there lets out that iron was familiar to his time. The *Odyssey*, too, evinces some more elevated conceptions and other manners than the *Iliad*, which have been variously explained as signs of a later date or of a separate origin. The *Iliad*, for example, shows the Oriental contempt of dogs as prowling scavengers; while in the *Odyssey* they are fierce but faithful guardians of a flock, and one hound, lit up to fame by a ray of sympathetic feeling, bears a name, Argos, such as in the *Iliad* is attributed to the horses of Achilles. All those questions as to Homeric personality, authenticity, date, and origin on the Ionian shores of Asia or elsewhere, must be passed over lightly here. There may have been one great poet whose mind made a refining crucible for the ore of legend; but scholars now rather incline to take Homer as no more real than his heroes —themselves perhaps half-real—his name covering a

long process of welding together old fables and traditions into a final form where imperfect fusion is betrayed by careless inconsistencies; and the evolved moral
ideas that hint a later date may perhaps have belonged
to some false dawn of thought, clouded over by recurrent
barbarism.

In those famous poems the Pantheon appears not
quite complete; but all its chief members have taken
their place, superseding an older generation of gods,
whose history was less edifying. Local cults, no doubt,
went on amalgamating, also perhaps arising afresh, and
in some cases spreading far, as when Athene, the patron
goddess of Athens, became reverenced over Greece,
and across the Adriatic was transformed into the Latin
Minerva. There were waves of foreign influence, like
the enthusiasm of the worship of Bacchus introduced
with the culture of the vine, whereas honey had made
the nectar of the old gods. The Orphic spirit in Greek
religion is a more mysterious infusion. It has been
supposed that Orpheus was a real teacher, who sought
to raise men's minds upon a cloud of mystic practices
and to refine superstition into a rule of nobler life.
Under his name, at all events, a movement of religious
zeal spread over the Hellenic world, probably allied
with the new doctrines of Pythagoras as to life after
death, marking one tendency of the Greek mind, while
another was manifested in the Ionian philosophers who
would have turned attention rather on rationalistic enquiries into the nature of matter and its phenomena.

About the middle of the millennium before Christ,
we come into the clearer light of Greece's great days,
when its hurling back of the Persian hosts called forth
a stronger sentiment of national life, and mental culture
went hand in hand with martial pride. A rapid develop-

ment of intellectual life seems marked by the first solid
history, the work of Thucydides, coming close upon
the legendary tales of Herodotus. Now Phidias almost
breathes life into the statues of the gods; Pericles
adorns their temples, whose priests, and the craftsmen
to whom those shrines bring no small gain, are concerned to keep up the old beliefs; but moralists are fain
to shake their heads over barbarous legends which the
great Athenian dramatists shape into statuesque tableaux
and choruses; while philosophy seems hard put to it in
reconciling them with new conceptions of duty and piety.
The philosophic mind, indeed, sublimating forms into
ideas, finds much to apologize for and to explain away
in the popular Pantheon, set in a new light by comparison with the gods of other lands. Pythagoras saw
Hesiod bound to a pillar in Hades as punishment for the
lies he had told about the gods; Plato was for banish-
ing the fabling poets from his ideal state. To Homer
himself, it will be remembered, Olympus furnished the
most comic scenes of his story. Later poets show consciousness that their favourite themes need a good deal
of " editing ", such as Homer, too, no doubt did in his
day according to its lights. Euripides raised applause
by dealing boldly with unedifying stories of the gods,
when yet the sophist Protagoras was prosecuted for
professing himself an agnostic as to their very existence. Plato suggests nobler myths of creation, and
purgatorial emendations on the incredible torments of
Hades: he may still speak of gods, but what he has in
his mind's eye is the archetypal godlike. More and
more, thinking men come to look on the divine as a
potency or tendency rather than a batch of personalities,
while the vulgar cling to old superstitions or even adopt
new ones with the eclectic spasms of decadence we see

at work among some of ourselves, who give up their orthodox faith to itch after exotic theosophies and wonder-workings.

About a century before our era, Apollodorus wrote in stolid prose a history of godlike and heroic doings, which has made *mémoires pour servir* for many more-spirited writers. Theocritus and other poets of a later age give a shapely turn to the old legends, as did Ovid in his *Metamorphoses*, that handed them down to the mediæval world. Prose writers like Apuleius, too, try their hand at fairy tales. Then, in the second century after Christ, comes a Lucian to assail Olympus with peals of laughter, and to caricature the absurd marvels of mythology. It is harder for us to understand the mental attitude of Pausanias, who, in the same century, made an alternately credulous and critical survey of the monuments of his ancestral superstition. By this time the wisest pagans were more or less unconsciously borrowing from Christianity, while early Christian teachers might take classic legends as texts for denouncing the works of the devil, but would not be concerned to put these stories in the best light. Purer morals brought new tests to bear. Modern moralists and poets are bound to pass lightly over the coarsenesses of a mythology that has offered many subjects for edifying discourse and enhancement by graceful fancy. Our artists, too, have touched up some of those time-worn myths, bringing out here a feature, and there covering up a fault, to fit in with their rules of composition or canons of the becoming.

So stands in what might be called ruinous repair that broken temple of the Grecian mind which, ages after it has seen a devout worshipper, makes one of the grandest monuments of the human instinct bidding—

"Build thee more stately mansions, O my soul,
  As the swift seasons roll!
  Leave thy low-vaulted past!
  Let each new temple, loftier than the last,
  Shut thee from heaven with a dome more vast,
  Till thou at length art free,
  Leaving thine outgrown shell by life's unresting sea!"

Theogony and Cosmogony

"The cosmogony or creation of the world has puzzled philosophers of all ages", pronounced the Vicar of Wakefield's learned acquaintance; but ancient poets have been readier with explanations, not wholly consistent. The books that reach us under the name of Hesiod set forth a formal series of conceptions, to a great extent incidentally borne out by Homer. The protoplasm of all things was Chaos, where Love soon began to stir and to call forth reproductive shapes. Night brought forth Day; Earth, besides her brood of mountains and seas, was the parent of the sky, that easily passed into a personage, Uranus, whose marriage with Gæa, or Gē, another allegory of the earth, founded a huge family of Titans, Cyclopes, and the like gigantic beings.

This prologue presents a rather misty scene, but the stage is now set for an historical drama in which the dynasty of the gods shows to disadvantage by quarrels between father and son more bitter than those of our eighteenth-century Georges. Uranus hated his monstrous progeny so much that he imprisoned them in a cave, and thereby drove Gæa to a treasonable plot, carried out by her youngest son Cronos (Saturn). Armed with a sharp sickle, he attacked and shamefully mutilated his father, from whose blood sprang fresh monsters. Here Hesiod breaks the main thread of his story to record the birth of Aphrodite from the sea, also the incarnation of the Fates, along with abstractions such as Necessity, Strife, Toil, and many of the other characters to figure in mythological romance.

We come back to the reign of Cronos, paired with his sister Rhea, who afterwards as Cybele became venerated as mother of the gods, representing the matriarchally conceived deity who was long supreme on the adjacent coasts of Asia. Her husband turned out a not less ruthless tyrant than his father. Warned that he should be dethroned by one of his own children, he made a practice of swallowing them at birth. The family thus suppressed were three sisters, Hestia, Demeter, and Hera, followed by three brothers, Pluto, Poseidon, and Zeus. He who was to be the heir is the youngest in Hesiod, like his father before him; but elsewhere Zeus is represented as the eldest son. Rhea, like her mother, was naturally ill-pleased by such treatment of her offspring; and when it came to the birth of Zeus, she played a trick upon the unnatural father by wrapping a stone in swaddling clothes, which he unsuspiciously swallowed, while the babe was smuggled off to be brought up in a cave on Mount Dicte in Crete. There reared to manhood, the young god fulfilled his destiny by coming back to dethrone Cronos, forcing him also to disgorge his brothers and sisters along with the stone representing himself, long treasured as a relic at the shrine of Pytho on Mount Parnassus, afterwards more famous as the oracle of Delphi.

The reign of Zeus was soon marked by civil war. He had released his gigantic uncles from their confinement; and a faction of Titans ill rewarded him by raising insurrection on behalf of Cronos. The ten years' conflict of Titans and gods is a famous episode, that

suggested to Milton his conception of the battle with
fallen angels. The scene of the struggle was imagined
as the mountains of Thessaly, where Olympus made
the fastness of the gods, while the Titans occupied the
Othrys range to the south, and were fabled to have piled
its summits on one another in their attempt to scale
heaven, but came to be beaten back by the thunderbolts
of Zeus, on whose side fought the hundred-handed giant
Briareus, the Cyclopes, and other monstrous warriors.
Finally the rebels were conquered and driven down to
confinement in Tartarus.

Zeus, now established as sovereign, gave to his
brothers, Poseidon and Pluto, the kingdoms of the sea
and of the dark underworld, while he kept earth and
heaven as his own dominion. But not yet could he reign
in peace. Fresh rebellion broke out under Typhon, a
hundred-headed monster begotten by Gæa and Tartarus;
then came another insurrection of giants ; so not for
long, Typhon being at last imprisoned under the burning
mass of Mount Etna, were the gods free to dwell at
ease beside their nectar ; and henceforth the history of
Olympus becomes rather a scandalous chronicle of
despotism tempered by intrigues.

From heaven we turn to earth, the early story of
which seems more edifying. Iapetus, brother of Cronos,
had four sons, two of whom took part with the rebellious
Titans, one being Atlas, punished by having for ever to
hold up on his shoulders the vault of the sky, or the
earth itself, as his doom came to be more easily pictured
in an illustration made familiar in the frontispiece to
early collections of maps, hence christened by his name.
His brother Prometheus fought for Olympus, yet later
incurred the anger of Zeus. While man is sometimes
spoken of as autochthonous, generated from the soil,

one story makes Prometheus his creator, who kneaded him of clay in the image of the gods, shaping his body to look up to heaven instead of down upon earth, and endowing him with the best of the qualities distributed by his brother Epimetheus among mere animals. At all events, Prometheus (Forethought) figures as the patron and champion of man, on whose behalf he stole away from heaven the gift of fire, grudged by Zeus, and in a hollow reed brought it down to be treasured on earth. The angry king of Olympus punished his bold vassal by fettering him on a cliff of the Caucasus for thirty thousand years, daily tormented by an eagle tearing at his liver.

Hesiod has to add a more grotesque offence given by Prometheus to the lord of heaven. Sacrificing an ox, he made two parcels of its flesh, one chiefly consisting of the bones covered with a slight layer of fat under the hide, then invited Zeus to choose one for himself; and though the god saw through the trick, none the less he held himself for insulted, and took this excuse to refuse the gift of fire, which then had to be filched by man's presumptuous friend.

To balance the irrevocable boon of fire, Zeus gave man a curse in the shape of that scapegoat on which early priests and poets so readily load the sins of our race. Woman was created and sent down to earth by the hands of Epimetheus (Afterthought).[1] The name Pandora denotes how she was endowed by the gods with beauty and accomplishments, instructed and dressed by Athene, while Hermes bestowed on her artful wiles and Aphrodite seductive charms. As outfit, she brought a box filled

---

[1] Plato relates a queer myth that man was originally created in a round shape, with eight limbs, and that, to abate his pride, Zeus cut him in two, dividing the race into male and female halves.

with plagues and vices, which she was forbidden to open;
but female curiosity was already as strong as in the days
of Bluebeard : she raised the lid, and out flew the germs
of widespread suffering for mankind.   When she shut it
up too late, only Hope remained at the bottom of the
fatal casket to be a balm for all those woes.

Consistency seems too much to expect of poets, and
from Pandora Hesiod goes on to give another history
of man, afterwards made more familiar by Ovid.   Our
men of science tell us how we must have risen from a
low estate through successive ages of stone tools and
weapons, improved by the use of metals, hammering out
more and more elaborate arts.   The poetic mind reverses
this progress, always looking back fondly on a golden
dawn of innocence and happiness, from which man fell
to the coarse realities of his present life.   The classical
age of gold was under Saturn, when the denizens of earth
had no need to envy Olympus.

> " Like gods they lived, with calm untroubled mind,
>   Free from the toil and anguish of our kind:
>   Nor e'er decrepit age mis-shaped their frame,
>   The hand's, the foot's proportions, still the same.
>   Pleased with earth's unbought feasts, all ills removed,
>   Wealthy in flocks, and of the bless'd beloved,
>   Death as a slumber pressed their eyelids down;
>   All nature's common blessings were their own;
>   The life-bestowing tilth its fruitage bore,
>   A full, spontaneous and ungrudging store:
>   They with abundant goods, mid quiet lands,
>   All willing shared the gatherings of their hands."

>   Hesiod's *Works and Days* (Elton's translation).

Next came the Silver Age, in which man became less
pious and less blessed, incurring the anger of the gods,
who now sent scorching winds and nipping frosts to blight
that early Eden.   In the Brazen Age that succeeded,

men took to fighting among themselves. Between this
and the more degenerate Iron Age from which he is
looking back, Hesiod inserts an Heroic Age, when Zeus
restored some of man's pristine virtue to carry him
through the great Trojan war and other semi-mytho-
logical exploits of early Greek history. Ovid, not so
much concerned with this period, reduces the ages from
five to four, going straight on from the Brazen to the
Iron Age, a change that has its basis of fact in the
gradual substitution of iron for bronze weapons. The
Roman poet's time gave him too plain a picture of human
depravity.

> " Enfranchised wickedness dominion hath,
> And puts to flight truth, modesty and faith:
> Fraud and deceit, and treachery and greed,
> And souls that covet others' good succeed:
> The sailor spreads the sail on seas unknown;
> From mountain slopes the patriarch trees fall down,
> Supinely fall, and bound the wave upon;
> And land which common was as air or sun,
> Man metes and measures, marks and calls his own.
> But not content to reap agrestan stores,
> He delves below, and Stygian gloom explores.
> Metallic ores—earth's secret heart within—
> He drags to light, provocatives to sin:
> The noxious iron, more pernicious gold,
> Parents of war and blood and deaths untold.
> Man lived by rapine: thresholds lost their awe,
> Nor safety gave to guest or son-in-law:
> Fraternal love was rare, and murders rife
> Through nuptial infidelity and strife:
> The step-dame culled the lurid aconites,
> The son conspired against parental rights:
> Prostrate was piety."
>
> Ovid's *Metamorphoses* (Rose's translation).

So crying grew the sins of mankind that Zeus saw
well to destroy the rebellious race. He who might have

tried the experiment of setting a better example, at first
was minded to use his celestial artillery, but feared to set
the heavens on fire as well as the earth : immortals living
in such glass houses could not safely throw thunderbolts.
So he sent a deluge that is curiously analogous to our
Bible story.　The fountains of the sky were opened by
a strong south wind ; the deep, too, was stirred to wrath
by the trident of Poseidon, called to his brother's aid ;
all the earth became submerged, so that fish swam in the
highest branches among the nests of birds, and the most
savage beasts of prey in vain huddled together seeking
flight from a common fate.

The few men who could escape that flood perished
by famine, all but one dutiful pair, able to find refuge
on the last spot of dry land at the head of Mount
Parnassus.　These were Deucalion, son of Prometheus,
and Pyrrha, daughter of Epimetheus.　When the waters
subsided under a north wind, they descended upon the
general wreck, and tearfully sought counsel at a ruined
altar of Themis, Titan-daughter of Uranus and consort
of Zeus.　There a dark oracle bade them veil their faces,
ungird their garments, and throw behind them the bones
of their mother.　The pious Pyrrha shrank from such
sacrilege ; but Deucalion rightly guessed the riddle as
meaning the bones of their mother earth.　Obeying the
oracle, they threw stones behind them that, taking human
form like statues, began to breathe with life, turned into
men and women according as they came from the hand
of Deucalion or of Pyrrha.　So arose a new breed of
humanity that, whatever its other qualities, had at least
the virtue of hardness and endurance to bear its lot.

The race thus re-created spread over the *orbis terrarum*,
taken to be not a globe but a round flat, environed on all
sides by the boundless river Oceanus, in which stars and

sun had their birth or setting. This disk was divided
lengthwise by the broken line of the Mediterranean con-
tinued into the Euxine, an idea of which we have some
trace in our use of *latitude* and *longitude*. To the north
of this chasm Greece was fringed by Illyrians, Thracians,
and other semi-barbarous folk, shading off into wilder
Scythians and Sarmatians, beyond whom lay dark-dwell-
ing Cimmerians, and still farther the fabulous Hyperboreans were understood to enjoy perpetual sunshine and
bliss given them by ignorance; or perhaps we have here
a hint of some glimpse of the far northern summer
with its midnight sun. Far to the south, the " blameless" Ethiopians were credited with some similar im-
munities ; hence, too, came vague reports of pygmies
who in our time have taken shape of flesh and blood;
the shores of Africa were inhabited by more familiar
races, while impassable deserts and mountains naturally
made homes for giants and monsters. Atlas bore up
the world near the Straits of Gibraltar, where the end
of all known land was marked by the Pillars of Hercules, beyond which indeed were caught dim glimpses
of Gardens of the Hesperides and blessed Islands of
Atlantis, perhaps not mere dreams if it be true that the
Phœnicians circumnavigated Africa two thousand years
before Portuguese mariners. The eastern walls of the
world were the Caucasus and Taurus ranges, hiding
dusky peoples brought to knowledge by the Persian
invasions, then more clearly by the conquests of Alexander. The cloudy prospect of Herodotus, who makes
no doubt of Europe being larger than Asia or Africa,
is bounded to the east by the deserts of Scinde, to the
west by the Cassiterides, "tin islands", that seem the
southern end of our own country. In that direction
classic views became extended, till Pausanias could tell

how on that shore of Ocean "live the Iberians and the Celts, and in it is the Island of Britain"—*toto divisos orbe Britannos.*

At the centre of all stood Greece, a focus of light for the outer barbarians, to whom yet she owed her strength and the seeds of her culture. The boss of the universe was the Thessalian Olympus, on which dwelt the gods in palaces of cloud turned by fancy to

> "golden houses, girdled with the gleaming world:
> Where they smile in secret, looking over wasted lands,
> Blight and famine, plague and earthquake, roaring deeps and
>   fiery sands,
> Clanging fights, and flaming towns, and sinking ships, and
>   praying hands".

Several mountains took the sacred name of Olympus, and poets soon began to make this a mere figure of speech, raising their gods' home into the skies, with the Milky Way as a highroad of approach. In Homer, Zeus threatens to hang up earth and sea in the air by a rope fastened to the crest of such a cloudy Olympus.

Either openly or in disguise, the immortals were much in the way of visiting our earth, and interfering with its affairs, as often as not selfishly or capriciously. Certain spots were taken as specially favoured by their resort, or as *penetralia* for the revelation of their will in mysterious oracles. One of the oldest of the oracles was the dark grove of Dodona in Epirus, where the sighing of the wind could be interpreted as the voice of Zeus. The most famous and influential came to be that of Apollo at Delphi on the slopes of Parnassus, a spot looked on as the earth's navel, the reverence of which went far beyond Greece, and must have been hoarier than the Olympian myths. In this theatre of stern scenery, walled by stupendous precipices, a cleft in the ground emitted mephitic vapour, rising about the tripod of the priestess who, when excited by the fumes, was understood to speak the god's mind. As in the case of other prophecies, her utterances were apt to be obscure, if not worded to fit more than one meaning that would cover doubtful events. Enormous treasures were offered at the temple of Delphi; and the profitable working of the oracle seems to have fallen into the hands of a local priestly caste, who in the end destroyed its credit by interfering too manifestly in politics, with a bias towards Sparta as against Athens. Another noted oracle of Apollo was that at Didyma, on the Ionian coast. The cave of Trophonius in Bœotia was also celebrated as a mouthpiece of oracular utterance.

The fur trader Alexander Henry gives an elaborate account of an American Indian pow-wow scene which strikingly matches with what we know of the classic oracles. The American Indians of the French and English wartime also drew omens from the bones and entrails of animals, as did those ancients at their sacrifices. All over the world the flight of birds has been interpreted in signs of good or ill luck, a notion surviving among ourselves, so feebly, indeed, that the appearance of such or such a number of magpies bears a different omen in separate parts of the country. How strong this particular superstition was of old is shown by the word *augur*, originally a diviner by birds; and, while the art was more regularly organized by the Romans, the Greeks also looked on birds as messengers of the gods, or as ministers of divine justice. Prometheus was not the only sinner fabled to be tormented by a vulture.

The legend of the Cranes of Ibycus is familiar to us through Schiller's ballad. The poet Ibycus, on his way to the Isthmian Games, was murdered by two robbers, in sight of a flock of cranes, to whom he commended the charge of vengeance. Sure enough, the unknown murderers sitting in the open theatre, the conscience of one was moved to exclaim, "The cranes of Ibycus!" as the vengeful birds came hovering over their heads; then he and his comrade, seized on suspicion, saw nothing for it but to confess their crime, and paid with their blood for that of the beloved poet.

> "Scarce had the wretch the words let fall,
> Than fain their sense he would recall.
> In vain; those whitening lips, behold!
> The secret have already told.
> Into their Judgment Court sublime
>   The Scene is changed;—their doom is seal'd!
> Behold the dark unwitness'd Crime,
>   Struck by the lightning that reveal'd!"

Marching to battle against Carthaginians, a Greek army was dismayed to meet mules loaded with a herb used to wreathe tombstones; but their leader turned off the omen by pointing out how the same plant made crowns for victors at the Isthmian Games; and confidence was fully established by the appearance of two eagles in the air. Not every hero was strong-minded enough, like Epaminondas when the sacrifices went against him, to quote Homer, that "there could be no better omen than to fight for one's country". Not every poet cared to copy the boldness of Euripides: "The best seer is he who makes a good guess". In the time of Socrates and Thucydides the Athenian attack on Syracuse was ruined by an eclipse of the moon, as the Spartans connected their naval defeat at Cnidus with an eclipse of the sun. From Thales to Alexander, indeed, eclipses are recorded as repeatedly influencing Greek history. A dream inspired Xenophon to take a lead among the retreating Ten Thousand. Lightning on the right might be hailed as a lucky omen, while thunder on the left uttered a warning. A people whose leaders and warriors were so easily moved by signs and wonders, would not neglect such active machinery of bane and blessing as charms, curses, amulets, and the like. In our time have been unearthed leaden figures pierced with nails, by which, ages ago, spiteful Hellenic hearts practised upon the lives of long-forgotten enemies, even as George IV's unloved queen, in less earnest mood, worked an ancestral spell upon a wax image of her husband.

Keenly as the Greek enjoyed the beauty and sunlight of life, his thoughts were much on death. Beneath the exultation of the pæan and the rapture of the dithyrambic chorus, we catch, in recurrent undertone, the "still, sad music of humanity". The poets, who for him took the place of a priestly caste such as dominated Oriental minds, are seldom without a vein of melancholy moralizing, and do not shrink from straining their eyes into the darkness beyond the grave. The kingdom of the shades made a congenial scene for myths. Any gloomy cave or volcanic chasm seemed fit to be an entrance of the fearsome underworld to which man must come, for all his shuddering. In famous legends were explored the incoherent horrors of Hades, and its lower deep, Tartarus. Round this region coiled the black Styx, over which the souls were ferried by Charon to enter the gates guarded by Cerberus; and within flowed Phlegethon river of fire, Cocytus swollen with salt tears, and the black flood of Acheron, both real streams whose scenery suggested a dreary Inferno. In Tartarus certain noted evil-doers were described as bearing ingeniously protracted torments, while other unhappy souls suffered rather through misfortune than for crime. But for the common dead Hades made no place of active punishment: their sad lot was the privation of light and joy and all of life but a shadowy form keeping consciousness enough to know what it had lost. Then as now, man had his commonplaces of consolation; but when the Greek spoke out his mind, he would agree with the ghost of Achilles in the sentiment which Matthew Arnold transfers to the Balder of Northern Mythology.

> " Gild me not my death!
> Better to live a serf, a captured man,
> Who scatters rushes in his master's hall,
> Than be a crowned king here and rule the dead."

That the soul, unless stained by extraordinary guilt, had as little to fear as to hope in the homes of the dead, is shown by the obol placed in the mouth of each corpse as passage-money for Charon, without which he left the ghost wandering miserably on the farther side for a hundred years. Within the realm of shades the brightest spot was the weird garden of its queen—

> " No growth of moor or coppice,
> No heather-flower or vine,
> But bloomless buds of poppies,
> Green grapes of Proserpine,
> Pale beds of blowing rushes,
> Where no leaf blooms or blushes
> Save this whereout she crushes
> For dead men deadly wine ".

For exceptionally favoured heroes, Homer has a glimpse of some dim Elysian asylum far set in the western seas, a scene copied by Tennyson in his island valley of Avilion:

> " Where falls not hail, or rain, or any snow,
> Nor ever wind blows loudly, but it lies,

Deep-meadowed, happy, fair with orchard lawns,
And bowery hollows crowned with summer sea".

Later poets improved upon this vague hint; and Hades
itself was furnished with a dark and a light side. There
stood out of the shade three stern judges, Minos, Rhadamanthus, and Æacus, distinguished for their justice on
earth, before whom the trembling souls were led by
Hermes to receive sentence according to their deeds.
Those who had done evil were scourged by the Furies
to their appointed torment; but the good passed into
blissful Elysian fields, where the joys of life lived again
for them, and the water of Lethe blessed them with forgetfulness. Fame, indeed, rather than virtue appears as
the title to a heavenly heritage, till philosophers like Plato
made conscience the tormenting vulture and saw souls
brought before those judges branded with the damning
record of their sins; then laughing Lucian reports the
tyrant Megapenthes sentenced by Rhadamanthus to go
without the blessed draught of Lethe that he might be
punished with memory of his past life. Such conceptions
came to be complicated by the Pythagorean idea of trans-
migration of souls, as by vague hopes engendered in
dreams of poetic prophecy and raptures of mystical initia-
tion; but, unless for choice spirits, any prospect of a
heavenly home would be dim and flickering in ages unwilling to look steadily through the gates of death.

How feebly the natural man pictures an abiding city
for his soul, is shown by the importance the Greeks put
on the body being laid to rest by funeral rites, without
which the dead might wander disconsolate, exiled even
from a home in Hades. In the wars that distracted their
states, the victors would commonly let the vanquished
bury their dead. The strange cruelty of Creon in for-

bidding the burial of Polynices called forth the displeasure of gods and men; another case marked as exceptional is the insolence of Achilles upon Hector's body. In the Gaulish invaders who came to found Galatia, nothing seemed more barbarous than their carelessness as to what became of their slain comrades. The Greek practice varied between inhumation and cremation; the latter, as ensuring the body from outrage, apparently preferable, till Christian ideas of resurrection quenched the funeral pyre. Both forms of burial might be elaborately carried out for such a hero as Patroclus; but in cases of haste or necessity a mere sprinkling with dust, as in the story of Antigone, could seem enough to satisfy religious sentiment. Homer and other authorities have hints of an ancient custom of embalmment in honey or oil.

As in other parts of the world, the rich and powerful might try to hoard up their memory in imposing tombs, like that famed *Mausoleum* erected for Mausolus of Caria; but the comparative want of slave labour in Greece and the democratic sentiment that, under one form or another, soon mastered its famous states, made such monuments less costly than those of the Asian and African kingdoms, while popular devotion and artistic skill filled this land with stately temples, palaces for the many deities, native or imported, crowding the Pantheon of its faith.

The Pantheon

In what might be called the Augustan age of Olympus, its dynastic founders had fallen into a shadowy background; and the divine family stood out in a new generation of dominant forms, shaped partly by differentiation of function and attributes, partly by accretion of kindred superstitions. The poets recognize twelve great gods and goddesses—sixteen is a fuller tale sometimes put forward—bearing over man and nature a rule limited by their own feuds, also now and then by a Fate mistily conceived as lord of all life, human or supernatural. Here follows a list of these divine personages, with some outline of their character and conduct, showing plainly how far man has since advanced in his religious ideas. Within brackets is given the, to us, more familiar name of the Latin deity, who, it must be remembered, had often undergone modification in the country of his adoption, or may have been originally a different personage adapted through the influence of that vassal that led the mind of its conqueror captive. But while Greek was long almost a dead letter to mediæval Europe, the Roman poets supplied their mythological names to point the morals and adorn the tales of clerical scholarship that handed on the dimmed lamp of learning through the dark ages.

ZEUS (Jupiter, Jove) was the king of earth and air, and overlord of Olympus, yet himself not wholly free from the power of what must be. He figures as a magnificent form, curled and bearded, sometimes crowned with oak leaves, holding in his hands the thunderbolts with which he scourged impiety. The "Thunderer" made one of his most familiar epithets; and Mr. J. C. Lawson tells us how in modern Greece—where Artemis has become St. Artemidos and St. Elias seems to have supplanted Helios—the Christian God is still conceived of as aiming celestial artillery. An eagle attends him as minister of his will, and for page or cup-bearer he has Ganymede, a boy so beautiful that Zeus grudged him to mankind, and by the agency of his eagle had him stolen from Mount Ida to make him immortal in heaven. The serpent is an apt symbol going with any god, and not wanting to Zeus.

Besides Hera, his recognized sultana, the father of gods and men had half a dozen other immortal consorts, Metis, Themis, Eurynome, Demeter, Mnemosyne, and Leto. This family did not hinder him from seeking secret brides on earth, to whom he was in the way of appearing transformed into a satyr, a bull, a swan, a shower of gold, and so forth: with sly humour Lucian makes the god complain that women never love him for himself but always in some unworthy disguise. Of one of his illicit loves, Semele, daughter of Cadmus, it is told that she, prompted by Hera's jealousy, desired to see her lover in all his Olympian majesty, and was burned up by the awful glow of that revelation. Another mortal maiden hardly treated was Callisto, turned into a bear, and in that shape hunted down by her mistress Artemis at the instigation of jealous Hera; then all the Olympian seducer could do for his victim was to place her and her son among the stars as the Great and the Little Bear.

The god's visits to earth, indeed, are sometimes on errands of justice or enquiry. A pleasing story is that of Philemon and Baucis, the Phrygian Darby and Joan who entertained him as an unknown stranger in their humble home, and by divine gratitude were warned to fly from the wrath about to come on their impious neighbours. Moreover, this worthy pair, invited to choose a boon, asked nothing better than to end their days together after spending them as ministers in the temple to which their hospitable cot was transformed. More awful was the example of Lycaon's fate, that cruel and unbelieving king of Arcadia who, to test his guest's divinity, placed before Zeus a dish of human flesh, and for such impiety was

turned into a wolf, his family being exterminated by lightning, as seemed not unfair to early moralists.   Another
victim of divine justice was Salmoneus, the overweening
king of Elis, who had sacrifices offered to him as a god,
and even haloed himself with artificial thunders and lightnings, amid which a veritable bolt from heaven scorched
up this ape of divinity with his city and all its people.

To common men, Zeus was represented by many
statues, the noblest of them the work of Phidias, which,
forty feet high, in gold and ivory, passed for one of the
Seven Wonders of the ancient world, and was hailed
by the Roman conqueror, Æmilius Paulus, as "the
very Jove of Homer".   This adorned the rich temple
at Olympia that became chief seat of the god's worship, while Dodona, as already mentioned, seems his
oldest oracle.   Another famous oracle was that of
Jupiter-Ammon in the sands of Libya; under this title
Zeus seems to have been fused with an Egyptian deity
and is figured with horns.   But indeed his epithets and
attributes are innumerable.   The Roman Jove, who bore
a graver character than his Greek fellow-despot, was
reverenced as Jupiter Optimus Maximus, his chief shrine
being a temple on the Capitoline Hill, the St. Peter's of
pagan Rome.

HERA (Juno) was the legitimate queen of Olympus,
who by all accounts led her husband a troubled life of
it, through the jealousy for which he gave her but too
much cause.   Her other leading characteristics were a
pride that kept her austerely virtuous, and a self-satisfac-
tion that, when infused with anger, too often soured to
vindictive hate; and always she proved quick to take
offence at any slight on the part of gods or men.   Her
special handmaid was Iris, the rainbow, that carried her

messages to earth; and her daughter Hebe served with Ganymede as cup-bearer at the celestial table. Another attendant came to be the peacock, when that gorgeous bird was brought as a novelty to Greece. The cuckoo was also a pet of hers.

The story goes that when Zeus courted Io, daughter of Inachus king of Argos, and transformed her into a white cow, the watchful Hera sought to foil her consort's intrigues by placing the animal under guard of the monster Argus, who had a hundred eyes, no more than two of them closed at a time. Zeus, on his side, employed Hermes to lull all the eyes of Argus to sleep with the spell of his lyre, and then to slay him; and in memorial of his ineffective service, Hera placed his hundred eyes on the tail of a bird that made an emblem of her own pride. Also she sent a gadfly to drive the unfortunate Io through the world, wandering like the horned moon, till at last that persecuted maiden found rest in Egypt, where she bore a son who was the founder of Memphis. This myth is typical of the punishments often inflicted by a so impeccable and implacable goddess upon frail mortals.

A prettier story than most of those told of her makes an old priestess drawn to Hera's temple by her two sons, Cleobis and Biton, since befitting white heifers could not be found to yoke in the car; then the mother was so touched by their filial service that she prayed her patron goddess to grant them the greatest boon of heaven, and on coming out of the temple found them dead where they had lain down to sleep off their fatigue. On this fable of Herodotus, Addison in the *Spectator* rather cynically remarks that had their death followed an act of disobedience, the moral would have been reversed.

The "ox-eyed Hera" is Homer's well-worn epithet

to denote the calmly imperial looks attributed to the queen of heaven. She was worshipped specially at Argos, at Samos, and in a temple at Olympia, older than that of Zeus. The Roman Juno takes a more matronly form, and appears rather as the protector of married life than as the spiteful chastiser of illicit love.

APOLLO—with Phœbus prominent among his many *aliases*—was the most beautiful and the most beloved of the Olympians, close kinsman to that radiant sun-god who shines out in so many mythologies. Beside his sister Selene, the moon, he figures openly as Helios, the sun, with the by-name of Hyperion under which Hamlet contrasts him with a satyr. He was the son of Zeus and Leto (Latona), who, driven to Delos by the jealousy of Hera, there brought him forth with his twin sister Artemis, so that this island became their favoured sanctuary. The mother being still persecuted by jealous Juno, Apollo was reared by Themis so thrivingly that at the first taste of nectar and ambrosia he burst his swaddling-clothes and stood forth a full-grown youth, demanding the lyre and the silver bow with which he is usually represented. His first great exploit was slaying the huge serpent Python, where afterwards arose the Delphic oracle; and he became peculiarly the god of prophecy, as, in a manner, the voice of heaven upon earth. He was also the source of life and healing, an attribute specially manifested in his son Æsculapius, father of the medical profession, who was, indeed, slain by Zeus for presuming to restore the dead to life; but he handed down his science and practice to his daughter Hygeia. The number of temples that came to honour Æsculapius, hints how this useful divinity was a double or deputy of the sun-god in his healing power.

Yet where the benignant sun burns fiercely at times, "far-darting" Apollo could hurt as well as heal, and his arrows might kindle pestilence, as in the camp of the Greeks before Troy. His chariot might be drawn by lions as well as by swans. He had a charge of flocks and herds, and generally of civilizing arts. But his chief renown was as the patron of song and music, hailed by the stirring chant of the pæan. Orpheus was his son; and for attendants he had the nine Muses — *Clio* (history), *Euterpe* (lyric poetry), *Thalia* (comedy), *Melpomene* (tragedy), *Terpsichore* (dance and song), *Erato* (love song), *Polymnia* (sublime hymn), *Urania* (astronomy), *Calliope* (epic poetry). The favourite haunts of this choir were Mount Helicon and Mount Parnassus with its Castalian spring, in which so many poets have sought to bathe; and few bards of ancient or modern times fail to invoke Phœbus as their patron spirit.

Pindar tells how, in his character of *Hyperion* (the Sun), Apollo happened to be out of the way when the gods were dividing the earth by lot, and, thus left portionless, he asked of Zeus the volcanic Rhodes, which he foresaw would rise from the waves. So this island of roses became his special sanctuary, renowned by its Colossus, a brazen image of him, a hundred feet or so high, another wonder of the ancient world, overthrown by one of the earthquakes that have worked havoc here with later monuments. He had other local phases, like that *Smintheus* of the Troad, who seems to have been a mouse-god, the propitiation of destructive rodents flourishing here as among the Philistines.

The sculptors, for whom this comely god made a favourite model, usually show him as a naked form in the bloom of noble and graceful manhood, crowned with laurel, like the famous Apollo Belvidere statue of the

Vatican. "Ever young and fair", Apollo seems to reflect the brightest side of Greek religion, and by his fine humanity to come closest in touch with its cultured worshippers. He had strongly marked traits of human nature, both good and bad. Celebrated was his affection for the fair boy Hyacinthus, whom he accidentally killed with a quoit as they played together, then as monument of him caused a blue flower to spring from his blood. Not less renowned was Apollo's love for the celibate nymph Daphne, who fled from him in vain, but was saved from his embrace by being turned into a laurel, to which the baffled god gave evergreen leaves. The gods seldom show to advantage in their love for mortal maidens, and this one was apt to treat his sweethearts too cavalierly, as in the case of Coronis, mother of Æsculapius, whom he slew on a report of her perfidy brought by a crow—originally a white bird, but now turned black as a punishment for scandal-mongering. Apollo was not only human but savage when he flayed Marsyas alive for presuming to compete with him in music. And his most unworthy exploit was joining his sister Artemis in the cruel revenge they took on Niobe by cutting off her whole flock of too loudly boasted darlings. But, on the whole, he appears in the beneficent character hymned by Shelley :—

> " I feed the clouds, the rainbows and the flowers
> With their ethereal colours; the Moon's globe,
> And the pure stars in their eternal bowers
> Are cinctured with my power as with a robe;
> Whatever lamps on Earth or Heaven may shine,
> Are portions of one power, which is mine.
>
> " I stand at noon upon the peaks of Heaven,
> Then with unwilling steps I wander down
> Into the clouds of the Atlantic even;
> For grief that I depart they weep and frown:

What look is more delightful than the smile
With which I soothe them from the western isle?

" I am the eye with which the Universe
Beholds itself and knows itself divine;
All harmony of instrument or verse,
All prophecy, all medicine are mine,
All light of art or nature;—to my song
Victory and praise in their own right belong."

ARTEMIS (Diana), Apollo's twin sister, like himself, drew into her name the character of several foreign deities, one of them that renowned Diana of the Ephesians, whose temple ranked among the Seven Wonders. Her name was also given to the cruel goddess of Tauris, a congenial guest at Sparta, where the hardy lads scourged even to death before her altar look to be a softened form of human sacrifice. The native Arcadian Artemis, again, was a goddess of hunting and wild life, who went kirtled to the knee on wooded mountains, followed by nymphs of like tastes. She was chaste to a fault, as would appear from the stories about her victims; and her fatal jealousy would be most easily aroused not by love but by presumption on the part of mortals. Actæon, who accidentally came upon her bathing, was turned into a stag to be torn in pieces by his own hounds. There is, indeed, some hint of tender passages between her and the giant hunter Orion; but varying stories of his fate make him the mark of her vengeful arrows; then he was set in heaven as a constellation along with the Pleiades, seven daughters of Atlas, her favourite attendants, whom this hunter had tried to pursue. A softer side to Artemis appears in her identification with the moon, in which character she let her coldness grow warm for the beautiful youth Endymion, kissed by her to sleep on Mount Latmus, to whom Zeus allowed a choice between death and perpetual youth in dreamy slumber, guarded by the enamoured goddess.

> " As I seemed to gaze on her,
> Nearer she drew and gazed; and as I lay
> Supine, beneath her spell, the radiance stooped,
> And kissed me on the lips, a chaste, sweet kiss
> Which drew my spirit with it.   So I slept
> Each night upon the hill, until the Dawn
> Came in his golden chariot from the East,
> And chased my love away."   —*Lewis Morris.*

ATHENE (Minerva) was another virgin goddess, whose cognomen Pallas may have been derived from an Athenian hero of that name, while her chief Greek title shows her specially at home in the city that honoured her with the renowned Parthenon.   The orthodox story about Pallas-Athene's birth was that she sprang full-grown and full-armed from the head of her father Zeus.   She is often represented in armour, with helmet, breastplate, and shield, and so has passed for the goddess of war; but rather she fostered the patriotic defence without which civilization were fruitless, her true spirit being for invention, the care of the arts and crafts, and woman's handiwork especially.   Justice and order grew up under her ægis, so that she was the protectress of cities.   As to her particular regard for Athens, it is told that Poseidon being her rival for the place of its godfather, a council of the gods settled that honour on whichever should offer the most welcome gift to man.   Poseidon struck the earth with his trident to call forth the horse, then Athene produced the olive, preferred as an emblem of peace and plenty, and bearing a quasi-sacred esteem in ancient Greece, as shown by the use of its wood for funeral pyres and of its leaves for crowns of honour.

The animals sacred to her were the serpent, the cock,

and the owl, hence the proverb "owls to Athens", translatable by our "coals to Newcastle", a phrase that may have been prompted by the owl stamped on Athenian coins. She was grave, austere, dignified, and as a rule beneficent, free from the scandals fixed on other goddesses; even wanton Cupid stood in awe of this virgin governess. Once indeed she lost her temper with Arachne, the Lydian spinster who presumed to vie with her; and she appears in a ridiculous light when, on her invention of the flute, she set Olympus laughing by the queer faces she made in playing it. But she seldom showed feminine weaknesses; and her martial figure had masculine outlines. She plays the hero in Homer's battles, from which other intervening goddesses fly in tearful dismay at their first taste of bloodshed. The Roman Minerva rather emphasized her patronage of letters, when a poet's verse could not hope to flow smoothly *invitâ Minervâ*.

APHRODITE (Venus), the goddess of love, was a daughter of Zeus according to one story, but an older myth makes her spring from the sea in the cataclysm that followed the overthrow of Uranus. Her name, "foam-born", bears out such an origin; and the fact of Paphos on Cyprus, Cythera, and other islands passing as her favourite homes, hints how she came across the Ægean, being no other than the lustful Astarte that scandalized the Hebraic conscience. To Greece she came dowered with soft charms, in a chariot drawn by doves or swans, adorned with flowers and fruit, and having as her special ornament the cestus or girdle, the loan of which was enough to inspire love, as when Hera borrowed it to enhance her charms in wheedling Zeus out of a favourable disposition towards the hated Trojans.

At first Aphrodite appears well dressed as becomes a matron; but soon her form made an excuse for sculptors and artists to display their mastery of the nude, in countless famous pictures and in statues like those known as the Venus of Milo and the Venus de Medici.

In song and story, too, the goddess of charms and caprice was bound to be familiar. The tritest tale of her loves, handled by Shakespeare, has Adonis for its hero, the beautiful youth incarnating, like Persephone, a myth of the alternation of growth and decay. For his sake Aphrodite abandoned heaven, and took to the woods like Artemis, where, instead of nerving the boy to hardy deeds, she would have had him hunt only such harmless animals as are the quarry of our noble sportsmen. But Adonis, not yet tangled in the wiles of love, was unwilling to toy in the shade with this fair charmer, and tore himself from her embraces to encounter a boar by which he was wounded to death. So moving was the grief of the goddess that Hades yielded up her darling to pass half the year with her above-ground. Another form of this poetical conception of the seasons makes Adonis an orphan placed under charge of Persephone, who grew too fond of him to let him go, till Zeus compromised the dispute by decreeing that he should spend four months with the queen of Hades, four with Aphrodite, and four at his own will, barren winter being left out of account in this view of earth's recurrent life. The same notion occurs in the myth of Persephone herself, one variant of which divides her presence between three seasons, while another regards only the successive change of summer and winter.

Cupid, the Greek Eros, best known by his Latin

name, who plays such pranks in myth, must have been
born to Venus somewhat late in life; and still later she
has about her in art a whole brood of such tricksy sprites.
The original *Eros* was a more serious personage, who
appears to have grown backwards into a fat and foolish
boyhood. We find Love styled now the oldest, again
the youngest of the gods. It is not very clear how
Cupid came into the family; but poets as well as artists
soon made much of this wanton imp, naked and winged,
his eyes sometimes blindfolded, with his torch to kindle
hearts, and the arrows he shoots in careless mischief,
some tipped with gold to quicken, some with lead to
palsy the pulse of love. The most famous story about
him, that of Cupid and Psyche, is not found before
Apuleius in the second century of our era, but no
doubt came from ruder myths the doings ascribed to
Cupid, that are of course much older than Hesiod or
Homer. Eros had a less famous brother, *Anteros*, conceived as the avenger of slighted love.

A more staid attendant of Aphrodite was *Hymen*,
who with his torch would lead the nuptial chorus.
For handmaidens she had the naked Graces, *Euphro-
syne*, *Aglaia*, and *Thalia*, daughters of Zeus, their Greek
title *Charis* sometimes appearing identified with the goddess herself, who passed through a gamut of phases from
the meretricious mistress of sensual pleasure to the
august mother of all life. Her official husband was
Hephæstus; but it seemed natural she should play this
sooty clown false in her favour to other Olympians.
The Latin Venus, originally of more humble rank,
became exalted as mother of Æneas, when Roman poets
transfigured him into a national ancestor. And Plato
reminds how there were two conceptions of the Greek
Aphrodite, the Uranian who represents the purer spirit

of Love, and the Pandemian, daughter of Zeus and the Titan Dione, who was more manifest to vulgar natures.

DEMETER (Ceres) was the daughter of Cronos by Rhea, through whom she inherited the misty awe of *Gæa*, the earth, oldest of deities, that mother-spirit wedded by the invading sky-god. She figures most famously in the myth of her beloved daughter *Persephone* (Proserpine), known also as *Corē* ("the maiden"), who

> "Gathering flowers,
> Herself a fairer flower, by gloomy Dis
> Was gathered ".

"That fair field of Enna " was in Sicily, recommended by its fertility as a favourite haunt of Demeter; but the scene of the rape of Proserpine is also put in Asia. Mother and daughter were highly honoured in Greece, especially at the Eleusinian Mysteries associated with Demeter's worship, which came to be the holiest rites of Greek religion, guessed at as a survival of its primitive awe developed into some mystic hope of immortality. This goddess of ancient date appeared one of the most beneficent, by her evident gift of growth, and by the agricultural arts she was fabled to have communicated to man through her nursling Triptolemus, who also gave the world a triple law called by his name: To honour parents ; to reverence the gods with sacrifices of their boons; not to harm man nor beast. As inventor, or introducer, of the plough, he stands for father of civilization; so Scott was humorously reflecting a classic idea when he christened the unwelcome improver of Shetland farming by the name of Triptolemus Yellowley.

HESTIA (Vesta), though named among the great gods,

does not much appear in their intrigues, being modest and domesticated, as became her office of cherishing the family hearth. Yet her maidenhood implied no want of charm, if it be true that she was wooed in vain by Apollo and by Poseidon. She was probably akin to the deity still worshipped by the descendants of Persian fire-worshippers, who look on fire as so sacred that a Europeanized Parsee lights his first cigarette with a sense of doing something daringly profane. In the Prytaneum, or town hall of Greek cities, a public hearth was kept burning, from which emigrants carried sacred fire to be the seed of their colony's religion. The Roman Vesta seems a more conspicuous goddess, of great antiquity, well known to us through the Vestal Virgins bound, under severe penalties, to keep her fire burning and their lives as pure as that of their mistress.

HEPHÆSTUS (Vulcan) was the god of fire in its industrial applications, the Tubal-Cain of the classic world. Some accounts make him spring from Hera in a non-natural manner, to match her husband's prodigious production of Minerva; but hers proved not a success, as the boy was born lame and so puny that she threw him out of heaven, to be reared by sea nymphs in a submarine grotto. Another story is that when Zeus chastised his nagging wife by hanging her from Olympus, her heels weighted with a pair of anvils, Hephæstus took his mother's part and was hurled down, to fall nine days—or only "from morn to dewy eve"—till he came on the island of Lemnos with a broken leg; but he returned to heaven to reconcile the quarrelsome couple. There is also difference of testimony as to his marriage: various beautiful brides are ascribed to him, among them Venus herself, as if in mockery. For this lame and ugly fellow played the low comedian of Olympus, at whose hobbling gait the more elegant gods burst into unextinguishable laughter. Rough and be-grimed as he was, there could be no question as to his usefulness. The palaces and jewels of Olympus were his handiwork, not to speak of the thunderbolts, as well as cunning devices like the net in which he caught Ares dallying with his faithless spouse, and for once turned the laugh on his side. For the heroes of myth he made such masterpieces as the shield of Hercules, the armour of Achilles, and the sceptre of Agamemnon. His workshops naturally came to be placed in volcanic islands, where the Cyclopes acted as his journeymen, the idea of them perhaps taken from craters, each with its burning eye. So Virgil places Vulcan's forge off the coast of Sicily, with the Ætnean fires as furnace :—

> "On their eternal anvils here he found
> The brethren beating, and the blows go round:
> A load of pointless thunder now there lies
> Before their hands, to ripen for the skies:
> These darts, for angry Jove, they daily cast—
> Consum'd on mortals with prodigious waste.
> Three rays of writhen rain, of fire three more,
> Of winged southern winds and cloudy store
> As many parts, the dreadful mixture frame;
> And fears are added, and avenging flame.
> Inferior ministers, for Mars, repair
> His broken axle-trees and blunted war,
> And send him forth again with furbish'd arms,
> To wake the lazy war, with trumpets' loud alarms.
> The rest refresh the scaly snakes that fold
> The shield of Pallas, and renew their gold.
> Full on the crest the Gorgon's head they place
> With eyes that roll in death and with distorted face."
> —*Dryden*.

ARES (Mars), son of Zeus and Hera, was the god

of war, apt to be at strife with his austere rival in that capacity, Athene, and indeed with all his Olympian kinsmen, among whom he gave his brother Hephæstus good cause for jealousy. In Greek mythology this blustering athlete cuts no noble figure, being beaten by Hercules and other earthly heroes, and showing something of the savage sullenness and stupidity that come natural to legendary giants. Even his father had a poor opinion of him, to judge by Homer's report of his reception in Olympus when he came complaining of his hurts got by meddling in the battle before Troy.

"Of all the gods who tread the spangled skies,
Thou most unjust, most odious in our eyes!
Inhuman discord is thy dire delight,
The lust of slaughter and the rage of fight;
No bound, no law thy fiery temper quells,
And all thy mother in thy soul rebels".

Mars rose to a loftier position at Rome, where, as father of Romulus and Remus, he took the same protecting part as Athene at Athens. But the Campus Martius of Rome was matched by the Areopagus of Athens, fabled to be so called because there the gods held a court to settle a dispute between Ares and Poseidon. At Sparta he would be made much of: it was there Pausanias found an image of him in fetters to prevent the god from deserting this martial state. In Italy he had for comrades *Quirinus*, a deification of Romulus, and *Bellona*, who seems to have been a native goddess adopted by the Romans; and in Greece, too, Eris, "Strife", was his twin sister, while Terror and Fear were his sons.

HERMES (Mercury) was another son of Zeus, by Maia, the eldest of the Pleiades. His special function was as messenger and herald of the gods, in which capacity he is represented as a handsome and agile youth, with winged sandals and a broad-brimmed hat also winged, bearing the *caduceus*, a staff wreathed with serpents, which he got from Apollo under singular circumstances. No sooner was Hermes born than he took to stealing, and set out on a raid against cattle belonging to his brother Apollo. Among the precocious babe's adventures on this sally was the finding of a tortoise and turning its shell into the seven-stringed lyre. Having stolen fifty oxen, he stoutly denied the theft, and Maia stood up for her sleeping infant's innocence, till Zeus brought the truth to light; then Apollo was so delighted with the tortoise-shell lyre, that he not only pardoned his knavish little brother, but in return for that invention gave him a wand of magic power. Autolycus, the cunning robber of Mount Parnassus, might well be called his natural son.

Hermes came to be looked on as the god of herds, also of commerce and of theft, a pluralism of functions natural enough when cattle made the standard of value, as shown in the history of our word *pecu*niary. He was moreover the guardian of roads, of gymnastic exercises, of clever inventions, such as the alphabet attributed to him; of eloquence, and of games of chance; in short he appears a god of all work, who amused his leisure hours by playing sly tricks on his fellow denizens of Olympus, as when he stole the trident of Poseidon, the girdle of Aphrodite, and the arrows of Artemis; yet for all his mischievousness he appears a favourite in the family, and his father's chosen henchman in his excursions on earth. Of his own dealings with mortals, one is moralized by Ovid in the story of his love for Herse, daughter of Cecrops, whose sister Agraulos offered to

betray her for a large bribe. But when Hermes came
back with the money, Athene had punished Agraulos by
setting the fiend Envy to poison her heart, so that she
now stood out against letting the god pass to her sister's
chamber, till he turned her into a black stone.

The most dignified office of Hermes was conducting
the shades of the dead to the world below. The Roman
Mercury seems originally to have been a patron of trade,
his name connected with *merx*; but he took on the light-
hearted and slippery ways of the Greek god, that have
given an *alias* to the metal quicksilver. His most
famous statue seems to have been that by Praxiteles,
found in a mutilated state at Olympia. Small images of
Hermes were very common in Greek life, set up on
roadways and at the gates of houses, their faces sometimes painted black and white to symbolize the offices of
the god above and below ground, and often perhaps
mere fetish blocks such as that on which Lucian tried
his prentice hand as a carver with sore result.

POSEIDON (Neptune) should have been introduced
earlier, as one of the oldest of the gods, brother of Zeus,
against whom he sometimes ventured to rebel, but as a
rule rested content with his satrapy of the sea, under
which he had a marvellous golden palace, its grottos
adorned with corals and sea-flowers, and lit with phos-
phorescent glow. Rejected as patron of Athens, in
favour of his accomplished niece, he was understood to
have a special regard for the Isthmus of Corinth, that
focus of navigation from east and west. His sceptre was
the trident fishing-spear of the Mediterranean; and he
rode forth in a chariot drawn by dolphins, sea-horses, or
other marine monsters. Horses came into his province
as well as waves, an idea not far to seek in the com-

parison of leaping and rearing billows that has occurred
to many a poet. Naturally, he had his moods, in some
of which he could be very terrible to maritime mortals,
for, besides storms, he raised disastrous floods and devouring monsters of plague and famine. His wife was
the sea nymph *Amphitrite*, who still accompanies him on
our crossing-the-line mummeries. By her he had *Triton*
and other sons; but he would not have been a right god
without giving her cause for jealousy, as against that unfortunate Scylla whom she got turned into a six-headed
bugbear haunting the straits of Sicily, a caverned whirlpool opposite the rock Charybdis, into which a daughter
of Poseidon had been transformed by angry Zeus. These
perils, not now so apparent to sailors, were noted in the
proverb, *Incidit in Scyllam qui vult vitare Charybdin*.

The powers of water take changing shapes, like that
Proteus, son of Poseidon, who, guarding his herd of seals,
had to be caught and held fast before he would give forth
his oracles. He might be confused with *Nereus*, a bene-
volent Old Man of the Sea, who presided over calm
weather, and with his fifty daughters the *Nereides*, was
ready to help friendly mariners. *Oceanus* was an older
god, son of Uranus, with an enormous family of Ocean-
ides, among them the *Electra*, whose tears were drops of
amber, through which her name passed to that force that
has been so heavily enslaved by modern science. *Glaucus*
seems a later deity, immortalized against his will by falling
into the sea. The eldest son of Oceanus was *Achelous*,
guardian of the largest Greek river, and rival of Hercules
for Deianira; he had some thousands of brothers, himself
the most famous among a large family of river gods.
Thetis, mother of Achilles, was daughter of one of those
slippery beings, whom Peleus won by being able to hold
her elusive form; then, *Eris* (Strife), not invited to their

marriage, played the part of the wicked witch in our fairy tales, as appears in the Tale of Troy. But Thetis is connected with a legend of peace. She it was that, when Halcyone threw herself into the sea after her shipwrecked husband Ceyx, changed them both into the birds whose nest was taken to float upon the sea in the calm of "halcyon days".

PLUTO, not having his seat on Olympus, hardly appears among the twelve great gods, large as this grim lord of the underworld must have loomed before superstitious minds. The name of *Hades* he shares with his realm; and *Dis* is another *alias* that at first seems to have belonged to Zeus. Another title of both realm and ruler, *Orcus*, is still very active in Italian folklore. The most dreadful of the gods was conceived as a dark-browed form, seated on an ebony throne, or driving in a chariot drawn by coal-black steeds; he brandishes a two-pronged spear; and among his possessions is a helmet that has the property to cast a spell of invisibility. Sacrifices to him were offered at dead of night, the blood of victims being allowed to run into trenches from which it might trickle down to his underground palace. The one bright spot in his life was his love for *Persephone*, whom he carried off to share his gloomy throne. But this fair form became infected by the spirit of the dark abode in which she must dwell half the year, so that in a shadowy manner she seems to pass into the fearsome form of *Hecate*, the goddess of witchcraft and other weird doings that haunts crossroads or lonely scenes of murder. Such an ugly shade, indeed, appears to flicker as cast either by Artemis or by Persephone, while it is as "handmaid" to the latter that Hecate appears in a so-called Homeric hymn.

DIONYSUS (Bacchus) was a god who came to Greece with the culture of the vine, and brought along with him eastern orgies that had their religious side. Son of Zeus by Semele, he was ever youthful, handsome and effeminate, clad in a panther skin, crowned with vine leaves and grape bunches round which his locks curled like tendrils, carrying as his sceptre the *thyrsus*, a wand wreathed with ivy or other vines; and his invocation was the excited dithyramb, contrasting with the sublime pæan of Apollo. Drama began with the choruses that celebrated his festival at Athens. The Dionysia, transported into Italy as Bacchanalia, were the Carnival days of the ancient world, when the Saturnalia of Rome gave a hint for our Christmas revelry. Bacchus had travelled far and wide, a long visit to India being one of his wanderings, on which he may have picked up the tigers, lynxes, or panthers that drew his chariot. His favourite attendants were goat-footed Satyrs, headed by the purple-faced Silenus, who made a disreputable boon companion. Also he led about a rout of wild women, who, as will be when people take to drink, were given to fits of scandalous excitement. These Mænads, Bacchants, or whatever they might be called, danced along intoxicated with a rabid frenzy that did not stick at the blood of any coldly prudent man who shunned their noisy enthusiasm. So it was with Pentheus, king of Thebes, who was for sternly putting down this exotic worship; but when he thought to spy on its rites in secret, the god beguiled him into shameful disguise as a woman; then his own mother headed the crew that pulled him from the tree in which he had ensconced himself, and tore him to pieces in their madness. Another king, Lycurgus of Thrace, who would have restrained such inspired excesses, was punished by being driven mad himself.

An amusing story is that of the pirates, who caught Dionysus and would have sold him as a slave; only their prudent steersman, guessing this to be a god, warned his comrades what might come of such impiety. Sure enough, the prisoner easily broke from their fetters, the ship's masts bloomed out in vines and ivy wreaths, the sails dripped perfumed wine, and all around rang the music of an invisible choir. By such prodigies the sailors' eyes were opened too late : their captive took the shape of a lion, backed by a bear that began by tearing the captain ; then the rest jumped overboard to be changed into dolphins, all but that considerate steersman, who at the god's request set him ashore at Naxos, where he had his celebrated meeting with Ariadne. A rare hint of temperance principles appears in the legend of Icarius, an Athenian who entertained this strange god, and being taught in return the power of the grape, was beaten to death by his ungrateful neighbours, who took their first experience of intoxication to be no better than poisonous; then his daughter Erigone, led to his grave by the dog Mæra, hung herself above it for grief, and as reward of her filial piety, she along with her father and the faithful dog were placed as stars in the Great Bear constellation.

Bacchus, like Cupid, belonged to a later generation of gods, their nature, indeed, in general so fissiparous that they had much power of adding to their numbers, while they were liable to a confusion of character and a multiplication of names. Zeus and the rest came to be regarded under a variety of attributes and epithets, which make them almost different personages in local worship. In the Greek world, confusion was confounded by the importation of avowed foreign deities like Isis and Serapis, till irreverent Lucian could represent the old gods as seriously disturbed through the intrusion of parvenu strangers, crowding Olympus with a mob of all nations and languages, so that nectar and ambrosia are like to run short. To abate this scandal, the satirist suggests a celestial committee of privileges, seven in number, three elected from the *ancien régime* of Saturn and four from the twelve great gods of the Jovian dynasty, who should be empowered to examine the titles of pretenders to godship. This task seems too hard for mere human patience; but before giving it up, we must at least mention certain divine or quasi-divine personages and conceptions that flit over the shifting background of classical mythology.

PLUTUS, the god of wealth, was a different personage from Pluto, understood to be in charge of the *irritamenta malorum* stored underground. He would not take his grimy form till the precious metals came into use as means of exchange; and the ancients made him blinded by Zeus, poets and moralists in all ages having reason to understand that riches do not always go with merit. In the Theban temple of *Tyche* (Fortune) he appears as a child in her arms, she also being represented as blindfold, sometimes winged, sometimes standing on a slippery ball, holding the Cornucopia, or horn of plenty, from which she pours out her gifts so carelessly. Plutus belongs, of course, to the same family of abstractions as *Momus* (mirth), *Comus*, the presiding genius of revelry, and that *Priapus*, whose figure did not strike the ancients as unfit for polite society, while he had serious functions as guardian of flocks, of swarming bees, and of fruitfulness in general.

A word should be said in passing as to certain

other names apparently peculiar to Roman mythology, though perhaps handed down from Etruscan superstitions of kindred origin to those of Greece. The most renowned of these is *Janus*, the god of gates, whose principal shrine at Rome was closed in time of peace, twice or thrice only, it is said, during seven centuries, and notably at the birth of Christ, as Milton proclaims in his ode for the Nativity. He is represented with two faces, to look both ways. Janus has passed for deification of an ancient hero-king; but was probably a sun-god who opened the gates of heaven; and he appears to have been originally the chief god of Rome till supplanted by Jupiter. *Terminus* was the god of boundaries and landmarks, not left without work in a land of small encroaching communities. *Libitina* presided over funerals, as *Lucina* over childbirth. *Fortuna* seems here to have come to higher honour than did her sister Tyche in Greece. The *Lares* were the Roman spirits of ancestors; the *Penates*, household gods; the *Manes*, shades of the dead, who appear in more ghastly shape as *Lemures*, *Lamiæ*, and *Larvæ*; then every Roman went through life attended by his *Genius*, as was the Indian by his *manitou* or totem spirit. In Greece, also, man's body was shadowed by his *Ker*, a ministering wraith whose invisible activities are hard to catch; and he might believe himself guided by his *Daimon*, a guardian spirit that for us has taken uglier significance.

Manifold, indeed, were the bodiless shapes called into imaginary existence by the Greek aptitude for personification. There was *Ananke* (necessity), before whom the very gods must bow. *Ate* (the spirit of evil) sowed crimes among men. *Nemesis* (retribution) came after the wicked with slow but sure foot. *Nike* (victory), *Dike* (justice), and *Themis* (law) were all vaguely conceived

as airy beings. Pausanias records altars or temples to
such abstractions as Energy, Mercy, Shame, Rumour,
and Persuasion. Death and his brother Sleep make a
metaphor as old as Homer or Hesiod; and Dreams
came from above as messengers, false ones issuing
through a flattering sheet of ivory, but the true from
a gate of horn, to whisper to mortals locked in the
arms of *Morpheus*. They were children of wide-
mantled Night, who readily became a personage, like
Eos (Aurora), the Dawn; *Phosphorus* and *Hesperus*, the
Morning and the Evening Star, and a host of other
shining ones, attendants of the Moon and the Sun,
whose four horses had their names and local habitation in the stables of the sky. So had the four winds,
Boreas, *Eurus*, *Zephyrus*, and *Notus*, children of Eos and
Astræa, the virgin star, those airy beings kept shut
up in the cave of *Æolus*, whence at command they
issued forth as winged youths to do the will of the
gods. The wife of Zephyrus was *Chloris*, who became
more famous as the Roman *Flora*, the flower goddess,
comrade of *Pomona*, whose spouse was *Vertumnus*, the
Season god, wooing her successively as a ploughman,
a reaper, a grape gatherer, and as an old woman white
with winter snows, at last in the composite present-
ment of a beautiful youth. The Seasons (*Horæ*) were
also incarnated as lovely maidens, *Eunomia*, *Dike*, and
Irene, daughters of Zeus and Themis, going along with
the Graces in attendance upon Aphrodite or Apollo.
The mostly animal signs of the Zodiac belong, of course,
to older observation than that of Greek fancy.

The Seasons sometimes appear as two or four; but
it has already been mentioned how the Greeks might
leave winter out of account. It is noticeable how their
imagination of female forms usually goes in triads, while

the same tendency was less marked in the case of gods. There were three Fates, *Moirai* (*Parcæ*)—*Clotho*, *Lachesis*, and *Atropos*—to spin and cut the thread of life. Three also were the Furies—*Tisiphone*, *Alecto*, and *Megæra*— whose proper title was the *Erinyes*, but men gave them the flattering name of *Eumenides* (the Gracious Ones), as our mischievous fairies were styled "the good people", or the "men of peace". The *Graiæ*, grey cousins of the Gorgons, may have been originally represented as two, having one eye and one tooth between them, but they also pass into a trinity. The Muses are three times three. Three goddesses contend for the prize of beauty, and Psyche, like Cinderella, has two sisters.

Modern Greek folklore, that but blurredly reflects the ancient mythology, runs much to the sets of three brothers, so familiar in our *märchen*, of whom the youngest commonly is the lucky one; whereas this feature is not marked in the old Greek stories, so far as male characters are concerned. There are three supreme deities; but Pluto seems not to rank with his brothers; and of the three judges in the lower world, only Minos and Rhadamanthus appear as holding regular sessions. Two brothers seem more common than three in ancient stories. Miss Jane Harrison suggests that three figures would lend themselves to artistic composition; but this hardly explains why Greek heroes are grouped in triads less often than heroines; and several scholars to whom I have put the point can offer no explanation. Mr. J. C. Lawson, in his scholarly comparison of ancient and modern superstitions in Greece, finds that there three has come to be a number of sinister associations.

It were a labour of Hercules to present a complete list of all those beings of earth and air, of water and

darkness, that flickered into imaginary shape. Every
river and fountain might have its nymph or Naiad,
every tree its Dryad; the mountains were haunted by
Oreades, as the forests by half-brutal Satyrs. Unknown
regions, then, were readily peopled by Giants, Centaurs,
Chimæras, Amazons, Sirens, Cyclopes, Hyperboreans, or
other fabulous creatures, such as long afterwards would
be looked for across the Atlantic by the contemporaries
of Columbus, in their turn taking *omne ignotum pro magni-
fico*, not to say *horrifico*.

Among what may be called the half-comic features of
mythology, stands out one figure that grew to singular
importance from humble beginnings. PAN (Faunus)
seems to have been a country sprite like our Puck,
a horned, sharp-eared, and goat-footed creature born
among the wooded hills of Arcadia, where, angrily disturbed in his noonday sleep, he would sometimes appear
to startle travellers, and no wonder, when the nymph
who bore him to Hermes was dismayed at the sight
of her misshapen offspring. His harsh voice was fabled
to have served as volunteered artillery at the battle of
Marathon, where it threw the Persians into *panic* fear.
Another word we get from him is the pan-pipe, which
he is said to have invented when the nymph Syrinx
fled from his arms, and, on her prayer for rescue, was
turned into a reed, which he adapted to such good
purpose as to rival the music of Apollo's lyre. He
came to be looked on as the god of woodland jollity,
of herds and flocks, of fertility, and of country life in
general. From being chief of the Satyrs, a hanger-on of
Dionysus, Aphrodite, and other unedifying high society,
he rose to rank as one of the most active of the gods.
By a confusion, no doubt, of his name with the word *pan*
(all), he was latterly looked upon as personification of

nature; and at the dawn of a new era "Universal Pan" had so far come to represent Olympus that a dubious legend makes the birth of Christ hailed by a supernatural voice proclaiming to Greece, "Great Pan is dead".

> "The oracles are dumb;
> No voice or hideous hum
> Runs through the arched roof in words deceiving.
> Apollo from his shrine,
> Can no more divine,
> With hollow shriek the steep of Delphos leaving".

But Pan was dethroned rather than dead, living on in Christian conceptions to shape the horned and cloven-footed devil of mediæval mythology. Nay, so great loomed this vanished fame in after ages, that there are traces of strange comparison between him and his conqueror, so that Milton does not stick at using this name to hymn the advent of our religion—

> "Full little thought they than
> That the mighty Pan
> Was kindly come to live with them below".

Demigods and Heroes

The foregoing account of the gods indicates how Greek mythology included many semi-divine personages, of whom less need be said here, since they figure largely in the tales that follow. A salient instance of this double nature is supplied by the *Dioscuri*, Castor and Polydeuces (Pollux), hatched from the same swan's egg with their sister Helen, that *teterrima causa* of so many souls going down to Hades before their time. Though they had Zeus for father, fate did not provide immortality enough to go round this family; and an oracle let the two brothers know that one of them was destined to rank among the gods, while the other must share the common lot as putative son of the Lacedæmonian king Tyndareus. The brothers, devotedly attached to each other, and ignorant which of them was mortal, had no wish but to die together. *Dis aliter visum*: in a quarrel with rival suitors Castor was slain, and all Zeus could do for him was to strike down the slayer with a thunderbolt. But Pollux took his brother's loss so much to heart, that means were found to compromise with the decree of fate by sharing the boon of divinity between them, so that they spent together day about on Olympus and in Hades. These semi-immortal personages were also inconsistently placed among the stars as the *Gemini*. On earth they rose to quasi-divinity, first at Sparta, the place of their human origin, and their worship spread far over the Greek world into Italy. Castor having been renowned as a charioteer and Pollux as a boxer, they were looked on as patrons of public games, along with Hermes and Hercules. It is less obvious how they came to be the special protectors of mariners, like that "sweet little cherub" sitting up aloft as agent of the modern Neptune's goodwill to poor Jack: sailors of the Latin nations still connect with their name the flitting gleams sometimes seen on a ship's rigging. On land, they appear as goodly youths nobly mounted on white chargers, who came to help of favoured armies at a critical moment. As Theseus rose from the dead to give ghostly aid to his Athenians on the plain of Marathon, so at the battle of Lake Regillus the Roman Dictator found that princely pair riding beside him to victory.

> " Back comes the Chief in triumph,
>   Who, in the hour of fight,
>   Hath seen the Great Twin-Brethren
>   In harness on his right.

Safe comes the ship to haven,
Through billows and through gales.
If once the Great Twin-Brethren
Sit shining on the sails."

Pausanias mentions a case of this belief being turned to hostile account : when the Spartans were celebrating the feast of Castor and Pollux, two young Messenians, dressed for the part in white tunics and purple cloaks, rode into the camp to be received with awe as immortals, then galloped through cutting and stabbing the deceived worshippers.

Three hundred years or so before our era, the Greek writer Euhemerus boldly applied to the national mythology an explanation identified with his name : that the gods had been magnified out of renowned men. The process appears in the case of Alexander the Great, who claimed descent both from Achilles and Jupiter-Ammon, and, out of policy or vanity, made a point of having his quasi-divinity recognized in Greece. We know how cheap deification came to be when not only emperors were thus raised to the skies as matter of course, but Antinous, the minion of Hadrian, had a temple built in his honour, and sacrifice was offered to the images of the famous physician, Hippocrates. A grateful pupil of the Academy erected an altar to Plato. In earlier times any benefactor or terror of men would readily take on a supernatural character, at whose tomb sacrificial rites seemed due. Everywhere the first sketches of history show heroic personages, real or fictitious, looming out in proportions that seem more than mortal, like Achilles and Æneas. Romulus and Remus precede our own Arthur in having ascribed to them some origin or end distinguished from that of common men. Hiawatha was an American Indian Triptolemus who played the same part in bringing the sacred boon of corn among his fellow Indians.

All over the world indeed the tomb of any hero tends to become a shrine. In Greece this hero-worship was manifolded by the number of rival states, each of them eloquently concerned to exalt its legendary worthies, whose names, if not invented by local pride, came down from a distant age when the gods were understood to move freely upon earth. The bards who sang before and after Homer had to earn praise or pudding by extolling the ancestors of their hearers—Homer himself had several legendary birthplaces, but not so many as Zeus. The Catalogue of the ships in the *Iliad* appears to have been inserted that no Greek state should be left out of that roll of ancient glory. Much later, Pindar's odes were addressed to victors in the athletic games of his day ; and he takes every chance of bringing in allusions to such legendary fame as might tickle the ears of his numerous patrons. Not that the lauding bard need have been mercenary: admiration is the natural attitude of dithyrambic chroniclers, as in the case of one whom in our own time we have seen working himself up to extol dubious heroes from Dr. Francia to Frederick the Great. But many a true worthy must have gone down into endless night, for lack of a sacred trump to sound his exploits.

> " For not to have been dipt in Lethe Lake,
> Could save the son of Thetis from to die;
> But that blind Bard did him immortal make
> With verses dipped in dew of Castalie."

Nor had the bards to please only limited audiences. Contests in music and song made part of the meetings for athletic prowess. The influence of the arts in ancient

Greece, reflected in the fame of Apollo, went to refine and to illustrate its early legends. They were no barbarians among whom so many stories show poetry in high honour. The names of Sappho and Anacreon are remembered better than their works. When Alexander destroyed Thebes, he bid spare the house reputed as Pindar's. It is told that the Spartans being directed by an oracle to seek a leader in war from their rival Athens, the Athenians sent them the lame schoolmaster Tyrtæus, as least likely to be of use to an enemy; but they had reckoned without his gift of impassioned song, that so inspired the Lacedæmonian soldiers as to lead them on to victory singing the chants of which some fragments have come down to us under his name. Terpander of Lesbos is famed as the inventor of the seven-stringed lyre, in its simpler form ascribed to the precocious infant Hermes. A more mythical minstrel appears Arion, said to have earned a fortune at musical meetings in Sicily.

Whatever poetical gains may have been, we owe a debt of gratitude to the " rhapsodists ",[1] actors in monologue, indeed, rather than poets, through whose chanting or recitation were handed down to us the strains attributed to Homer, which seem to have been finally stereotyped in the form given them by ceremonial delivery at the Panathenaic gatherings, whether or no they were edited under the direction of Pisistratus. We have specimens, or at least the titles of other epics, sometimes ascribed to Homer, that were authority for some traditional characters and incidents of legend. And as there were heroes before Agamemnon, so after Homer there were esteemed poets, such as Archilochus, Stesi-

---

[1] In the literal meaning of *rhapsodist*, "stitcher together", seems to be a hint of argument for controverters of "Lewis Carroll's" opinion, that the works known as Homer's, if not written by him, were by "another man of the same name".

chorus, and Simonides, whose works, though lost to us, unless in fragments or allusions, no doubt went to colour the old stories, not to speak of extant but neglected poems like the *Argonautica* of Apollonius, an epic that should be better known as model for Virgil's *Æneid*.

It will not be amiss to say a word about those primarily athletic contests that did so much to foster a national life and common religion among the jarring cities of the Greek world, the competitors coming not only from Greece but from its colonies in Asia and Sicily. The four great meetings of the Greek world were :—

The *Olympic Games*, held on the templed plain of Olympia, near Pisa in Elis, where the Alpheus flows to the western coast of the Peloponnesus. These seem the oldest of all, traced back to the eighth century B.C., but their origin is lost in immemorial antiquity ; one fond tradition made them founded by Zeus in honour of his prevailing over Cronos. Other Panhellenic meetings apparently date from the sixth century.

The *Pythian Games* at Delphi, its old name Pytho, were given out as founded by Apollo. Like the Olympic Games, they took place every four years, whereas the next mentioned were at intervals of two years.

The *Isthmian Games*, held on the Isthmus of Corinth in honour of Poseidon.

The *Nemean Games*, in Argolis, taken to be founded or revived by Hercules after his killing of the Nemean lion.

There were also the Panathenaic Games, peculiar to Attica and her dependencies, and doubtless many other local celebrations which did not succeed in establishing themselves as national and historical landmarks.

Among these the famous Olympic Games were the most important as a festival at once social, political, and religious, held at intervals of four years, which period, styled an *Olympiad*, was used in dating events, like the five-year *Lustrum* of the Romans, the successive Olympiads running from 776 B.C., when the games first appear as fully organized. We know how, in the effort to make a " living Greece " once more of the modern kingdom, they came to be revived at the end of the nineteenth century, having died out in the fourth century of our era.

" You have the Pyrrhic dance as yet—
Where is the Pyrrhic phalanx gone?"

The ancient ceremonies lasted for a month, beginning with the first full moon of the summer solstice. Both place and period were held as sacred, no armed force being suffered to approach. This national truce, indeed, might be disturbed by an old quarrel between Pisa and Elis for the presidency of the meeting, which once, in 364 B.C., came to be broken up by a collision of implacable feuds, turning the games into a battle.

In the athletic contests which filled the first half of the month, all freeborn Hellenes might compete; but they were not open to barbarians, a word implying all people who did not speak Greek. " Pot-hunting " and "gate-money" did not corrupt the sport of early days, though something like " professionalism " seems to have been developed. The prize was a simple crown of wild olive; but the winner deemed himself rich in the general applause and in that of his fellow citizens, who hailed his victory as a special triumph for his native state, where henceforth he lived in honour and privilege; and more substantial rewards were not always wanting, while his fame might be embalmed in a statue. The first and chief contest would be the foot race, followed by wrestling, boxing, hurling the spear and the discus, horse races, chariot races, and other exercises, altered or modified at different times. There were competitions for boys only, and at one time a race for girls; but as a rule women were held aloof from the lists. The *pancration* made a medley of boxing and wrestling, and the *pentathlon*, a succession of five separate contests, victory in either of which came to be the ardent ambition of athletes. Nor was personal prowess the only title to fame. Rich men, and magnates of outlying colonies, trained horses for races, where their success gave the owner such pride as comes from possession of a Derby winner. But the excitement of our Epsom or Newmarket faintly reflects the eagerness with which the Greek world fixed its eyes on the contests of Olympia.

The second half of the month was taken up with processions, sacrifices, and such religious ceremonies, ending with a banquet to the successful competitors. During the festival it was customary for authors to read their compositions as at a Welsh *Eisteddfod*; and the History of Herodotus is doubtfully said to have been published in this manner. The huge concourse attracted on such an occasion lent itself, likewise, to commercial dealings, which gave it the character of an inter-state fair. Works of art, also, were exhibited at what made the Greek form of an Exhibition, while such sanctuaries as Olympia and Delphi became permanent museums of national art and history.

The whole scene was thickly set with temples and statues, in part votive offerings, but often furnished by fines for bribery or foul play, which seem not to have been unknown. Besides metal, wood, clay, and stone, ivory was used in combinations, like the famous chryselephantine (gold and ivory) statue of Zeus by Phidias. Pausanias, who plays Bædeker for us among the memorials as they stood at his day, mentions one athlete, Theagenes, as having won 1400 crowns at the various games of his time. He began his career as a schoolboy by taking down a brazen statue in the marketplace and carrying it home on his back; but when he came to have a statue of his own after death, an enemy was less lucky in dealing with it, who used to vent his spite by scourging the brazen image every night till it fell over and crushed him. Milo of Croton is the competitor whose name has come down to us most renownedly, for his feats of strength and for his miserable end: trying to hold open a split trunk, he got his hands wedged into it, and was held a helpless prey for wolves. Sometimes a town appears hard up for a hero, as that one whose boxing champion, having killed his adversary at the Games, was sentenced to lose the prize, then went so far out of his mind for grief, that after returning home he performed Samson's exploit with the pillars of a school and pulled down the roof upon threescore children. The indignant people pelted him with stones to take refuge in the temple of Athene, where he hid himself in a chest that when broken open was found empty; and an oracle bid his fellow citizens honour him as no mere mortal. Even in such sports, we see how hero-myths might take shape; then where minstrels and priests met, as well as athletes and lovers of horse-flesh, the occasion naturally made an exchange for legends jumbled together from the superstitious imagination of different districts.

These intercommunications go to explain the form in which many myths have come down to us, their outlines blurred, their colours run together, and sometimes changing like a chameleon with the ground on which they are set. The confusion would be increased by migrating tribes bringing their legendary heroes to new seats. There seems to have been a movement both of amalgamation and differentiation of traditions. Local heroes got to be identified with more widely famed ones, whose exploits in turn might be adopted to swell the renown of some minor champion, while new sprouts of glory could find credit by being grafted on to a time-honoured heroic stock.

The characters and deeds of the heroes had, of course, to fit local pride and jealousy, as when Minos, who in general mythology presents the type of a just judge, figures in the story of Theseus as a cruel tyrant wreaking his spite against Athens. " Thus it seems ill to earn the hate of a city great in eloquence and poetry ", remarks Plutarch, whose life of Theseus is strikingly critical in tone. The recent discoveries in Crete, showing this island to have been a seat of maritime enterprise before the rise of the Greek states on the mainland, pave the way to some historic basis for Athens having been in such a tributary position towards the powerful Minos dynasty, as might well leave a grudge against their name. The vengeance of Minos, by the way, is attributed to the fact of his son Androgeos having been murdered by resentful competitors whom he had beaten at the Athenian games.

The Muses are not to be trusted as historians. If heroes were promoted to godship, phantoms might take vague heroic form, like that of Pelops, legendary lord of the Peloponnesus, who appears in fable as boiled by his father Tantalus to make a sacrilegious meal for the gods, and again as winning an Olympic race by bribing his opponent's charioteer to run foul. For further instance of how we must pick and choose among variant legends, four different impieties are alleged as cause of the punishment to which Tantalus was so famously doomed. Nor can we be sure that we have all the versions once current. Some tales are known to us only by casual allusions in the poets; and some are best known as freely handled for the Athenian stage. Here and there we may surmise the moralizing or refining touch of an author. The brutal Polyphemus of the *Odyssey* must have grown softer of heart when he combed and shaved himself for love of the fair Galatea, though indeed his savage nature came out in the revenge he took on his favoured rival, Acis, as the happy pair sat listening to the love-lorn Cyclops' song. The painful stories of Niobe's children, and of Philomela, might both seem blended less shockingly in that of Aedon, the jealous sister, who would have slain Niobe's first-born, but by mistake killed her own son Itylus, a tragedy she laments for ever in the plaintive notes of the nightingale; and this tale also takes more than one form. Sometimes a patch can be detected as let in to an old story, the fable of "The Choice of Hercules" for example, ascribed to a sophist of the fifth century B.C., and evidently out of keeping with the sanguinary tissue of the original legend.

The figure most like a national hero is that of Hercules, who varyingly appears as born at Tiryns and at Thebes, but never settled down at any city that could take the full credit of his exploits, his wanderings carrying him far and wide, beyond the bounds of Greece. Outside of it was he honoured, as in his great temple at Tyre; but indeed Herodotus notes two separate incarnations of this great name. His descendants the Heraclidæ are made to conquer the Peloponnesus, dividing its kingdoms between them—probably a mythical view of the Dorian invasion—and the list of that progeny, as enumerated by Apollodorus, is so long that it could have supplied heroic worthies enough to serve all the Greek states.

Many an ancient bard may have done violence to his conscience by ennobling liberal patrons with the blood of such an illustrious ancestor; and Hercules strangling the snakes in his cradle came to be a favourite device on the coins of Greek cities and colonies. The story of Perseus, still more that of Theseus, look like local variants of the long list of prodigious exploits that from many quarters came to be tacked on to a more widely famous name.

Thus we may have similar exploits recorded of different personages, and varying, often contradictory versions of what seems the same tale. That, of course, is no new thing in mythology. The classical writers who had to handle this medley of tradition, were more or less free to "edit" it according to their own tastes and prejudices. Wild work was made of chronology by the need of bringing such and such a hero to some place at a certain time, and of putting certain heroes together on the same scene. Tiresias, the blind seer, for instance, figures like a Methusaleh in many generations. The charms of Ninon de L'Enclos did not hold out so long as Helen's, who for a century or so, if all poets are to be trusted, might by generations be prayed "make me immortal with a kiss!" Hercules appears a contemporary of many heroes, some of whom must have been too old or too young to be very serviceable among the Argonaut crew that had him for a shipmate. The enterprise of the *Argo*, by the way, suggests how some early commercial voyage to the inhospitable Euxine may have made a core for such a snowball tale of marvel and adventure, as the siege of Troy very probably was a real prelude to the later struggles between Greece and Asia. Several cities, indeed, are now seen to have stood successively on the site of Troy, always likely to be a scene of collision between eastward adventurers and the holders of a stronghold commanding the entrance to the Hellespont.

Homer stands above other bards in appealing to a national patriotism, though there may be some trace of *particularismus* in his opposition of the northern Achilles to the Peloponnesian lord of Argos. Not less remarkable is the *Iliad*'s advance from the barbarism of less refined legends. Poisoned arrows have gone out of common use, while there are hints of these in the *Odyssey* and in the cureless shafts bequeathed by Hercules to Philoctetes; warriors exchange courtesies as well as insults when about to engage; woman is no mere thrall; and human sacrifice occurs only in the exceptional case of the funeral of Patroclus, whose death indeed rouses Achilles for once to insult the body of a gallant foe, yet he repents before the grief of a suppliant father.

So much being hinted as to the Protean nature of the materials here to be handled, in the following stories the critical attitude must be laid aside. We have to take these legends as we find them. The writer's task is to reproduce the chief features of this mythology, treated on a given scale, usually after the best-known version, yet sometimes with an eye to the taste of readers who will not so readily stomach the grossness that did not offend ancient hearers. In a certain amount of selection or suppression, one is justified by classic example; but, as far as may be, the attempt is to present the Greek mind as shown in its famous fables, and to make familiar the names and characters so often cited in poetry, oratory, and history.

PHAETHON

A proud youth was Phaethon when his mother Cly-
mene let him know how for father he had no mortal man,
none less than the god Phœbus-Apollo that daily drove
across our world in the Sun's dazzling chariot. But the
lad's companions mocked him when he boasted such
high birth; then, at his mother's bidding, he sought
out that heavenly sire to demand a boon through which
all should know him as of divine race.

Before dawn he came to the golden palace of Phœbus,
where the purple-mantled god sat on his ivory throne,
amid a rainbow sheen of jewels. Round him stood his
ministers and henchmen, the Hours, the Days, the
Months, and noblest of all, the Seasons: Spring wreathed
with fresh blossoms, naked Summer clothed in leaves
and crowned with ears of corn, Autumn stained by the
clusters of fruit he held in his sunburnt arms, and shiver-
ing Winter with snow-white locks. Phaethon's eyes were
dazzled before such magnificence, so that he durst not
approach the throne till his all-seeing father called him by
name.

"Welcome, my son, to the halls of heaven!" quoth
Phœbus, laying aside the crown of sunrays on which
mortal sight could not bear to gaze. "But say, what
brings thee from earth?"

Thus encouraged, the beardless boy drew near to
falter out his request, and soon waxed bolder in the god's
smiling face. He made his complaint that men would

not believe him Apollo's son, unless his father gave him a pledge of his birth that might be seen by the whole world.

"Before the whole world," cried the god, "will I own thee for my son. Well hast thou done to seek a proof of favour, which thy father grants unheard: so I swear by the Styx, that oath that binds even the gods. Ask, then, and have!"

"Father," exclaimed Phaethon eagerly, "grant me my dearest wish, for one day to be trusted to drive the chariot of the Sun!"

A shade fell on the radiant face of Phœbus, and once and again he shook his glowing head before he answered.

"Rash boy, that knows not what he would dare! That charge is too great for heedless youth, nay, for any mortal, since not even to the gods may it be safely committed. Jupiter himself takes not in hand the reins of the Sun's coursers. Among all the sons of Olympus, I alone can stand firm in the burning car and rule aright its fiery steeds on their steep and toilsome path. Renounce, I beseech thee, such a perilous boon. Ask anything else in heaven or earth, and again I swear by Styx it is thine."

But the froward youth, with pouts and entreaties, held fast to his audacious wish, and would not let himself be moved by fatherly counsels. So at last, the lord of the Sun, bound by his oath, was fain to consent, though sorely fearing what would come of trusting such steeds to so weak a hand.

It was time to be off on that daily journey, for already Aurora began to draw back the rosy curtains of the East, as Phœbus led his son to Vulcan's masterpiece, the golden chariot studded with sparkling gems, all so rich and beautiful that Phaethon's head was turned by his good fortune to be its master for one day. The vanishing of the stars and the fading of the moon's horns were signal to lead out the four coursers of the Sun, pawing and neighing to show how, full fed with ambrosia, and refreshed by the night's rest, they came eager for their accustomed task. While the swift-fingered Hours fitted on their clanking bits, and harnessed them to the chariot-pole, fond Phœbus anointed the youth with a sacred balm that would enable him better to bear the heat of his glowing course. Meanwhile the god plied him with warnings, to which his impatient son hardly gave ear.

"Keep heedfully the straight path marked by fear-some signs of beasts. Beware in going by the horns of the Bull and the mouth of the roaring Lion, and the far-stretched claws of the Scorpion or the Crab. Shun the South Pole and the North Pole; hold the upper arch of the sky from east to west; safest ever is the middle way. Sink not too far down, lest the earth catch fire; rise not too high to scorch the face of heaven. Spare the goad, and draw tight the reins, for my horses fly of themselves, and all the labour is to hold them in. Now mount the car—or no, dear son, bethink thee in time! It is not honour thou shalt win, but punishment and destruction. Leave the chariot to me, and be content to watch its course like thy fellow men!"

But already the presumptuous stripling had sprung up to grasp the reins; and when Thetis drew the bar of heaven, he let the chafing horses bound forth, throwing back a hasty word of thanks and farewell to his anxious father.

Boldly Phaethon urged that mettlesome team through the morning mists, with the east wind following to sweep him on his proud career. But soon the swift-

ness took away his breath, while under his light weight
the car shook and swayed like a keel without ballast,
till his head began to turn. And too soon the fiery
coursers felt how their reins were in an unpractised
hand. Rearing and starting aside, they left their wonted
way; then all the earth was amazed to see the glorious
chariot of the Sun speeding crookedly overhead as a
flash of lightning.

Before he had gone far, the rash charioteer sorely
repented his ambition, and would have asked no greater
boon than to be saved from that perilous honour.
Too late he saw how wisely his father had warned him.
His head whirled, his face grew white, and his knees
shook as he looked to earth and sea spread out
beneath, and to the boundless sky above. In vain he
tugged at the tangled bridles; in vain he cried to
the horses which he could not call by name. Heated
by the wild course, they no longer minded his un-
masterful hand, but took their own way through the
air, prancing hither and thither at will. Now they
soared up towards the sky, so that the clouds began
to smoke, and the Moon looked out with dismay to
see her brother's car so strangely guided. Then turning
downwards, as if to cool themselves in the ocean, they
passed close over a high mountain, that in a moment
burst into flames.

Thus fearsome disaster fell upon the earth. The
Sun, instead of holding his stately beneficent course
across the sky, seemed to rush down in wrath like a
meteor, blasting the fair face of nature and the works
of man. The grass withered; the crops were scorched
away; the woods went up in fire and smoke; then
beneath them the bare earth cracked and crumbled,
and the blackened rocks burst asunder under the heat.

The rivers dried up or fled back to their hidden fountains; the lakes began to boil; the very sea sank in its bed, and the fishes lay gasping on the shore, unless they could gain the depths whence Poseidon thrice raised his head and thrice plunged back into his shrinking waves, unable to bear the deadly glow. Scythia was not shielded by its frosts, nor Caucasus by its snows, licked up beneath the passage of that scorching whirlwind. Mighty Atlas, they say, had all but let the red-hot world fall from his writhing shoulders. On that day the earth was scorched, and, ever since, one stretch of it has been a sandy desert, where neither man nor beast can thrive. But all over the habitable world the Sun's charioteer spread woe and ruin, as its cities were consumed one by one, and the people in their torment swarmed here and there, like ants, among the ashes of their homes. Never had such a calamity fallen on man since Zeus and Poseidon drowned his impiety under the flood in which only Deucalion and Pyrrha found dry land!

By now the wretched Phaethon had given up hope to check or guide his baleful course. Blinded by terror and by the glare spreading beneath him wherever he sped, seared by the heat till he could not stand on the glowing car, he threw down the useless reins, to fall on his knees with a pitiful prayer for his father's help. But his prayer was lost in the cry that went up from the whole earth, calling upon the lord of heaven to save mankind from destruction.

Not unheard rose that cry. All-powerful Zeus was sleeping away the noonday hour; but quickly he awoke and raised his head and saw what had befallen. Snatching a thunderbolt that lay ready to his hand, he hurled it through the smoky air, and struck senseless Phaethon from this chariot he could not control. Down the youth dashed with blazing locks, swift as a falling star, to be quenched like a firebrand in the river Eridanus. Then the horses of the Sun shook off their yokes, breaking loose to seek their stalls in the sky; and for once at noon night fell upon the earth, lit only by the flickering fires kindled through Phaethon's folly.

So, on that woeful day, ended the vainglorious son born to Phœbus-Apollo, who was fain to hide his countenance for shame of his fatherly fondness. But some there were who mourned the rash youth's end. When the nymphs of the Eridanus had buried him on its banks, his mother, frantic with grief, came thither to pour out her heart's blood in sorrow. His three sisters, too, wept so bitterly, that the pitying gods changed them into poplar trees dropping tears of amber upon the water. And his friend Cygnus dived so often into the river to gather up Phaethon's charred members, that when he pined away for grief, it was granted him still to haunt the stream in the shape of a swan.

PERSEUS

I. The Gorgon

Acrisius, king of Argos, was sore troubled through an oracle declaring that by the hand of a grandson he should die; then, having but one child, his fair daughter Danaë, he thought to cheat that doom by keeping her unwedded. To make sure, he shut her up in close prison, a cave underground, or, as some say, a brazen tower, never to see the face of man while she lived. But the gods can make their way even where the light of day is shut out. Danaë was visited by Zeus in the form of a shower of gold, and here she bore a son, who was to be the famous hero Perseus.

When the infant's crying came to the ears of the king, and he learned how a grandson had been born to him for all his watchfulness, his cowardly soul was filled with dismay. Not daring to have the boy's blood on his hands, nor yet to let him live, he had mother and child put together in a chest and sent drifting out to drown or starve upon the stormy sea. But Zeus watched over them; and at his bidding Poseidon stilled the winds and waves that gently bore their frail ark eastward, till it came washed ashore on the island of Seriphos in the Ægean archipelago.

Here Danaë and her babe were found by a fisherman named Dictys, who treated them kindly, and took them to his house to bring up Perseus as his own child. And so well throve this young stranger that the men of Seriphos could guess him to be of royal birth, nay, son of a god. In sports and combats he soon vanquished all his playfellows, and grew up to full strength and stature, his mind set on brave deeds by which he might prove himself a hero among men. In dreams he was inspired by Athene, who strung his heart to choose the deadliest perils in the flower of youth, rather than inglorious ease and safety.

Soon he was to have his desire. His foster-father Dictys had a brother, Polydectes, the chief of the island, but of less noble nature. He, at first friendly to the strangers cast on his shore, came to love Danaë, and would have forced her to be his wife. But all her heart was given to her son, and such a wooer seemed unworthy of one who had been loved by a god. The cunning Polydectes bethought him how to get rid of this manly youth who stood as a guard to his mother's honour. To have Danaë in his power he set Perseus upon a fearful adventure, from which the bravest man was little like to come back alive.

The task given him was to slay the monster Medusa, one of the three Gorgon sisters, she alone of them mortal, but her very looks deadly to the best-armed foe. For, to punish an impious outrage on Athene, her hair had been turned into vipers writhing about a face so horrible that whoever set eyes upon it was stiffened to stone before he could strike a blow. Yet Perseus did not fear to face the Gorgon, when his patron Athene gave him wise counsels how he should accomplish that perilous quest.

"Not without help of the gods can the bravest man assail such a foe," she bid him know, when the bold youth would have made light of all he must dare.

For now the goddess appeared to him in radiant majesty, accompanied by her brother Hermes, and they lent him certain powerful talismans in proof of their favour. Hermes girded on to him his own crooked sword that could cut through the stoutest armour, and fitted the youth's feet with his winged sandals to bear him swiftly over land and sea. Moreover, from the realm of Pluto he brought him a wonderful helmet that made the wearer of it invisible. Athene gave him her polished shield, which he must use like a mirror so as to strike Medusa without looking straight in her horrific face. Also she provided him with a goatskin bag to hide the Gorgon's head, that even in death would freeze the blood of all who beheld it, friend or foe.

Thus equipped, he was bidden first to seek out, in their icy home of the north, the frostbound Graiæ, half-sisters of the Gorgons, who alone could tell him the way to the far-off isle where Medusa had her lair. Not an hour did he lose in setting forth, only begging of Athene to watch over his mother till he brought back Medusa's head. With such heavenly aid, he could make no doubt of victory.

Springing into the air from the cliffs of Seriphos, lightly he flew to the north, till he came among snows and mists and mountains of ice where no mortal man can dwell. There, on the edge of the Hyperborean sea, he found the Grey Sisters huddled up together, dim and shapeless forms, of which his eyes could hardly tell whether they were two or three. Clothed only in their long hair, white and bristling with ice, so old were they and so doting that they had but one eye and one tooth left between them, which their fumbling hands passed from each to other with groans and murmurs, as in turn they needed to munch the snowflakes or to peer through the blinding mists. This Perseus knew from Athene; and as she had bidden him, he stole up to the old hags, invisible in his helm of darkness, then suddenly snatched away their eye, as they wrangled which should have it to see whose steps came clanging on the frosty shore.

"Tell me the way to the Gorgons," demanded he, "or I take your tooth also, and leave you to starve in this wilderness."

A miserable outcry those Grey Sisters made, when they found themselves thus robbed by an unseen hand. With threats and curses they bid him give up their eye; but he held it firm, till, since so it must be, they mumbled out directions by which he might find the Gorgons' Isle. For thanks he gave them back their eye, but they saw him not, for he was gone before they could nod their feeble heads, falling asleep like blocks of ice.

Now he must fly far to the south, where the mists and snows soon melted away, and the earth lay green with fields and forests, and the blue sea shone and sparkled under a glowing sky. Hot and hotter grew the air as he flew over land and sea towards the other end of the world, all its rivers and mountains stretching out below his feet, and at last a great ocean upon which no sail was spread. There, following the course given him to steer by the sun and the stars, he spied out the island whereon lived those hateful sisters, among lifeless images of men and beasts whom their looks had turned to stone.

Swooping down in the brightness of noonday, he saw the three Gorgons fast asleep, Medusa in the middle. But on her he did not dare to fix his eyes. As Athene

Phoebus Apollo
Page 34

Perseus and Andromeda
Page 81

The Return of Persephone
Page 125

Hylas and the Water Nymphs
Page 155

The Golden Fleece
Page 166

Echo and Narcissus
Page 220

Clytemnestra
Page 284

The Last Watch of Hero
Page 368

had bidden him, he drew near with his back turned, holding her shield so as to make a mirror for that blood-curdling head, with its mane of vipers curling and writhing about it even in sleep. Fearfully beautiful was Medusa's face as well as horrible; but as she tossed to and fro in her dreams, Perseus saw how her body was clad in loathsome scales and brazen plumage, and how her limbs ended in cruel claws; and her mouth open in a bitter smile showed fangs like a serpent's, bristling round her forked tongue.

He durst not look longer for fear she should open her blood-freezing eyes. Marking in his mirror how she lay, he struck backwards, and with one sweep of the crooked sword of Hermes had cut clean through her neck so swiftly as to choke her one shrill cry. Then with averted looks and shuddering hands he stowed away the bleeding head in his goatskin bag, and rose into the air with a shout of triumph.

That cry awoke the two sister Gorgons to find Medusa's headless body lying between them, and to hear the exulting voice of the foe who had done this deed. Hissing and howling, they spread their wings like monstrous birds of prey to seek him out with their iron talons. But Perseus, hid from them by his helm of darkness, was soon beyond reach of those revengeful monsters, that, unlike their sister, could not be slain by mortal hand.

Fast and far the hero flew with his prize, the way soon leading over a boundless desert on which he could see no green thing nor any living creature. But as the Gorgon's blood oozed through the goatskin, gouts of it dropped upon the thirsty sand, and there bred venomous snakes and scorpions, ever since to plague that barren soil. Huge pillars of whirling sand rose up to mark how the raging Gorgons chased him in vain; for

Perseus soared above them invisible, nor set foot on earth till he came at evening to the westernmost bounds of the known world.

Here night and day knelt the old giant Atlas, holding up by pillars the weight of the sky. Of him Perseus, wearied by his long travel, begged leave to stay and rest in the famed garden of golden apples which Atlas kept jealously enclosed under guard of a dragon. But the churlish giant bid him begone.

"I am a son of Zeus, and I have done a deed to earn better welcome," pleaded Perseus.

"A son of Zeus is fated to rob my garden!" growled the giant, remembering an oracle of old, which was indeed to be fulfilled by Hercules.

"If so chary of what is thine, take thou a gift from me!" And with this Perseus drew forth the Gorgon's head to hold it full in the giant's face.

Not another word did Atlas speak. This hugest of Titans had in an instant been turned to a stony peak, his tall head white with snows, his beard stiff with ice, his rocky ribs bristling with forests. And so he stands to this day, a lifeless mountain bearing up the clouds.

II. Andromeda

His face set to the east, Perseus held an airy way, feeling himself truly invincible, now that to the god-given talismans he had added the spell of Medusa's head, which even in death could appal the strongest foe. When he had passed over the desert, and crossed the green edges of the Nile, he came next to the land of the Ethiopians, and other exotic peoples; and soon the rising sun showed him a marvellous sight. Against a black rock on the seashore washed by every wave, the

form of a sunburnt maiden stood like a statue, nor
moved as he swept down towards her, so that but for
the tears in her eyes and her long locks stirred by the
wind, he might have taken her for carved out of stone.
He saw how, veiled in sunlight and spray, she blushed
at his approach, faintly struggling as if she would have
covered her face with her hands, but could not, for she
was fast chained to the rock.

"Fair maiden, how comest thou in such a plight?"
he cried, wondering at her beauty, not less than her woe.
"Why these chains for a form more fitly arrayed in
wedding garlands? Thy name and race? asks one who
would fain set thee free from such unworthy bonds."

The maiden strove to speak, but once and again
tears choked her voice, and shame tied her tongue.
But, when the hero put on his helm of darkness and
thus became invisible to her downcast eyes, she at last
found voice to answer.

"I am Andromeda, only daughter of Cepheus the
king; and here am I set to suffer for words not my
own. It was my mother Cassiope who, in her pride,
boasted of me as fairer than the Nereids, daughters
of the sea. They, out of spite, worked on Poseidon
to send a cruel sea-monster, ravaging our coasts, and
scaring the people from their homes. Then my father
sought the oracle of Ammon in the Libyan sands, and
had for answer that by the sacrifice of his daughter alone
could the pest be stayed. Long my parents were loath
to devote me thus; but the people cried out so sorely
that they were fain to obey the oracle. So here I stand
helpless, awaiting the monster, that is to devour me at
sunrise, then leave the land in peace. And there he
comes!" she ended with a shriek, as afar off rose a
shapeless black bulk from the sea depths.

"Not helpless, fair Andromeda!" quoth Perseus, and
with his magic sword cut the chains that bound her as
lightly as if they were thread. "By heavenly aid, I have
slain the Gorgon, and so will I do to this monster, be it
ever so fearful."

Now the maiden stood still and calm, trusting that
here must indeed be a son of the gods sent to deliver
her. But her cry of alarm had come echoed back from
the cliffs, on which stood the woeful parents with a crowd
of people, waiting to see her cruel end. Their warning
shouts told how that the monster made speed towards
the victim, who closed her eyes when she saw its back
cleaving the waves like a swift galley.

With one word of cheer to Andromeda, Perseus made
ready for the fight that should deliver her. He laid
aside Medusa's head, veiling its horror in seaweeds that
afterwards were found changed into coral branches.
Drawing his sword, he sprang lightly into the air, and
flew to meet the monster as it rushed upon Andromeda
with foaming jaws and grinding teeth. But when from
above the hero's shadow fell upon the sea, the creature
checked its course to rage against this unlooked-for
enemy. Down swooped Perseus like an eagle, piercing
its scaly neck with his keen blade. The monster roared
and lashed and writhed, turning on its back as it vainly
tried to get him into its horrid jaws, while again and
again the sword goaded it to fresh fury upon the waves
purpled with its blood; and to those looking on with
affrighted eyes it seemed as if the whole sea were stirred
by a storm.

At last, when all was still, the weeping parents ventured down from the cliff to see what had befallen. They
found their daughter trembling but unharmed, and beside
her Perseus stood wiping his sword, where out of the

heaving red water stood up the monster's body, now still as a huge black reef.

"Dry your tears and take back your daughter, loosed by my sword," was the greeting of Perseus. "But her whom I have won from death, I claim for a kinder embrace. I am son of Zeus and Danaë, one whom ye might not despise for her husband, even were she free to choose."

The grateful parents willingly agreed to give such a champion not only their daughter, but all the kingdom if he desired it as dowry. With tears, now of joy, they led him to their palace, where a feast was soon prepared to grace the marriage of Perseus and Andromeda, more lovely than ever in her bridal array.

But their wedding feast was troubled by a clang of arms, when into the hall burst Phineus, kinsman of the king, by whom the maid had before been sought in marriage. Backed by a throng of armed henchmen, he demanded his promised bride, hotly defying the favoured lover.

"No stranger is worthy to win the daughter of our land!" he declared; and not a few of the guests cried out on his side.

"Thou didst not woo her when chained to the rock!" taunted Perseus. "Neither suitor nor kinsman stood by her against the monster from whose jaws I won Andromeda to be mine."

For answer Phineus hurled his spear, that stuck quivering in a post beside Perseus as he stood with his shield held over Andromeda. His sword flashed out like lightning, and in a moment the hall was filled with uproar. Song and mirth gave place to the clash and hiss of weapons, and the tables ran red with blood instead of wine. So many were the followers and well-wishers of Phineus that the king's men could not withstand them; then over the din rose the hero's voice:

"Let all who are my friends turn away their eyes!"

He held up the Gorgon's head, and in the twinkling of an eye those enemies had been turned to stone as they stood, one brandishing a sword, one flinging a dart, and Phineus, last of all, upon his knees as he fell to beg for his own life when he saw what befell his comrades in rebellion. Not thus could they now disturb the marriage banquet.

> "Beautiful, eager, triumphant, he leapt back again to his treasure;
> Leapt back again, full blest, toward arms spread wide to receive him.
> Brimful of honour he clasped her, and brimful of love she caressed him,
> Answering lip with lip; while above them the queen Aphrodité
> Poured on their foreheads and limbs, unseen, ambrosial odours,
> Givers of longing, and rapture, and chaste content in espousals."
> — *C. Kingsley's "Andromeda"*.

III. The Minister of Doom

Men say that the rock from which Perseus loosed Andromeda may still be seen at Joppa below Jerusalem. However that may be, in the kingdom of Cepheus he built a ship, on which to carry home his bride to Seriphos. He reached the island to hear heartstirring news. His mother was still alive, but Polydectes had made her a slave, ever persecuting her with his hateful love, so that she had been driven to take sanctuary from him in Athene's temple. Spurred by wrath, Perseus strode to the hall of that tyrant, and found him revelling among his drunken companions.

"Ha, foundling, whom we never thought to see again!" was his scornful welcome. "Hast brought the Gorgon's head?"

"Behold!" said Perseus sternly, as he uncovered the blood-curdling trophy, before which those mockers were forthwith turned to stone; and there they stand in a ring, washed evermore by wind and weather.

In place of Polydectes, Danaë's son made the good Dictys chief of the island. Now, from his joyful mother he learned how he was grandson of the king of Argos, and set out forthwith to claim his rightful heritage. But first he piously restored the magic gifts of the gods; and to Athene he gave the head of that Gorgon foe of gods and men, to be set as a boss in her dazzling shield, and serve her as the dread Ægis thrown over the innocent in the eyes of those who would do them wrong.

Acrisius had heard with dread of his grandson being still alive and on his way to Argos. Always bearing in mind the words of the oracle that he should die by this hand, he waited not his coming, but fled to Larissa in the land of the Thessalians. Thither Perseus followed, hoping to persuade his grandfather that he meant him no harm. He came to Larissa when its king was holding games, at which old Acrisius sat among the onlookers. The young stranger joined in these sports, and all wondered how easily he bore off the prize in racing and wrestling. But when his name ran from lip to lip, Acrisius shrank into the shade and covered his face, fearing to be known by that fated offspring.

It came to throwing the quoit, and again Perseus hurled far beyond all his competitors. But there rose a sudden gust of wind that carried his strongest cast aside, so that the quoit struck Acrisius, him and no other among the throng; and such a hurt was enough to end his old and feeble life.

Perseus stood horror-struck to learn how by chance he had been the death of his own grandsire. After burying the body and purifying himself by due rites from his unconscious guilt, he went back to Argos, but could not with a quiet mind keep the inheritance thus won. He exchanged his kingdom with the neighbour king of Tiryns, and built for himself the great city Mycenæ. There his life was long, in honour and welfare, when

> " Peaceful grew the land
> The while the ivory rod was in his hand,
> For robbers fled, and good men still waxed strong,
> And in no house was any sound of wrong,
> Until the Golden Age there seemed to be,
> So steeped the land was in felicity ".
>
> —*W. Morris.*

Many famous heroes sprang from one whom men came to look on as half-divine ; and after their death, Perseus and Andromeda, with Cepheus and Cassiope, were placed by the gods among the bright stars that guide wandering mariners.

ARACHNE

The Lydian Arachne, daughter of a famed dyer in purple, was herself still more famed for rare skill in weaving. Not common country folk alone, but nymphs of the woods and the streams came to watch how deftly she plied her loom, and with what wonderful art she used the needle to embroider rich patterns on her webs. So high rose her name that it reached Pallas-Athene, the goddess of such arts, to whose inspiration, men said, this humbly-born maiden must owe her skill. But to say that she needed any teacher hurt Arachne's pride.

"Pallas, indeed!" she would cry, tossing her head. "There is none in heaven or earth with whom I fear to compete. Let Pallas come, if she will, to try her hand against mine!"

"Nay, speak not so rashly," said a grey-haired old woman who stood by leaning on her staff, as the boastful damsel once uttered such a challenge. "Age and experience ever bring wisdom. Be ruled by me and own the power of the goddess, for she has graces to give to mortals who bend before her. No human work is so good that it cannot be bettered."

"Foolish old crone, keep thy counsel till it be asked for!" hotly spoke back Arachne. "Folks lose their wits, also, by living long. To thy slave or thy daughter, play the mistress. For me, I need no lessons from doting age, nor yet from Pallas. Why shrinks she from a contest of our skill?"

"She is here!" rang out a queenly voice; for lo! the seeming grandam had changed to Pallas herself, who stood forth with flashing eyes and majestic bearing. In that disguise of feeble age, she had come to spy on her earthly rival's handiwork; and now, stung to haughty disdain, she offered to match her art against the Lydian spinster's.

Arachne had at first flushed for astonishment, but soon she recovered her confidence and boldly accepted the challenge. The contest began forthwith: two looms were set up, at which these eager rivals plied their best craft and cunning, with such swiftness that ere long on each the growing tissues shone in all the hues of the rainbow woven into marvellous devices, and shot with threads of gold.

For her design Pallas chose the gods ranged upon the Acropolis at Athens, Jove's awful majesty in the midst, Poseidon smiting the rock with his trident, herself in full panoply among the rest, who was shown calling forth the olive tree that made her best gift to man. About this central group were pictured scenes of impious mortals brought to confusion, rebellious giants turned to mountains, and, for a hint to her presumptuous rival, prating girls changed to screeching fowl. Round all ran a border of olive foliage, as sign of whose handiwork this was, with which few would dare to vie!

The irreverent Arachne, for her part, had picked out stories that cast shame or derision upon the gods. Zeus and his brethren were shown wooing mortals in unworthy form, Apollo humbly serving as a shepherd on earth, Dionysus playing his drunken pranks, nay, scandalous memories of old Cronos himself. From such ancient tales she could choose but too many to fill out her picture, all enclosed by a border of ivy leaves and flowers.

But these scenes were worked in with so cunning art,
that one could believe to see real animals and real waves
standing out before the eye upon that accusing web, the
more offensive for its truth.

So Pallas-Athene felt when she rose to examine the
other's work. With a cry that was half envy and half
indignation, she snatched at the too faithfully coloured
cloth, tearing it to pieces, and showering blows upon
the sly maker of such a masterpiece.

How might mortal maiden stand before the fair-
haired goddess when her eyes blazed with wrath? Thus
unfairly beaten, Arachne could not bear her spiteful
shame. She stole away to hang herself in despair.

Nor even then was the wrath of Pallas glutted. She
bid her rival live, yet in what hateful form! For a spell
was woven round her bloated body, her human features
disappeared, her hair fell off, her limbs shrunk up, and
thus poor Arachne hung as a spider, doomed for ever
to spin as if mocking the skill that had moved Olympian
envy.

MELEAGER AND ATALANTA

I. The Boar Hunt

In Calydon, fair country of Ætolia, to King Oineus and his wife Althæa was born a son whom they named Meleager. And when the babe was not a week old, there came to the house three lame and wrinkled old women, busy night and day with their distaffs, spinning the thread of men's life. For these were no other than the Fates, who, as they bent over the new-born child, croned out his fortune thus :—

"He will grow a goodly man, like his father," quoth the first.

"He will be a hero renowned through the world," murmured the second.

"He will live," muttered the third, "only so long as that firebrand on the hearth remains unconsumed."

The anxious mother's ear caught those words ; then no sooner had the weird sisters vanished, than she rose from her bed to seize the firebrand, quench it in water, and hide it away among her most secret treasures.

Young Meleager grew up, as had been foretold, a son to be the pride of any mother. He made one of the band of heroes who went with Jason to seek the Golden Fleece ; and when they came home, another feat of arms awaited him to celebrate his name by the slaying of the Calydonian boar.

In his son's absence, King Oineus had drawn upon

himself the wrath of a goddess. As thanksgiving for a
fruitful year, he loaded the altar of Demeter with corn,
to Dionysus he poured out wine, and to Athene oil;
but he forgot any sacrifice to Artemis, and that haughty
maiden avenged herself on the mortal who had failed
in doing her honour. She sent into his country a monstrous boar with glowing eyes and foaming jaws, its
bristles strong and sharp like sword points, its tusks
long as those of an elephant, its breath so fiery as to
scare man and beast when it broke crashing through the
woods. Wherever it ravaged, the crops were trampled
down, the herds scattered at its onset, the shepherds
fled from their flocks, and the husbandmen durst not
venture out to pluck the fruit of their vines and olives,
left to hang rotting on the trees.

So when Meleager came home from Colchis, it was
to find his father's land laid waste by the fear of this
monster. At once he set about gathering hunters and
hounds to track it to its lair, as no man had yet dared
to do. He was readily joined by several of his fellow
venturers on the Argo, not yet tired of perilous quests;
and in all Greece could be seen no such gallant band
as now joined together to hunt down the Calydonian
boar.

Among the rest came the maiden huntress, Atalanta,
of whom strange tales were told. Her father, too, was
a king, and had hoped for a son like Meleager to be
his heir; so, when a daughter was born to him, in his
anger he threw her out to die upon a wild mountain.
But there the child, men say, was suckled by a she-
bear, then in its den found by hunters, who brought
her up to their own rude life. Thus she grew manlike and hardy, careless of wind or weather, not less
bold than beautiful, skilled to handle bow and spear,

and more willing to face the fiercest beast than to listen
to tender words. All her heart was set on hunting and
strenuous exercises, and she thought of men only as
comrades in sports, at which few youths could surpass
her by strength or courage. More than one, rashly
seeking to woo her, had rough handling to take for his
answer.

"Happy the man who can find such a mate," was
Meleager's first thought when he saw Atalanta, with her
brown face like a lad's, her hair loosely tied back upon
her broad shoulders, bearing a spear as lightly as if it
were a spindle, and carrying bow and quiver slung about
her sturdy sun-tanned limbs. But others murmured
that their quest was none for women; and grudges
rose against this unknown companion, who only asked
a chance to prove her prowess. It was no time, indeed,
for wooing nor for quarrelling, so without delay the
whole band set forth to seek their fearsome quarry.

No hard task was theirs to find the boar, that soon
came raging through the forest to meet those champions. The nets were spread to catch it; the hounds
were turned into the thorny thickets; but the monster
needed no rousing. Out of a bed of reeds it broke
upon them, a grisly sight that set the dogs turning tail,
when their masters stood fast to hurl a cloud of darts,
and the first spear-point that drew blood was Atalanta's.

Maddened by wounds, with heaving sides and gnashing jaws, the boar dashed among them like a thunderbolt, laying low three or four with its dripping tusks
before they could fetch a blow. One was fain to save
himself by swinging up into the boughs of an oak, on
the trunk of which the horrid foe sharpened its deadly
tusks in vain, till a rash hound came within reach to be
tossed howling into the air. One dog after another,

too, was hurt by their own masters, as the spears flew amiss. Running on with axe heaved above his head, one bold hunter slipped upon the grass wet with blood and lay a helpless victim in the monster's way. But when the men gave ground before its charge, Atalanta's arrow flew with so true an aim that the bristling boar again stopped short to rage out its pain.

"Verily, maiden, thou art the best man of us all!" cried Meleager; and the rest, ashamed to be outdone by a woman, once more closed to the attack.

A score of wounds in turn brought the monster to the ground; and when it got to its feet it was to stagger and turn round and round, blinded by blood. Red froth poured out of its jaws, choking its angry growls; its fiery eyes grew dim; and when at length Meleager thrust his sword to the hilt in its reeking sides, the huge beast lay writhing in its own gore mingled with that of its conquerors, never more to be a terror to the land.

The boar's death-throes were hardly at an end before Meleager planted his foot on its neck with a shout of exultation. Making haste to cut off the bleeding head and to strip away the bristly skin, he offered these trophies to Atalanta as the one that of all had best deserved them, though they fell to himself whose fortune was to give the fatal stroke. But against this some of the hunters cried out in displeasure, loudest of all the two Thestiades, brothers of Althæa and uncles to Meleager.

"This is no woman's work, nor is its prize for a maiden!" clamoured the jealous men; and those sons of Thestios made bold to tear the spoils from Atalanta's hands.

Thus began a brawl in which the heroes turned on

one another their weapons still warm from the boar's blood. So hot waxed the quarrel, that Meleager in his own defence shed the life blood of both those kinsmen, who would have scorned the fair huntress. So all their jubilation was changed to bitterness and grief for friends slain over the body of their foe.

An ill day was that for the house of Oineus, on which its brave son made an end of the boar. When the news came to Althæa, she had gone out to the temple to give proud thanks, but on the way fell in with a mourning train that bore her dearly loved brothers to their funeral pyre. Too soon she learned by whose hand they had fallen; then, beside herself for sorrow, she was moved to curse her own son. Beating her breast and tearing her hair with wild outcry, she broke open the secret place in which she kept hidden away that quenched firebrand that measured his days of life. Furiously she ran with it to where the sacrificial fire burned on the altar. In her madness she scarce knew what she did, yet thrice, four times, she drew back from her unnatural purpose, the mother and the sister warring in her breast. But as her eyes fell on the blood-stained corpses of her own mother's sons, with shuddering hand and averted face she hurled that brand upon the flame. Quickly was it burned to ashes; then as quickly her rage melted to heartbreaking repentance. When soon she heard what came of her vengeful frenzy, the woebegone mother saw nothing for it but to end her own days, dying with her brethren, beside the embers on which she had quenched the life of her son.

For as Meleager came bringing home in triumph the spoils of the great hunt, suddenly his steps had faltered and his eyes grew dim as if blinded by the smoke of that consuming firebrand. A hot fever filled his veins, while his heart dried up and his spirit withered away as a dead leaf. With a groan of amazement he fell like the trunk of some thunder-stricken oak, to breathe his last without a wound, nor ever knew how he had come to so untimely death. And thus was accomplished the decree of those fatal sisters that looked upon his birth.

II. Atalanta's Race

When the boar of Calydon had been quelled by Meleager's doughty band, Atalanta would have gone back to her savage haunts, caring not to consort with men since he was dead who alone had stirred her heart. But that feat had come to the ears of her harsh sire Iasos, who might well be moved to pride in such a daughter. He sought her out and brought her home to his kingdom, still without an heir.

Many were the suitors willing to win a bride so fair and so famous, daughter of a sonless king, and well able to hold her own in arms. But Atalanta would have none of them, choosing to remain a virgin, like the goddess of hunting to whom she was vowed. Still she practised manly exercises, scorning all softness, and having no skill in women's work. When her father pressed her to wed, she made one and another excuse; then at last agreed to take the wooer who could outstrip her in running; but death to be his lot if he failed to win the race.

Even on such hard conditions, brave and agile youths came forward to run for their lives against Atalanta's hand. She, fleet as a fawn, lightly outran the swiftest footed; and one after another they paid their rashness by a cruel end, for, while the suitor must run naked and unarmed, the fierce maiden bore a spear, with which she goaded them not to victory but to death. Still, the sight of their heads set up as a warning by the goal did not chill the hearts of other adventurers, hoping to win the prize where so many had shamefully failed. Among the rest was young Hippomenes, who, while acting as judge at such a contest, had let his own heart be inflamed by Atalanta's scornful eyes.

Before he offered himself to the trial, not trusting wholly in his breath and sinews, like the rest, Hippomenes had implored the favour of Aphrodite on that strange course of love. And the goddess heard and helped him with a gift, that by her counsel should serve him well. Three golden apples she gave him to carry in his hands as he ran, and what he was to do with them came from her knowing how to win the heart of this woman.

Away went youth and maiden, racing towards the goal. Before long Atalanta was like to pass her competitor, who then slyly threw down one of the golden apples to roll across her way. Tempted by wonder or curiosity, she stooped to pick it up, while Hippomenes pressed swiftly on. After brief delay it was easy for her to catch up with him, but now he threw away the second apple, and again she halted to seize it. Again she followed hot-foot, when he, panting towards the goal, let the third apple fall before her. And lo! while once more she tarried to gain that glittering prize, her wily suitor had won the race.

Thus taken in her own snare, the manlike maiden could not but give her hand to Hippomenes, who hoped to win her heart withal. But he, poor youth, had short joy in his fortune. For, as Oineus neglected to propitiate Artemis, so this exultant bridegroom forgot to give thanks to Aphrodite for her favouring aid. Thereon the resentful goddess no longer smiled but frowned upon their love. She led them into offence against Rhea, mighty mother of the gods, who transformed that bold runner and his ungentle bride into a pair of lions, harnessed to her car when she drove forth amid a wild din of horns and cymbals.

HERCULES

I. His Youth

Hercules, whom the Greeks called Herakles, was
the strongest man on earth, being indeed of the blood
of the gods. Amphitryon, king of Tiryns, passed for
his father, who had married Alcmene, granddaughter
of Perseus; but his true sire was Zeus himself, who
had deceived this queen in the form of her husband.
When his birth was at hand, the ruler of Olympus proclaimed that the child born that day should be lord over
all Greece. Then Hera, in hatred of her secret stepson, brought about that his birth was hindered, and that
his cousin Eurystheus came into the world before him,
whereby afterwards Hercules was doomed to serve that
unworthy kinsman.

Alcmene so well guessed how the jealous mistress
of heaven would plot against her son, that she durst
not nurse him at home, but had him exposed in a field,
trusting that Zeus would not fail to protect his own
offspring. There, then, came by Hera and Athene,
wondering at this sight of a naked, new-born child.
Hera, unaware who it was, caught up the babe to hold
it to her breast, but it sucked so violently that she threw
it down in anger. Athene, more patient and pitiful,
carried the unknown Hercules to the city, and gave
him to his own mother to be brought up as a foundling.

Joyfully Alcmene undertook to rear her child, hoping

that the few drops of Hera's milk he had sucked would save him from the goddess's ill-will. But when Hera came to know who was the babe she had saved from death, her heart was hot with spite. She sent two snakes to kill him in his cradle. While his mother slept, those ministers of her vengeance had twisted themselves about the child's neck. The nurse sitting by could not move nor speak for horror. But Hercules awoke with a shout that roused his anxious mother to see how her lusty babe had caught one snake in each hand, and laughingly strangled them before they could do him harm. Alcmene's cries in turn brought in her husband with drawn sword, who might well stand amazed at such a feat of infant strength. He sent for Tiresias to cast the child's fortune; and that blind seer now let him know the origin and destiny of Hercules.

Henceforth Amphitryon spared no pains on the bringing up of so wonderful a foster-son. He himself taught the boy to tame horses and to drive a chariot. The most famous teachers of arts and exercises were sought out for him all over Greece, among them Linus, son of Apollo, to be his master in music. But when Linus one day would have chastised this sturdy pupil, Hercules smote him to death with one blow of the lute, thus early indulging the hot temper that was to cost him dear. After this Amphitryon sent him from home to dwell among his herdsmen on the mountains, where he grew taller and stronger than any man in Greece, able to fell an ox with his fist, and never missing his aim with the bow or the spear. He is also said to have made one of that fellowship of young heroes who were schooled in the cave of the wise Centaur Cheiron.

There came a time when the full-grown youth must choose whether his strength should be turned to good or evil. Wandering alone, he met two beautiful women, each beckoning him to follow her on a different path. She who spoke first was full-fed and richly arrayed ; her eyes shone with pride and lust ; and her wanton charms seemed heightened by meretricious art.

"My name," spoke she, "is Pleasure, loved by the most of men. See how my path is broad and easy and soft to the feet ! Take this way and thou shalt never want rich food and drink, nor fine raiment and soft beds, nor any cheer of life, and all without pain or peril. For I lead my friends far from strife and suffering, and give them only sweet things for which other men have toiled. Come, then, with me ! "

The youth looked willingly at this fair temptress, yet before taking her hand, he turned to the other, who pointed out an opposite way. She appeared more modest and maidenly, clad in simple white without gauds or jewels, and in a low voice she spoke thus :—

"My name is Duty, whom no man dares to scorn, yet few learn to love. My path indeed will prove steep and thorny, and on it I promise not ease and pleasure, but labour and smarting, without which no man gains the best gifts of the gods. Yet pain bravely borne shall turn to joy and pride for him who faces the foes of life, wrestling with his own fate, and bearing the burdens of weaker men. So shall he who follows me win honour and peace upon earth, and at last his birthright among the gods."

"Say rather how he may come to die betimes on that perilous path of thine ! " cried Pleasure with a mocking laugh.

"Aye," whispered Duty, "but those worthy to go with me think noble death better than to live in sloth and folly."

For a moment the hero stood in doubt, then his swelling heart went out to Duty, and he gave her his hand. Thus was made the Choice of Hercules, whose sorest sufferings would come when he strayed from that toilsome path.

II. His Labours

Having chosen Duty as his guide, Hercules followed her to become the most famous champion of his age. He slew cruel giants, he exterminated fierce wild beasts; everywhere he hastened to help the oppressed. Gods as well as men hailed his mighty deeds. Athene equipped him in armour from her own temple; Hermes gave him a resistless sword; Apollo furnished him with sharp arrows; and he bore a famous pictured shield, the work of Hephæstus at the bidding of Zeus. Thus arrayed, he flew to the aid of Thebes when it was threatened by an invader haughtily demanding tribute. This city, indeed, was dear to Hercules, since his reputed father Amphitryon, his own kingdom given up, had made his home there. In the battle for its defence Amphitryon fell; but the prowess of his son gained the victory. The grateful Creon, king of Thebes, gave Hercules his daughter Megara in marriage; and it seemed as if he had no more to wish for on earth.

But nothing could make Hera forget her hatred to this son of Zeus. She sent upon the hero a furious madness, in which he threw his own children upon a fire and drove his wife from him in horror. When his frenzy passed away, letting him know what he had done, he fell into deep melancholy, and for a time was seen no more among men, while he sought pardon and healing from the gods. As penance it was appointed him to

become vassal to his kinsman Eurystheus, he who, by
Hera's cunning trick, had gained the birthright promised
by Zeus. Humbly Hercules stooped his pride to serve
that poor-spirited and faint-hearted lord, spending now
the best years of his manhood in labours beyond the
power of any but himself. On ten weary errands must
he go at the bidding of Eurystheus, before he could be
his own man again : such was the decree given forth from
the oracle at Delphi.

The first task set him was to slay the Nemean lion,
a savage monster that had long kept the land of Argolis
in dread; it was invulnerable to all weapons, being of
the blood of that hundred-headed Typhon buried by
Zeus beneath the roots of Etna. Armed only with his
bow, and with a wild olive tree he tore up by the roots
to make him a club, Hercules hunted through the forest
of Nemea where the lion had its lair. Before long its
fearsome roar led him to a thicket, from which it burst
towards him open-mouthed, with jaws and mane dripping
blood. Hercules drew his bow with true aim, but one
and another arrow fell harmless from the creature's hide,
that could not be pierced by the sharpest point. But
with his club the hero laid it low in the act to spring;
then, flinging away his weapons, he threw himself upon
the writhing beast, cast his arms round its neck, and
choked it to death. He had much ado to tear off its
skin, hard as iron; but when he had flayed it with its
own sharp claws, he hung the skin about him as a garment and helmed himself with its head. By these spoils
and by his huge club, this lion-killer was henceforth
known wherever he went. So terrible did he appear
bringing back such trophies, that the cowardly Eurystheus shrunk from meeting him face to face, but sent

out his further commands for Hercules by another's
voice.

The second task laid upon Hercules was to quell
a monster haunting the marshes of Lerna. This was
the Hydra, that huge snake with nine heads, one of
which could not be hurt by any weapon, and the others
would grow again as fast as they were cut off. Accompanied by his nephew Iolaus, the hero set out for Lerna
in a swift chariot, and soon found the wooded hill where
the Hydra kept itself hidden. Leaving his nephew
beside the horses, with fiery arrows he fetched the creature from out of its hole, to swoop upon him, hissing
and spitting from all its heads, that waved like branches
in a storm. Undismayed, Hercules met its onset and
mowed down the twisting heads one by one, yet as fast
as he cut them off two grew up in place of one, while
it twined its loathsome body round his limbs and almost
stifled him with its foul breath. He was fain to call for
the help of Iolaus, who ran up with a torch; then as
Hercules shore off the bristling heads, his nephew seared
each bleeding wound, so that they could not grow again.
At last the raging Hydra was left with that one head no
iron could wound; but he crushed it with his club, and
tore it off and buried it in the ground under a heavy
rock. In its poisonous blood the conqueror dipped his
arrows, to make the hurt from them henceforth incur-
able.

His third labour was to bring in alive the golden-
antlered and brazen-hoofed stag Cerynitis, that roamed
free upon the Arcadian hills. A bold man he would
have been who should slay that beast, sacred as it was
to Artemis. For a year Hercules chased it in its native

haunts and far beyond; it led him out of Greece to
Thrace; and on over barbarous wildernesses, and deep
into the northern darkness. Foiled again and again, he
had nothing for it but to lame the agile stag with a dart,
then could catch it to bear home on his shoulders. By
the way he fell in with Artemis, wroth against him for
hurting a beast under her protection. But a hero can
soothe even an offended goddess; and she let him carry
the stag to Eurystheus.

The fourth labour was to catch a grimmer beast,
that boar that ravaged the Erymanthian mountain ridge
between Attica and Elis. On his way to this adventure,
Hercules brought on a strange battle, against his will.
He was entertained by a Centaur named Pholus, who set
before him meat enough but no wine, for he had only
one cask, the gift of Dionysus, which belonged to the
Centaurs in common, and must not be opened unless all
the race were there to share it. Yet Hercules persuaded
his host to broach that cask; and when the fumes of
strong wine spread through the woods, the other Centaurs came trampling up, armed with rocks and fir
branches. In their anger over the broached cask, they
would have fallen upon the stranger, who stoutly defended
himself, and his invincible arrows drove them to take
shelter in the cave of Cheiron, his old teacher. That
good Centaur, in the fray, was hurt by a chance arrow,
which, dipped in the Hydra's poisonous blood, killed him
in slow agony, all his own arts of healing being in vain.
Pholus, too, the kindly host, died from handling one of
those deadly arrows, which he let fall on his foot. Having
mournfully done the last offices to those friends on whom
he had brought such suffering, Hercules held on to the
haunts of the Erymanthian boar, which he drove from

the forests up to the bare crests, and wearied it out with chasing in deep snowdrifts till he could bind it with cords to bring alive to Eurystheus.

His fifth labour was cleansing in a single day the stables of Augeas, king of Elis, who kept three thousand cattle, but for thirty years had not taken the trouble to clear out the enclosures heaped with their filth. When he saw Hercules present himself for a task so unworthy of a hero, Augeas laughed, and lightly promised him one-tenth of his herds, if he would do the work that seemed beyond a giant's power. But Hercules was crafty as well as stout. He saw how the rivers Peneus and Alpheus flowed hard by, whose waters he brought by a new channel to sweep through the Augean stables, and thus cleansed them out in a day. Now that Augeas heard how he came sent by Eurystheus for this very task, he was for refusing the promised reward; but Hercules held him to his offer, calling to witness against him his own son Phyleus, in whose presence it was made; and when Phyleus testified truly, the angry father drove him from home, along with the hero who had done him so good service. Years later, Hercules came back to teach that churlish lord how ill he had done in breaking his word with such a servant.

The sixth labour was hunting out the Stymphalides, those same arrow-feathered birds of prey that troubled the voyage of the Argonauts. Lake Stymphalis in Arcadia was their breeding place, which Hercules found black with such a throng of the mischievous fowl that he knew not how to deal with them. But Athene, goddess of invention, came to his aid, giving him a huge pair of brass clappers made by Hephæstus, to raise a rattle louder than all the screeching of the birds. Taking post on a hill, Hercules startled them up by the clappers, then, as they rose in the air, shot them down with his deadly arrows; and those that flew away were so scared as never again to be seen in Greece.

The seventh labour was to master a bull wandering madly about the island of Crete. Minos, its king, willingly gave him leave to chase down this pest that worked havoc through his dominions, and no man had yet been able to tame it. But Hercules caught the bull, and mounted its back, and rode it through the sea to Greece. There Eurystheus turned it loose, again to be a terror to the people, till it was hunted down on the plain of Marathon by Theseus, him who ever took pride in doing deeds after the pattern of his great kinsman.

The eighth labour of Hercules was to catch the mares of Diomedes, a Thracian chief, who reared his horses to be savage as himself by feeding them on human flesh. The hero first took Diomedes captive and gave him as food to his own wild mares, which after devouring their master, let Hercules drive them away quietly as kids. Yet they were not wholly weaned from their fierce nature, as, while he made a stand against the Thracians pursuing him, the troop of mares tore in pieces his companion Abderus, set to guard them; and Hercules had to tame them afresh. Men say that a horse of this breed was that Bucephalus long afterwards mastered by Alexander of Macedon.

The ninth labour was to win for Eurystheus's daughter the girdle of Hippolyte, gift of Ares to that queen of the warlike Amazons, who lived far away in Asia. So unwomanlike were they as to kill all their male children; and they burned away their right breasts not to be hindered in the use of the bow. Hippolyte was so charmed by the looks and bearing of this foe that she offered to give up her girdle freely. But Hera, taking the form of an Amazon, stirred up the virago people against him, nor could her stepson bring off that trophy without a hard battle. As he carried it back to Greece, Hercules passed by Troy, and there saved the daughter of its king Laomedon from the claws of a monster, as Perseus freed Andromeda. This king, also, cheated the hero of his promised reward; then Hercules vowed to come back and leave no stone of Troy standing upon another, as he did in after-years.

The tenth labour for Eurystheus, that should have been the last, was to bring a herd of red cattle belonging to the giant Geryon, from the island Erythia by the western ocean, where they fed under guard of the two-headed dog Orthrus; and Geryon himself was so monstrous that he had three bodies, three heads, six arms, and six feet, being the son of Chrysaor, a giant engendered from the blood of Medusa, slain by Perseus. The more Hercules toiled for his kinsman, the more that cowardly king hated him, envying his prowess; and now Eurystheus hoped to be rid of him, sent so far against such a foe. But Hercules set out cheerful and undismayed, undertaking by the way exploits that would have appalled most men. Reaching the straits of Gades, he there set up two landmarks henceforth famed as the pillars of Hercules. Thirsty after long wandering through waterless deserts, the heat of the sun so irked him that he dared to point his arrows against Phœbus, lord of the sky. Yet noble Apollo took no offence at his boldness,

but favoured him with a golden boat in which he passed
over to Erythia, where he slew the three-headed giant
and his two-headed dog, nay, shot an arrow into the
breast of Hera's self, who came to the aid of that monster
against the man she ever hated.

Geryon's herd he then drove home over seas and
rivers and mountains, yet not without fresh perils on the
way. As he passed through Italy, the fire-breathing
giant Cacus stole part of the cattle while their keeper
lay asleep. To leave no plain trace of the theft, he
dragged them into his cave backwards by the tail. Deceived by this trick, when he had searched all round,
Hercules gave them up for lost; but as he drove the
rest of the herd past that hidden cave, the beasts shut
up within lowed back to their fellows. To seek them
out was to put himself face to face with Cacus, who
found too late how ill it was to rob such a stranger.
Having slain the thievish giant, Hercules went on with
the herd, and still had much ado to keep them together,
for Hera sent a gadfly to drive them wild among the
hills ; and she flooded a water on his way, which he could
not cross till he had filled up the channel with stones.
It was then that he wandered far into the wilds of
Scythia, and there dealt with another monster, half-
woman, half-serpent. But in the end he brought the
herd safe to Greece, to make for Eurystheus a rich
sacrifice to that ungracious queen of heaven.

When now the hero hoped to be free, that mean-
minded king still claimed his service. Two of the tasks
he had accomplished Eurystheus refused to count among
the ten : the slaying of the Hydra, because then Hercules
had his nephew's help ; and the cleansing of the Augean
stables, because for that he had taken hire. So he must

undertake two more labours, making twelve in all; and the last were the worst.

He was next sent to pluck three golden apples from a garden given by Gaia, the earth-mother, to Zeus and Hera on their marriage. The Garden of the Hesperides it was called, from those four nymphs, daughters of Night, who kept it; and for warder it had a sleepless hundred-headed dragon. No man even knew where this garden lay; and Hercules, in search of it, had to wander far and wide, everywhere slaying giants and monsters with his mighty club, nay once he came to blows with Ares himself, but Zeus by a thunderbolt parted those kinsmen of Olympian blood. At last the friendly nymphs of the Eridanus counselled the hero to ask his way from Nereus, Old Man of the Sea, who knew all things. So Hercules did, coming upon Nereus while he slept clad in dripping seaweeds, to bind him and hold fast his slippery body for all the changing forms it was his way to take, till, weary of the struggle, he told how to find the island Garden of the Hesperides in the western ocean.

Further directions he should get from Prometheus, who now for thirty years had been chained to an icy crag of the Caucasus, exposed by turns to scorching sun and freezing winds, while daily tormented by the talons of an eagle, or as some say, a vulture, the minister of Zeus. As Hercules strode across those giant mountains, he saw this bird flying on its cruel errand, and shot it with one of his fatal arrows. Thus guided to the place of punishment that should last for ages, it was easy for the hero to tear Prometheus loose; nor did Zeus resent that boldness of his son, but laid aside his ire against the friend of man. The grateful prisoner, wise with age and lonely sorrow, repaid his release by good counsels for Hercules, bidding to seek out Atlas and ask him to fetch the golden apples from the Hesperides, who were thought to be his children.

So the messenger of Eurystheus held on to Africa, and first he came to Egypt, where the king, Busiris, had harsh welcome for strangers. Years before, a famine falling on his land, a certain soothsayer from Cyprus told how the gods' anger might be turned away by yearly sacrifice of some man not born on the soil. Busiris made this soothsayer his first sacrifice; and every year some stranger was marked for death. So Hercules, taken as a goodly victim, was brought to the sacrifice with laughter in his heart, for he burst the bonds like thread, killed the king at his own altar, and went his way from among the terrified Egyptians.

In Africa he overcame a doughtier foe, the giant Antæus, who challenged all-comers to wrestle with him for life or death, and could vanquish most men by the fresh strength it was his nature to draw in as often as he touched his mother-earth. But the hero had craft as well as strength to hold Antæus up in the air and there choke the breath out of him, so that he troubled travellers no more. Hercules also cleared the Libyan sands of wild beasts, as was his wont wherever he came.

So, after long travel, he found Atlas, where that weary giant bears up the weight of the world. Hercules offered to take the burden for a time on his own shoulders if Atlas would go for the golden apples, as he consented to do. But when he came back with three apples robbed from the garden, Atlas was unwilling to shoulder his heavy load again, now that he had felt what it was to stretch his limbs freely. The hero had to use cunning when force would not serve him. Feigning to be content, he only asked Atlas to hold the world for a little, while he wound cords about his own aching head to ease the pressure.   The dull-witted giant did so; but no sooner had he the world on his back again, than Hercules made off with the golden apples, leaving Atlas taken by his own trick.

When once more he came back safe and successful, his unkind kinsman saw with despair how from all the perilous labours laid upon him Hercules but won more glory and goodwill as a benefactor of men.   To make an end of him, Eurystheus chose a task that seemed beyond the might of any mortal; he sent his ever-victorious champion to fetch from the nether world Cerberus, the three-headed hound of hell.   For this enterprise, Hercules piously prepared himself by visiting Eleusis, there being initiated into its mysteries and cleansed from the guilt of the Centaurs' blood.   He then went to Tænarum, the southernmost point of the Peloponnesus, where a dark cave opened as one of the gates of Hades.   The god Hermes led him below into that chill under-world, where the thin shades fled in affright from a being of flesh and blood; but Medusa stood to face him, and he would have drawn his sword upon her, had not Hermes held his hand, bidding him remember how ghosts could no more be hurt by iron.   The shade of Meleager, too, ventured up to whisper to him a message of love for his mourning sister Deianira, of which more was to come than he knew.

Near the gates of Hades, Hercules was amazed to find two living men chained to the black rock, and still more when he recognized them as his old comrades Theseus and Peirithous.   For Peirithous, king of the Lapithæ, who fought their great battle with the Centaurs, had been so exalted with pride that he ventured to woo Persephone in hell itself, and his dear friend Theseus accompanied him on the too daring errand; then, seized by Pluto, they were both condemned to endless prison among the dead. Hope shone in their eyes at the sight of Hercules; pitiably they cried to him for help, which he did not grudge. He caught Theseus by the hand to tear him loose from his chains; and the king of Athens could thus win back for a time to the upper world. But when the hero would have freed Peirithous also, the rocks shook as from an earthquake, and he must leave that presumptuous man fast bound to his fate.

Yet so bold was he that he slew a bull of Pluto's cattle, pouring the blood into a trench for the wan ghosts to get a taste of life; and when the herdsman would have hindered, Hercules crushed his ribs, hardly letting him go but at the entreaty of his mistress Persephone. In such manner the hero stormed through hell till he came at last face to face with its dark-browed king, who barred his further passage. The undaunted one shot an arrow into Pluto's shoulder, making him roar for pain never felt before. Thus aware that this was an asker not to be denied, on learning his errand grim Pluto gave him leave to carry away Cerberus, if he could master it with his hands alone, using no weapon. Then at the mouth of Acheron, Hercules gripped that hellish watch-dog by the throat, and, for all the terror of its three barking heads, its poison-dripping teeth, and its stinging tail like a scorpion's, he swung the loathly monster over his back and brought it up to earth to cast before the feet of Eurystheus.

This king, aghast at the very sight, could do nothing with Cerberus but let it go. As for Hercules, triumphant in every ordeal, Eurystheus gave up in despair his mastership over such a hero, and set him free on condition that he put back the monster at its fearsome watch post.

III. His Death

Thus released from his long servitude, Hercules still wandered about the world doing mighty deeds of strength to aid his fellow men. Yet ever Hera's ill will followed him, clouding his mind, so that here and there he turned aside from the chosen path of virtue. Athene for her part stood by him with help and counsel; and Zeus looked kindly upon the feats of his son, nor did he spare to chastise his spiteful queen when she took on her to send storms upon the hero's course. How he sailed with the Argonauts, how he dealt with the false king of Troy, how he brought back Alcestis to the house of Admetus, are famous tales often told.

Long ago, he had parted from his wife Megara, when he madly slew her children; and in time he sought another bride, Iole, daughter of King Eurytus, who in his youth had taught him the use of the bow. This renowned archer offered his daughter's hand as prize to whoever could shoot better than himself and his three sons. Hercules came to the trial and beat his old master. But when he claimed Iole, Eurytus was unwilling to let her marry a man known to have brought such woe on Megara. Among the king's sons, Iphitus alone took the part of him whom he loved and admired beyond all men; then, his bride being denied him, Hercules went away in wrath.

Forthwith it chanced that certain oxen of Eurytus were stolen by the noted thief Autolycus. The king made sure of this as done by Hercules in revenge; but Iphitus would not believe such villainy of his friend. He sought out Hercules, and they joined together to hunt down the true robber. On their chase they had mounted a tower to look out for the stolen herd, when the hero's old madness returned upon him, and taking Iphitus as to blame for the ill will of his father, he hurled him from the tower in sudden fury.

When he came to himself and found that he had killed his best friend, Hercules passed into melancholy remorse. He pilgrimaged from one shrine to another, seeking to be purified from that sin. The oracle at Delphi at first refused to answer so blood-stained a suppliant; whereupon he threatened to rob the temple, to carry off the tripod and to set up an oracle of his own; then Zeus had some ado to make peace between his fierce son and the offended Apollo. In the end Hercules wrung from this god's priestess a sentence that his guilt could be purged away only by selling himself as a slave for three years, and giving the price to the children of Iphitus.

Willingly the hero stooped to this penance. In charge of Hermes, taking ship for Asia, where he was little known, he let himself be sold for three talents to Omphale, Queen of Lydia. She soon found out what a strong slave she had, who rid her land of robbers and beasts of prey as easily as another would bear wood and water. But when she knew that this was no other than the world-renowned Hercules, she would have kept him for a spouse rather than a servant. Then, alas! in the softness and luxury of eastern life, the hero forgot his manhood, and let Omphale make sport with him. While she took his club and lion-skin as toys, he put on woman's clothes and gauds to sit at her feet spinning wool, or amusing her and her maids with stories of how he had strangled snakes in his cradle, and laid low giants, and quelled monsters, and gone down to face the king of death in his dark abode.

So three years passed away in shameful ease; then at once Hercules came to his right mind, like one awakening from a dream. He tore off the womanish garments in shame; he dropped the distaff from his knotty hands; and, turning his back on the idle court of Omphale, strode forth once more to seek deeds that might become a hero. But again a woman was fated to be this strong man's undoing.

In his later wanderings he came to Calydon, and saw Deianira, daughter of King Oineus, to whom he bore a message from her brother Meleager in Hades. From him Hercules had heard of her beauty; now he loved her well and carried her away as his wife, after a hot fight for her with a rival wooer, the river-god Achelous, who changed himself into a snake and a bull, but in any form could not withstand the son of Zeus.

As if that beaten river-god would still do him an ill turn, his road brought him to a stream in flood, where the Centaur Nessus stood offering to carry wayfarers across on his back. For himself Hercules scorned such a ferry; he flung over his club and lion-skin on the farther bank, that he might lightly swim the swollen water; but his wife he trusted to Nessus. Then that rude Centaur, inflamed by her beauty, would have borne her off; but Hercules heard her cry, and with one of his envenomed arrows brought Nessus to the ground. In his death throes, the vengeful monster whispered to Deianira a lying tale: he bid her dip a shirt in his blood, and if ever she lost her husband's love, that should prove a charm to bring it back.

Hercules ended his labours by taking amends from those who in past years had done him wrong, among them King Eurytus, whom he conquered and slew, and made his daughter Iole a captive. When Deianira heard how her husband's old love lay in his power, she was moved by jealousy to try the spell of the Centaur's blood, which in truth had been poisoned by the hero's own deadly arrow. She sent him a shirt dipped in this venom, begging him to wear it as made by her hands. Without suspicion he put it on, when he came to offer sacrifices of thanksgiving for his victory.

Then, as soon as the fire on the altar had warmed the envenomed blood, burning pains seized him and shot through every vein, till, for once in his life, he could not but roar for agony. Vainly he struggled to pull off the fatal garment; it stuck to his skin like pitch, and he was fain to tear away the tortured flesh, beneath which his veins hissed and boiled as if melted by inward flames. In his rage he caught the servant who had innocently brought this gift from his wife, and hurled him into the sea. Seeing that he must die, with his last strength he tore down tree trunks to make a funeral pyre, on which he stretched himself, begging his companions to kindle it beneath his still living body. His armour-bearer, Philoctetes, alone had heart to do him this sad service, which Hercules rewarded with the gift of his deadly bow and arrows, that should one day be turned against Troy.

"Hera, thou art avenged: give me a stepmother's gift of death!" were his last words, as the flames rose crackling about him; and a terrible storm of thunder and lightning broke out above, through which Pallas-Athene's chariot bore the demigod to Olympus.

On the pyre lay the ashes of what part of him came from his mother. The immortal part he had from Zeus now dwelt in heaven. There even Hera's hatred died away, so that she welcomed him among the gods, and gave him in marriage her daughter Hebe, the spirit of eternal youth.

When poor Deianira knew what she had unwittingly done to her too dearly loved husband, she killed herself for remorse, goaded by the upbraiding of her own son Hyllus. By the dying wish of Hercules this son married Iole; and from them sprang a famous race of heroes, known to after-ages as the Heraclids.

But the children of Hercules long inherited their father's hard fortunes. They were chased from city to city by the hatred of Eurystheus, so that they must wander over Greece under the guardianship of Iolaus, now grown old and feeble, yet ever faithful to the memory of his dead comrade and kinsman. At last Demophoon, son of Theseus, gave them refuge in Athens, and with Hyllus gathered an army to defend them against Eurystheus. An oracle declaring that a maiden of noble birth must be sacrificed as the price of victory, Macaria, daughter of Hercules and Deianira, did not fear to devote herself to death. And in the hot battle Iolaus prayed Zeus to give him back for one day the strength of his youth; then, his prayer being heard, no foe could stand before a champion worthy to follow that peerless hero. The host of Eurystheus was set to flight, and its lord brought to a miserable end.

Still the Heraclids found themselves dogged by evil fate, as if the sins of their great father rose up against them. It was long before the curse of the race seemed to have worn out. Not till generations had passed, were warriors of the blood of Hercules able to conquer the Peloponnesus and divide its kingdoms among their chiefs.

ALCESTIS

Time was when great Apollo had so grievously offended his father Zeus that as punishment he must for nine years serve a mortal upon earth. Thus the god became herdsman to the Thessalian king Admetus, who made such a good master to him that, his term of service up, as parting gift Apollo won for Admetus from the Fates a boon never yet granted to man. When his day came to die, this king might live on if he could find any soul who loved him so well as to go down to Hades in his stead.

The day dawned when Death's messenger brought to the house of Admetus that word that strikes dumb king as well as beggar. Then eagerly he sought one willing to take his place. None of his friends would go down into darkness for his sake. His people had no more to give him than due pity and lamentation. His old father and mother clung fast to the few dim years they might yet have to live. Only his wife Alcestis, in the bloom of her beauty, joyful mother of children as she was, declared herself ready to sacrifice her life for his; and so it was to be.

As the black shape of Death drew near the doors to lead her away, the noble queen washed herself in running water, put on her festal attire and choicest ornaments to come forth for the last time into the light of day. With heartbroken woe she embraced once more her tearful children; of her servants too she took kind farewell; and these were her last words to Admetus :—

118

"Since thy life is dearer to me than my own, I die willingly, not caring to take another husband, nor to abide with thy orphaned children, as well loved by thee as by me. One thing only I ask: give them up to the grudge of no second wife, for a serpent may be kinder than a stepmother."

The weeping king vowed that in death as in life Alcestis should be his only bride; and with this promise of comfort she fell into a mortal swoon.

While all the house was now busy with preparing her funeral rites, there arrived at it an ill-timed guest, who but Hercules bound on one of his mighty errands! Struck by the signs of mourning that met his eyes, he would have turned away; but Admetus, true to the duty of being hospitable, dissembled his grief, giving Hercules to think that the dead woman was only a visitor. Led into the guest chamber, crowned with flowers, and well supplied with wine, the hero carelessly fell to boisterous drinking and singing, till an old servant rebuked him for such unseemly riot in a house whose mistress had just been carried out to burial. Struck sober by contrition, and by the generosity of his host, Hercules asked which way Death had gone, then hurried after, bent on wresting from him his victim; and the house of Admetus was left hushed in its woe.

> "Night wore away
> Mid gusts of wailing wind, the twilight grey
> Stole o'er the sea, and wrought his wondrous change
> On things unseen by night, by day not strange,
> But now half seen and strange; then came the sun,
> And therewithal the silent world and dun
> Waking, waxed many-coloured, full of sound,
> As men again their heap of troubles found,
> And woke up to their joy or misery."

—W. Morris.

Admetus was sitting alone at daybreak in his silent home, overwhelmed by sorrow, also by shame that his wife had shown him the courage to die. Now again Hercules entered his gates, this time leading a veiled woman at his side.

"Oh, king!" he greeted Admetus, "it was ill done of thee to hide from me that thy wife lay dead; and I did thee wrong by revelling in a home darkened by such a loss. Here, to make amends, I bring a woman whom I won in a hard contest. Take her for thine own; or at least keep her for me till I come again."

"Lead her to some other friend!" cried Admetus, waving her away; and as he fixed his eyes on the veiled figure, he broke out: "I could not bear to see in my house one whose form so strongly recalls my own wife, that the very sight of her sets me weeping afresh."

"Nay, dry these tears," quoth the jovial hero. "Mourning brings not back the dead; but for the living there are still gifts of joy. Take, then, this woman to wife, and forget what has gone before."

"Never can I love any woman save Alcestis!" vowed the king; but his voice rose in a cry of joyful amazement, as Hercules drew off the veil to show him the living face of her he loved so well.

Alcestis it was and no other, whom for once a half-divine hero had been able to tear out of the arms of Death. Three days she lay breathing yet speechless, as if dazed by the dread of what she had seen through the gate of Hades. Then she rose and spoke, and went about the house which her life filled again with gladness.

PYGMALION AND GALATEA

Pygmalion, king of Cyprus, had more fame as a sculptor than as a warrior. So devoted was he to his art that he cared not to marry, declaring that no living woman could be so beautiful as the figures he fashioned with his own hands. And at one ivory statue he wrought so long and so lovingly that it became the mistress of his heart, till he would have spent all he had in the world to give it breath as well as silent grace and beauty. All day he laboured to put new touches of perfection to the senseless form; and all night he lay sighing for the power to make it flesh and blood.

Galatea was the name he gave his statue, in vain hoping to call it to life. In vain he sought to kiss warmth and motion into its shapely limbs. He decked it with costly tissues, made its neck and arms sparkle with precious jewels, wreathed its cold head with flowers of every hue; but all in vain. The image remained an image, that seemed less fair the more he hid its white form in gold and purple.

There came the feast of Aphrodite, great goddess of the island. Then Pygmalion presented himself in her temple, bearing rich offerings and sending up a passionate prayer with the incense smoke that rose from the altar.

"Queen of love, take pity on one who has too long despised thy power! Give me for bride the work of my own hands; or, if that may not be, a maiden of earth as lovely as my Galatea!"

As if in favourable answer, three times the altar flame leaped up in the air, making Pygmalion's heart beat high with joyful hope. He hastened home to stand before the statue that a hundred times had almost cheated his eyes into belief it might be alive.

"Galatea!" he cried for the thousandth time, stretching out his arms; then had almost shrunk back in dread of what he so long desired.

For now as he gazed, a change came over the ivory shape. Its breast heaved; its veins ran with blood; its eyes no longer stared upon him like stones. It was no cheat. He pressed the hand that grew warm and soft in his. He could feel the pulses throbbing under his touch. He smiled to the face that smiled back again. He spoke, and his Galatea's lips had breath to answer—

"Aphrodite hath worked her miracle!"

> "Speechless he stood, but she now drew anear,
> Simple and sweet as she was wont to be,
> And once again her silver voice rang clear,
> Filling his soul with great felicity;
> And thus she spoke, 'Wilt thou not come to me,
> O dear companion of my new-found life,
> For I am called thy lover and thy wife'."
>
> —*W. Morris.*

THE RAPE OF PERSEPHONE

An ill trick it was Aphrodite played on gods and men when she bid her mischievous son shoot his dart at Pluto, that even in his gloomy kingdom should be known the power of love. From such a mountain-mouth as breathes fire and smoke over Sicily came forth the stern King of Hades, to drive in his iron chariot across that fair isle, where the ground heaves beneath fruitful crops, and ruin is strangely mingled with the richest green.

There, in the Vale of Enna, his lowering looks fell upon Persephone, sweet daughter of Demeter, blooming like the flowers she plucked among her sportive companions. But she dropped her lapful of violets and lilies when that fearsome wooer caught her up into his chariot, striking his forked spear upon the ground, that opened in a dark cleft through which he bore her away to his dwelling in the nether world. A cry for help, too late, brought up Demeter to see that her beloved daughter had vanished from the face of the earth.

"Persephone! Persephone!" she cried in vain. No answer came but the rumble of the earthquake and the stifled roar of the volcano hailing that tyrant's retreat to his kingdom underground.

All day the woeful mother sought her lost child, and all night she went calling Persephone's name, lit by torches kindled at the fires of Etna. Many a day, indeed, she now wandered over land and sea, but neither sun nor moon could show her the darling face, never forgotten in her heart. At last, coming back to Sicily, she found a trace of Persephone, what but her girdle floating on a stream into which one of the girl's playmates had wept herself away, and could give only such silent token of her friend's fate!

But the nymph of another stream had power to speak, fair Arethusa, who, pursued by the river-god Alpheus under the sea, had fled to Ortygia, and there was changed by Artemis into a sacred fountain. She in pity told Demeter how, when drawing her springs from the deep caverns underground, she had seen young Persephone throned by Pluto's side as the queen of Hades, adorned with gems and gold in place of flowers, and had through that chill darkness heard her sighing for the sunlit vale whence death's king so roughly snatched her away. What power could bring her back from his cold embrace?

In wild despair Demeter cursed the earth, and chiefly the soil of Sicily that had swallowed up her child. Her tears fell as a plague upon field and grove, so that they no more yielded fruit for man or beast. The people wasted away in famine, crying upon the gods, who feared to lose the reverence and sacrifices due to them. Zeus himself pled with Demeter in vain: she would not return to her seat on Olympus, but went madly up and down the world, scathing and blighting where she was wont to bless.

"If a mother's tears touch thee not, be mindful of a father's pride!" was ever her prayer to Zeus. "She is thy daughter as well as mine, doomed to so untimely fate; and thy honour as well as my woe calls for redress against the insolent robber of our child."

At last the father of the gods was fain to appease this ceaseless suppliant. He sent Hermes to fetch

Persephone from the nether world and restore her to her
mother's arms; yet so it might be only if she had eaten
nothing in the kingdom of Pluto.   Alas! that very day
she had been tempted to taste the seeds of a pomegranate; and thus was she still held in the power of
her grudging spouse.

Once more the miserable mother filled heaven with
her entreaties, and earth with her wrath.   Again Zeus
gave a decree that should content both his brother and
the goddess of fruitfulness.   Persephone's life must
henceforth be divided between her mother and her husband, and with each of them she should spend half the
year: no otherwise might it be than life and death for
her in turns.

Joyful was Demeter to clasp her fair daughter,
brought back from the gloomy realm of Pluto; and
glad was the earth of her joy.   For now again the land
grew green like a jewel set in its rim of blue sea; the
withered trees budded and blossomed; the naked mountains were clothed with leaves; sweet flowers sprang up
in valleys for children to gather freshly; the fields and
gardens bore goodly food for man, and all the world
smiled back to the bright sky of summer.

But, in turn, came year by year their darkening
days, when the goddess gave up her daughter to that
tyrant of the shades.   Then all the earth must mourn
with Demeter, laying aside the gay garlands of summer
and the rich robes of autumn for wan weeds that ill kept
out the winter cold, till again the welcome heralds of
spring let men hail Persephone returning to her mother's
arms.   And so it goes with the world, while men still
live and die.

Other wondrous tales men tell of what befell Demeter
in those weary wanderings, to and fro, when long she

sought her vanished child over the face of the earth.   As
this : that coming one day to a cottage, disguised as an
old beggar woman, she was scornfully given a bowl of
mush at the door, where the son of the house, like the
rude boy he was, laughed to see how hungrily she ate
such humble food ; then the seeming crone flung the
bowl in his face with an angry word, at which, lo! he
had been changed into a spotted lizard, to teach him and
his that poverty may hide a goddess.

But another home gave less churlish welcome to this
beggar, old and poor.   At Eleusis, in Greece, it was that
a kindly housewife took her in, and would have had her
stay as nurse to the new-born son, named Triptolemus.
Bereaved Demeter came to love this child almost as her
own, so that she was minded to bestow on him in secret
the gift of immortality.   His own mother, waking up
one night, stood amazed to find that nurse holding her
babe in the flames of the fire; then with screams of terror
she snatched him away, knowing not how his limbs had
been bathed in nectar, and a charm breathed over him so
that the fire should but temper his life to deathlessness.
Now the stranger shone forth by the hearth as a goddess,
to tell what purpose it was had thus been brought to
nought ; and forthwith she passed away upon her long
quest.

But when her mind was set at ease by the return of
Persephone, Demeter sought out that nursling at Eleusis
to show through him new favour to mortals.   In her
dragon-chariot she sent Triptolemus out with the gift of
corn for men, and to teach them the use of the plough
and the sickle, so that no more should they be in danger
of famine.   And in his native land she set on foot the
sacred Eleusinian festival, by which for ages to come its
people should remember Demeter and Persephone.

ORPHEUS AND EURYDICE

Orpheus the Thracian was famed as sweetest minstrel of old. Son of the muse Calliope, he was born under Mount Rhodope, yet often wandered about Olympus, home of the gods, enchanting also with his song the wooded slopes on Parnassus and the sacred spring of Helicon. The tale goes how when, with the skill taught by his mother-muse, he struck the golden lyre given him by Apollo, fierce beasts of the forest would come forth charmed to tameness; the rushing streams stood still to listen; and the very rocks and trees were drawn after that witching music, that softened the hearts of savage men.

The singer who could breathe life into a stone, readily won the heart of fair Eurydice, not the less since he had shown himself brave as well as gifted when he followed Jason on the quest of the Golden Fleece. But all too short was the happiness of that loving pair. As she danced at their bridal feast, a venomous snake, gliding through the grass, stung the heel of Eurydice, her only among the merry guests, so that she died on the night she was wedded.

The lamenting husband bore her to the grave, playing mournful airs that moved the hearts of all who followed that funeral train. Then, life seeming to him dark as death without his Eurydice, Orpheus pressed on to the very gates of Hades, seeking her where no living man might enter till the day of his own doom.

127

But at this man's tuneful strains, Charon silently ferried him across the Styx, that black stream that divides our sunlit world from the cold realms of Pluto. So moving were the notes of his lyre that the iron bars slid back of themselves, and Cerberus, the three-headed guard of death's gloomy portal, sank down without showing his teeth, to let the lulling music pass. Without check or challenge Orpheus stole boldly into the world of the shades, flitting about him from all sides to fix their dim eyes on the man who could work such a spell even among the dead.

Fearsome and gruesome were the sights he saw in the dark caves of Tartarus, yet through them he held on undismayed, straining his eyes after Eurydice alone. He came past the daughters of Danaus, who, all save one, had stabbed their husbands on the wedding night, and for such a crime must do eternal penance by vainly pouring water into a sieve; but, as the Thracian singer went by, they had a brief respite from their bootless task, turning on him looks which he gave not back. So, too, his music made a moment's peace for Tantalus, that once rich and mighty king, that for unspeakable offence against the gods was doomed to suffer burning thirst in a lake whose waters ever fled from his lips, and in his hungry eyes bloomed clusters of ripe fruit shrinking and withering as he stretched out his hand to clutch them; and over his head hung a huge stone threatening in vain to crush him out of his misery. Again, Orpheus passed where Sisyphus, for his life's burden of wickedness, had to roll uphill a heavy rock always slipping from his arms to spin down to the bottom: he, too, could pause to wipe his hot brow as the singer's voice fell on his ears like balm. Nor did the spell of music fail to stop Ixion's wheel, bound to which that treacherous murderer must

for ever whirl through the fiery air in unpitied torment.
Then for once, they say, were tears drawn to the dry
eyes of the Furies, those three chastising sisters, whose
very name men fear to speak.

> " Heavenly o'er the startled Hell,
> Holy, where the Accursed dwell,
> O Thracian, went thy silver song!
> Grim Minos with unconscious tears,
> Melts into mercy as he hears—
> The serpents in Megæra's hair
> Kiss, as they wreathe enamoured there;
> All harmless rests the madding throng;—
> From the torn breast the Vulture mute
> Flies, scared before the charmèd lute—
> Lulled into sighing from their roar
> The dark waves woo the listening shore—
> Listening the Thracian's silver song!—
> Love was the Thracian's silver song!"
>
> *—Schiller.*

But Orpheus looked not aside, and the thin ghosts
ever made way for him as he pressed on till he came
before the throne where the dark-browed King of Hades
sat beside his queen Persephone, her fair face veiled by
the shadows of that dire abode. Then, striking his
softest notes, the suppliant minstrel raised a chant to stir
the hardest heart, beseeching its sovereign for once to
loose the bonds of death.

"Love", he sang, "gives me strength to seek the
shades before my time; love, that if tales be true, has
had power even here, when stern Pluto came forth to
win a bride snatched from the world of life. Let me
take back my loved one, doomed too soon by fate! Or,
if that may not be, oh! dread king, in mercy accept two
victims for one, nor bid me return alone to the upper
air."

Black-browed Pluto nodded to his prayer, when Per-

sephone whispered a pitiful word in her consort's ear.
Then the lyre of Orpheus was silenced by a hollow voice
proclaiming through the vaulted halls a boon for once
granted to mortal man. All Hades held its breath to
hear.

"So be it ! Back to the world above, and Eurydice
shall follow thee as thy shadow ! But halt not, speak
not, turn not to look behind, till ye have gained the
upper air, or never mayst thou see her face again.
Begone without delay, and on thy silent path thou wilt
not be alone."

In grateful awe, the husband of Eurydice turned his
back upon death's throne, taking his way through the
chill gloom towards a faint glimmer that marked the gate
of Hades. Fain would he have looked round to make
sure that Eurydice came behind him, fain would he have
halted to listen for her footfall. But now all was still as
death, save his own hasty steps echoing dreadfully as he
pressed on to the light that shone clearer and clearer
before him like a star of hope. Then doubt and impatience clouded his mind, so that he could not trust the
word of a god. He had not yet gained the gate, when,
giving way to eager desire, he turned his head and saw
indeed behind him the shrouded form of her he loved so
fondly.

"Eurydice !" he cried, stretching out his arms, but
they clasped the cold thin air ; and only a sigh came back
to him, as her dim shape melted away into the darkness.

In vain the twice-bereaved lover made Hades ring
with Eurydice's name. He was never to see her more
while he lived. Out of his senses for despair, he found
himself thrust into the daylight, alone. There he lay
like an image, for days unable to speak, or to sing, with
no desire but to starve himself back to death.

At last he rose and took his way into the world of men. Now he went silent, the strings of his lyre broken like his heart. He shunned all dwellings and scenes of joy, nor would he look upon the face of women, though many a maid smiled kindly to bid him forget his lost Eurydice. Henceforth, his solitary haunts were the mountain forests of Thrace, where beasts rather than men would be his companions among the rough thickets.

But ere long, as he would have retuned his lyre to strains of woe, the rocks rang with a clamorous din, and forth upon him burst a troop of Mænads, women frenzied by the rites of Dionysus, to whom, with jangling cymbals and clanging horns, they yelled a shrill chorus *Evoe, Evoe!* Clothed in fawnskins, and garlanded with vine leaves, they danced towards the stranger; but he rose in horror to fly from their flushed faces, nor heeded the wild outcry with which they called on him to join their revel. Furious at this affront, the maddened votaries of Bacchus followed him like fierce hunters closing on a deer. They stoned him to the ground, they broke his lyre in pieces, and, their drunken rage heated by the sight of blood, that ruthless crew ended by tearing their disdainer in pieces. His limbs were flung into a stream which bore them to the sea; and they tell how his head, still breathing Eurydice's name, was washed ashore on the isle of Lesbos, there to be buried by the Muses in a tomb that became a sacred shrine, on which the nightingales sang more sweetly than elsewhere.

MIDAS

Midas, king of Phrygia, was rich above all men in the world, yet, like others who have much, his heart was set on more. Once he had the chance to do a service to a god, when in his garden was found old Silenus, who, strayed from the train of his patron Dionysus, had lain down here to sleep off a drunken bout. Midas sportively bound the wandering reveller with roses, and, after filling him with the meat and drink he loved, took him back to the god of wine; then so well pleased was Dionysus to see that jovial companion, that he bid the friendly king choose any reward he liked to ask. Midas did not think twice.

"Grant me this boon then," he cried eagerly: "that whatever I touch may turn to gold!"

"So be it!" laughed the god, pledging him in a cup of wine; and Midas left his presence exulting to know that henceforth his wealth was boundless.

Impatient to test his new-given power, as he walked through the woods he tore off a twig, and lo! at his touch it had turned to yellow gold. He picked up stones from the path, then they, too, became pure gold, and every clod he handled was at once a glittering nugget; he grasped an ear of corn to find it hard as gold; and when he plucked fruit or flowers they were like the apples of the Hesperides, so that soon his attendants went groaning under the burden of gold he gathered on the way. Weighed down by his golden robes, he himself would fain have been borne along, but when he mounted a mule it stood a lifeless image, and the litter on which they laid him was too heavy for the strength of all his men. Almost beside himself with pride and greed, he got home to his palace, where, as he brushed through the portal, its posts turned to golden pillars; and when he threw himself on the nearest seat, it was henceforth such a costly throne as any king in the world might envy.

Fatigued by his journey and its excitements, Midas called for food. Obedient menials made haste to spread a table, while others brought basins in which as their lord plunged his hands, the water froze forthwith into golden ice. So it was when he sat down to eat. He smiled to see how his plates and bowls changed to gold, as beseemed; but his smile became a frown when the first savoury mouthful met his lips as tasteless metal. In vain he tried to swallow such rich fare; the sweetest morsel crunched between his teeth like ashes; and when he would have drained a cup of wine, the drink was solid gold.

Tormented by hunger and thirst, he rose from that mockery of a banquet, for once envying the poorest kitchen-boy in his palace. It was no comfort to visit the growing mass of his treasures; the very sight of gold began to sicken him. If he embraced his children, if he struck a slave, their bodies turned in an instant to golden statues. All around glared hateful yellow in his eyes. It was a relief when darkness came to hide that now-abhorred wealth. Then, flinging off his heavy golden robes, he sank with a sigh upon a soft couch that at once grew hard and cold; and there he tossed restless all night, the richest and the most wretched man alive.

In sleepless despair, with the first light of dawn he

hastened to Dionysus, earnestly beseeching him to take back his gift of splendid misery.

"So men's dearest wishes oft prove unwise!" railed the god. "But once more I grant thee thy desire. Seek out the source of the Pactolus, and by bathing in its pure waters thou mayst undo the spell laid upon thee."

Scarcely waiting to thank him, Midas set off for that healing stream. Driven on by the gnawings of hunger, over mountain and plain he panted till he came to the Pactolus, whose sandy bed was streaked with gold wherever he trod; and men say that scales of gold may still be turned up to mark his footsteps. When he reached its cool fountain and hurled into it his fevered body, the crystal water was stained as if by gold. But no sooner had his head plunged beneath it, than that fatal gift was washed away; and to his unspeakable joy Midas came out able to eat and drink like other men.

This king was not always so fortunate in his dealings with the gods. Cured of his greed for gold, yet no wiser in his mind, he took to roaming the green woods, and there came upon Pan at strife with the great Apollo. For that rude Satyr had presumed to boast his pipe of reeds against the god's lute; and they took Midas for judge which of them made the sweetest music. After listening to their strains, the dull-eared mortal gave judgment for Pan; then Apollo, in displeasure, punished him by decking his head with the ears of an ass, even as the Muses spitefully turned the daughters of Pierus into birds, when these mortal maidens would have contended with them in song on Mount Helicon.

The first pool into which Midas looked showed him how shamefully he had been transformed; but this time he could hope no favour from an angry god. Slinking into his palace by night, the king would have hid from all

that he bore those long, hairy ears. His head he kept
wrapped night and day in a turban such as makes a shield
against the sun for men of the hot East. None knew
why Midas went thus arrayed, save only his barber, to
whom he could not but disclose the truth, binding him
by oaths and threats never to breathe it to human ear.

But the barber, for his part, could not bear the weight
of such a secret which he must not tell. Itching to let
it out, yet fearing his master's wrath, he stole down to
the lonely bank of the river and scooped out a hole, into
which he whispered " *Midas has ass's ears* ", hoping to
be heard by no man. But where he had opened the
ground, there grew up a clump of reeds that, as often as
they were stirred by the wind, kept on murmuring,
" *Midas has ass's ears* ".

SCYLLA

Of Megara, Euclid's birthplace, it is told how in old days it was besieged by Minos of Crete. Long the siege lasted, for the Fates had decreed that the city should not be taken while it contained a talisman, which was no other than a lock of purple hair growing on the head of Nisus, its king; and that secret he had told to his daughter Scylla. So, month by month, the Cretan army lay encamped without the walls; but all their attacks were thrown away.

From the highest tower of the city, Scylla so often looked down on the array of her father's foes, that she came to know the leaders by sight and by name. Always her eyes sought out Minos, the famous king, who, enemy as he was, seemed to her the most goodly and gallant man she had ever seen. Her heart followed her eyes, and her dreams kept the hero's image in mind by darkness as by daylight, till the love-sick maiden thought more of this stranger than of her own country or kin.

"Were it not well to end the weary war?" she told herself. "With me for a captive, would not the King of Crete grant us peace? And what could he refuse to her who put into his hands the secret of victory?"

Brooding over such thoughts, at last poor Scylla strung herself up to betray her native city, for the sake of one whose voice she had never heard, save raised in menace against its defenders. At the dead of night she stole to her sleeping father's couch. Softly she shore off the shining purple lock that glittered like a star among his grey hair. Cautiously she slipped out from the gates, and made her way to the enemy's camp, demanding of the sentinels to lead her into the presence of Minos.

With beating heart she knelt before the king, whose love she hoped to buy at such a price. But when she held out to him the purple lock, explaining how on it lay the safety of her father's kingdom, and by looks rather than speech would have given him to know why she thus played traitress to her own people, the noble Minos repelled that gift with scornful indignation.

"A treacherous daughter is worthy of no brave man's love!" he declared. "Begone from my sight, dishonour of thy race and thy sex! Minos gains not victory by baseness."

Now that Megara lay at his mercy the generous foe offered it peace, and, without striking another blow, made ready to sail away to Crete. Scylla, wild with shame and remorse, not daring to face her father, begged in vain to be taken on board the fleet.

"The ship that bore thee would never come safe to port," answered Minos sternly. "Such a one as thou must be cursed by the gods, to find no resting-place on sea nor on land."

"I deserve indeed to die," pleaded the miserable maiden; "yet for thee it was I sinned against father and country—leave me not to their wrath!"

The proud king turned away without a word. When she saw his ship set sail, Scylla in despair leaped into the water, clinging to its rudder as it stood away from her native shore. But down swooped an eagle to strike her with its beak and claws, so that she let go her hold and would have been drowned, had not some god changed her into a sea-bird. In that form is she doomed to fly homeless and restless over the waves, ever pursued by the eagle, that is none other than her betrayed father, to whom the gods granted such endless vengeance. So say some; but others tell how the traitorous daughter was transformed into a cruel monster haunting the strait between Italy and Sicily.

BELLEROPHON

It seemed as if a curse rested on the house of Sisyphus, king of Corinth, who for his tyranny and treacheries had been doomed to endless labour in Hades. His son Glaucus was famed for love of horses, which at last brought him to a cruel end, when the mares which he had fed on human flesh turned madly upon their master and tore him in pieces. The son of Glaucus was Bellerophon, a valiant and comely youth, who yet could not escape the evil fate of his race. For, having slain one of his countrymen in a chance fray, he must needs fly from Corinth, to take refuge with Prœtus, king of Argos.

This king gave him kindly welcome, sheltering him from the avengers, and offering solemn rites to cleanse his guilt of bloodshed. Bellerophon's youthful charm won not only the favour of Prœtus, but the sinful love of Antea, the dark-eyed princess whom he had brought from Asia to be his queen. But in vain she tempted the loyal guest to secret wickedness. When all her wiles could not make him untrue to honour and hospitality, her love turned to hate, and with a lying tale she would have stirred her husband's wrath against his foully slandered friend. The deceived Prœtus was in a strait what to do. He had come to love this gallant youth so well, that he could not bear to have him slain in his own sight. Yet, the false wife poisoning his mind, he was moved to wreak his jealousy by another's hand.

Without letting Bellerophon guess his changed mood, he sent him to visit his father-in-law, Iobates, king of Lycia, charged with a tablet on which was written in secret characters the bearer's doom.

All unsuspicious of harm, Bellerophon made the long journey by sea and land, that at last brought him to the city of the Lycian king. Iobates received the stranger like a courteous host, asking not who he was, nor whence he came, nor on what errand. Nine days he entertained his unknown guest freely with feasts and games, since Bellerophon's noble bearing showed him worthy of honour at a king's hands. Not till the tenth day did he declare his name, giving over to Iobates the tablet on which Prœtus had drawn a secret message, to be interpreted by his wife's father alone.

"*He who bears this token comes deserving death at thy hands. See to it!*"

The king of Lycia, in turn, had come to love that winsome Greek so well that he was dismayed to learn how he had been sent here for execution. To his son-in-law who gave him such a charge Iobates was so beholden that he durst not refuse to do his bidding; yet loath was he to punish, for an unknown crime, one who had already become his friend.

Unwillingly, he cast about for some plan of having Bellerophon killed without shedding his blood by his own hands; nor had he long to seek. The outskirts of Lycia were then being ravaged by a fire-breathing beast called the Chimæra, that had devoured every champion set out against it. The very sight of it indeed was enough to appal the stoutest heart, for it had the head of a lion, the hinder parts of a dragon, the body of a monstrous goat, rough with scales and bristles; and with its breath it scorched all who ven-

tured to face it. Iobates, then, believed himself giving
up Bellerophon to certain death when he begged him to
rid the land of such a plague; and his heart smote him
to see how gladly the gallant youth took upon himself
that fatal adventure.

The very gods had pity on an innocent man thus
sent to so cruel death, none the less when by pious
sacrifices he invoked their aid on his perilous quest.
Before going far he came upon the winged horse
Pegasus, sprung from the blood of that Gorgon slain
by Perseus. Bellerophon would fain have made his own
such a goodly steed; but Pegasus, never yet backed
by man, reared and flung and sprang, and would not
let itself be caught. Tired out by his vain efforts to
tame it, he had fallen asleep beside a fountain, when
Athene appeared to him in a dream, who seemed to
lay a golden bridle at his side and to whisper in his
ear—"*Wake, take, tame*".

He woke up, and lo! beside him lay the golden
bridle, while Pegasus was still feeding by the fountain.
As he softly stole up to it, the horse did not now dash
away from him, but, lowering its proud neck, let him
slip the bit into its mouth, and stood still for him to
leap upon its back. By divine aid he had mastered the
horse of heaven.

Mounted on such a courser he soon reached the
haunts of the Chimæra, that came out raging against
him, vomiting fire and smoke. But now that monster
had to do with an invincible foe. Soaring in the air
beyond reach of hurt, Bellerophon shot down sharp
arrows, till the ground, burning under the creature's
breath, was quenched in its blood. Then the hero dis-
mounted to cut off its hairy head and scaly tail, which
he bore back in triumph as proof of his victory.

Iobates, half-glad to see him return with such spoils, half-concerned to find the victim still alive, soon took excuse to lay upon him another perilous adventure. He charged him with war upon the Solymi, a race of fierce mountain robbers who infested the borders of Lycia, and had slain the king's bravest fighters in many a battle. But they could not stand against the darts of this flying champion; and when he had rooted them out of the land, he again came back unhurt.

Next, Iobates sent him far off against the Amazons, that nation of women warriors who had overthrown kings and their armies. But them, too, Bellerophon conquered, and again came back in triumph. On his way home an ambush was laid for him by Iobates, still striving to do his son-in-law's desire; then the hero slew these assailants as easily as he quelled all other enemies.

"This can be no evildoer deserving punishment, but rather a man dear to the gods," the heart of Iobates told him; and when once more Bellerophon came back victorious over every foe, the king no longer sought his death. Joyfully he hailed him as worthy of all honour, gave him his daughter to wife, and shared with him his kingdom and riches, as if the stranger were his own son.

Thus raised to power and wealth, Bellerophon might surely rest in peace after the trials of his youth. But he who had borne himself so well in adversity, fell away from virtue when life became smooth and soft for him. It seemed as if that old guilt of bloodshed ever rose up against him. With years he grew not wise but proud, forgetting the gods to whom he owed his good fortune, that therefore came to be clouded by their ill will. His eldest son grew up a brave champion like the father, only to fall in battle with savage robbers. His daughter was slain by a shaft of offended Artemis. Heedless of these warnings, Bellerophon thought to fly to heaven on his winged steed. Then Zeus sent a gadfly to sting Pegasus, so that it reared in the air and threw off its presumptuous rider, tumbling to earth alive but sorely hurt. Now made aware of the gods' anger, the down-fallen hero henceforth shrunk from the looks of men. Crippled and feeble, he wandered about like a madman in solitary places, till at last death ended his miserable age, of which Homer has to tell how—

" Woes heaped on woes consumed his wasted heart ".

ARION

After Orpheus, fabled as son of a Muse, the most famous singer in ancient Greece was Arion, who lived much with his chief patron, the wise Periander, king of Corinth. But Arion had a mind for showing his skill in other lands, and, for all Periander could say to keep him at Corinth, he sailed away to take part in a great musical contest held in Sicily.

There this minstrel gained such prizes and so rich gifts that it was a treasure of gold and silver he had to take back from the land to which he brought nothing but his harp. To carry his wealth safe home, he hired a ship of Corinth, trusting Periander's countrymen rather than strangers not to play him false. But the sailors were covetous and treacherous; and the sight of that treasure turned them to pirates.

All went well with the ship; and Arion little guessed that he were safer on the stormiest waves. Halcyon weather and gentle breezes were bearing him round the southern point of Greece, when at once those wicked men threw off the mask of kindliness. With drawn swords they fell upon their passenger, declaring how they had hatched a plot to rob him of all he possessed.

"Take my gold, but spare my life!" he entreated them to no purpose.

"Then how should we face Periander?" was their mocking answer. "Thy gold will we bring safe to Corinth, but not the owner, who might tell tales. Choose

forthwith: either slay thyself and get from us the boon
of a grave on shore, or we throw thee overboard without more ado."

All his promises and prayers being lost on them, the
poor rich man asked one last grace, that he should be
allowed to deck himself in his costliest robes, and to sing
to the harp his sweetest song; then he would leap into
the sea and save them the guilt of bloodshed. To this
the rough sailors agreed, not unwilling to hear for once
the strains of a renowned minstrel who had won all
that wealth they hoped now to make their own.

So Arion robed himself in purple, and perfumed his
hair, crowned with a triumphal wreath he took as the
noblest of his winnings. Thus arrayed, he stood upon
the poop to sing his death-chant. Poets tell that, when
he sang in wood and field, the lamb and the wolf would
stand together to listen, yea, the stag and the lion, the
hare and the hounds, while overhead the dove and the
hawk hung still to listen in the air. Now, so sweetly his
golden harp resounded over the sea, that not only were
those cruel men half-stirred to pity, but a shoal of dolphins gathered about the ship, drawn after the music as
if by a cable. When it came to an end, taking one last
look at the bright sky, harp in hand, Arion leapt overboard.

The pirates let their sail fill and stood on for Greece,
pleased to be so well rid of him. But Arion had not
sunk under the waves. He was caught on the back of
an admiring dolphin, that carried him safe and dry over
the sea to Tænarum, the nearest point of land. So
works the magic of song for men favoured by Apollo.

Thus set on shore, Arion travelled through the Peloponnesus and came to Corinth a day before the ship.
The returned minstrel was gladly welcomed by Periander,

who, indeed, could ill believe his story of strange escape
from drowning. When now the ship sailed into harbour,
those robbers, summoned before the king, were asked for
news of Arion. Boldly they declared that they had left
him honoured and prosperous in the new Greece beyond
the sea. But as the false words came from their lips, he
stepped forth before them clad as they saw him lost overboard, and still bearing the harp of marvellous power.

The amazed sailors no longer durst deny their crime;
but fell on the ground praying for mercy, and for pardon
from their victim, whom they took for a god. The
harper's heart was not tuned to vengeance; but the king
was stern in justice. He ordered the treacherous crew
to a death more cruel than they had designed for Arion,
in memory of whose wonderful preservation was erected
at Tænarum a brazen monument of him riding on the
dolphin's back.[1]

---

[1] Pausanias speaks as if he had seen this monument, and adds that he had himself
known "a dolphin so full of gratitude to a boy, by whom he had been healed of wounds
received from some fishermen, that he was obedient to his call and carried him on his
back over the sea whenever he wished".

THE ARGONAUTS

I. Jason's Youth

In a cave high up the rocky and snowy sides of Mount Pelion dwelt Cheiron, oldest and wisest of the Centaurs, that wondrous race that were half-horse and half-man. When the brute strength of his lower part began to fail, the white-bearded Centaur's head was richly stored with knowledge and experience, and his hands had rare skill in playing on a golden harp, to the music of which he gave forth wise counsels in human speech. So great was his fame that many a king's and hero's son came to be trusted to his care for rearing in all that beseemed a noble youth. From him they had lessons in duty, to fear the gods, to reverence old age, and to stand by one another in pain and hardship. He was a master of the healing art, and this they learned as from the lips of Æsculapius himself. He taught them to sing, to make music, to bear themselves gracefully in the dance, but also to run, box, and wrestle, to climb the dizzy rocks, and to hunt wild beasts in the mountain forests, laughing at all dangers as they scorned sloth and gluttony, and cheerily facing the sharpest storms of winter as they plunged into foaming torrents under the hot summer sun. So in all the world there were no goodlier lads than they who grew up under the care of Cheiron to be both skilful and strong, modest as well as brave, and fitted to rule by having rightly known to obey.

Among that youthful fellowship, goodliest in his day was Jason, a boy of princely race, nay, a king's son by right. For his father Æson had been born heir of Iolcos, yet let this kingdom be stolen from him by his wicked half-brother Pelias, who would have slain Jason to make that wrongdoing sure. But Æson had saved the child by flight, hiding him in Cheiron's cave, where for years he little guessed how it was his own heritage of rich plain and well-peopled seashore on which he looked down from the cloud-wrapped ridges of Mount Pelion; nor did Pelias know what a champion was growing up within sight of his usurped realm.

But when the sturdy lad had shot to full stature, and his mind, no longer set on boyish sport and mirth, turned eagerly to the wide world in which he might prove his manhood, old Cheiron saw the time come to let him know the secret of his birth, and how he was destined to avenge on Pelias the wrong done to his father. The young hero heard in amazement; then not a day would he delay in setting out on the adventure in store for him. Taking leave of his envious playmates, he dutifully received his old master's parting counsel.

"I need not wish thee fearless before enemies; but remember how it becomes a king's son to be friendly to all other men, and helpful in their need."

The youth's heart beat high with hope, as under the bright morning sun he took his way down the mountain, where every step brought him nearer in view of the unknown world below. Lightly clad in a close-fitting vest beneath a panther's skin he had won by his own spear, his feet shod with new sandals, his long hair streaming in the wind, Jason bounded from rock to rock, and stepped out under the cool shade of pine woods, and pushed through thickets of tangled shrubs, all familiar to him,

for Cheiron had taught his scholars to know every flower
and leaf on their mountain home. But when the steep
paths had brought him down to the lowland country, he
found it covered with fields of corn, lush meadows, groves
of fruit trees, and such signs of human habitation. Yet it
was his hap to meet no soul to bid him speed, till on the
bank of a rushing river he found an old woman in mean
rags, who rocked herself feebly as she sat and cried out
beseechingly—

"Alas! who will carry me across?"

With disdain Jason looked at this poor crone, and
with doubt at the foaming torrent, swollen by the melting
of the snows above. But to his mind came Cheiron's
word that he must be helpful to all kindly folk; and the
youth took shame to himself that he had turned proudly
from one who rather called on him for pity.

"My shoulders are broad enough for such a light
load!" said he heartily. "Up with thee, old mother,
and, the gods aiding, I will bear thee safe!"

Without more ado, before he could raise a hand to
lift her up, the seeming helpless beggar sprang on his
back; and with her arms clinging round his neck, he
strode boldly into the stream. He slipped, he staggered
as it took him to the knees, to the waist, to the shoulders;
and he had almost been put to swimming for it, while the
old hag moaned and shrieked for terror, crying out that
he was drowning her, and abusing him crossly for wetting
her worthless rags.

"Hold on fast!" was his cheery answer, though she
half-choked him by her clutching fingers.

For a moment he had a mind to throw off this thank-
less stranger, and take his own chance of buffeting the
flooded torrent. But he knew that thought for unworthy,
and struggled on sturdily to gain at last the further bank.

Here as he scrambled to shore, all dripping and breathless, and would have gently laid down his burden on the grass, she sprang from his back to take on a wondrously altered guise. For when he looked to see a wrinkled and bent crone, with hardly a word to thank her helper, lo! there stood before him a tall and stately form, like no daughter of woman, her rags changed to jewelled robes, and her eyes now smiling on him so radiantly that he knew her as of divine race.

"Yes," she said, reading his mind. "I am indeed Hera, the queen of heaven, to whom thou hast done such service unaware. Not in vain was thy spirit humbled and thy back bowed for one appearing to be poor and helpless. In thine own hour of need, call upon me, and see if a goddess can be grateful."

Speechless, the youth fell upon his knees, his eyes dazzled by the vision of glory that, as he gazed, went up in a shining cloud; and when he could see clearly, he was alone on the river bank.

Thanking the gods that he had been true to his better nature and to the teaching of his master, Jason took his way onwards to a city whose towers stood out before him upon the plain. But now he limped along more slowly, for he found he had lost one of his sandals, left sticking in the slimy bed of the torrent, where a sharp stone had cut his bare foot. Schooled as he had been to make light of such mishaps, he bound up his hurt with soft leaves, and held on through shade and sunshine till towards evening he reached the gate of Iolcos.

There he found all astir with a great feast held by Pelias in honour of the gods. Many an eye was cast curiously on this comely youth, as he wandered through the streets, sun-tanned and dusty from the long way. He thought these trim citizens despised him for being but half-shod, for he knew not what was known to them, how an oracle had foretold that Pelias should lose his ill-gotten kingdom to a stranger who came wearing but one sandal.

Seeking his way to the palace, he presented himself before Pelias, who, amid all his royal state, might well start at the sight of this half-barefooted youth, since night and day his guilty mind never forgot what sign was to mark the avenger.

"Thy name and lineage?" he faltered forth.

"I am Jason, son of Æson, come to claim my rightful heritage," declared the youth boldly.

The king's heart sank within him, for he was as full of fears as of falsehood and cruelty. But, hiding his dismay, he made a show of welcoming this nephew with joy, and bid him sit down at the feast beside his own fair daughters. To-morrow, he said, would be fitter time to talk about the affairs of the kingdom. Meanwhile, let all be joy and mirth to hail the return of a nephew long given up for dead.

Simple and honest himself, Jason was won by his uncle's fine words and by the charms of his new-found cousins. Their seeming kindness turned his head, so that he let his heart go out to them, believing Pelias must have been slandered as a faithless usurper. He ate and drank among them friendly, then, flushed with wine, listened eagerly to the minstrels who cheered the banquet. A song that set his pulses beating was the tale of the Golden Fleece: how Phrixus and Helle, a king's son and daughter, were persecuted by their cruel stepmother Ino; how they fled from her on a golden ram, sent by a friendly god; how poor Helle, turning giddy as they flew over land and sea, fell from its back into the Hellespont, that has ever afterwards been known by her name; but Phrixus safely reached Colchis at the farther end of the dark Euxine Sea; how he sacrificed the ram to Zeus, and hung up its fleece in a sacred grove by the river of the Colchians, among whom henceforth he lived and died. There it was jealously treasured by Æetes, king of that distant land, whose own life, said an oracle, depended on its safe keeping, so that he had it guarded night and day by a sleepless serpent, as by other perils no hero had been found bold enough to face; but never would the ghost of dead Phrixus be laid till the Golden Fleece were won back to his kinsmen in Greece. This song had been sung by command of Pelias; and keenly he watched his nephew's flashing eyes as the moving tale was told.

"Ah!" exclaimed the crafty king, "time was when I would have dared all for such a prize. But I am old, and the sons of our day are not as their fathers. Where lives the man who will venture to bring back the Golden Fleece?"

"Here!" cried Jason, leaping to his feet. "I will seek the Fleece, if I have to pay for it with my life."

His cunning uncle made haste to embrace him, with feigned pride and joy in a youth worthy of their heroic stock. Yes, let him bring the Golden Fleece to Iolcos; and he himself would gladly give up the kingdom to the hero of such a deed! So he promised, secretly trusting that his brave kinsman would never come back from that perilous errand; and thus by guile and flattery he hoped to make himself sure of his stolen power.

When, after a night's sleep, he came to think calmly over his undertaking, Jason might well see its rashness, and maybe he suspected how his uncle had thus schemed to get rid of him. But the old Centaur had taught him never to draw back from his word, and what he had spoken in haste he must strive to perform by dint of courage and prudence. He sought the aid of a cunning shipwright called Argus, who from the tall pines of Mount Pelion built him a fifty-oared ship, so strong that it could bear the buffeting of winds and waves, yet so light that it might be carried on the shoulders of its crew. This was named the *Argo*, after its builder. To man it, Jason sent out to his old schoolmates and to other heroes of Greece, summoning stout hearts and arms ready to join him in the quest of the Golden Fleece.

While they came together, Jason betook himself to Hera's sacred grove at Dodona, beseeching her promised favour, of which he was assured by the Speaking Oak that made her oracle. As proof of her gratitude, he was bidden to tear away a limb of that oak to make a figure-head for his ship; and this lifeless wood had the power of speech, through which, when in doubt or danger, he might be counselled by the goddess. Moreover, she procured the goodwill of wise Athene to inspire Argus in building the ship, which should set out under such high auspices.

For comrades he had the best and bravest of the Grecian youth, sons of gods and men, a band henceforth to be known as the Argonauts. Among those heroes were names of fame—Hercules, the twin-brethren Castor and Pollux, Theseus, Orpheus, Peleus, Admetus, and many more, fifty in all, one to each oar of the galley, in which their seats were fixed by lot. Argus himself made one of the crew, and Acastus, the son of Pelias, stole off to join them against his father's will. Tiphys was their steersman; sharp-eyed Lynceus their pilot. With one voice they would have chosen Hercules for captain; but he gave the leadership to Jason, and all were content. After due sacrifices to the gods, and farewells to their friends, they launched forth the *Argo* into the blue sea, its prow set towards the clouds hiding that far-off eastern land whence they must tear the Golden Fleece. Orpheus put heart into them with his songs; but there was a tear in Jason's eye, as he saw the mountains of his fatherland fade away behind their track.

II. The Voyage to Colchis

'Twere long to tell all that hindered those heroes on their far course, and how one and another were cut off by mishaps, never to reach the Colchian land. Turning from the shores of Thessaly, they stood across the Ægean Sea to the rocky island of Lemnos, where a strange snare was set for them. The women of the island, maddened by jealousy, had slain all their men folk, and, now vainly repentant, hailed the newcomers as husbands for their defenceless need. Jason and most of his crew, going among them, gave way to their endearments, and amidst pleasures and feasting were tempted to forget what work they had on hand. But stouthearted Hercules had stayed by the ship; and when he came on shore to chide his comrades, they took shame for their softness, and tore themselves away to face the cold sea winds like men, who for a moment had been caught by womanly wiles.

Bending afresh to their oars, they passed through the Hellespont and came to a haven in the Propontis Sea, where Cyzicus, the young king of the Doliones, received them gladly and would have them stay to his wedding feast. But Hercules, again on watch in the ship, saw how here too there was a snare set. For a race of giant savages came down from the hills, and were blocking up the harbour mouth with huge stones, when

Hercules gave the alarm, and with his arrows kept off these foemen, who fell or fled when the whole band had gathered to defend their ship. And worse was to betide here, for when the *Argo* steered forth into the open sea, a storm drove her back by night, and their late friendly hosts, the Doliones, taking them for enemies, set upon them in the darkness, so that Jason unaware slew the young king at whose marriage he had sat a guest. Daylight showed both bands how they had mistaken each other; then for three days the Argonauts tarried to celebrate the funeral rites of those unhappily slain.

But soon they were to lose stout Hercules, who more than once had served them so well. As he tugged at his oar in the stormy waves, it broke, and not easily could another be found to match his brawny arms. When next they went on shore and his companions were being feasted by the hospitable Mysians, Hercules strode off into the forest to cut for himself a new oar from some tall pine tree. With him went the beautiful boy Hylas, whom he loved like a son, and also another of the crew named Polyphemus. While Hercules stripped himself to fell the tree he had chosen, young Hylas turned aside to a spring from which he would have drawn water for their supper. In this spring dwelt a bevy of water nymphs, who, as they saw the boy leaning over with his brazen pitcher, were so taken by his beauty, that they cast their arms round him and dragged him down into the water, never again to be seen of men. Polyphemus heard his last cry, and hastened to tell Hercules that the lad was being caught by robbers or wild beasts.

In vain these two searched for him through the forest, shouting and raging against the unseen foe who had laid hands on the hero's darling. Meanwhile their shipmates impatiently awaited them, for the wind had turned fair. When the hours passed and Hercules came not, they fell to quarrelling among themselves, for some said they should not go without that tower of strength, but others were for leaving him behind. So, in the end, they did, and with quiet minds after the sea-god Glaucus had risen from the waves to disclose to them how Hercules was not destined to share the gaining of the Golden Fleece. That hero had glory enough awaiting him elsewhere.

On their next landing, Hercules might have found a task worthy of him, for this was the country of the Bebrycians, whose brawny king's humour was to challenge all strangers to box with him, never yet having met his match. But Pollux took up the challenge, and after doughty blows on both sides, smote the boaster to the ground; then his angry people would have avenged him with their weapons; but the Argonauts drove them away like wolves. Before letting him rise, the hero made that churlish king swear to handle strangers more courteously henceforth.

A more unfamiliar combat it was they undertook on coming to the home of the blind king Phineus, who was tormented by winged Harpies that pounced upon his food to snatch or defile it ere he could carry a morsel to his mouth. But two of Jason's band were winged men, able to rise in the air and drive away those monstrous birds, letting the blind old man eat in peace his first meal for many a day. In gratitude, he warned them of dangers on their course, and first of the Symplegades, two islands of floating ice-rock that would open like a monster's jaws to close upon their ship and crush it, unless they could speed through at the nick of time. By his advice they took a dove on board to show them the opening of the perilous passage. Loosing the dove, they saw it fly through those heaving rocks, that closed to snap off but its last feather and again drew asunder in haste; then the Argonauts pulled hard at their oars, and their wary steersman brought them darting between the icy walls that in another moment would have clashed upon them.

Holding their way along the coast of the black Pontus, they met with other mischances and delays. Where king Lycus entertained them at the mouth of the Acheron, Idmon, the diviner, blind to his own fate, was slain by the tusk of a wild boar. Here, too, their steersman Tiphys died of short sickness; and days were spent on the funeral piles. Well for the heroes, it may be, that they did not linger in the land of the Amazons, for these fierce women were more ready to wield sword and spear than distaff or needle; yet with them some of the crew would have tried a bout, as if they had not perils enough that could not be passed by! Also they skirted the coast of the Chalybes, those sooty iron smiths that night and day forge arms in the service of Ares. Next, standing out to sea, they were attacked by a flock of prodigious birds, called the Stymphalides, that cast their brazen feathers from them like darts to wound the men at their oars. But while half of them rowed on, the other half stood on guard, and raised such a din by smiting spear upon shield, that the birds were scared away, and the *Argo* could anchor safely by an island near the east end of this sea.

Here they drew near to their goal, and now they fell in with new comrades that would stead them well. For, shipwrecked on this island, they found four naked youths, the sons of Phrixus, him who had brought the Fleece to Colchis. Clad and fed by Jason, these four

agreed to guide his company to the home of Æetes, yet
not without dread, for they knew how jealously that
cruel king guarded the Fleece on which hung his own
life.   But the Argonauts, come safe through so many
perils, made light of all Æetes could do against them;
and with the sons of Phrixus for pilots, they stood across
the sea to where the ice-topped Caucasus echoed the
groans of Prometheus chained upon a cloudy crag.   And
so at last the *Argo* entered the Phasis, river of Colchis,
and by its bank her crew saw the dark grove sacred to
Ares, in which gleamed that Golden Fleece they had
come to fetch away.

III. The Winning of the Fleece

Leaving the most of his men to guard their ship,
Jason went forward to the city with a few companions,
among them the four sons of Phrixus, who were here
at home.   Forth to meet them came King Æetes, for
from his towers he had seen the *Argo* reach the Colchian
shore; and an evil dream had warned him of her errand.
With him came his young son Absyrtus, also his two
daughters, Medea the witch-maiden, and Chalciope, the
widow of Phrixus.   Right glad was she to see her sons,
whom she had mourned as lost.   As her sister had done
on Phrixus years before, Medea looked kindly upon
Jason, for in a dream she had foreseen his coming, and
no such goodly man could she see in Colchis.   Their
dark-minded sire had little joy to hail those strangers,
yet hiding his ill will, he led them to the lordly halls of
his dwelling, and set food and drink before them.

Not till the guests had eaten, did he ask what brought
them to Colchis.   Then with Medea's eyes ever fixed
upon him, Jason told of their voyage, and all the perils

they had come through for the sake of the Golden Fleece, which he boldly demanded as their reward. To this the frowning king made answer:—

"Verily, it is a vain errand to come on from so far. What ye have borne is but child's play to that which the man must dare who would prove himself worthy of such a prize. Listen, stranger, if thou have the heart even to hear the trial appointed for that rash hand that may not touch sacred things till he have proved himself more than man. Two brazen-hoofed bulls, breathing fire from their nostrils, must he tame and yoke to a plough. Thus must he plough four acres of stony field, and sow the furrows with the teeth of a venomous dragon. From these teeth will spring up forthwith a crop of armed foemen, to be mowed down before they can slay him. All this must he accomplish between the sun's rising and setting; then if he still dare, he may strive with the serpent that guards the Fleece night and day. Art thou the man?"

Jason's heart quailed within him as he listened to this tale of terrors, that indeed seemed more than mortal strength could affront. But he showed no fear, and, trusting in the favour of Hera and his own arm, he let the king know that he was ready for that ordeal, the sooner the better. Since it must take the whole day, this was put off till next morning; and the hero went back to his ship to rest before meeting those unearthly adversaries.

But while he slept, others in Colchis were wakeful. Chalciope wept in sore dismay, fearing lest, if Jason failed in his attempt, Æetes would slay all the Argonauts, and among them her sons who had guided their ship to Colchis. Therefore she sought the aid of her witch sister to work some spell on behalf of the strangers.

Nor did Medea need persuading to pity, for at first sight she had loved Jason, and was minded to save him from the death designed by her cruel father.   At nightfall she wandered among the woods gathering herbs and roots, out of whose juices she knew the art to make a magic salve, that for one whole day could keep a man scathless from fire and sword, and temper all his arms against the doughtiest stroke.   Her charms duly worked, wrapped in a veil she went towards the harbour at the earliest peep of dawn, and there met Jason coming forth to see the sun rise once more, if never again.

"Wilt thou go to death?" whispered a veiled woman in his ear.

"I had not come to Colchis, did I fear death," answered Jason.

"A bold heart alone will not avail.   But one friend hast thou in this land, else thou wert lost," murmured the witch-maiden; and Jason knew her voice for that of the king's daughter whose dark eyes had met his so kindly.

Hastily she gave him to understand how by her aid he might pass through the sore ordeal unhurt.   Then the longer he listened, the more ready he was to trust her counsels, daughter of an enemy as she was.   When in whispers she had told him all he must do, Medea put into his hands the magical salve, and fled back to her father's house as day began to break.

Jason lost no time in putting her spell to the proof. After bathing in the sea, he anointed himself from head to foot with that salve, also his shield, his helmet, and all his weapons.   This done, he let his comrades try their utmost upon him arrayed in the charmed armour. The strongest of them hacked at his spear without being able to break it with the sharpest sword; the mightiest blows made no dint on his polished shield; and he stood like a rock against the brawniest wrestler of the band. Seeing, then, how Medea had been true with him so far, he did not doubt to follow out her bidding to the end; so his heart was high as he presented himself to the king at sunrise.

"Hast thou not repented?" asked Æetes with a sneer. "I had hoped to find thee stolen away through the night with all thy presumptuous crew. It is no will of mine that a stranger must perish miserably. Bethink thee once again!"

"The sun is in the sky; and I am ready," answered Jason.

Without more ado, the king led him to a field where were laid out the brazen yoke, the iron plough, and the goad with which he must tame those fiery bulls, whose bellowing could be heard from their stable underground. All the beholders drew back, while Jason stuck sword and spear in the earth, hung to them his helmet, and, throwing off his mantle, stood nude like a marble statue with only his shield in hand.

Out came the brazen-footed bulls so suddenly as seeming to rise from the ground, that shook beneath them as they bounded upon Jason, snorting red flames from their nostrils, and roaring like thunder amid a cloud of hot smoke. But the hero fled not nor flinched at their onset. He held up his shield, against which they dashed their iron horns in vain, and behind it he stood unhurt by their scorching breath. All other eyes were half-blinded in the smoke and dust, but they could see anon how the hero caught one bull by the horn to bring it on its back by sheer strength, and how he flung down the other to its knees, wrestling against both of them with hand and foot. They being thus overthrown, he forced upon their necks the strong yoke, and harnessed them to the heavy plough, and, goading them forward, though they bellowed and struggled like a storm wind, he ploughed up the field with deep and straight furrows, to the wonder of all looking on and the secret joy of Medea, who in the background kept muttering magic spells on his behalf.

Even scowling Æetes could not but marvel at such feats. But wrath was in his heart as he saw half the appointed task done, and still it was but noon. Yet he trusted that the other half were beyond this bull-taming champion's strength. When the weary beasts had been driven back to their underground cave, he gave Jason a helmet full of dragons' teeth to sow in the fresh furrows. Strange seed that was, for no sooner had the earth covered it than the whole field began to stir and swell as if it were alive, and from every heaving clod glistened blades that were not green grass but sharp bronze and iron, the bare ground quickly bursting forth with a crop of helmets and spears which rose higher every moment, and grew up above shields and clanging mail till every furrow bristled with a rank of armed warriors, to be mowed down by Jason ere the sun sank over the sea.

And now Medea's secret counsel served him well, for he took not spear nor sword in hand, but, when the warriors were full grown and stood like bearded corn ripe for the sickle, he pitched amidst them a huge stone, such as might have made a quoit for a giant. The rattle and crash of it was drowned by the yells of the armed men, turning here and there to ask who had cast this missile against them. So hot for fight were they that forthwith they fell blindly upon one another, wrestling together and plying sword and spear on the joints of each other's harness. Thus madly and blindly they fought, some springing up from the ground only to be reaped in death. So, while Jason leant on his spear to watch how these prodigious foes struck down their own brethren, the fight went on till the furrows were filled with blood and the field lay strewn with corpses, laid low as under a hailstorm. And when the sun set, the earth had swallowed up that monstrous brood, where now green grass grew over their bones.

Black were the brows of Æetes as Jason came to demand the Golden Fleece, since he had fulfilled the hard task set him.

"We will speak of that to-morrow," answered the king, turning away sullenly to his halls, while the Grecian heroes, proud and glad, went back to their ship.

There, as they sat at supper, into the blaze of their fire stole Medea with breathless haste to warn them what was afoot. Her father, she disclosed, was secretly gathering his warriors, and meant to set upon them next morning with overwhelming might. If they would win the Fleece, it must be now or never. She herself would guide Jason to the grove where it hung, and by her spells she could lull its fearsome guardian to sleep. Then he must seize it and fly before the sun rose.

This witch-maiden having already schooled him so well, Jason could not doubt again to do her bidding. His comrades left to unmoor the *Argo* and make all ready for instant flight, he alone let Medea guide him to the sacred shrine. With her had come her young brother Absyrtus; and he too followed, trembling for fear.

At dead of night they entered the gloomy grove of Ares, where at once they heard the blood-curdling

hiss of that watchful serpent, whose coils glittered like
lightning about the tall tree on which hung the Golden
Fleece, turned to silver in the moonlight.   Lightly as
they trod through the tangled thicket, before they came
in sight by flitting moonbeams, the monster had raised
his fearsome head and opened his poison-breathing jaws.
But Medea stole up to him with a soft, low chant that
charmed his ears, and she sprinkled his eyes with a
magical potion brewed from honey and herbs, and let
its drowsy odour rise through his jaws, till soon this
potent drug filled him with sleep.   The serpent stretched
out his measureless coils to lie still as any fallen branch,
overpowered by the arts of the murmuring enchantress.
When his hissing had changed to deathlike silence, Jason
stepped warily over the scaly bulk, nor did that fierce
guardian stir as he laid hands on the Golden Fleece,
and tore it down from where it had hung since Phrixus
nailed it there.

"Away!" was now the word, before the grisly serpent
should awaken from the spell cast upon him.   But as
Jason turned exultingly towards his ship, Medea held
him back, and her song broke into lamenting.

"Well for thee that canst speed homeward to friends
and honour!   But woe is me, poor maiden, whom an
angry father will slay when he knows how I have helped
the stranger against him!"

"No stranger to one for whom thou hast played such
a friendly part!" quoth Jason.   "Fly with me, Medea,
as my bride, without whose aid I might have gone back
dishonoured.   Thus I shall bear home two treasures for
one, and be most envied among the sons of Greece.
Speak, wilt thou share my fortune?"

She answered not, but a maiden's silence may be
more than speech.   So, bearing up the Fleece with one

hand, he cast the other around her, and it needed no force to draw away the daughter of Colchis, who might never see her father's land again. Side by side, the pair hastened down to the harbour; and the weeping boy Absyrtus clung to his sister, knowing not where she went.

With the first beam of dawn they came to the *Argo*, where the crew, sitting ready at their oars, hailed the Golden Fleece with a shout of joy to waken all Colchis. Medea and her brother being led on board, and the trophy fastened to their mast, Jason cut the cable by one stroke of his sword, then away went the *Argo* like a horse let loose, soon bounding beyond sight of that eastern shore.

IV. Medea

King Æetes was early astir, arming himself and his men to fall upon those presumptuous strangers when they should come to demand the Fleece. But daybreak showed him the *Argo* flying across the sea; and hot was his wrath to learn that she had carried off his daughter and his son along with the chief treasure of Colchis, on which hung his own life. Quickly making ready his fleet, he launched forth to follow with so many ships that they covered the dark water like a flock of sea-gulls.

The Argonauts, seeing themselves pursued, hoisted every sail and tugged their best at the oars. But now it was ill for that crew that they had lost stout Hercules as well as other strong arms. For all they could do, the Colchian ships gained upon them so fast that one-half of Jason's men had to stand on guard grasping spear and shield, while the other half rowed with all their might.

"On, on!" ever cried Medea, fearing to fall into her father's hands; and when his ship drew so near that she could see his stern face and hear his threatening voice, the cruel witch did a deed from which Jason might know, as he would know to his sorrow, what a fierce and ruthless bride he had stolen away. In spite of the boy's tears and entreaties, she hurled her brother Absyrtus overboard; nay, some say that she had him torn in pieces and thrown upon the waves that their father might be delayed by gathering up the dead body for pious burial.

So it was; and thus the *Argo* escaped from mortal foemen, soon to be hidden in a cloud of thunder with which the gods proclaimed their wrath against that hateful crime. Henceforth, for long, Jason's crew wandered as under a curse, abandoned for a time, it would seem, even by Hera's favour, when the king of heaven frowned upon them. They were driven astray by storms, blinded in mists, and tossed on many a strange sea, ere the guilt of innocent blood could be washed away from their ship. Broken and befouled, it came on the rocks of an unknown land; and no man can well tell how and where its crew made their way onward. Some say that Medea had enchantments to drive it over the land as on the sea.

With no guide, unless it were that marvellous figurehead speaking as an oracle, the Argonauts travelled now up a great river and across mountains and deserts, their ship dragged with them, till once more they could launch it in the Mediterranean Sea, repaired and rigged afresh for another voyage. Still trouble and danger were their penance, even when by sacrifices and holy rites they had appeased the gods for the death of Absyrtus. Many strange adventures befell them among the same perilous straits and giant-haunted islands as were afterwards known to the wandering Ulysses; they had to steer past Scylla and Charybdis and the luring Sirens; then but for Medea's crafty spells those stout hearts might never have won home to Greece. They were wrecked on the desert shore of Libya, and once more had to drag their battered *Argo* over its barren sands. Launching again, they came past Crete, to find this island guarded by the giant Talus, whose monstrous body and limbs were of red-hot brass, but for one vulnerable vein in his heel. When the Argonauts would have landed for food and water, from the cliffs he hurled mighty rocks at their vessel, that would have been sunk had they not sheered off in haste. But Medea, boldly going on shore, laid Talus fast asleep by her magical incantations, then wounded his heel of flesh to spill all his life-blood, so that the heat went out of his huge body, and it rolled from the rocks, crashing and splashing into the sea.

So many years had passed, that when at last they saw Iolcos, the band of hopeful youths who followed Jason came back weary and toilworn men, grown old before their time. They were hardly to be known by their friends, as they stepped on shore amid cries of amazement, welcome, and triumph at the sight of the Golden Fleece they brought as proof of their achievement.

Pelias had long given them up for dead, never having thought they could come back alive with such a trophy. He himself was now drawing near to death, yet his palsied hands clung to the ill-gotten sceptre, and, for all his promise, he would not yield up the kingdom to Jason. But Medea had wiles deeper than his own. He and his looked askance on the Colchian witch, till she offered by her magic to make him young again, as she did for a ram which, boiled in a caldron with certain herbs, came forth under strange incantations a tender lamb. Thereby she persuaded the daughters of Pelias to do the like with their old father, who thus perished miserably, slain by the hands of his own children. But some tell how Æson, Jason's father, was indeed restored to youth by the Colchian witch, and that he reigned again at Iolcos.

Jason himself had no mind for a kingdom gained by so wicked arts; and it might well be that his heart grew cold to such a cruel wife. Once more wandering from home, he fell in love with Glauce, the daughter of Creon, king of Corinth. He hoped to make Medea content with his second marriage; but not yet did he know the stern-hearted stranger he had taken to his side. Dissembling her hate, the enchantress sent to Glauce a rich wedding robe, steeped in poison, which was the death of that woeful bride, vainly striving to tear the splendid torment from her flesh. Then, in the madness of jealousy, Medea slew her three young sons with her own hand; and when Jason furiously turned from their bodies to take vengeance on the unnatural mother, he saw her for the last time borne away through the air in a chariot drawn by dragons.

So a hero's life on which such bright suns had risen, was to set in dark clouds of affliction. Some say that in his frenzy he killed himself by the corpses of his children and of his murdered bride. But others tell how, as he sat by the seashore beside his good ship *Argo*, thinking sadly on the glorious days when she had borne him to Colchis, the rotten figurehead broke off and crushed him: so his protecting goddess sent death as the best gift to a man whose work was done.

PYRAMUS AND THISBE

In neighbour houses dwelt Pyramus and Thisbe, he
the briskest youth, she the fairest maid of Babylon.
Long had their eyes spoken what from childhood grew in
their hearts; but the fathers of both frowned upon their
wooing and forbade them to meet, as they could not be
forbidden to love. Nay, love's flame burned but the
hotter for being covered up, till it lit for them a way by
which they could at least promise each other to be faithful
to death.

The two houses were parted by a wall of sun-baked
clay, in which the lovers found a chink to let them hear
one another's voices from side to side. Daily, when all
else was still, through this chink they exchanged sighs
and whispers, and spoke of kisses that could not meet.
Often they complained against the rough wall sundering
each from the other's eyes; yet again were they fain to
be thankful for the cleft where lip and ear were pressed
by turns.

So for a time they nursed their secret love, yet could
not bear for ever to be denied what both would buy at
any cost. Through the wall a night was fixed between
them to give their guardians the slip: singly and by
separate ways, they should steal from home, to meet at
the tomb of Ninus, that known landmark in the woods
outside the city; then never more would they consent
to be parted.

So was agreed, and so was done. Thisbe, in her

impatience, set out before the hour. With her veil
wrapped close about her, slinking hurriedly through the
streets in dread of every shadow, she first reached the
place of meeting, where the moonlight showed a fountain shining beside the tomb, and over it hung a tree
loaded with white mulberries. She looked round for
Pyramus, but he came not yet by the silvered glades
of the wood. She bent her head to catch the tread
of his footstep; then what horrid sound of a sudden
broke upon her ears, echoed by a shriek of horrified
terror!

It was a roaring lioness that bounded out of the
thicket where it had been gorging its prey. The startled
maiden did not wait to see its fiery eyes and its dripping
jaws. Throwing off the long veil that hindered her
flight, with screams she ran wildly through the trees,
and never stopped till she could hide her beating heart
and trembling limbs in a dark cavern which opened a
refuge.

The full-fed lioness did not care to give chase.
But that savage creature fell upon Thisbe's white veil,
left on the grass, befouling and tearing the fine stuff
with blood-stained fangs, before it passed on to quench
its thirst at the fountain, then betook itself to its hidden
lair among the rocks.

As he hastily drew near from the city, Pyramus
had heard the fierce roaring and the cry of that voice
he knew so well. Drawing his sword, he sped forward
to the tomb, where now all was still.

"Thisbe!" he murmured; "Thisbe!" he exclaimed.
But no answer came, and no living form moved under
the moonlight.

Soon, to his consternation, he saw the ground freshly
marked by a lion's claws. And there, beside the foun-

tain, lay Thisbe's veil, all stained and torn. Horrified to frenzy, he made no doubt that the lion had borne away his beloved. Rashly he searched the dark wood, calling on the fierce beast to seize him for its prey rather than that helpless maid. Bitterly reproaching himself for not having been first at the meeting-place, he came back to shower tears and kisses on the veil of her he took for dead.

"Let me not live, after leading thee into such peril!" he cried. "At least our hearts' blood may be mingled together, now we are free to meet in death!"

With desperate hand he drove the sword deep into his breast, and fell expiring at the foot of the mulberry tree. His blood gushed out upon the roots, that sucked it up to turn the white berries into dark purple, as if the tree itself mourned for those unhappy lovers.

Day was breaking when Thisbe found courage to come forth from her hiding-place, and, starting at every crackle of a twig beneath her feet, made her way back to the tomb where she hoped to be safe beside the arm of Pyramus. All her fear now was he might think she had played him false. Her heart throbbed with joy as she saw him lying beneath that tree as if asleep; but misgiving fell upon her with the sight of the white mulberries turned black, and she stooped down to know him writhing in his death-throes upon her veil wet with his blood.

"Pyramus!" she cried wildly, raising his head. "Speak to me! Say this is but an ugly dream!"

At her voice he opened his dim eyes, he tried to smile and speak, but that effort was his last.

When no answer came, she tore her hair, she filled the wood with lamentations, she mingled her tears with his blood, she laboured to kiss him back into life; and when all was in vain, she saw the sword sheathed in his breast.

"Death, too, sought to part us, but that neither death nor the living can do. Ah! cruel parents, at least ye will not grudge us to rest for ever side by side. And thou, oh! pitying tree, stand ever with black berries as a monument of Pyramus and Thisbe."

With these words she drew the blade from her lover's wound and plunged it, still warm, into her own heart. Thus were they found locked together under that mournful tree; then the gods moved their parents to grant Thisbe's last prayer. They lay side by side on the funeral pyre; and their ashes were mingled in the same urn.

> "Here may ye se, what lover so he be,
> A woman dare and can as well as he."

ION

Cecrops, Pandion, and Erechtheus were the first kings of Athens, under whom it chose Pallas for its guardian deity. This race was said to have sprung from the earth, so deep in the past darkness, that men knew of them no more than their names, nor even clearly how they stood to each other in descent. But there came a time when their children seemed like to die out. For Erechtheus had only daughters, and all but one fell victims to Poseidon, who bore a grudge against the city that had preferred Athene to himself.

The one survivor was Creusa, who passed for childless. But she in secret had been wooed by Apollo, and to him bore a son, whom, dreading her father's wrath, she had abandoned, hidden in a dark cave, where she laid him swaddled in a basket, thus trusted to the protection of Apollo. Herself deserted by that faithless celestial spouse, in time she was openly wedded to Xuthus, a neighbour prince who had done service to Athens in war, and thus seemed worthy to be its king. Years went by without an heir being born; then often Creusa thought wistfully of that babe she had left to die, as seemed like, for she knew not what had become of him.

But the child was not dead. Apollo felt more compassion for his helpless offspring than for the betrayed mother; and by the hands of Hermes he had it carried to Delphi to be laid as a suppliant on the steps of his own temple. There it was found by the priestess, who adopted and reared this boy under the name of Ion. He grew up dedicated to the service of the temple, sprinkling its pavements, sweeping them with laurel branches, and scaring away birds from the consecrated offerings. Then early he showed such piety and dutifulness as to endear him to his foster-mother, not less than did his winsome looks and modest bearing.

When Ion had grown to his full stature, there came to the temple a band from Athens, its leaders no other than Xuthus and Creusa, seeking at the oracle some remedy for their childless lot. Creusa stood without, and talked with that fair-faced acolyte, whose voice and looks so stirred her heart that fain she would have learned how he had been brought up in the god's service. But he knew nought of his origin, and as yet she could not guess that he was her lost child. Meanwhile, Xuthus had entered the inner shrine, where, putting his case to the inspired priestess, he was bidden take for his own son the first he should meet on leaving the temple. He rushed out, then his eyes fell upon Ion, whom he made haste to embrace, hailing so goodly a stripling as a welcome heir given to his prayers.

But Creusa did not share her husband's joy. Now she looked askance on Ion, her mind darkened by suspicion that this temple sweeper must be a natural son of Xuthus, whom he had planned with the priestess to pass off on her as a gift of the god. So strong was her mistrust that she began to hate the youth to whom at first her heart had gone out kindly. She took counsel with an old servant of her house, a man to stick at nothing for his mistress; and he engaged to poison Ion at a feast with which the king would have celebrated his adoption. A deadly poison the queen had about her in two drops of the Gorgon's blood given to her father by Pallas.

Ion, at first troubled and amazed by the embraces of one he took for a madman, had come to understand that in some sort he must look on himself as the king's son. When the wine-cups were filled at the banquet, Creusa's servant, as if to do him honour, handed to the new-made heir a rich golden bowl in which he had mingled one drop of the Gorgon's fatal blood. Then, before drinking, the pious youth poured on the ground part of the costly wine as libation to his guardian god. A flock of sacred pigeons were ever fluttering about the precincts of the temple, and now one of them lighted down to taste this offering. No sooner was its beak wet by the envenomed wine than it beat its wings with a shriek of pain that drew all eyes to see it quivering in deadly convulsions.

At this sight Ion flung down the cup, tearing his garments and indignantly demanding who sought to take his life. He turned on the old man that had offered him the poisoned draught; then Creusa's servant, seized by the other guests, under wrathful threats confessed that he had done this at her bidding. A cry arose against the stranger woman; and the elders of Delphi declared that she must be stoned to death as having planned to violate the sanctity of the temple by making away with its innocent minister.

When she heard how the executioners were in search of her, Creusa fled as a suppliant to Apollo's temple, and, crouched at the altar, took sanctuary amidst a crowd clamouring for her blood. Then as Ion stood plying her with reproaches and questions why she had conceived such wicked intent against him who had never done her wrong, from the shrine burst forth the Pythia, for once deserting her tripod to speak openly before all. Amid reverent silence she disclosed the secret of her nursling Ion being laid on the steps of the temple, a nameless babe, and brought forth the basket in which she had found him.

Creusa's heart began to beat, as she heard how this boy was of the same age as her own child; and she uttered a cry at the sight of the swaddling clothes she had wrapped about him years ago. The recognition was complete, when on these garments she traced patterns worked by her own hands. Ion, whom in jealous anger she would have murdered, could be no other than her long-lost son.

The youth proved slower to believe that this must be his mother; but the proofs were clear; and with proud astonishment he heard how his father was Apollo himself. Thus at last mother and son came to each other's knowledge; and all doubt was ended by an appearance of Pallas sent to speak for her brother god, who might well shame to tell his own tale. Bidding Ion go to Athens and take up the heritage of its kings, the goddess foretold that he should be the father of a widespread people known after him as Ionians; and to Xuthus and Creusa she promised another son named Dorus, from whom would spring the Dorian race. And so it came to pass, if poets tell true.

THESEUS

Ægeus, the old king of Athens, was believed to have no children, so the sons of his brother Pallas, known as the Pallantids, looked to seize the throne on his death. But years ago, Ægeus had made a secret marriage with Æthra, daughter of Pittheus, king of Trœzen, moved thereto by an oracle that also promised him from that union a son destined to rare renown. Yet soon he left poor Æthra, taking leave of her at a huge rock on the seashore which he rolled away to hide beneath it his sword and his sandals.

"Should the gods grant us a son," he charged her, "let him not know his father till he be strong enough to move this stone; then let him seek me out at Athens, bearing the sword and sandals as tokens."

In due time Æthra bore a son named Theseus, whom she kept in ignorance of his race, and among her own people he passed as being the child of Poseidon, to whom special reverence was paid at this seaport of Argolis. The boy, indeed, grew up so lustily that he might well be thought of more than mortal birth. While he was still a child, Hercules visited Trœzen, who was his kinsman by the mother's side; and the sight of such a famous champion and the tales of his exploits filled young Theseus with longing for the like adventures. While other children shrank from the lion's skin the hero wore, he flew upon it with his little sword, taking this for a lion indeed, when one day Hercules had thrown it off his brawny limbs. All through his youth Theseus kept that hero before him as pattern of what he would be; then in after-life he held it an honour to be friend and companion of Hercules.

Deserted by her husband, the mother's comfort was in a son known as the stoutest and boldest lad in the land, prudent, too, and trustworthy beyond his years. For all that Theseus was loved by Æthra, she did not forget how the time for their parting drew on. When he was full grown, she took him to the rock by the shore and bid him roll it away, as he did with ease, to find beneath it the sword and sandals hidden here by Ægeus. Then first she told him his true father's name, and that he must seek out the king at Athens, taking the sword and sandals as tokens of his birth.

Full of pride to know himself the son of such a king, and of eagerness to see the world, Theseus made light of his old grandfather's counsel that he should go to Athens by sea. Greece in those days had sore trouble from tyrants, robbers, and wild monsters; and the youth's heart was set upon ridding the country of pests such as he might expect to meet on his way by land.

"So shall I be like Hercules," he told his anxious mother, "and come more welcome to my father if I bring his sandals worn by travel and his sword stained with blood."

The mother sighed, but let him take his way. He would not even choose the easiest road, but went up into the mountains behind Epidaurus on the east coast of Argolis. There he had not gone far, when out of a wood rushed the robber Periphetes, brandishing a huge club and calling on him to stand. Theseus stood firm, sword in hand, and when they closed in hot tussle, that club-bearer for once met his match. The youth nimbly avoided every crushing blow, drove his sword through the robber's heart, then went forward bearing the club of Periphetes and his bearskin cloak as trophies.

With this cloak he felt himself like his model Hercules; and before long it served him well, when he came to the isthmus of Corinth, haunted by a wretch named Sinis, of whom men spoke with dread as the "pine-bender", for it was his wont to slay what unfortunates fell into his hands after a cruel manner: bending down two pines he would fasten the man between them, and let them spring up to tear his members asunder. But when he would have so dealt with Theseus the young hero felled him to the ground, bound him with his own cords, and let his bones be shot into the air to feed the kites.

Before leaving the isthmus, Theseus turned aside to hunt down a fierce wild sow that ravaged the fields and had been the death of all other hunters. The country people, glad to be rid of this pest, warned him of another foe upon his way. Going from Corinth to Megara, on a narrow ledge of rock above the shore he would pass the giant Sceiron, whose humour was to bid wayfarers wash his feet, and to kick them over into the sea while so obeying him. To hear of such a peril was enough for Theseus, who now would not be persuaded to take any road but this. He went to meet that churlish giant, and, when called on to wash his feet, hurled him over the steep into the sea, to be changed into a rock washed for ever by the waves.

Next he came to Eleusis, where the people, pitying so gallant a youth, would have had him slink past without being seen by their tyrant Cercyon, who, trusting in his mighty bones and sinews, challenged every stranger to wrestle with him, and none had yet come alive out of his clutch. But Theseus was not one to pass by such an adversary. He went up to the palace, ate and drank with the king, and willingly stripped for a struggle in which the insolent Cercyon fell never to rise again; then the citizens, delivered from that oppressor, would have had Theseus stay with them as their king.

But Theseus would not tarry, hastening on to Athens past the den of another monstrous evildoer, to fall in with whom he was all the readier for the warnings given him. This was Procrustes, or the "Stretcher", who would lie in wait for harmless travellers and with friendly words lure them to his dwelling as guests, there to divert himself upon them with a cruel device. He had two beds, one over long, the other too short for a grown man's body. Were the stranger short of stature, this giant's way was to put him into the longer bed and stretch out his limbs to fill it; but if tall, he was laid on the smaller one and his legs were cut down till he fitted that.

"Such a one were well brought to an end by his own tricks," quoth Theseus to himself, when, as his wont was, Procrustes came out offering hospitality to this wayfarer.

The youth, feigning to be deceived, cheerfully turned aside with him, then staggering and gaping as if he were tired out, let himself be led into the torture chamber.

"Friend," chuckled the giant, "you see how it is! This other bed of mine is too short for a youth of your inches; yet can I soon make that right."

But as he would have laid Theseus on the shorter bed, suddenly he found himself caught in a grasp of iron, flung off his feet, thrown down and bound for the stranger to hack and hew him with his own axe, and so he came to the miserable death he had wrought on many another.

This was the hero's last exploit on his way to Athens. On the banks of the Cephissus, he next fell in with friendly men, who refreshed him after his toils, washed him clear of blood and dust, and sent him on with good wishes, nor without pious rites and sacrifices to purify him if he had done aught amiss on that adventurous journey.

Yet a deadlier danger than all awaited him when at last he came to his father's home. Ægeus, wellnigh in his dotage, was no longer master at Athens. Treason and rebellion filled the streets of the city, where his nephews the Pallantids took on themselves to rule with insolent pride, while in his palace the old king had fallen under the power of Medea, that wicked witch-woman, who lighted here after flying from Jason at Corinth. By her magic arts she had foreseen the coming of Theseus; and she knew at once who must be the noble youth that now presented himself in the king's hall. It was easy for her to make the feeble old man take this for some secret foe bent on his harm. Then the enchantress mixed poison in a bowl of wine, which she offered the stranger as welcome, whispering to Ægeus that thus they should be surely rid of him.

But before Theseus drank, he drew forth the sword glittering in his father's sight, not so dim but that Ægeus remembered it as his own; and his dull eyes grew bright as he guessed this goodly young man for his long-forgotten son. Coming to himself, he dashed the poisoned drink on the ground; and in a moment father and son were in each other's arms.

The cunning witch-queen might well scowl at their happy meeting. She felt that her power over the doting king was gone; and in her dragon-chariot she fled away from Greece for ever. Theseus, hailed as his father's

heir, was soon able to quell the disorders of the kingdom. He drove out of Athens the insolent Pallantids,
who already bore themselves as kings ; and, young as he
was, he showed himself so worthy that all the citizens
were content to obey a ruler blessed with such a son
to uphold him. The first service he did to his new
country was to rid it of the fierce bull of Marathon, the
dread of which had long kept the husbandmen from till-
ing their lands. Many a hunter had sought that monster
to his own hurt, before Theseus, setting out alone against
it, brought the bull alive from its lair, led it as a show
through the streets, and offered it as a sacrifice to the
gods that had given him such strength and valour.

Ere long, the heir of Ægeus had the chance to do
a greater deed for Athens, a deed never to be forgotten
in song and history. Years before, on Athenian ground
had been treacherously slain Androgeos, son of the mighty
Minos, king of Crete. Some say that this crime sprang
from jealousy, since the Cretan prince had beaten the
athletes of the country in their own games. The father,
to avenge his blood, had made war on Athens, to which
he granted peace at the price of a sore tribute. Every
nine years, seven of its finest youths and fairest maidens
must be sent to Crete, there to be delivered to the
Minotaur, a fearsome creature, half-beast and half-man,
by which they were savagely devoured. Now, for the
third time, this tribute had to be paid, the victims chosen
by lot among the noblest families of the city. But when
it came to drawing lots, Theseus stood forth to offer
himself freely.

"The lot falls first on me, as son of your king!"
he declared. "I will head the tribute band, and let
the Minotaur taste my sword first of all, that has slain
as fierce monsters."

His generous devotion filled the citizens with gratitude, but the old king was loath to risk his only son on such a perilous chance. In vain he begged Theseus to hold back; the hero's spirit was keen and steadfast as his sword. So on the appointed day, he embarked for Crete among the tale of luckless youths and maidens, followed by the prayers of their woeful parents. His own father, hardly hoping to see him again, made him promise one thing. The ship that bore this doomed band was wafted by black sails in sign of mourning; but if it should be their lot to come back safe, they were to hoist a white sail, that not an hour should be lost in showing good news to those on the watch for their return.

With winds but too fair for so forlorn an errand, the ship came safe to the city of Minos. There he kept the Minotaur in his famous labyrinth, a maze of winding passages in the rock, made for him by Dædalus, that cunning artificer of old, who, when he had served the Cretan king long and well, offended him to such wrath, that with his young son Icarus he had needs fly away to Sicily. The crafty Dædalus knew how to fit wings to their shoulders, fastened by wax; and thus they sped over the sea, the father coming safe to land, but when heedless Icarus flew too near the sun, the wax melted, and, losing his wings, he fell into a sea thenceforth called the Icarian, after his name. His body was wafted far away over the waves, to be in time drawn ashore by Hercules, who gave it burial on an island also named from him, Icaria. Dædalus, grateful for this friendly service, fashioned and set up at Pisa a statue of the hero so lifelike, that when Hercules saw it in the twilight, he took it for a threatening foe and dashed it to pieces with a stone. Such an artist was that Dædalus whose name became a proverb for skill; and the world knew no other such work as he left behind him in the Cretan labyrinth.

Minos might well be proud to see the prince of Athens offer himself to glut his revenge; yet even his stern heart took pity on this noble youth, so boldly claiming as a right to be first to face the ravenous monster.

"Bethink thee, ere it be too late," he warned Theseus. "Naked and alone, thou must seek out the Minotaur, that has torn in pieces every victim turned into its haunt. And even couldst thou escape such an enemy, no stranger, venturing within the labyrinth, has ever been able to find his way out of its dark secrets."

"So be it, if so it must be!" answered Theseus; and that night was set for his dreadful ordeal.

But not in vain had the hero, at the bidding of an oracle, invoked for his enterprise the protection of Aphrodite, goddess of love. One friend he had in Crete, before ever a word passed between them. Ariadne, daughter of King Minos, looked with kind eyes on this gallant stranger, and her heart was hot to save him from so miserable death. Seeking him out by stealth, she whispered good cheer and counsel in his ear, giving him a clue of thread which he should unroll as he passed on into the labyrinth's windings, then, his task done, he might follow that helpful clue till it brought him back to the free air. Moreover, she put into his hand a magic sword, with which, and with none other, the Minotaur might be slain. And, if he came out safe, she made him promise to carry her away from her father's anger, as Theseus willingly agreed, when the very favour of so bright eyes seemed a charm to bring him safe through all dangers.

Thus equipped and heartened, he took his way alone into the mouth of the labyrinth, leaving the youths and maidens, his comrades, to await what should befall him. With tearful eyes they saw him swallowed up in the darkness, and heard his steps die away within. Then all was silence, till there burst forth an awful roar echoing through those hollow windings, to show how the Minotaur was aware of his foe. The time seemed long while fearfully they stood listening to a distant din of bellowing and clattering and gnashing, as if a thunderstorm were pent up in the cavern's inmost *penetralia*. Again, all fell silent; and, quaking at the knees, his companions hardly hoped to see their leader come back from that chill gloom that in turn should be their own grave. But what was their joy at last to catch his voice raised in triumph, then he strode forth into the starlight, his sword dripping with blood!

The hero threw himself on Ariadne's neck to thank her for the aid without which he would never have overcome that monster, nor made his way out of its darksome lair. But she bid him lose no moment in hastening beyond the power of her father and all his men. The watchmen she had made heavy-headed after draughts of strong wine; and now, by her counsel, the crew of Theseus bored holes in the Cretan ships that they might be in no state to pursue. This done, taking Ariadne with them, the Athenians got on board their own vessel, and had hoisted sail before Minos awoke to see them already far at sea.

And now the pair who had loved each other at first sight would fain have been wedded; but their love went amiss. For Theseus became warned in a dream that his Ariadne was destined as the bride of no mortal man, but of a god. So he hardened his heart to put her ashore on the island of Naxos, and there left her asleep by the strand, sailing away without a word of farewell. Some say that when poor Ariadne awoke to know herself thus deserted, she fell into such despair that she saw nothing for it but to take her own life. But the tale as told by others is that on Naxos she was found by Bacchus, who kissed away her tears and made her his wife, and so she came to shine among the stars.[1]

However the truth be, Theseus held on his course with a heavy heart, the joy of victory all overcast for him by Ariadne's loss. And in that sorrow he forgot his father's charge to hoist a white sail if he should come back safe. Day after day, when the ship might be expected, old Ægeus sat upon a high point, straining his weak eyes on watch for her return. At last she came in sight, and lo! the sails were black as death. The king gave up his son for lost. With a cry of despair he flung himself over a cliff into the waves, still known by his name as the Ægean Sea.

So mournful news met Theseus when he sailed into the harbour in triumph, all Athens pressing down to learn how it had fared with him. With thanksgiving to the gods for their speeding, he had to mingle the funeral rites of his father; and never could the son pardon himself that fatal forgetfulness that made him king of Athens.

As king, Theseus ruled wisely and well, so that in his reign Athens first began to grow great. Many more adventurous feats he did far and wide, of which the

---

[1] Among the various apologies for Ariadne's desertion, Plutarch includes a most unromantic one of her being so sea-sick that Theseus had to put her on land, then himself was blown out to sea by a storm—an accident common enough in fact on those squally waters. A modern commentary, suggested by the recent discoveries in Crete, is that the vast rambling palace built for its Minos kings may well have suggested the poetical idea of a labyrinth.

most celebrated is his war against the Amazons, and the wooing with his sword of their queen Hippolyte to be his loving wife. After her death he married Phædra, daughter of Minos, who revenged on him his desertion of Ariadne, when the time came that his glory set in clouds of misfortune. Deceived by that wicked stepmother, he cursed his innocent son Hippolytus, who came soon to a violent end, flung out of his chariot and dragged to death on the seashore when Poseidon sent a monster out of the waves to scare his horses; then too late the mourning father learned how false Phædra had beguiled him. In his old age the fickle citizens of Athens turned against the hero to whom they owed so much; and so deep did he lay their ingratitude to heart, that he turned his back upon the city, betaking himself to an island where a treacherous enemy did him to death. Not till ages had passed were his remains brought to Athens, and a famous temple came to be built there to his memory.

PHILOMELA

At Athens was told an older tale, and a sadder, than that of Theseus. The founder of the city was taken to be one Cecrops, from over the sea, whose grandson Pandion had two daughters, Procne and Philomela. In his reign Athens was hard beset by barbarians and delivered only by help of Tereus, a fierce king from Thrace, to whom grateful Pandion could not but offer as reward either of his daughters in marriage.

Tereus chose Procne, the elder; and the wedding was held forthwith, yet with evil auspices, for though Tereus had the god Ares for father, Hymen came not to bless the feast, nor Hera and her attendant Graces; but the chief guests were the dread Furies, and a hoarse owl hooted on the roof of the bridal chamber. The rude Tereus, making light of these omens, bore his bride away to Thrace. They had one son, named Itys, and for years they lived together without mischance.

But, when years had passed, Procne began to weary among the half-savage Thracians, who could not make her forget Athens and her dear sister Philomela. At last, her longing grew so strong that she coaxed Tereus to let her go home on a visit. He harshly denied her request; but by dint of tears and kisses she won him over to consent that Philomela should be brought to see her sister in Thrace.

Tereus sailed to Athens, where he found the old king loath to part with his other daughter, even for a time. With misgivings he gave way to the plea of Procne's love of her sister, who for her part was not less eager to see Procne once more. Before letting her go, Pandion made Tereus swear to keep his dear child from harm, and to send her back safe to Athens; then he took leave of her with tearful farewells, as if fearing never to embrace her again.

Too truly he feared, for the barbarous Thracian's oath was as false as his love. No sooner had he set eyes on Philomela in the bloom of her maidenhood, than his heart took flame, and he repented his choice of the elder sister. As they sailed across the sea, he set himself to woo the younger, who, in her innocence, took all his endearments as offered for Procne's sake, and smiled upon him in the joyful hope soon to meet her sister. But once he had her on land in his own wild forests, Tereus no longer disguised his wicked desire to put her in her sister's place.

The sorrowful Philomela would have none of his hateful love; but she cried in vain for help to the gods; and when with drawn sword he would have forced her to his will, she fell on her knees beseeching of him death rather than dishonour. From that one crime the fierce tyrant shrank, yet with his cruel blade he cut out her tongue that it might not betray his falsehood. To make surer, he shut her up in a lonely prison far among the woods, where Procne might never learn that she still lived.

To Procne he told that her sister was dead; and when this news came to Athens, the old father died of grief. Well Philomela guessed how Procne had been deceived; but her watchful keepers gave her no chance to escape, so for a year the queen mourned both sister and father as lost to her in the tomb, till at last with horror she learned the truth. Dumb Philomela's wits were free, and so were her hands. She got leave to spend her prison hours in weaving, then on a white web she wrought with purple threads the story of her woeful case. When her work was done, for pity, or bribes, she found a messenger to carry it to the queen.

Tereus was away from home when this woven letter came to Procne's hands, painting for her how she had been deceived and how her beloved sister was still alive. With the messenger for guide she hurried to the prison, tore Philomela from her keepers, and brought her home, the miserable sisters mingling their tears, while Procne alone could raise her voice in threats of vengeance against the husband who had so foully wronged them both. She, erst so gentle and loving, now vowed to slay Tereus in his sleep, to burn his house, to curse him before the gods who too long had let such wickedness go unpunished.

As they reached the gates there ran out to meet them Itys, Procne's son, the darling of his rough father, and his image in features. That likeness to Tereus inflamed the mother's wrath, and when she saw how her sister could not speak a word to greet the wondering boy, her fury broke out upon this innocent one. Like a tigress she sprang at him, and, maddened by woe, struck a dagger into the throat of her own son. One wound was enough; yet Philomela, also, fed her heartburning on the boy's blood. These two raging women tore Itys limb from limb, and boiled his flesh in a caldron, all their minds hot for revenge on the father. When Tereus came home, Procne set before him that horrid meal. He ate unsuspecting, and only when gorged to the full, thought of asking what game this was she had cooked so well.

For answer burst in speechless Philomela, to fling the gory head of his son at the king's feet, and Procne brandishing the torch with which she had kindled their marriage bed. The looks of the two wronged women told their tale as plainly as a hundred tongues. With cries and imprecations the father leaped to his feet, overturning the table in his blind horror of the unnatural food. He drew his sword upon the sisters, who fled before him from the accursed house, now filled with smoke and flame.

Tereus fiercely followed them into the woods, where, as minstrels tell, the gods worked a miracle to mark the guilt of this house. Procne was turned into a swallow, and Philomela into a nightingale, flying ever pursued by a long-billed hoopoe that was no other than the false husband with his blood-rusted sword. But old Pausanias has another tale: "Procne and Philomela melted away in tears, lamenting what they had done and suffered, and the story of their being changed into a nightingale and swallow comes from these birds having a sorrowful and plaintive note"—such as well might tune the unhappy sisters' song.[1]

[1] This painful story is told in different ways, Procne and Philomela exchanging their parts in one version.

THE TRAGEDIES OF THEBES

I. Cadmus

It is told of Cadmus, the Tyrian, that he first taught the use of letters to Greece. And a strange errand it was that brought this stranger from his home beyond the sea.

His father, king Agenor, had one young daughter, Europa, on whom fell the eyes of Zeus, and he plotted to bear her away to be his own. As Europa was sporting with her companions on the seashore, the god appeared to her in the shape of a milk-white bull, so gentle and goodly that she fell to stroking it and decking its head with flowers, while it licked her neck, lowing as if to breathe a spell upon the Tyrian maid that gave back a kiss to this kingly creature. As it lay down on the grass, the playful girl made bold to mount its broad back. But she screamed with fright when at once it leapt to its feet, and galloped away with her like a spirited courser. Europa did not dare to throw herself off, still less when the bull plunged with her into the sea. Heedless of her cries, it bore that light burden across the waves, clinging to its flower-wreathed horns and looking back wildly to the shore, soon lost for her in tears. She would see her native land no more.

With dolphins and Nereids gambolling on the track, and Tritons blowing their horns in bridal glee, all night the bull swam swift and strong as a galley, then at daylight set Europa on an island, which indeed was Crete. There the bull vanished, Zeus taking his own godlike form to tell her how he had done this for love. Aphrodite, too, appeared to comfort her with a promise that a whole new quarter of the world should be called after her name. So the maiden let herself forget her Asian home, and in time became the mother of Minos and Rhadamanthus, who were to sit in Hades as stern judges of the dead.

But the king of Tyre never ceased to mourn his lost daughter. When her scared playmates came running back, crying out what had befallen her, he was beside himself for wrath and grief. Bitterly reproaching his three sons, Cadmus, Phœnix, and Cilix, with having kept no better guard over their sister, he sent them out in search of her, and bade them not return home unless they brought back Europa.

The three youths set out together, and with them went their woeful mother Telephassa, who could not rest while her dear daughter was so strangely missing. For weeks they hastened here and there, for months and years, seeking everywhere to hear of Europa, but no one had seen her in any haunt of men. First Phœnix grew tired of their long quest, dropping off from it to make himself a home in the land called from him Phœnicia. Then Cilix in turn wearied of long bootless wandering, and fixed himself in the country of Cilicia. But Cadmus and his mother held on, till she, worn out by sorrow and travel, lay down to die, her last words a charge to him not to give up the search.

With a few faithful servants who had followed him from Tyre, Cadmus crossed the sea, and came into

Greece; but there he could still hear no news of his sister, so that at last he lost all hope to find her alive. Without her he might not see his father's face, and he knew not where to turn for a home. Coming to the renowned Delphic oracle of Apollo, he sought its counsel, and was bidden to follow a cow he would find feeding alone in a meadow hard by: where the cow first lay down he should build a city and call its name Thebes.

He soon found the cow, that walked on before him, leading him and his men many a league through fields and hills, into a land of mountains and plains which came to be called Bœotia. There at last the cow, lowing to the sky, laid itself upon the grass as token for Cadmus that his long wandering was at an end. Thankfully he fell down to kiss the strange earth a god seemed to give him for his own.

But the place had a fearsome lord with whom he must reckon. Proposing to offer sacrifice to Pallas-Athene, that she might be favourable to him, he sent his servants to draw water from a stream which rushed out of a dark cave, its mouth hidden in a thick grove of mossy oaks never touched by the axe. The men entered the grove, but came not back; and from within he heard a sound of hissing, and saw wreaths of foul smoke spreading among the trees. He bounded forward to find his servants lying dead before the cave, scorched by the breath of a huge dragon that stretched towards him its three fiery heads, each bristling with three rows of teeth through which it breathed poisonous fumes, its eyes shining like fire, and its red crests glowing in the shadow of the cave mouth, as it pushed out its long neck to lick the bodies of the slain.

"Ah! poor companions, either must I avenge you, or be your mate in death!" cried Cadmus, and snatched up a heavy rock to hurl it at the monster, from whose horny scales it bounded back without doing them harm; but all the dark wood echoed with an angry roar.

Undaunted, the hero flung his spear so straight and strong that black blood gushed from the dragon's breast to mingle with the foam of its fury. Now it uncoiled all its monstrous length, and issuing from the cave, reared its horrid heads like trees to fall upon the man who dared to face its wounded rage. But Cadmus held his ground, smiting with all his might at the fiery jaws, till he drove his sword through one poison-swollen throat to nail it to an oak trunk. The monster twisted its necks and lashed its tail so as to bend the thick tree double, but the roots held firm, and the sword stuck fast; so there it writhed helplessly while its fiery breath was quenched by its own blood.

All unhurt, Cadmus stood over the dead body, when he was aware of Pallas at his side, come down from Olympus to found a city that should grow great under her ægis.

"Sow the dragon's teeth in the earth," she bid him. "From them will spring up a race of warlike men to do thy will."

Much wondering at such counsel, Cadmus did not disobey. He dug deep furrows with his sword; he plucked out the dead dragon's teeth; he sowed them in the earth drenched by its gore. Forthwith the ground began to heave and swell and bristle with spear points; then quickly there sprang up a crop of armed men, their weapons clashing together like corn beaten by the wind. Cadmus, in amazement, made ready to defend himself, but again a divine voice murmured in his ear—

"Sheathe thy sword: let these do after their kind."

No sooner were the new-born warriors full grown out

of the furrows, than they fell on each other in their lust for battle. So fiercely they fought that, before the sun was set, all but five had fallen dead on the bosom of their mother earth. These five, weary with bloodshed, dropped their weapons and offered themselves to serve Cadmus in place of his followers slain by the dragon.

With their aid he built here the citadel that came to be called Thebes, and thus founded a kingdom in the Bœotian land. There are those who say that this Cadmus, "man of the east", came not from Tyre, but from famed Thebes in Egypt, whose name he brought into Greece. But others have it that the name was given by Apollo's oracle.

The new city throve, yet its first lord had to suffer from foes, both in heaven and on earth. The dragon-serpent slain by him was sacred to the god Ares, who long bore ill will to Cadmus for its death. In time Cadmus seemed to have made amends for that sacrilege, so that he got to wife Harmonia, daughter of Ares and Aphrodite. All the gods came to the marriage; and among the gifts were a necklace and a veil made by Hephæstus for Aphrodite's sake, gauds that became too famous heirlooms as charged with misfortune for whoever wore them. And though Ares, at the bidding of Zeus, appeared to be reconciled with Cadmus, a curse rested on his house. His children and his children's children came to evil ends, among them Ino, who drowned herself after her husband in madness killed their son, and Semele, consumed by the fierce glory of Zeus, when she became the mother of Dionysus.

Cadmus himself, they say, was dethroned by his own grandson Pentheus. In his old age, the many-woed king had again to go forth homeless, yet not alone, for with him went his faithful wife Harmonia. They wandered into the wild northern forests, till this once dauntless hero, bowed down by infirmities and burdened with the curse of that dragon's blood, was fain to murmur—

"If a serpent be so dear to the gods, would I were a serpent rather than a man!"

At once he sank upon his breast, his skin turning to scales and his limbs to speckled coils. As Harmonia saw how her husband was transformed, she prayed that she too might become a serpent; and her prayer likewise was answered. There they dwell still among the rocky woods, hurting no man, nor hiding from the sight of men who were once their fellows.

II. Niobe

Thebes, thus founded in bloodshed, had a long history written in letters of blood by the hate of rival gods. It was the fate of Pentheus to be torn in pieces by the women of his house, his own mother their leader, because he frowned on their wild worship of Dionysos.

Another queen who worshipped the wine-god was Dirce, wife of the usurper Lycus. The daughter of the rightful king was Antiope, beloved by Zeus, to whom she bore twin sons, Amphion and Zethus, brought up humbly as shepherds on Mount Cithæron, while their mother wandered in lonely exile, and in the end, they say, went mad through her misfortunes. At one time she fell into the power of Dirce, who in her hatred for the captive she had wronged, ordered her to be dragged to death by a wild bull at the hands of Amphion and Zethus. But when they knew the victim for their mother, they led a band of herdsmen against the city, slew Lycus, and tied cruel Dirce to the horns of the bull to make her perish by her own device.

So Amphion became king at Thebes, which he walled about through the power of music, being so skilled to play on a lyre given him by Hermes, that at its enchanting sound the very stones were drawn to move as he bade them. But on his children, too, fell a curse of wrath and woe.

Amphion had married Niobe, daughter of the doomed Tantalus, who was himself a son of Zeus. She bore seven noble sons and seven fair daughters; then, too proud of this goodly brood, she made bold to exult over Leto, as mother of twins and no more. But these twins were the divine Apollo and Artemis, on whom their despised mother called to avenge her against that presumptuous queen.

"Enough!" Apollo cut short her tearful tale. "Complaining but delays chastisement."

Wrapt in dark storm-clouds, brother and sister flew to overlook Thebes, where on an arena outside the walls, the seven sons of Niobe were exercising themselves in chariot racing, wrestling, and other sports. They had no warning unless the clank of the god's quiver, before the eldest was pierced to the heart by an arrow from the sky, and fell without a groan among the feet of his horses. The second turned his chariot to fly, but that did not avail him, struck by Apollo's unerring aim. So, also, it went with the third and fourth brothers, transfixed by a single shaft. The fifth and sixth sons ran to raise the bodies of their fallen brethren, but were themselves laid low before they could embrace the dead. The youngest only remained, a long-haired, fair-faced stripling, who, guessing how he had to do with an angry god, threw himself on his knees to beg for mercy, but the fatal point was already winging to his breast.

The news of this sudden slaughter quickly spread

through the city. Amphion stabbed himself for despair at the loss of his sons. Niobe, gathering her scared daughters about her, as chickens under the wings of a bird, hurried out to the field on which her seven boys were stretched lifeless around the altar of Leto. At the sight of them, rage spoke louder than grief, and raising her head against the gods who had so avenged their mother, she cried bitterly—

"Triumph, cruel Leto; but even now my offspring surpasses thine!"

For answer twanged the bow of Artemis, and the eldest daughter fell as she stood tearing her hair over her slain brothers. Next, the second with a sharp cry put her hand to her heart; then the third sister, who would have held her up, sank beside her, bleeding from an invisible arrow. One by one, all the daughters were shot down, till only the youngest in terror hung to her mother, whose pride now gave way; tears burst forth, and she stretched out her hands in suppliant prayer—

"Spare me but one, the last of so many!"

As she spoke, the last shaft of pitiless Artemis reached the child on the mother's bosom. Without a wound, Niobe herself sank as dead, her heart broken, her limbs motionless, her eyes staring, the blood gone from her face, where only her tears did not cease to flow. Sorrow had turned her to stone. For ever, they say, as the hot rays of the sun and the cold moonbeams pour down by turns on that stone image, it weeps for the children of whom Niobe had boasted against the jealous gods.

III. Œdipus

After the destruction of Amphion's race, Laius was brought back to his forefathers' throne, from which he had been driven into exile. Among all the descendants of Cadmus, the most famous and the most unhappy was this king's son, doomed by an oracle to be the death of his own father and the husband of his mother. Fore-warned of such a fate, when his queen Jocasta bore a boy, Laius had him cast out on Mount Cithæron, with his feet tightly bound to make the child more helpless against speedy death. But the goatherd charged with this cruel errand took pity on the wailing infant, and, though he told the king that his bidding was done, in truth he had given it to another herd, who took it to his master Polybus, king of Corinth. By him the boy was kindly received, and brought up under the name of Œdipus ("Swollen foot"); while Laius and Jocasta, making sure he had been torn to pieces by wild beasts, believed themselves to live childless, and thus hoped to cheat the oracle.

Polybus and his childless wife Merope adopted the outcast boy as their own son; then, as years went on, few at Corinth remembered how he was not so in truth. Œdipus grew to manhood never doubting but that these foster-parents were his father and mother, till one day, at a feast, some drunken fellow mocked at him for a base-born foundling. In wrathful concern he sought to know from Merope whose son he truly was. She tried to put him off, yet could not deny that he was a stranger by birth. The dismayed youth turned to Polybus, who also gave him doubtful answers, bidding him ask no more, since it would be a woeful misfortune if ever he came to know his real parents.

But these hints only made Œdipus more eager to learn the truth, and he bethought himself of Apollo's oracle. Leaving Corinth secretly, he travelled on foot to Delphi, where the priestess vouchsafed no plain answer to his question, but only this fearful warning—

"Shun thy father, ill-omened youth! Shouldst thou meet with him, he will fall by thy hand; then, wedding thine own mother, thou wilt leave a race destined to fresh crimes and woe."

Œdipus turned away with a shudder. Now he believed himself to understand why Polybus and Merope had made a mystery of his birth. Fearing affliction for them, who loved him well, he vowed never to go back to Corinth, but to seek some distant land, where, if madness came upon his mind to drive him to such wicked deeds, he might be far from the parents he took for threatened by so dire a curse.

From Delphi he was making towards Bœotia, when in a narrow hollow way where three roads met, he came upon an old man in a chariot, before which ran an arrogant servant bidding all stand aside to let it pass. Œdipus, used to bid rather than to be bidden, answered the man hotly, and felled him to the ground; then his master flung a javelin at this presumptuous youth. With his staff Œdipus struck back, overturned the old man from the chariot, and left him dead by the roadside. In the pride of victory Œdipus went his way, ignorant that the proud lord he had slain in a chance quarrel was no other than his own father, Laius. A traveller who found the king's corpse buried it where it lay; and the news was brought to Thebes by the charioteer, who, having fled from that one bold assailant, to excuse his own cowardice gave out that a band of robbers had fallen upon them in the hollow pass.

Wandering from city to city, Œdipus reached Thebes, to find it all in mourning not only for the death of its king, but from the dread of a monster that haunted the rocky heights beyond the wall. This was the Sphinx, which men took to be a sister of Cerberus, that three-headed hound of Hades. To anyone coming near it, the creature put a riddle, which if he failed to answer, it devoured him on the spot. Till some man should have guessed its riddle, the Sphinx would not be gone; and so long as it brooded over the city, blight and famine wasted the fields around. One or another Theban daily met death in setting his wit against this monster's, and its last victim had been a son of Creon, Jocasta's brother, who for a time ruled the kingless land. Seeing himself unable to get rid of the Sphinx, Creon proclaimed that whoever could answer its riddle, were he the poorest stranger, should have as reward the kingdom of Thebes, with all the dead king's treasures, and the hand of his widow, Jocasta, in marriage.

As Œdipus entered the city, a herald went through the streets to make this proclamation, that set the friendless youth pricking up his ears. Life seemed not dear to him; all he desired was to escape that destiny of crime threatened by the oracle. At once he presented himself before Creon, declaring that he was not afraid to answer the Sphinx.

They led him outside the walls to the stony wilderness it haunted, strewn with the bones of those who had failed to guess its riddle. Here he must seek out the creature alone, for its very voice made men tremble. Soon was he aware of it perched on a rock, a most grisly monster, with the body of a lion, the wings of an eagle, and the head of a woman. But Œdipus, caring little whether he lived or died, shrank not from its appalling looks.

"Put thy riddle!" he cried; and the Sphinx croaked back—

"What creature alone changes the number of its feet? In the morning it goes on four feet, at midday on two, in the evening on three feet. And with the fewest feet, it has ever the greatest strength and swiftness."

Fixing her cruel eyes on the youth, she frowned to see him not at a loss,—nay, he smiled in her stony face, answering forthwith—

"The riddle is easy. It is man that in childhood goes on all-fours, then walks firmly on two feet, and in his old age must lean upon a staff."

Furious to hear her riddle guessed for the first time, the Sphinx gave a shrill scream, flapped her gloomy wings, and vanished among the rocks, never more to be seen at Thebes. With shouts of joy the watching citizens poured out to greet that ready-witted youth that had delivered them from such a scourge. They hailed him as their king; and he was married to the widowed Jocasta, the more willingly on his part, as he believed himself thus made safe against the unnatural union predicted by the oracle, for he held Merope to be his mother, for all her denial.

Years, then, he reigned at Thebes in peace and prosperity, gladly obeyed by the people, who took this young stranger for a favourite of the gods. He loved his wife Jocasta, older than himself as she was; and they had four children, the twin-sons Eteocles and Polynices, and two daughters, Antigone and Ismene. But when these were grown to full age, the fortune of the land seemed to change. For now a sore plague fell upon it, so that the people cried for help to their king, who sent to Delphi his brother-in-law, Creon, to ask of the oracle how the pestilence might be stayed.

The answer was that it came as punishment for the unatoned blood of Laius. Now, for the first time, Œdipus set on foot enquiries as to his predecessor's death. Vowing to do justice on the criminal, whoever this might prove to be, he consulted Tiresias the seer, struck with blindness in his youth because he had spied upon the goddess Athene, who again, taking pity on him for the loss of his eyes, gave him marvellous sharpness of ear, so that he understood the voice of all birds, also she filled his mind with mystic knowledge of things past and of things to come. But the blind seer was loath to tell what Œdipus sought to know.

"Bitter is knowing when ignorance were best. Let me go home, with a perilous secret hid in my bosom!"

In vain the people besought him, in vain the king bid him speak. At last Œdipus angrily reviled him as having himself had a hand in the murder he would not disclose. This rash accusation made the old man speak.

"Hear then, oh king, if thou must learn the truth. Thou thyself art the man that slew Laius in the hollow way to Delphi. For thy sake, and no other, this curse is come upon the city."

Now with a start Œdipus remembered that old lord in the chariot whom he had slain in quarrel as he came from Delphi. Anxiously he pressed Jocasta with questions about her first husband. She described his grey hair, his haughty bearing, his black steeds; she told that he had been killed by robbers in a hollow pass where three ways met; and every word made Œdipus surer of the truth. But his wife mocked at the seer's wisdom.

"Even the god's oracle may speak falsely," she said, "for Laius was warned at Delphi that he should fall by the hand of his own son, who, moreover, should marry his mother. Yet we never had but one child, and he was thrown out to die on Mount Cithæron when not three days old, that thus our house should escape so dark a doom."

Among the bystanders chanced to be that goatherd charged long ago with the child's death; and him Jocasta called to confirm her words. But the old man fell on his knees, confessing how he had not had the heart to leave a helpless babe to be torn by wolves and eagles, but had given it alive to a servant of the king of Corinth.

Jocasta raised a cry, for she knew her husband passed for a son of that king, and she began to guess the truth, now clear to the awestruck Œdipus, that he and no other had unwittingly fulfilled the oracle by slaying his own father and wedding his mother. While he stood aghast, veiling his face for shame and horror, she fled to her chamber, like one out of her senses, barring herself in with her unspeakable woe. When the door was broken open, she had hanged herself with her girdle rather than look again upon the husband who was no other than her son.

"Thy sorrows are ended; but for me death were too light a punishment!" he wept upon her dead body. And with the buckle of Jocasta's girdle he bored out the sight of both his eyes, so that night came upon him at noonday.

A blind old man, his hair grown suddenly grey, Œdipus groped his way out of the palace, poorly dressed as he had entered it a travel-worn youth; and leaning on the staff with which he had been the death of his father. His people turned away from him shuddering. His own sons held aloof. Only his daughters, Antigone and Ismene, followed him tearfully, begging him to stay. He would not be entreated; and when they had led him out of the city, Ismene took leave of him and went back to her brothers, already quarrelling over the kingdom.

But Antigone vowed that she would never desert her father, and with him she wandered away from her birthplace. Led by her, he went from city to city as a blind beggar, till they came to Athens, where Theseus was king. He gave the exiles refuge in a temple at Colonos. In this sanctuary Œdipus lived on for some years, poor and sorrowful, pitied by his neighbours as a victim of fate, and gently tended by Antigone till death came to end his strange misfortunes.

IV. The Seven against Thebes

After the death of her old father, Antigone went back to Thebes, where she found her twin-brothers at hot strife. Eteocles and Polynices had agreed to share the kingdom between them, ruling year about, but ever they looked jealously on each other, and their uncle, Creon, could not keep them friends. By and by Eteocles, in his turn of office, drove his brother from the city, where he henceforth reigned alone.

Thus exiled, Polynices sought refuge at Argos, hoping for the help of its king, Adrastus. As by night he came before this king's palace, he ran against another fugitive, Tydeus of Calydon, son of King Oineus and brother of Meleager, who through chance slaying of a kinsman had also had to fly from his native land. In the darkness these two strangers took one another for enemies and drew their swords; then the clash of arms brought out Adrastus and his men to part them. As soon as the torchlight showed those warriors' shields, the king uttered a cry of amazement.

" Who and whence are ye ?"

This Adrastus had been troubled by an oracle, giving out his two daughters as destined to marry a lion and a boar. Now Polynices bore a lion's head on his shield, and on that of Tydeus was a boar's, cognizance of his part in the great Calydonian boar hunt led by his brother. On seeing their devices the king of Argos joyfully hailed the strangers as sent to fulfil that oracle in a manner not to be feared. He made them welcome to his house; and, learning that they were of kingly birth, he forthwith married them to his daughters, Argia and Deipyle, both glad to have so gallant husbands in place of fierce beasts.

Grateful for such a son-in-law, Adrastus warmly took up the cause of Polynices against Eteocles, and called on kinsmen and allies to gather an army for restoring him to his kingdom. Seven were the captains of that host—Adrastus, his brothers Hippomedon and Parthenopæus, his nephew Capaneus, his brother-in-law Amphiaraus, Tydeus, and Polynices himself, they who came to be famed as the Seven against Thebes.

One only of these heroes had hung back from the enterprise—Amphiaraus, renowned both as warrior and as seer. Divining by his art that only one of the Seven would come back alive from Thebes, Amphiaraus, to escape the king's importunities, hid himself in a secret place known only to his wife Eriphyle. When Adrastus would not march forth without one whom he esteemed the eye of the army, Polynices bethought himself of winning over Eriphyle, believed to have power on her husband's will to make him do whatever she desired. The son of Jocasta had brought from Thebes an ancestral treasure, no other than that fatal necklace made by Hephæstus for Harmonia, wife of Cadmus.

With this dazzling gaud he bribed Eriphyle to disclose her husband's hiding-place and to persuade him to go against Thebes.   Unwilling at heart, Amphiaraus then joined the host; but so resentful was he of his wife's treacherous vanity that, before setting out, he made his son Alcmæon swear to kill Eriphyle, if the father should not come back alive.

In sight of Thebes, the allied host encamped on Mount Cithæron; and Tydeus went forward as a herald to demand that Polynices should be received into his kingdom.   Eteocles sent him back with an insolent answer of defiance, for the city, full of armed men, was fortified by a high wall with seven gates, behind which the usurper felt sure of his defence.   Yet to hearten the citizens, he called on the blind soothsayer, Tiresias, who gave out a dark foreboding—

"Thebes stands in dire peril, to be averted only by the youngest son of its royal house; his life alone is the sacrifice that, freely offered, can save the city."

At this utterance, none was more dismayed than Creon, Jocasta's brother, for he thought how his darling son Menœceus was the youngest of the fated family. He proposed, then, to send him off to Delphi, there to be kept safe under sanctuary of Apollo.   But the brave stripling had at once devoted his life to his native city. The oracle no sooner heard, he hastened to the highest tower of the walls, and hurled himself over among the assailants.

And that sacrifice seemed to avail for the safety of Thebes.   Each of the seven heroes stormed at a different gate; but all were driven back by the defenders, who, sallying out, spread death and rout among their enemy.   So many brave warriors fell, that when once more the Argive host came on, Eteocles sent a herald to propose that the quarrel should forthwith be settled by single combat between him and Polynices.

Thus it was agreed: the brothers met outside the walls, and fought before the two armies with such fierceness, that sweat burst in thick drops on the brows of the onlookers, loud in uproar as each party shouted to hearten its own champion. They clashed together like boars; they broke their spears on one another's shields; they took to their swords, closing in desperate thirst for a brother's blood that poured out from all the joints of their armour, till both sank dying on the field.

Both sides now claiming the victory, in their dispute they fell to fighting with more fury than ever. Again the invaders were routed, and fled, all their leaders, save Adrastus, having fallen, as Amphiaraus had foretold. Yet the Thebans, too, suffered such loss that a battle won so dearly came to be known as a Cadmean victory.[1]

V. Antigone

The sons of Œdipus being no more, Creon again took over the kingdom, as he had done after the death of Laius. His first order was that, to mark the infamy of Polynices in warring against his mother's city, his body, and those of his allies, should lie unburied, a prey to dogs and vultures. So, while they bore Eteocles to the tomb with royal pomp, his brother's corpse was left to be parched by the sun and drenched by the dew, a guard set over it night and day to see that, on pain of death, no friend should give it sepulture.

But Antigone, faithful to her brother as to her

---

[1] The heavy losses of Pyrrhus, in one of his Roman battles, gave the same significance to the phrase " a Pyrrhic victory".

father, had stood beside the dying Polynices; and with his last breath he had made her promise to do for him those funeral rites without which his soul might not rest in peace. No threats of Creon could appal her sisterly heart. Ismene wept with her over their brother's fate, but had not the boldness to share her pious task. Alone, in the moonlit night, Antigone stole forth to the field strewn with corpses, among which she searched out her brother's. Washing it with tears, she strove to drag it away; but her strength failed her, and she must make haste, not to be seen by the watchmen. All she could do was softly and silently to sprinkle the body with dust; but that seemed enough to save it from miserable wandering on the bank of Styx.

In the morning, one of the guards came in fear to tell Creon that, for all their watchfulness, Polynices' body had through the night been lightly covered with earth, by whose hands they knew not. Creon wrathfully bid them uncover it, and keep better watch: their own lives should be forfeit if they again let anyone touch the body. With this threat the man went back to his post, glad to get off so lightly; for the king's resentment against Polynices was so well known, that the guards had cast lots which of them should take on himself the perilous office of bringing news of his command set at nought.

Through the day sprang up a mighty whirlwind, filling the air with dust. Antigone again ventured out, to find, as she feared, that her brother's body had been stripped of its thin coat of earth. Again, now in broad daylight, she was trying to cover it, when the guard seized her and brought her, bound, before Creon, who stormed like a tyrant on learning by whom he had been thus defied.

"Rash girl!" he cried, "knew'st thou not the law made but yesterday?"

"I know a higher law that is neither of yesterday nor to-day," she answered with unshrinking eye, "the eternal law of pity, that forbids me to leave the dead son of my mother unburied."

"If such be thy love for a brother, thou shalt go to love him in Hades!" stormed the king.

"Death is the worst thou canst do to me; but my name shall live as that of one who feared not to do a sister's duty. And to die before my time were welcome in a world of such woes."

Enraged by her boldness, Creon gave command that she should be walled up in a cave and there left to die. He was obeyed, for the shuddering citizens did not venture to cross his vindictive mood, though all men whispered against him that there was no honour in warring upon the dead. But Ismene now found heart to withstand him, clinging to her sister, falsely accusing herself as an accomplice in the pious crime, and demanding to share her fate. Then came another to plead for her, Creon's son Hæmon, who was betrothed to Antigone, and loved her more than his life. Reverently addressing his father, he besought him to consider how all men would cry shame on him for such cruelty: the Thebans murmured, though they durst not speak out, mourning over the sister that little deserved death for her care not to leave a brother's body to wild beasts. King as he was, let him remember that he could not scorn his people's goodwill, as the tree that holds stiff against winds and waves comes to be uprooted, yet might stand firm by bending.

"Would the boy teach me wisdom?" his furious father cut him short. "I see how love for that traitress blinds thee; but thou shalt not have my foe for a bride. Too late shall she learn it is better to obey the living than the dead."

When Antigone had been borne off to her doom, there came yet another to bend Creon's stubborn will. This was the blind Tiresias, whose inner vision warned him of fresh calamities for Thebes, polluted through the innocent fate of Antigone and the sacrilegious exposure of Polynices to beasts and birds. The gods were wroth, he declared, at the wrong thus done to a king's children. But, like Œdipus, the king spoke bitterly to the rebuking soothsayer.

"Who hath bribed thee to scare me with lying auguries?" And that insult stung the old man to speak plain.

"Before the sun sets, thou shalt pay for double impiety—yea, two corpses for one! Their blood be on thy head! Lead me far from him who defies the gods!"

Without another word, the seer turned away, leaning on a boy who had brought him into the king's presence. So solemn had been his warning, that Creon, left alone, began to falter in his ruthless purpose. He called the elders of the city into council, and of them deigned at last to ask what he should do.

"Bury the body of Polynices, and set Antigone free from her living tomb!" they answered with one voice.

Since all men were against him, Creon sullenly gave way. He ordered Polynices to be honourably buried beside his brother, and went himself to the cave in which Antigone had been walled up. Hæmon, her lover, ran on first of the crowd bearing axes and bars to set her free; then peering through a cleft, he uttered a lamentable cry for what he saw within. Too late the wall was broken down, letting all see how the noble Antigone had strangled herself with her veil twisted into a noose. Hæmon in speechless despair drew his sword, and, before the father could hold his hand, had fallen upon it over the body of his beloved one.

When his mother, Creon's queen, heard what had befallen, she, too, killed herself for grief; thus Tiresias spoke truly that, before the sun set, the king's house should pay two corpses for one. All the city was one cry of mourning, amid which the bereaved Creon hardened his heart, and in his gloomy rage, once more forbade the burial of those slain foes about the city.

But again the widowed and childless king had to bend his obstinate will. Adrastus, by the swiftness of his horse, had escaped to Athens, and as a suppliant sought help from its king, nor was Theseus deaf to his prayer. With a strong army he marched to Thebes, summoning Creon to let the dead be buried, that their spirits should have rest. The Thebans were in no heart for further fighting; and their tyrant had nothing for it but to consent. The fallen followers of those seven heroes were heaped into seven piles, to be solemnly burned on the field, with due rites. Of Evadne, the widow of Capaneus, it is told that woe drove her to hurl herself upon her husband's funeral pyre. Over the ashes, Theseus built a temple to Nemesis, genius of Retribution; then he withdrew with his allies; and for a time Thebes had peace to lament its evil destiny.

VI. The Fatal Heirlooms

Thebes was still to suffer from the bane laid on its kingly house, that spread far beyond its own soil. Polynices had left a son, Thersander, to grow up in exile at Argos. When years had passed, he and other sons of the heroes slain before Thebes began to hatch revenge upon the hated city, and made against it a new war known as that of the Epigoni, or offspring of the Seven.

Of those Seven, Adrastus was still alive, but too old to lead the army. He sought counsel of the oracle at Delphi, that bid choose as chief Alcmæon, son of Amphiaraus, the seer. But Alcmæon shrank from this honour put upon him, while also the oracle reminded him how he had pledged himself to revenge upon his mother Eriphyle the death of his father, betrayed by her to death for the bribe of that fatal necklace, but his dreadful vow was still unfulfilled. Eriphyle had some strange spell to throw over the will of her son, as of her husband. And, as against her husband, so she could be bribed to persuade her son. Thersander had one more Cadmean heirloom to bestow, the rich veil which was another wedding gift of Aphrodite to Harmonia. With this he bought from Eriphyle that she should win over her son to lead the Epigoni.

Alcmæon, then, consented to be their chief, putting off his dark purpose to slay that bewitching mother. He marched to Thebes, where this time the war went for its invaders. The Thebans came out to meet them, but were driven back with the loss of their leader Laodamas, son of Eteocles. The blind Tiresias, now over a hundred years old, gave forth the worst auguries. He bid his fellow citizens send out a herald to propose terms of peace, and under this pretence, to fly from their walls by night. So they did, escaping to seek new homes elsewhere. Thersander entered in triumph the abandoned city, where now he ruled as the last heir of Cadmus, and lived to fall in the great war against Troy.

His fate was happy beside that of Alcmæon, who went back victorious, brooding over the secret vow to slay his mother. To this fell duty, he believed himself urged by the oracle; and it steeled his heart when he came to learn how she had been bribed by the veil of Aphrodite to send him forth in arms. He slew her with his own hand, thus at last performing the long-deferred pledge to his father. But no more could he live in the home made horrible to him. He left Argos and wandered forth alone, taking with him those crime-inspiring gifts.

Then, wherever he went, the gods frowned on him as profaned by his mother's blood, and he was haunted by the Furies into restless madness. In time he seemed to be at peace in a city of Arcadia, whose king Phegeus did purifying rites to cleanse him from his guilt, and gave him in marriage his own daughter Arsinoe. But though his madness had left him, the curse he bore from place to place fell upon the land that thus granted Alcmæon asylum. It was blighted by famine, through his pollution of it; so said the oracle, declaring that this exile could find rest only on ground which should have arisen since he took his mother's life.

Once more he wandered into the world, leaving with Arsinoe those fatal gifts. After long search, he found at the mouth of the river Achelous an island newly sprung above the water, unseen by the sun when he raised his hand against Eriphyle. Here he fixed himself, and seemed now to be free from his curse.

Yet fresh troubles came with relief from the Furies' scourge. Forgetting his wife Arsinoe, he married Callirrhoe, daughter of the river-god Achelous, and she bore him two sons, Acarnan and Amphoterus. They might have lived happily but for Callirrhoe hearing of the famous necklace and veil he had left with Arsinoe, which she coveted so as to give her husband no peace till they should be her own.

Driven by her importunity, Alcmæon went back to Arsinoe, and demanded those fatal gifts on pretence of offering them to Apollo at Delphi, as a sacrifice by which he might be purged of the madness that, as he feigned, alone kept him apart from her. Arsinoe readily gave up her treasures, which he was for carrying off to his new home. But a disloyal servant betrayed to her father how his master had another wife, to be decked with the gifts of Aphrodite. Arsinoe's two brothers followed Alcmæon, slew him taken at unawares, and brought back the necklace and the veil to their sister. She, who loved her false husband still, gave them such bitter thanks for that service, that her also they sent to death, cruelly and shamefully, in their wrath at the dishonour done to their house.

And still the flow of blood was not stanched. When Callirrhoe came to know how she had been deceived and bereaved, beside herself with rage, she prayed Zeus, by her kinship with the gods, to make her two boys grow up at once to men that they might lose not a day in avenging their father. Zeus nodded consent; and the sons who lay down careless children rose next morning bearded men, stern and strong. Setting out forthwith on their errand of bloodshed, they fell upon Arsinoe's brothers carrying her necklace and veil to Delphi. Acarnan and Amphoterus killed them both, before they knew they were in danger ; then went on to root out their father's house.

Thus the fatal gifts at last came to Callirrhoe. But her father, the wise Achelous, would have none of their baneful charm. He bid carry them, after all, to Delphi, to be hung up in the temple of Apollo ; and this being done, the curse, passed on through the Cadmean house, was charmed away from the race of Amphiaraus, whose grandson, Acarnan, settled the Acarnanian land, as Cadmus had been founder of Thebes.

ECHO AND NARCISSUS

To the river-god Cephissus was born a son named Narcissus, who seemed to his fond mother the most beautiful of children, and anxiously she sought from the blind prophet Tiresias to know his fate.

"Will he live to old age?" she asked; to which the dark-seeing prophet made answer—"If he shall not have known himself!"

What these mystic words meant, time only would show. The boy grew up rarely beautiful, not only in his mother's eyes but in all that were not blind. There was no maiden but cast loving looks upon him; and less favoured youths must envy the charms that, alas! made Narcissus vain above all sons of earth. Blushes, sighs, and sparkling eyes were heeded by him but as tributes to his loveliness; and when he had bloomed to the flower of manhood, he was in love with himself alone.

Shunning all who would fain have been his companions, it was his wont to walk apart in solitary places, lost in admiration of the graceful form which he thought no eye worthy to behold but his own. One day, as he wandered through a wood, unawares he was spied by the wood-nymph Echo, who loved him at first sight, but was dumb to open her heart till he should ask its secret. For on her a strange fate had been laid: Hera, displeased by her chattering tongue, took away from her the power of speech unless in answer to some other voice. So now, when Echo slunk lightly among the thickets, shadowing the steps of that beautiful youth, eager as she was to accost him, she must wait for him to speak first, nor durst she show herself but at his desire. But he, given up to his sweet thoughts of self, strolled on silently, and the maiden followed him lovingly, unseen, till at last, as he halted to drink from a cool spring, his ear was caught by a rustle in the branches.

"Who is there?" he exclaimed, raising his eyes to peer into the green shade.

"*There!*" came echoed back; but he saw not who spoke.

"What do you fear?" he asked; and the invisible voice answered—

"*Fear!*"

"Come forth here!" he cried in amazement, when thus his words were given mockingly back to him; and still the voice took no shape.

"*Here!*" was the reply; and now glided forth the blushing Echo, to make as if she would have thrown her arms round his neck.

But in the crystal pool the youth had caught another form that better pleased his eyes; and he roughly brushed away the enamoured nymph, with a harsh word.

"What brings you?"

"*You!*" she faltered, shrinking back from his frown.

"Begone!" he bid her angrily. "There can be nothing between such as you and the fair Narcissus."

"*Narcissus!*" sighed Echo, scarcely heard, and stole away on tiptoe to hide her shameful looks in the deep shade, breathing a silent prayer that this proud youth might learn for himself what it was to love in vain.

When left alone, Narcissus turned eagerly back to

that spring in which he believed to have seen a fairer face. Like a silver mirror it lay, shining in sunlight, framed by a ring of flowery plants, as if to guard it from the plashing tread of cattle. On his knees at the edge, he stretched himself over the bright well, and there looked down upon a face and form so entrancingly beautiful, that he was ready to leap into the water beside it. A priceless statue it seemed, of one at his own blooming age, every limb chiselled like life, with features as of breathing marble, and curling locks that hung above ivory shoulders.

"Who art thou that hast been made so fair?" cried Narcissus; and the lips of the image moved, yet now came no answer.

He smiled, and was smiled back to. He flushed for delight, then the face in the water was overspread with rosy blood, its eyes sparkling like his own. He stretched out his hands towards it, and so the beautiful form beckoned to him; but as soon as his touch broke the clear surface, it vanished like a dream, to return in all its enchantment while he was content to gaze motionless, then again growing dim beneath the tears of vexation he shed into the water.

"I am not one to be despised," he pleaded with his coy charmer, "but such a one as mortal maidens and nymphs, too, have loved in vain."

"*Vain!*" resounded the sad voice of Echo from the woods.

Again and again he leaned down to clasp that lovely shadow in his arms, but always it eluded him; and when he spoke entreating it to his embrace, it but simulated his gestures in unfeeling silence. Maddened by so strong allurement of his own likeness, he could not tear himself away from the mirror in which it ever mocked his yearning fancy. "Alas!" was his constant cry, that always came sighing back from the retreats of the woeful nymph. Hour after hour, day after day, he hung over the pool's brink, nor cared to let food pass his lips, crying all in vain for that imaginary object of adoration, till at last his heart ceased to throb with despair, and he lay still among the water lilies that made his shroud. The gods themselves could not but be touched with pity for so fair a corpse; and thus was Narcissus transformed into the flower that bears his name.

As for poor Echo, who had invoked such punishment on his cold heart, she gained nothing but grief that her prayer was heard. Out of sight, she pined away for despised love, till all left of her was an idle voice. And that still haunts the rocks where never since can she be seen by startled eyes; but always she must be allowed the last word.

This was not the only tale told of Echo's bootless love, for of old, too, love went often blind and deaf.

> "Pan loved his neighbour Echo—but that child
> Of Earth and Air pined for the Satyr leaping;
> The Satyr loved with wasting madness wild
> The bright nymph Lyda,—and so three went weeping:
> As Pan loved Echo, Echo loved the Satyr,
> The Satyr, Lyda—and thus love consumed them.
> And thus to each—which was a woeful matter—
> To bear what they inflicted, justice doom'd them;
> For inasmuch as each might hate the lover,
> Each loving, so was hated.—Ye that love not
> Be warn'd—in thought turn this example over,
> That when ye love, the like return ye prove not."
> —*Moschus, trans. by Shelley.*

THE SACRED OAK

Every forest tree was held in respect by the men of old, for they could not be sure but that it were the home of some Dryad or other woodland nymph, whose life hung upon its flourishing. So poor Dryope learned to her woe, when, plucking a bright blossom for her child, she saw the sap run red, then found her own limbs putting forth leaves and flowers, as on the spot she became turned into a tree by the wrath of a nymph she had unwittingly wounded; and in vain she struggled to fly: rooted to the ground, she felt her voice failing, as with her last human words she begged that the child might often be brought to play beneath the sighing shade of her branches. Of many another hapless maid was it told that she suffered the same fate, like Daphne who, as a laurel, escaped the pursuit of Apollo, or like that Thracian Phyllis, betrothed to Demophoon, son of Theseus, but when he tarried away from her too long, she killed herself in hasty despair, and was transformed as a tree, hallowed by her overpowering love.

Bold was the crime and prodigious the punishment of Erysichthon, he that recklessly laid low a huge and venerable oak sacred to Demeter, in honour of whom the light-footed Dryads came often to dance round it in a moonlit ring. A giant it was among trees, towering high above its fellows, as they above the bushes, its branches thickly hung with votive tablets and garlands in sign of gratitude to the beneficent goddess. Yet that presumptuous churl bid his servants hew it down; and, when they hesitated in awe, himself snatched an axe to fetch the first stroke, crying—

"Were it the goddess herself, to the ground her tree shall come!"

The mossy bark gave out a deep groan as it felt the blow; the leaves turned pale; the branches trembled and dripped with sweat; blood burst from the trunk at every wound. The horrified bystanders vainly besought Erysichthon to throw down the axe. He struck one of them dead who would have held his hand, and kept urging on his thralls to the impious task, till at last the sacred oak fell with a crash echoing far around to drown the dying voice of the nymph that was its indwelling spirit.

To Demeter hastened the mourning Dryads of the grove; nor was the goddess deaf to their prayers for vengeance on the destroyer. She sent an Oread to fetch Famine from the ice-bound deserts of the north; and this gaunt shape she charged to plague the life of Erysichthon. As, weary from his day's bad work, he lay dreaming of costly banquets, Famine hovered over him and breathed into his vitals a madness of insatiable greed.

He woke up with a raging hunger which no food could stay. The more he devoured, the more ravenous he felt, as if every mouthful but added fuel to the flame of his appetite. In vain his table was loaded with all the fruits of the earth, with the flesh of every creature that ran, or swam, or flew; whatever he ate was lost like the rivers in the sea, and he never could have enough to appease the greed that tormented him night and day. When he had swallowed what would feed whole towns, he still felt hungry, as he vainly toiled to fill himself with emptiness. Thus the Dryads were avenged, while their beloved tree went to feed cooking fires that burned not so fast as his unquenchable voracity.

"More! More!" was his cry, if ever he had to wait a moment for the morsels that choked him into silence.

The once rich man was not long in eating himself poor. He had to sell his land, his goods, his house; and still unavailing gluttony preyed on him like a vulture. The day came when he had nothing left but his only daughter; and her, too, he sold as a slave to buy food with the price of her. And this resource she could spin out through the favour of Poseidon, who had bestowed upon her the power of changing herself into whatever form she pleased. Once in the hands of a master, she could soon slip out of them in some transforming disguise—a horse, a cow, a hind, a bird, or what not—and make her way back to the famishing father that he might sell her again to play the same trick on some other purchaser.

But at last her tricks wore themselves out, the story says not how; and the unhappy man had nothing for it but to devour his own flesh, consuming himself in less time than it had taken to hew down that sacred oak. So he perished miserably; but his name lives as a warning to men who mind not what is dear to the gods.

THE TALE OF TROY

I. Paris and Helen

The father of the Trojan race was Dardanus, who wandered across the Hellespont into Mysia, and married a daughter of the shepherd king Teucer. Their grandson Tros had a son named Ilus; and on a height by the river Scamander he built a city named Troy, or Ilion, or sometimes Pergamum, the "tower", its people known as Teucrians, Dardanians, or most famously as Trojans. For his new seat Ilus besought of Zeus some sign of favour; and in answer fell from heaven an image of Pallas-Athene which, under the title of the Palladium, was to be treasured as the luck of Troy.

But soon Troy had ill luck, brought upon it by the son of Ilus, Laomedon, a crooked-minded king dealing falsely both with gods and men. He it was who gave walls to the city, and for that task hired Apollo and Poseidon, when, driven from Olympus by the displeasure of Zeus, they had been condemned for a year to serve some mortal upon earth. Poseidon surrounded Troy with strong walls, while Apollo pastured the king's herds in the valleys of Mount Ida. But after their year's service was up, Laomedon denied them the promised reward, driving them away with threats and insults, so that, when restored to their place in heaven, these gods bore a bitter grudge against Troy, by one of them never forgotten.

Before long, Poseidon's ill will was shown, for he sent to lay waste the land a ravening monster that could be driven away, spoke an oracle, only by the sacrifice of the king's daughter Hesione. She was already chained to a rock as its trembling victim, when to Troy in the nick of time came Hercules, who undertook to deliver her, as he did by slaying the monster among his many feats and labours. For this deliverance Laomedon had promised him a team of matchless horses given by Zeus to his grandfather Tros. But, the monster slain, again this deceitful king broke faith, and Hercules angrily went his way without the horses, being bound to the service of Eurystheus.

Years later, the hero came back to take vengeance for that deceit. He stormed the city, killed its faithless king, and gave Hesione to his own follower Telamon, who carried her away to Salamis in Greece. But at Hesione's entreaty he let her ransom one of her brothers, Podarces, "the swift-footed", who, now under the name of Priam, "the ransomed", became king of Troy.

Priam and his wife Hecuba had many children. The noblest of her sons was Hector, but the comeliest Paris, before whose birth Hecuba dreamed that she bore a firebrand. That dream being interpreted by a seer as foretelling destruction for Troy, Priam and Hecuba agreed to save the city by exposing the helpless babe to death on the heights of Mount Ida; and so was done through the hands of a slave.

But Paris did not die. Suckled by a bear, they say, the child was found alive after some days, and reared among their own sons by the herdsmen of Mount Ida. In this rude life he grew up hearty, handsome, and strong, a youth of mark above his fellows, though

ignorant that he was a king's son. When he came to
manhood he did such feats against the robbers of the
mountains, that he won for himself the by-name of
Alexander, " helper of men ". He married the mountain
nymph Œnone, and for a time lived happy among the
herds, content with his simple lot and humble home.

> " There lies a vale in Ida, lovelier
>   Than all the valleys of Ionian hills.
>   The swimming vapour slopes athwart the glen,
>   Puts forth an arm, and creeps from pine to pine,
>   And loiters, slowly drawn. On either hand,
>   The lawns and meadow ledges midway down
>   Hang rich in flowers, and far below them roars
>   The long brook falling thro' the clov'n ravine
>   In cataract after cataract to the sea.
>   Behind the valley topmost Gargarus
>   Stands up and takes the morning: but in front
>   The gorges, opening wide apart, reveal
>   Troas and Ilion's columned citadel,
>   The crown of Troas."   —*Tennyson.*

One day, as Paris fed his flocks in such a leafy glen
of Mount Ida, there appeared to him three stately and
beautiful women, whom, even before hearing their names,
he was aware of as more than mortal. With them came
a noble form, whose winged feet and the herald's staff
he bore showed him no other than Hermes, messenger
of the gods. In their presence the shepherd stood with
beating heart and awestruck eyes, while Hermes thus
addressed him—

" Fear not, Paris; these are goddesses that have
chosen thee to award among them the prize of beauty.
Zeus himself bids thee judge freely which of the three
seems fairest in thine eyes; and the father of gods and
men will be thy shield in giving true judgment."

With this the god put into his hands a golden apple.

At the wedding of Peleus and Thetis, parents of Achilles, Eris alone among the immortals had not been bidden to the feast; then the slighted goddess of strife threw among the guests this golden apple, inscribed *For the fairest!* As was her design, three daughters of Olympus had quarrelled to which it should belong; and now they came agreed to take the judgment of that bright-eyed shepherd, who stood before them scarcely daring to raise his eyes till they heartened him with appealing voices.

"I am Hera, the queen of Olympus," spoke the proudest of the three, "and I have queenly gifts to bestow on the humblest mortal. Give judgment for me, and, shepherd lad as thou art, thine shall be the richest realm on earth!"

"I am Athene, goddess of arts," said the second. "Adjudge the prize to me, and thine shall be fame as the wisest and bravest among men!"

"I am Aphrodite," said the third, with an enchanting smile, "and I have gifts sweeter than these. He who wins my favour need only love to be loved again. Choose me for the fairest among gods, and I promise thee the most beautiful daughter of men as thy wife!"

Paris might well stand in doubt before three so dazzling claimants; but he did not hesitate long. He gave the golden apple to the goddess of love, who thanked him with a radiant smile, and confirmed her promise by an oath such as not even gods may break. But Hera and Athene turned frowning away, and henceforth were enemies to all the Trojan race.

The glorious vision having vanished, it now seemed to Paris like a dream amid the toils of his daily life, in which he might have forgotten the promise of Aphrodite. As yet he knew no woman fairer than his loved wife. But soon came a change in his fortunes, when he despised poor Œnone, and left her to weep out her broken heart upon the wild mountain side.

For the first time since his birth, Paris went down to the city of Troy to try his strength in games held there by King Priam. As prize of one of the contests was proclaimed the herdsman's favourite steer, and he could not bear to think of its passing into the hands of a stranger. Not only that prize he won but others, surpassing even the king's sons, his own brothers as they were, had he but known it. They, for their part, might guess him to be no common clown, that bore himself above them all. One of his sisters, Cassandra, had the gift of divination; and she it was who recognized in this sunburnt mountaineer the child cast forth to die; then his parents were too glad of such a goodly son to remember what had been foretold of him by the oracle.

Thus restored to his birthright, Paris came to stand so high in Priam's favour, that the king sent him to Greece in command of a great fleet, charged to demand that Hesione, borne off by Hercules, should be given back to her home, after many years. Alone Cassandra denounced this expedition, foretelling how a quarrel with the Greeks would bring them against Troy; but Apollo, who had bestowed on her the gift of prophecy, had again cursed it with the fate that her warnings should never be taken for true.

Paris sailed forth, full of hope and pride, on an errand he did not perform. For he turned aside to visit Menelaus, king of Sparta, married to Helen, the most beautiful woman on earth. At the first sight of this handsome stranger, richly arrayed in purple and gold, Helen was ready to forget her marriage vows. And when his eyes met hers, he forgot his true wife

Œnone, weeping lonely on Mount Ida, forgot his father's commands, forgot his own honour; he forgot all but the enchanting face which he was ready to take for that of the goddess herself—alas! to be famed for ages as

> "The face that launched a thousand ships,
> And burnt the topless towers of Ilium".

The honest heart of Menelaus was so trustful that, going upon some expedition, he left his guest with his queen, to steal one another's love by soft words and kindling looks. He was soon to learn how ill that long-haired Eastern prince could be trusted. Before the king came back, Paris had fled, after breaking into his house by force, carrying off its treasures to the Trojan fleet, among them the dearest of all, the wife so little unwilling to follow a new master, that she left behind the young daughter Hermione she had borne to Menelaus.

With such a prize on board, the love-sick prince no longer minded the mission on which he had been sent by his father. Now that Aphrodite had fulfilled her promise, he gave himself up to dalliance with this fairest of all mortal fair ones. It was long before he steered for Troy to show her with pride to his own people. Spending the stolen wealth of Menelaus in idle pleasure, these two would fain forget their kin and country. Yet Paris went not without warning. As he sailed over a summer sea, of a sudden it grew so calm that the ship seemed nailed to the water, from which rose the sea-god Nereus with dripping hair and beard, to utter fearful words.

"Ill omens guide thy course, robber of another's good! The Greeks will come across this sea, vowed to redress the wrong done by thee and to overthrow

the towers of Priam.   How many men, how many
horses I foresee dead for thy sin, how many Trojans
laid low about the ruin of their city!"

II. The Gathering at Aulis

Helen's matchless beauty had drawn about her in
youth so many hot suitors that they prudently bound
themselves by an oath to honour whatever husband
might be chosen for her, and to stand by him against
any who should wrong his wedlock.   So when Menelaus
learned how his wife had been stolen, he could call on
a host of fellow rulers to take arms for recovering her
and punishing that violator of his home.   He and his
elder brother Agamemnon, king of Argos, sons of Atreus
and descendants of Pelops, were the mightiest lords in
the Peloponnesus.   Agamemnon, husband of Helen's
sister Clytemnestra, stood out as greatest above all the
kings of Greece; and when he summoned its princes to
gather their ships and men for war with Troy, few ventured to slight his command.   Two of the chiefs, indeed,
held back at first, yet they were the two who in the
end would be most famous among the champions of that
war.

One of these was Odysseus (*Ulysses*), who, having
married a loving wife, Penelope, was loath to quit her
and his young son Telemachus for a war which he
foresaw as long and toilsome.   So when Palamedes,
friend of Menelaus, came with Agamemnon's summons
to the rocky island of Ithaca, its crafty chief feigned to
be out of his mind, in token of which he was found
ploughing with an ox and an ass strangely yoked together, and sowing salt in the furrows.   But Palamedes,
too, was wily.   He brought out the child Telemachus

to lay him in front of the plough, then the father so carefully turned it aside as to show himself no madman. It is said that Odysseus never forgave that trick, though he seemed to forget it, and that years afterwards he took a chance of working fatal vengeance on Palamedes. But now, betrayed out of his pretence, he had to go with him to the gathering host, for which he soon could enlist a nobler champion.

Achilles was son of Peleus, a mortal married to the goddess Thetis, at whose wedding Eris threw down among the gifts that golden apple to be the seed of so much strife. His mother foretold that either he might die young after heroic deeds, or live long in ignoble ease; and eagerly the boy chose a short and glorious life. She sought to make him invulnerable by dipping him in the water of Styx; then the heel by which she held him remained the one mortal spot in his body. He was brought up with other heroes by old Cheiron, who fed him on the hearts of lions and the marrow of bears, and taught him gentle arts as well as the stern trade of war. Among all his companions he was noted for courage and pride, for generosity and hot temper, as for strength, beauty, and activity that won him such epithets as the "swift-footed", and the "yellow-haired" Achilles.

When the Trojan war was hatching, Thetis, aware that it should lead him to his death, would fain have kept her son away. So she sent him, dressed as a maiden, to be hidden among the daughters of the king of Scyros. There cunning Odysseus sought him out in the disguise of a merchant, who among rich clothes and other womanish gauds carried a store of bright weapons; then, while the true women had eyes only for adornments, Achilles revealed himself by snatching

at sword and spear among all those wares.   His sex thus
disclosed, it was not hard for Odysseus to bring him
to the army, leading a band of warlike and devoted
Myrmidons from his native Thessaly.

Another service the Ithacan prince undertook in
going with Palamedes and Menelaus as an embassy to
demand of Priam that Helen should be given back.
The king of Troy and his people heard them with
amazement, as now for the first time they learned what
Paris had done in Greece; and Priam would give no
answer till his son came home to speak for himself.
For his part, he had to complain of his sister Hesione
held captive, for whom Helen might rightly be kept a
hostage, if she were brought to Troy.   And while the
father tried to speak them fair, to the threats of these
Greeks the Trojan princes gave back high words, so
that they had almost come to blows had not grey heads
checked the hot blood of youth.   The ambassadors,
courteously treated and put under guard against the
insolence of the common folk, had to depart without
their errand, bearing messages of defiance that made not
for peace.   As to Hesione, they told Priam how she
was long happily married in Greece, and that her son
Teucer was among the leaders of the host gathering to
take vengeance on Troy.

After long lingering in foreign lands and seas, Paris
brought home that bewitching bride, over whom the old
king shook his head, and would fain have frowned on
the darling son who had so ill done his mission in
Greece.   But his brothers, bribed by the wealth Paris
had stolen from Sparta, and by the smiles of Helen's
handmaidens given to those still unmarried, were loud
against letting her go back to Menelaus.   Their mother
Hecuba was set to learn from her own lips whether

she followed Paris by free will; and when Priam heard
that it was so, he agreed with his sons to defend her
against all the power of Greece. His people feared the
trials of the war now threatened; and as Paris strode
through the streets of Troy, many a stifled curse followed
him, who cared not that he brought such woe upon the
city; yet even the grey-beards who frowned on Helen
could not but turn their heads to look after so lovely
a stranger. But the princes were deaf to the ominous
warnings of their sister Cassandra. Among them Hector
stood out as chief leader, now that his father was too
old for war; and of the allies Troy called to its aid, the
most illustrious was Priam's son-in-law, Æneas, prince of
the neighbouring Dardanians, who had no less a mother
than Aphrodite.

Meanwhile, the Greek ambassadors had returned to
Aulis, a harbour on the Euripus, where more than a
thousand ships were gathered to carry a hundred thousand warriors across the sea. Years had passed before
this mighty host could be brought together. All being
at length ready, and the Trojans having shown no sub-
mission, the chiefs were for setting sail forthwith. But
Agamemnon, their leader, going on shore to hunt, had
hurt the pride of the goddess Artemis, by killing a hind
sacred to her. The offended goddess brought about a
dead calm, so that for weeks not a ship could stir from
the strait, on whose shore so many warriors chafed in
idle impatience. Then Calchas the diviner, in virtue of
his art, gave out that Artemis would not be appeased
without the sacrifice of Agamemnon's eldest daughter,
Iphigenia: only at the price of her blood could they
buy a fair wind.

The horrified father at first would have chosen rather
to lay down the command than devote his daughter to

such a doom. But Menelaus, eager for revenge on Paris, hotly upbraided his brother's soft-heartedness, till Agamemnon was won to concede the cruel sacrifice.

He sent for his wife Clytemnestra, bidding her bring Iphigenia to Aulis, on pretence that she should be married to Achilles. Then, relenting in his purpose, he sent another message bidding her pay no heed to the first. But that second message was intercepted by watchful Menelaus, who again heaped reproaches on the wavering Agamemnon as untrue to the common cause. As they stood quarrelling, it was announced that Iphigenia and her mother were at hand. So moving was the father's distress, that now Menelaus himself pressed him to forego that sacrifice; but when the brothers had been reconciled with tears, the elder declared his heart steeled to let the maiden die.

Soon arrived Clytemnestra and Iphigenia with her infant brother Orestes; and again the king's heart was wrung by the joyful embraces of his daughter, who could not understand why they called forth no answering smiles. Clytemnestra better knew her husband; and his gloomy looks filled her with suspicion, the more so when, seeking out Achilles, she heard from him that he knew nothing of the feigned betrothal to Iphigenia. Next she fell in with the slave prevented by Menelaus from carrying her husband's second message, and he told how Iphigenia was doomed for sacrifice.

When the queen had wrung all the truth from Agamemnon, loud was she in wrath and woe. The daughter clung about her father's knees, praying for mercy. Achilles burst into the tent, offering to shield her against the whole host already clamouring for her blood. But Agamemnon now stood like a rock against threats and entreaties : he remembered that he was a king as well as a father, nor yet a despot, but one who must consult with those who followed him in war. And Iphigenia, drying her tears, rose to stand upright before him, saying with firm voice—

"Since so it must be, I am willing to die; then shall I be called the honour of Greek maidenhood, who have given my life for the mother-land. Let the fall of Troy be my marriage feast and my monument!"

She turned away, her young brother Orestes clasped in her arms, leaving their mother prostrate on the ground in helpless despair. Iphigenia's last words were a promise to stand still as a lamb when brought to the altar; while Achilles, who had come verily to love this patient victim, spoke hotly of rescuing her by force under the knife of the priest, yet must fear that even his fierce Myrmidons would shrink from violating a sacred rite.

> "I was cut off from hope in that sad place,
>   Which yet to name, my spirit loathes and fears;
>   My father held his hand upon his face;
>   I, blinded with my tears,
>
> "Still strove to speak: my voice was thick with sighs,
>   As in a dream. Dimly I could descry
>   The stern black-bearded kings, with wolfish eyes,
>   Waiting to see me die.
>
> "The high masts flickered as they lay afloat;
>   The crowds, the temples wavered, and the shore;
>   The bright death quivered at the victim's throat;
>   Touched; and I knew no more."
>
> —*Tennyson.*

The Grecian host had been drawn up on a plain beside Aulis, where stood the altar of Artemis decked for ceremony. Iphigenia was led forth. Calchas unsheathed his sacrificial knife. The anguished father hid his face. A herald had proclaimed reverent silence, but not a man could speak or move as the noble maid stretched forth her neck to the blade that already glittered above her like the hard eyes of the slaughterer. Then lo! a wonder. Artemis had taken pity on this innocent victim: Iphigenia vanished, borne off by the goddess in a cloud to serve in perpetual maidenhood as priestess of her temple at Tauris. In the maiden's place, a milk-white fawn lay writhing before the altar, sprinkled with its blood. Calchas, with glad astonishment, proclaimed Artemis to be appeased. The victim she had sent was burned with fire upon her altar; then, as the last spark died out, a breath from heaven moved the air, and the ships could be seen tossing on the water where they had so long lain becalmed. A wind was springing up that at once set the camp astir.

Clytemnestra heard how her daughter had been carried away, never to see her more. Without waiting to take leave of her husband, she set out for his city of Mycenæ; ill blood rankling in her heart that in later years was to work long woe for the house of Agamemnon. But he and his warriors, delivered from the spell cast on them, joyfully embarked, to sail with a fair wind for the coast of Troy.

There another victim was called for. The Greek who first set foot on Trojan soil, so an oracle had declared, was doomed to die. Even the bravest might well fear to defy fate, till dauntless Protesilaus first leaped on shore, to fall forthwith by a spear flung by Hector. Long his faithful wife Laodamia mourned that he sent no word home; and many a hero who now hailed the bristling walls of Troy, would never again see wife or child. They had vowed not to cut their hair till these walls fell before them; but little thought the " long-haired Achæans " that the siege of this strong city would take them ten toilsome years.

III. The Wrath of Achilles

On the Trojan shore, at the confluent mouth of the rivers Simois and Scamander, the Greeks hauled up their ships, placing them orderly in rows, propped on beams and stones, with lanes between the squadron from each city; and each leader lived among his own followers, in tents or in huts of wood and earth, thatched with reeds, so that the camp was like a town, built over against the high-set battlements of Troy. In the midst was left an open space for public gatherings and for the altars of the gods. At either end it was guarded by Achilles and by the huge Ajax, as trustiest champions of the besiegers. Agamemnon, that "king of men", had his quarter, as beseemed, in the centre, among the tents of Ulysses, Menelaus, Diomede, Nestor, and other warriors from all parts of Greece.

> " Oh! say what heroes, fired by thirst of fame,
>   Or urged by wrongs, to Troy's destruction came.
>   To count them all demands a thousand tongues,
>   A throat of brass and adamantine lungs."

Between the city and the camp, the two rivers enclosed an open plain that made arena for many a fray. Again and again the Trojans sallied forth to hot battle beneath their walls. Each army was led on by its champions whirling up the dust in their war-chariots, from which often they would spring down to meet one another hand to hand in single combat, while all the rest stood still to look on, mingling their shouts with the clang of arms. Now one, now the other party got the better, and drove its enemy out of the field. But when years had passed, and many souls of heroes had gone down to Hades before their time, not yet were the Greeks able to break through the walls of Troy.

Besides battles before the city, the invaders made raids for plunder far and wide in the countries around. In one such foray was captured Chryseis, daughter of Chryses, a priest of Apollo, and she fell to Agamemnon's share of the booty. Her old father came to the camp seeking to ransom her; but the haughty king refused to yield up his captive, and harshly bade the sacred elder begone. Then as Chryses turned away sorrowful along the moaning shore, he prayed the god whom he served to reward his devotion by avenging him upon those arrogant strangers.

> " Such prayer he made, and it was heard.   The god
> Down from Olympus, with his radiant bow,
> And his full quiver o'er his shoulders slung,
> Marched in his anger; shaken as he moved,
> His rattling arrows told of his approach.
> Like night he came, and seated with the ships
> In view, despatched an arrow.   Clanged the cord,
> Dread sounding, bounding on the silver bow.
> Mules first, and dogs, he struck, but aiming soon
> Against the Greeks themselves, his bitter shafts
> Smote them.   The frequent piles blazed night and day."
> —*Cowper*.[1]

When the pestilence had raged for nine days, the Greeks met in council, and Calchas was called on to reveal the cause of the god's anger against them.   The seer knew, but was loath to tell what might offend one he feared.   Only when Achilles bid him speak out, promising to be his shield against any man in the

---

[1] This and the two succeeding chapters make the theme of Homer's *Iliad*. Quotations of celebrated passages, where not marked with the translator's name, are from the familiar version of Pope, which, with all its faults, remains one of the most spirited: in the selection of versions, the aim is to illustrate the different manners in which Homer has been treated.

host, were it Agamemnon himself, did Calchas declare
how Apollo's wrath was on account of Chryseis and the
wrong done to her suppliant sire; nor would the plague
be stayed till she had been freely restored with sacrifices
and prayers to appease the god, injured in the person
of his priest.

On this, Agamemnon flared into wrath, for he had
come to love his fair captive well. Not less hotly did
Achilles demand that the maid should be given back;
and thus broke out a quarrel between those heroes, long
jealous of each other. Since the general voice was
against him, the king sullenly agreed to resign his prize;
but in return he masterfully claimed Briseis, another
captive damsel who had been given to Achilles as his
share of the spoil.

Such a demand stirred Achilles to quick anger; and
before all the chiefs, he denounced the selfishness of their
leader.

> " O, impudent, regardful of thy own,
> Whose thoughts are centred on thyself alone,
> Advanc'd to sovereign sway for better ends
> Than thus like abject slaves to treat thy friends.
> What Greek is he, that, urg'd by thy command,
> Against the Trojan troops will lift his hand?
> Not I: nor such inforc'd respect I owe;
> Nor Pergamus I hate, nor Priam is my foe.
> What wrong from Troy remote, could I sustain,
> To leave my fruitful soil, and happy reign,
> And plough the surges of the stormy main?
> Thee, frontless man, we follow'd from afar;
> Thy instruments of death, and tools of war.
> Thine is the triumph; ours the toil alone:
> We bear thee on our backs, and mount thee on the throne
> For thee we fall in fight; for thee redress
> Thy baffled brother, not the wrongs of Greece.
> And now thou threaten'st with unjust decree,
> To punish thy affronting heaven, on me.

To seize the prize which I so dearly bought;
By common suffrage given, confirm'd by lot,
Mean match to thine: for still above the rest,
Thy hook'd rapacious hands usurp the best,
Though mine are first in fight, to force the prey;
And last sustain the labours of the day.
Nor grudge I thee the much the Grecians give;
Nor murmuring take the little I receive.
Yet even this little, thou, who wouldst ingross
The whole, insatiate, envy'st as thy loss.
Know, then, for Phthia fix'd is my return:
Better at home my ill-paid pains to mourn,
Than from an equal here sustain the public scorn."

—*Dryden.*

"Let him go," haughtily retorted Agamemnon; "the host would be well rid of such a quarrelsome and wilful comrade."

"We need not such a friend, nor fear not such a foe."

But in any case he must give up his Briseis, if the king had to tear her away with his own hands. At this threat the wrath of Achilles could not readily find words. He leaped to his feet, he laid hand upon his sword, and he stood torn between rage and loyalty, half in a mind to unsheathe against the leader of the host, when Athene swiftly descended to his side, visible to him alone, as she held him back by his yellow hair, bidding him restrain his hasty rage, and promising that prudence should not go without reward. Thus secretly counselled, the son of Peleus put up his sword, yet in bitter words he vented the swelling of his heart against that insolent king.

"Swoln drunkard! dog in eye but hind in heart,
Who ne'er in war sustain'st a warrior's part,
Nor join'st our ambush; for alike thy fear
In war and ambush views destruction near,

More safe, 'mid Græcia's ranks th' inglorious toil,
To grasp some murmurer's unprotected spoil.
Plunderer of slaves—slaves void of soul as sense—
Or Greece had witness'd now thy last offence.
Yet—by this sceptre, which, untimely reft
From its bare trunk upon the mountain left,
Bark'd by the steel, and of its foliage shorn,
Nor bark nor foliage shall again adorn,
But borne by powerful chiefs of high command,
Guardians of law, and judges of the land:
Be witness thou, by this tremendous test
I ratify my word, and steel my breast—
The day shall come, when Greece, in dread alarm,
Shall lean for succour on Pelides' arm:
Then, while beneath fierce Hector's murderous blade
Thy warriòrs bleed, and claim in vain thy aid,
Rage shall consume thy heart, that madd'ning pride,
Dishonouring me, thy bravest chief defied."

—Sotheby.

In vain Nestor, oldest and wisest of the Greeks, grey with experience of three generations of men, and reverenced as the familiar friend of bygone heroes— in vain with weighty words he strove to reconcile the threatening leaders. Vowing to fight no more for any woman's sake, Achilles, with his bosom friend Patroclus, withdrew to his tent, where presently he had the pain of seeing Briseis fetched away by the messengers of Agamemnon. The other chiefs consented to let it be so, since now Chryseis was given back to her father, and the god being duly propitiated, his fiery arrows ceased to fall upon the camp.

Such open indignity had driven Achilles beside himself. Going far apart along the shore of the sounding ocean, with tears of spite and sullen groans he called up his goddess mother from its depths. She rose like a mist to hear his tale of hurt honour and rankling pride. Thetis wept in sympathy with her injured son, whose cause she willingly agreed to further in the court of Olympus. He asked her nothing less than this, to make interest with Zeus that the Greeks should now suffer such loss as might teach them what it was to serve so hateful a king, and to want the help of their bravest champion.

Thetis promised to fulfil his mission as soon as Zeus should have returned from a feast he was holding among the blameless Ethiopians. After twelve days, then, she soared to Olympus, clasped its king by the knees, and begged of him to avenge her son's disgrace. Zeus, at first unwilling, gave way to her entreaties, consenting it should be as she desired, yea, confirming his decree with a nod that shook the skies. But he bid her begone in haste, not to be spied by his jealous queen, who, never forgetting the slight put on her by Paris, was impatient for the fall of Troy.

Hera indeed had marked the coming of the silver-footed Thetis, and she distrusted that resounding nod; but when she would have questioned her spouse what favour he had thus granted, the Thunderer sternly silenced her curiosity. There had nigh been a quarrel in heaven, but for Vulcan's handing round a bowl of nectar with such awkward goodwill, that his hobbling gait sent all the gods off in peals of laughter; and the rest of the Olympian day went merrily by in feast and song.

Soon would it be known on earth what Zeus purposed against the Greeks. When all the other gods slept he lay awake, turning over in his mind how to carry out that promise wrung from him by the fond mother of Achilles; and it seemed best to send a false dream to Agamemnon, by which he was bidden lead out the host for a battle that should humble the walls of Troy.

" For now no more the gods with fate contend;
   At Juno's suit the heavenly factions end.
   Destruction hangs o'er yon devoted wall,
   And nodding Ilion waits the impending fall.
   Awake; but waking this advice approve,
   And trust the vision that descends from Jove!"

Roused by such a lying phantom, the exultant king called all the chiefs to council. Then, to try men's temper, he first spoke of their toils, their losses through nine fruitless years: he asked if it were not well to give up this weary siege and hasten back to the wives and children who pined for them in their homes over the sea. To his dismay, the Greeks heard him but too gladly. With loud applause they hailed his feigned retreat; and the whole army moved towards the shore in rushing waves, eager to embark. Already they had begun to launch their rotting ships, when Pallas-Athene, sent by Hera, swooped down to hold them back. Odysseus she found still steadfast, and him she stirred to check the shameful flight. Into his hands Agamemnon gave the sceptre of authority, with which the hero flew among the broken ranks, reproaching, commanding, or beating back the dastards and laggards, crying on them to obey their leader's voice alone, and not

" That worst of tyrants, a usurping crowd".

One man only ventured to speak out against him. The squint-eyed Thersites, that hobbling hunchback, was ever a mocker and reviler of his betters. He now spitefully raised his voice to ask why men like him should fight for a rich king, who grasped the rewards of war, but left its toils to harder hands. With a threat to have him stripped and scourged to the fleet, Odysseus laid the heavy sceptre on his crooked back so sturdily that

Thersites shrank into tearful silence; and that example cowed all discontent.

The rout thus stayed, Odysseus eloquently called to his comrades' minds their vows, their hopes, the favourable omens that promised the fall of Troy. Old Nestor also addressed the warriors, bidding them forbear all strife but against the foe. Agamemnon no longer wasted his breath on crafty speech, but plainly ordered battle array. After offering sacrifice to the gods, and taking a meal that for many a man might be his last, the Greek host, as was their wont, advanced silently and sternly in close ranks, wrapt in a cloud of dust, while the Trojans came out to meet them like a noisy flock of cranes, with boastful cries and idle clash of arms. But he who should have led the Achæans on to victory, now sat sullenly in his tent.

IV. The Battles of Gods and Heroes

The armies being drawn up face to face, ready to set on, Paris, wearing a panther's skin over his bright armour, stepped gracefully forth from the Trojan ranks to challenge the bravest of the Greeks. At the word, Menelaus sprang from his chariot and bounded forward like a lion upon the spoiler of his home. But when Paris, erst brave as beautiful, saw the hero in all the fierceness of his wrong, conscience turned him coward; he flinched from the encounter, and would have shrunk back among the thick of his own people, had not Hector sharply up-braided him for shirking the foe he had brought on their native city by his tricks and graces.

> "Thou wretched Paris, though in form so fair,
> Thou slave of woman, manhood's counterfeit!

Would thou had'st ne'er been born, or died at least
Unwedded; so 'twere better far for all,
Than thus to live a scandal and reproach.
Well may the long-haired Greeks derisive laugh,
Who think thee, from thy outward show, a chief
Among our warriors; but thou hast in truth
Nor strength of mind, nor courage in the fight.
How was't that such as thou could e'er induce
A noble band in ocean-going ships
To cross the main, with men of other lands
Mixing in amity, and bearing thence
A woman fair of face, by marriage ties
Bound to a race of warriors; to thy sire,
Thy state, thy people, cause of endless grief,
Of triumph to thy foes, contempt to thee!
Durst thou the warlike Menelaus meet,
Thou to thy cost should learn the might of him
Whose bride thou didst not fear to bear away:
Then should'st thou find of small avail thy lyre
Or Venus' gifts of beauty or of grace,
Or, trampled in the dust, thy flowing hair.
But too forbearing are the men of Troy;
Else for the ills that thou hast wrought the state,
Ere now thy body had in stone been cased."

—Lord Derby.

His brother's scorn goaded Paris back to pride; and he nerved himself to fight out the quarrel in single combat with Menelaus, its issue to decide the war. A parley was called, a truce proclaimed, and the two armies ranged themselves about the lists in which that eventful duel should end so much slaughter. From the walls of Troy, old Priam looked anxiously on; and to him came Helen, who, as she sat weaving her story into a web of golden tapestry, had been called to witness the battle between her rival husbands. Sitting by Priam's side, she named to him the chiefs of the Greeks, once her familiar friends, kingly Agamemnon, gigantic Ajax, wise Odysseus; but she looked in vain for her brothers

Castor and Pollux, cut off by fate since she left their Spartan home.

When all was ready, Priam turned away, for he could not bear to behold the peril of his darling son. But Helen kept her place, gazing through tears upon her first husband, who now again seemed dear to her in his manly wrath. Lots being drawn for which of her lovers should cast the first javelin, the chance fell to Paris, and her eyes followed the shining dart as it sped through the air to bound back from the Greek's ringing shield. With a prayer to Zeus to guide his weapon well, Menelaus next threw with such forceful aim that the point pierced through shield and armour and garment, and but for drawing deftly back, Paris had felt a deadly wound. As he staggered under the shock, the son of Atreus was upon him with drawn sword. The keen blade splintered against the prince's crest, and broke off short in the hand of Menelaus, who then grasped Paris by the helmet and would have dragged him off among the exulting Greeks.

Already their shouts hailed the downfall of Troy's champion, when Aphrodite came to the aid of her favourite. With unseen touch she burst the golden strap of the helmet, that came away empty in the grasp of the Greek, who flung it hastily down, again to aim a dart at the Trojan's breast. But as it whizzed to its mark, the goddess had caught up Paris and carried him off hidden in a cloud, to lay him fainting on the bridal bed, where Helen came to tend him, her heart torn between love of the winsome form, and contempt for the craven spirit.

The Greeks now claimed the victory, as well they might after the flight of Paris; and in Olympus the gods held council about putting an end to the war. Zeus was for having Helen surrendered to the besiegers without more ado; but Hera pressed her ill will against Troy, offering her spouse in return for its destruction to let him ruin her own best-loved cities, Argos, Mycenæ, and Sparta; and for the sake of peace in heaven its king gave way. Pallas was sent down to rekindle the war, as she did by stirring the archer Pandarus to aim an arrow at Menelaus, that drew blood from a hurt quickly stanched. That treacherous shot broke the truce; then Agamemnon, filled with grief and rage when at first he took his wounded brother for dead, cried on the Greeks to battle.

Hot was the combat in which gods took part as well as men. The hero of that day was Diomede, whom Pallas healed, at a touch, of a mortal wound, so that he had strength to heave a stone, not to be lifted by two men of his degenerate posterity. He hurled it at Æneas, brought to his knees by its crushing weight, to be saved by his mother Aphrodite, who screened him behind her veil; but he saw his god-given chariot horses carried off as trophies to the Greek camp. Diomede did not fear to assail the goddess herself, and wounded her with a dart, not less keenly with insolent words.

> "The field of combat is no scene for thee.
> Go, let thy own soft sex employ thy care,
> Go, lull the coward or delude the fair.
> Taught by this stroke, renounce the war's alarms,
> And learn to tremble at the name of arms!"

Giving her son to be guarded by Apollo, the queen of love fled horror-struck to Olympus in the chariot of Ares, who, fighting for Troy, got a hurt that made him bellow for pain. Hera herself had come down to join in the fray, taking the form of Stentor, the loudest-lunged of the Greeks, and with his voice taunting them for cowardice, while Pallas, hidden under her helmet of darkness, served Diomede as his charioteer to charge against Mars. But when the god of war, sorely pierced by his own darts, fled to Olympus with groanings and complaints, the goddesses, too, saw well to leave the field.

The earthly warriors went on fighting till Simois and Scamander ran red with blood. It was then that Diomede encountered the Lycian prince Glaucus, grandson of Bellerophon; but on learning of the old guest-fellowship of their sires, they forbore to shed each other's blood, and even exchanged armour, the brazen mail of the Greek for the golden trappings of the other, worth ten times as many oxen, thus plighting faith to be friends, foemen as were their people. But there was no ruth nor kindness in the heart of Ajax, as he raged among the Trojans, smiting down young and old, great and small, so that for a time Achilles went unmissed by friend as by foe.

From the heat and dust of that hurly-burly, Hector hastened back to Troy, where he vainly set Hecuba and her attendants upon a solemn procession to the temple of Pallas, that she might be besought to check the doughty Diomede's career. In the palace Hector found Paris idly polishing and playing with his arms at Helen's side; then once more he broke out upon that unworthy brother, for whose sake so many brave men were meeting death, while he carelessly sat apart among the women. Stung by sharp reproaches, Paris promised to follow him to the battle; and his wife herself spurned the laggard forth, with warm words to Hector.

" Brother of me the abominable, accurst!
Would that from heaven a sweeping storm had burst,
And wrapt me away for ever to the hills,
In that day when my mother bore me first,

Or, where the wave roars and the hurricane shrills,
Had in the deep waste drowned me, ere I bred these ills!

"But since the gods ordained them, why not then
Give me a husband better and more fit,
That knew shame, and the burning tongues of men?
This hath not, will have never, a sound wit,
And he will reap his folly.   But now sit
On this chair, O my brother, for our crime
Hath most thy soul to ceaseless sorrow knit;
And now with him I to such misery climb,
Men shall make songs upon us in the after-time."
                                            —*Worsley.*

But Hector would not stay; before all he must seek
out his own wife Andromache for one short greeting that
might be the last.   He found her not in their home,
but on a tower of the walls, eagerly watching the turns
of a battle in which her husband's life was exposed to
the same swords that had already slain all the men of
her father's house.   Beside her, borne in the arms of his
nurse, was her young son Astyanax.   In vain she pled
with her husband to remain within the walls, as guard for
Troy and for his dear ones.

"While Hector still survives, I see
My father, mother, brethren all in thee!"

It could not be, he told her; his part was to stand
foremost in the field; and much as he loved her, honour
was dearer still.   So, with heartfelt forebodings of disaster,
he took farewell of wife and child, perhaps doomed to
slavery, did his arm fail to shield them.

"So said the glorious Hector, and stretch'd out his arms for the
      infant—
But back-shrinking, the child on the deep-veil'd breast of the damsel
Cower'd with a cry, and avoided in horror the sight of his father,
Scared at the shine of the brass and the terrible plumage of horse hai1

Tossing adown, as he stoopt, from the crest of the glittering helmet:
Then did the father laugh right forth—and Andromache also;
But soon glorious Hector had lifted the casque from his temples,
And on the ground at their feet it was laid, the magnificent head-
piece;
Then in his hands he receiv'd him and kist him and tenderly
dandled;
Which done, this was his prayer unto Zeus and the rest of the
godheads:—

"'Zeus! and ye deities all! may your blessing descend on mine
offspring!
Grant estimation to him, as to me, in the land of the Trojan!
Gallant in arms may he be, and his reign over Ilion mighty.
Let it be spoken of him, when they see him returning from battle,
Bearing the blood - stain'd spoils, having slaughter'd his enemy
fairly;—
This is the first of his lineage, more excellent far than his father.
Such be the cry—and in him let the heart of his mother be
gladden'd!'

"Thus pray'd he, and surrender'd the child to the hands of the
mother,
And she receiv'd him and prest to the fragrant repose of her bosom,
Smiling with tears in her eyes; and the husband beheld her with
pity,
Gently caressed with his hand, and bespake her again at departing:—
'Dearest and best! let not trouble for me overmaster thy spirit.
None, contravening the doom, prematurely to Hades shall send me,
Nor, full sure, can the sentence of Fate be avoided by mortals,
Whether for good or for ill, firm fixt from the hour of our birthtime.'"[1]

—*J. G. Lockhart.*

[1] The reader may be interested in comparing with a later translation of this
famous passage the version of old Chapman, who in some respects is judged to have
rendered Homer better than most of his rivals.

"This said, he reach'd to take his son, who of his arms afraid,
And then the horse-hair plume, with which he was so overlaid,
Nodded so horribly, he cling'd back to his nurse, and cried.
Laughter affected his great sire; who doff'd and laid aside
His fearful helm, that on the earth cast round about it light;
Then took and kiss'd his loving son; and (balancing his weight
In dancing him) these loving vows to living Jove he us'd,
And all the other bench of gods: 'O you that have infus'd

With this, bidding her return to her household tasks, he laced on his helm and strode away, while Andromache went home to weep with her maids for the well-loved lord she had seen for the last time alive.

Hector and Paris having come back to the fray, it soon blazed up afresh, and for a time victory was bandied about by stirring feats of arms on either side. It was Hector that now defied the bravest of the Greeks to single combat; and Menelaus would have taken up the challenge, had not his heedful brother Agamemnon held him back from encountering such a peerless champion. But when old Nestor called shame on the warriors for faint hearts, minding them of the dead heroes of his own time, they were spurred on to agree that their nine mightiest should draw lots which must face the Trojan leader. The lot fell on huge Ajax, the very man who would have been chosen by every voice; and he with joy and pride armed himself for the trial.

More fiercely than when Paris was the skulking foe, these two met before the gazing armies. Long and mightily they fought with spears and darts and flaming swords, and when these were broken or blunted, with

Soul to this infant; now set down this blessing on his star:
Let his renown be clear as mine; equal his strength in war;
And make his reign so strong in Troy, that years to come may yield
His facts this fame;—when rich in spoils, he leaves the conquer'd field
Sown with his slaughters:—These high deeds exceed his father's worth.
And let this echo'd praise supply the comforts to come forth
Of his kind mother, with my life!' This said, th' heroic sire
Gave him his mother; whose fair eyes, fresh streams of love's salt fire,
Billow'd on her soft cheeks, to hear the last of Hector's speech,
In which his vows compris'd the sum of all he did beseech
In her wish'd comfort. So she took into her odorous breast
Her husband's gift; who, mov'd to see her heart so much oppress'd,
He dried her tears; and thus desir'd: 'Afflict me not, dear wife,
With these vain griefs. He doth not live that can disjoin my life
And this firm bosom, but my fate; and fate whose wings can fly?
Noble, ignoble, fate controls: once born, the best must die."

big stones caught up to crush the other beneath their shattered shields; but before either had got the better, darkness fell upon them, and they drew apart with courteous salutations and exchange of gifts, promising to fight out their duel some other day, now broken off at the bidding of sage elders on either side.

> " Forbear, my sons, your further force to prove,
> Both dear to men, and both beloved of Jove!
> To either host your matchless worth is known,
> Each sounds your praise, and war is all your own;
> But now the Night extends her awful shade;
> The goddess parts you: be the Night obeyed."

There was little rest that night for either army. A truce had been agreed upon that each should gather its dead for burning and burial in honoured mounds. The Greeks, warned by their losses, had made haste to throw up a wall and trench round their camp, where before long they might find themselves besieged instead of besiegers. The Trojans held confused council, in which it was proposed that Helen should now be given back, that with her their land might be freed from the plague of war. Paris could by no means consent to part with his bride, but he was willing to yield up the treasures of Sparta, if so much would content the enemy; and the doting Priam sent a herald to offer this wealth, and more, as the price of peace. But the Greeks were not to be bribed by gold; and now fortune brought them a fleet of ships freighted with generous wine to warm their hearts into forgetfulness of pains suffered and to come.

Meanwhile, Zeus called a council of the gods, whom with threats he forbade to take further part on either hand. Yet, when daylight again awoke the war, moved by his promise to Thetis, he himself interfered with thunders that dismayed the Greeks. 'Twere long to tell all the ebb and flow of that day's battle. Enough to say that after fresh slaughter and countless heroic deeds, at nightfall the once exulting invaders were driven back behind their new-made defences, and the Trojans lay on the field they held as victors.

> " Many a fire before them blazed:
> As when in heaven the stars about the moon
> Look beautiful, when all the winds are laid
> And every height comes out, and jutting peak
> And valley, and the immeasurable heavens
> Break open to their highest, and all the stars
> Shine, and the Shepherd gladdens in his heart:
> So many a fire between the ships and stream
> Of Xanthus blazed before the towers of Troy,
> A thousand on the plain; and close by each
> Sat fifty in the blaze of burning fire;
> And champing golden grain the horses stood
> Hard by their chariots waiting for the dawn."
>
> *—Tennyson.*

While the Trojans already looked forward to spoiling the Grecian camp, those within it were beset with dismay. Agamemnon sent out whispering messengers to summon the chiefs, who found him tearfully downcast; and in words broken by sighs he put to them, now in good earnest, that there was nothing for it but to embark and fly, since the very gods fought for their foe.

He was heard in silence; but then up started Diomede, keenly reproaching the king with cowardice. Let him to whom the gods had given power and wealth but not a steadfast soul, let him and those like-minded take to craven flight! He himself would stay and fight out the fate of Troy, and one friend he had, Sthenelus, who would not let him fight alone. His bold words stirred outspoken assent, amid which rose Nestor to take the right of age in declaring to Agamemnon's face that all their misfortunes were owing to him, in that he had wronged Achilles and estranged their bravest warrior.

The contrite king listened meekly, and answered by confessing his fault, for which he was now willing to make amends. To the hero who held sullenly aloof in his secluded tent, he proposed to send an embassy of reconciliation, with gifts worthy of his fame, ten talents of gold, twenty golden vases, seven sacrificial tripods, twelve matchless steeds: moreover Agamemnon would let him have back his Briseis along with seven more fair captives, and twenty others he might choose from the captives of Troy; then, when they returned home in triumph, Achilles should marry any one of the king's own daughters, with seven cities for her dowry; only now let him come to help against the terrible Hector.

Nestor spoke the general approval, naming three chiefs to carry such princely offers, the wise Odysseus, the bold Ajax, and Phœnix, who had been tutor of Achilles in youth. Attended by two heralds, those ambassadors took their way along the wave-beaten shore to that silent end of the camp, where the Myrmidons had lain chafing in idleness while the tide of war rose and fell close at hand. They found Achilles in his tent playing the lyre as if all were peace, and singing to Patroclus, the friend of his heart, who alone kept him company. At the sight of the messengers he laid aside his lyre, rose to give them courteous greeting, made them sit down on richly spread couches, and bid Patroclus fill out wine for his guests. Nor would he listen to their errand till they had eaten as well as drunk the best he had to set before them.

> " Princes, all hail! whatever brought ye here,
> Or strong necessity or urgent fear.

Welcome, though Greeks! for not as foes ye came,
To me more dear than all that bear the name."

Supper over, Odysseus rose to drink the health of
their noble host, and went on to lay before him those
royal offers as proof of Agamemnon's repentance. If
the hero despised such gifts, let him remember that on
him lay the weal or woe of his people; and if that did
not move him, could he bear to hear proud Hector's
boasts that no Greek was his peer.

Achilles listened regardfully, but answered with un-
relenting pride. He rehearsed his wrongs: the Greeks
had chosen to affront him, and must do without the aid
of his arm; for shield against Hector let them trust
to the wall they had been fain to build, now their best
champion had left the open field; for leader let them
look to the insolent king, whose hateful gifts he spurned;
had he come to Troy to seek wife or wealth, he could
win them for himself. In vain old Phœnix tried to
move him by memories of his docile youth. In vain
blunt Ajax reproached his sullen obstinacy. Courteously,
but firmly, Achilles dismissed them with a parting cup;
and they went back to tell Agamemnon that the hero's
heart was still hardened against him.

Diomede alone was undismayed by the news, for he
felt in himself a champion to match Hector. While the
common men slept, Agamemnon went restless from tent
to tent, taking counsel with the leaders; and Odysseus
and Diomede stole among the drowsy foe to spy out
their strength and to bring back a trophy of snow-white
horses, after slaying Dolon, an adventurous young Trojan
whom they encountered bent on a like errand of darkness, and forced him to disclose, in vain hope of mercy,
the position of the hostile army.

Next morning Agamemnon, donning his richest

armour, with the courage of desperation, led forth the
Greeks to battle that at first went in their favour. But
the king, wounded by a spear, had to withdraw from
the field; stout Diomede too was hurt; and Hector in
turn charged so hotly that he swept all before him.
Paris this day shook off his softer mood to play the
warrior. The Greeks were driven back behind their
wall, which already the storming enemy had almost
broken through, when Poseidon came to its defence,
passing sea and land in a few bounds of his chariot.
Never had the god of ocean forgotten his old grudge
against Troy; and now, taking the form of Calchas,
their reverent soothsayer, he heartened the Greeks to
rally about Ajax the Great, and his namesake, Ajax the
Less, who for a time kept off the assailants with showers
of arrows.

Nor was Poseidon the only god that strove against
Troy. Fearing lest Zeus should after all grant victory
to the city of hated Paris, Hera beguiled her spouse by
borrowing the girdle of Aphrodite to throw round her
such a spell of enchanting smiles that the Thunderer
sank to sleep in her arms. When he awoke he found
the Greeks once more led on by Poseidon to victory,
the Trojans flying, Hector lying senseless, stunned under
a stone hurled at him by Ajax. But again Zeus made
haste to turn the scale. Angrily reproaching his wife
for her deceit, he sent Iris to bid Poseidon back to his
own watery domain, and Apollo to revive Hector and
cheer on the Trojans. With the sun-god for leader,
they again pressed the Greeks to their entrenchments,
through which they burst in pursuit, so that soon a hot
fight raged about the ships, last hope of Greece, and the
prowess of Ajax and his brother Teucer was hard put to it
to keep their fleet from being set on fire.

From the prow of his own ship, Achilles had watched the battle, unmoved to take part save by sending Patroclus to seek news. But Patroclus could not bear to stand idly by, watching the ruin of Greece. With tears of rage he begged his friend at least to let him lead forth the Myrmidons, who even yet might turn the day, now that Ajax's galley could be seen flaming at the farther end of the camp.

Still feigning indifference, Achilles gave him leave, even equipped him in his own armour and mounted him on his chariot, driven by the famed charioteer Automedon. He charged him, indeed, to do no more than beat back the Trojans from the ships, the burning of which would cut off the Greeks' return; but when he saw the fierce Myrmidons as eager to be let loose as a pack of famished wolves, the hero's stubborn heart began to warm within him, and he sent his friend forth with a prayer for victory and safe return, a prayer that was to be half granted and half denied. Another heartfelt prayer he had made in the martial passion he strove to conceal; and his charge to Patroclus was to forbear facing Hector, worthy to die by no sword but his own.

> "Oh! would to all the immortal powers above,
> Apollo, Pallas and almighty Jove,
> That not one Trojan might be left alive,
> And not a Greek of all the race survive;
> Might only we the vast destruction shun,
> And only we destroy the accursed town!"

At the head of the Myrmidons, Patroclus rushed forth; then the very sight of him, mistaken for the champion whose armour he wore, was enough to strike panic among the Trojans. Driven from the ships, they fled before his onset, streaming back over the wall and the ditch choked with broken chariots and wounded

horses. Once more the tide of battle had been turned.
With red slaughter, Patroclus chased off the foe to Troy,
nay, he even strove to break through its walls, but drew
back in awe when here he was confronted by the blazing
ægis of Apollo, proclaiming that neither by him nor by
Achilles was the city fated to be overthrown. He drew
back, yet only to rage afresh against mortal foes, and
forgetful of Achilles' charge, he met Hector face to
face. It was the god himself that, hidden in a cloud,
stunned the Greek hero by a crushing blow, and laid
the borrowed plume of Achilles in the dust. Before he
could save himself, Hector was upon him, whose lance
made an end; and with his last breath Patroclus gasped
out a warning to the exultant foe, that ere long his soul
would follow to the shades.

> " I see thee fall, and by Achilles' hand."

A crowd of champions closed over the body of
Patroclus, for which strove the Trojans led on by Hector,
now proudly clad in the stripped armour; and the Greeks,
rallied round mighty Ajax, would have borne it off under
cover of their shields locked together. So fierce was this
tug-of-war that Zeus hooded it beneath thundering darkness, in which the slaughterers groped blindly, and Ajax
cried with suppliant tears—

> " If Greece must perish, we thy will obey,
> But let us perish in the face of day!"

At his prayer, the god let daylight return; then at
last the Greeks were able to drag away their hero's corpse
out of reach of insulting hands. And when on the
walls of the camp the Trojans saw arise the dread form
of Achilles, and heard his voice uplifted thrice like a
trumpet, they fled in such confused rout as to crush

one another to death under the press of chariots and armour.

Soon they would have the whole Greek host sweeping forth upon them in waves of steel—

" As from air the frosty north wind blows a cold thick sleet
   That dazzles eyes, flakes after flakes incessantly descending;
   So thick helms, curets,[1] ashen darts and round shields never ending,
   Flowed from the navy's hollow womb; their splendours gave Heaven's
     eye
   His beams again; Earth laughed to see her face so like the sky;
   Arms shined so hot, and she such clouds made with the dust she cast,
   She thundered—feet of men and horse importuned her so fast."
                                 —*Chapman.*

The prince of heroes was arming himself for battle.

V. Hector and Achilles

In his lonely tent, which was rather a spacious hall built by the Myrmidons of pines and reeds, its entrance barred by a huge trunk that only he could lift aside, Achilles had sat awaiting the triumphant return of Patroclus. But when instead of him came Antilochus, son of Nestor, an unwilling messenger for heavy news, who shall tell how the hero heard of his friend slain and his own armour gone to deck the proud Hector!

" He grasp'd the ashes scatter'd on the strand,
   And on his forehead shower'd with either hand,
   Grimed his fair face, and o'er his raiment flung
   The soil that on its splendour darkly hung,
   His large limbs prone in dust, at large outspread,
   And pluck'd the hair from his dishonour'd head;
   While all the maidens whom his arm had won,
   Or gain'd in battle with Menetius' son,
   Left the still shelter of their peaceful tent,
   And round Pelides mingled their lament,

---

[1] Breastplates.

Raised their clasped hands, and beat their breasts of snow,
And, swooning, sunk on earth, o'ercome with woe;
While o'er him Nestor's son in horror stood,
And grasp'd his arm, half-raised to shed his blood.
Deep groan'd the desperate man, 'twas death to hear
Groans that in ocean pierced the sea-nymph's ear,
His mother's ear, where deep beneath the tide,
Dwelt the sea-goddess by her father's side.
She heard, she shriek'd while, gathering swift around,
Came every Nereid from her cave profound."

—*Sotheby.*

Thetis had hurried to comfort her son, promising to
bring him new celestial armour, in which he might take
vengeance on Hector; and Iris, sent by Hera, stirred
him from his abject misery to make that appearance on
the walls that had scared the Trojans like the ægis of
some god. But again the hero seemed beside himself
when they brought in the body of his friend. All night
he lamented over it like a lioness robbed of her young,
washing with his tears the cold limbs, begrimed and
gory, which now could be laid out for a funeral to be
bathed in Trojan blood.

" One fate the warrior and his friend shall strike,
And Troy's black sands must drink our blood alike.
Me, too, a wretched mother shall deplore,
An aged father never see me more!
Yet, my Patroclus, yet a space I stay,
Then swift pursue thee on the darksome way.
Ere thy dear relics in the grave are laid,
Shall Hector's head be offered to thy shade!"

Meanwhile Thetis had hied her to Vulcan's smithy,
where, at her entreaty, in one night the god of fire forged
for her son matchless armour of mingled metals, and a
wondrous shield on which were wrought pictured labours
of peace as well as war. Such a godlike gift she brought

to Achilles at dawn, and the very sight brightened his eyes like the shining mail, while the clanging touch thrilled his heart as a trumpet.

Without delay he sped to Agamemnon, calling the chiefs to arms as he went. Face to face with the king, Achilles briefly spoke out how his heart was unburdened from a wrath that had cost so dear to the Greeks. Agamemnon, too, owned his fault, laying it on a mind blinded by fate. Amid general acclaim, the heroes made friends. The king again offered atoning gifts; but all Achilles asked was instant battle, that might wipe out in blood the woe of their quarrel. Prudent Odysseus proposed delay, ceremonies of reconciliation, and a hearty meal to strengthen the warriors for fight. Let who would feast, vowed Achilles, he himself would neither eat nor drink till he had avenged his dead friend.

Hungering for slaughter, he hurried back to his tent, did on the flashing armour of Vulcan, and snatched up his mighty spear, which Patroclus had left untouched, not to be wielded but by the hero's own hand. Roused to fresh fury by the sight of restored Briseis weeping over that lifeless friend, he mounted his chariot, with a sharp word to the noble steeds, demanding of them not to leave him on the field as they had left Patroclus. For a moment the mettled coursers stood still, then lo! a marvel, when one of them was inspired to answer its master back in human speech with a boding that, if they bore him safe that day, his doom was yet not far off. The horse spoke, but the dauntless hero cried—

> "So let it be!
> Portents and prodigies are lost on me:
> I know my fates: to die, to see no more
> My much loved parents and my native shore—

Enough—when heaven ordains, I sink in night.
Now perish Troy!"

When like a storm the Grecian host poured out on
the plain, Achilles flashing at their head in a golden halo
shed upon him by Pallas, on Olympus was held high
council, at which Zeus, unable to control Fate, gave
leave for the gods to range themselves openly on either
side in this greatest of battles about Troy, else, the
Thunderer saw, it must fall forthwith before that hero's
rage of grief. Hera, Pallas, Poseidon, Hermes, and
Hephæstus fought now for the Greeks, while Ares,
Aphrodite, Apollo, and Artemis shone in the Trojan
ranks. And men strove like gods, high above all Achilles,
from whose sword Æneas was saved only in a mist thrown
over him by Poseidon, in pity for this Dardanian prince
that shared not the offence of Troy. So, too, Apollo
for a time hid Hector in clouds from his fellest foe.
Raging like a conflagration, his chariot wheels smoking
in blood, Achilles charged through the routed Trojans,
and he spared neither suppliant nor fugitives, neither
old nor young, save twelve chosen captives set aside,
bound with their own belts, for sacrifice at the tomb
of Patroclus.

So great was the carnage he made, that the river-
god Scamander, his stream choked with corpses, rose
against him in gory flood, before which the hero was
fain to turn and fly, and had been swept away but for
catching at an elm to swing himself on to the bank.
Even then, the offended river pursued him over the
plain, calling his comrade Simois to aid, till Hephæstus
helped Achilles by sending fire to scorch up the wooded
banks; and the hissing waters fainted before the breath
of flame. What wonder this, when Pallas-Athene herself,
heaving a huge boundary stone, threw down with it

Ares, his mighty limbs sprawling over acres of ground; and Aphrodite coming to help him up, was laid low by a touch from the same doughty goddess; and scornful Hera buffeted and scolded Artemis to fly in tears to the throne of Zeus, who meanwhile looked down careless on the dreadful arena that was sport for him. But Apollo could disdain the ire of his fellow deities, for to a challenge from Poseidon he replied—

> " To combat for mankind
> Ill suits the wisdom of celestial mind;
> For what is man? Calamitous by birth,
> They owe their life and nourishment to earth;
> Like yearly leaves that now, with beauty crowned,
> Smile on the sun, now wither on the ground.
> To their own hands commit the frantic scene,
> Nor mix immortals in a cause so mean!"

Yet Apollo stood to guard the gate of Troy, when the beaten Trojans poured through it, flying wildly before the terrible Achilles. Hector alone stayed at bay without, though from the walls his father and mother stretched their hands, imploring him to seek shelter. The hero himself, rearing his head, like a trodden snake's, felt his heart quail as that mightiest of foes came on : prudence and policy bid him draw back, while shame and despair held him fast. But when he stood face to face with the irresistible Achilles, suddenly panic-stricken, Troy's champion turned and fled, as he had never thought to fly before mortal man.

Like a panting dove before a falcon he fled. Through their tears his parents and comrades saw him run thrice round the walls of Troy, pressed hard by Achilles, who bid the Greeks stand aside, since this prey was for no meaner hand. Apollo nerved Hector's limbs for that desperate race ; and the gods, watching from Olympus, hesitated whether or no to snatch him from death, till Zeus weighed his fate in golden scales that sank the hero's soul to Hades. Then Hector, with one vain look at the gate from which Achilles always cut him off, turned for his last fight, Pallas, indeed, deceiving him to his doom, for she stood beside him in the false form of his brother, Deiphobus, on whose help he vainly relied. As he confronted Achilles, he sought a moment of parley: now that one or other of them was to die, let the victor swear not to dishonour the corpse of the vanquished. To this his furious foe:

> "Accursed, speak not thou to me of compact, or of troth!
> No faith 'twixt men and lions, 'twixt wolves and lambs is none;
> But ever these the other hate to harry or to shun:
> So love and peace shall never 'twixt me and thee be blent,
> Till thou or I on earth be strew'd,
> And we the War-god rough and rude with the rud-red blood content."
> —*Dean Merivale.*

Without more ado they hurled darts that went amiss, then closed upon each other. Achilles, all aflame, burned more fiercely to see that adversary wearing his own armour torn from Patroclus. Ere long his blade found a joint to pierce between neck and throat. Hector fell, gasping out his life with a bootless prayer for pious burial. The last words he heard were Achilles' bitter threat that his body should feast the dogs and vultures; and his own last murmur warned the Grecian hero that he too was doomed to die before Troy.

All who saw held Troy already fallen, from whose towers rose a din of lament, drowned in the exultation of the Greeks, pressing round as Achilles stripped the body; yea some who durst not have looked on Hector living were now forward with blows and spurns upon his noble corpse. Achilles himself, still maddened by

lust of revenge, bored through the fallen chief's feet
to tie them by thongs behind his chariot; then holding
up to view the gory spoils, he dragged the naked limbs
in the dust, before the eyes of his old parents, shrieking
and tearing their thin locks. Andromache was sitting
at her loom when she heard the mournful outcry, to
bring her in haste to the walls, half-guessing what she
should see, that when seen, blinded her eyes in swooning misery.

Hector's mangled and defiled body was cast on the
shore beside the bier of Patroclus, round which Achilles
made his chariots and Myrmidons circle thrice in honour
of the dead hero, before they took food or rest. When
the weary chief lay down to sleep, his friend's restless
shade appeared at his side, urging him no longer to
delay due rites of burial.

> "Sleep'st thou, Achilleus, nor rememberest me?
> Living, thou lov'dst me; dead, I fade from thee:
> Entomb me quick that I may pass death's door;
> For the ghosts drive me from their company,
> Nor let me join them on the further shore:
> So in the waste wide courts I wander evermore.
> Reach me thy hand, I pray; for ne'er again,
> The pile once lit, shalt thou behold thy mate:
> Never in life apart from our brave train
> Shall we take counsel: but the selfsame fate
> Enthralls me now that by my cradle sate.
> Thou too art doomed, Achilleus the divine,
> To fall and die by sacred Troia's gate.
> Yet one thing more, wilt thou thine ear incline;
> Let not my bones in death lie separate from thine."
> —*Conington.*

The haunting ghost was soon to be laid. Next day
Agamemnon sent out a band of men to hew down wood
for a wide-piled funeral pyre. On this the body was

laid, strewn over with locks of hair which his comrades cut from their own heads as offerings to the shade. Oxen and sheep, four noble steeds, and two household dogs were sacrificed to be thrown on the heap, and with them the twelve hapless Trojan captives. The pile was slow to light till the son of Thetis prayed for favouring winds, Boreas and Zephyrus, that flew to fan it into crackling blaze. Oil and wine were poured upon the flames burning all night, while beside them Achilles watched restless; then in the morning he quenched the ashes with wine to gather them in a golden urn, above which should be heaped a mound hiding the remnants of the fire.

Nor was this all. Funeral games must be held, with rich prizes given by Achilles, for which Agamemnon himself did not disdain to contend in honour of the dead. Henceforth the two chiefs were friends; and Achilles led the host when again it marched forth against Troy.

Within Troy now all was woe and wailing, as day after day the insatiable avenger could be seen dragging the body of its champion thrice round the pile sacred to Patroclus. Pitying gods preserved Hector's corpse from decay, and when twelve days had gone, Zeus was moved to save it from dishonour. He sent Thetis to soften her son's heart that he might agree to let it be ransomed. Then from the walls, in a chariot loaded with rich gifts, came forth old Priam to throw himself at the feet of Achilles, clasping his knees and praying him, as he revered his own father, to give up the body of that noblest son.

He bent his grey head, ready to take death for an answer, and those looking on feared that the rage of Achilles might burst forth upon this helpless suppliant of the hated race. But at once the stern hero's mood was turned by gentle compassion. He raised the old king, he granted his request, he had a couch laid for him in his tent, where Priam slept for the first time since Hector's death. Yet early in the morning, fearing to fall a prey to the pride of Agamemnon, he stole away with the body, now washed and anointed, and brought it safe within the gates of Troy.

The generous Achilles had promised a twelve days' truce, that Hector's body might be duly buried. So this hero's spirit, too, could sleep in peace, honoured by solemn rites and warm tears. And among all the farewells of his friends and kindred, none spoke from the heart more than the stranger Helen, for whose sake he had died.

> " Ah, dearer far than all my brothers else
> Of Priam's house! for being Paris' spouse,
> Who brought me (would I had first died!) to Troy,
> I call thy brothers mine; since forth I came
> From Sparta, it is now the twentieth year,
> Yet never heard I once hard speech from thee,
> Or taunt morose, but if it ever chanced,
> That of thy father's house female or male
> Blamed me, and even if herself the Queen,
> (For in the King, whate'er befell, I found
> Always a father,) thou hast interposed
> Thy gentle temper and thy gentle speech
> To soothe them; therefore, with the same sad drops
> Thy fate, oh Hector, and my own I weep;
> For other friend within the ample bounds
> Of Ilium have I none, nor hope to hear
> Kind word again, with horror view'd by all."
> —*Cowper.*

Here ends the story of Homer's *Iliad*. But others tell how fresh heroes came to take the place of Hector as shield of Troy. There came the warlike Amazons, led by their queen Penthesilea, before whom the Greeks could not stand, till she fell by the spear of Achilles. But on tearing off her helmet, he stood as if spellbound in sorrow for the withering of so fair a face; and when Thersites, after his kind, jeered at the hero's ruth, Achilles struck this vile mocker dead with a single buffet.

Next Priam's nephew Memnon, the noble Egyptian, brought a band of dusky warriors to the aid of Troy. Him, too, the son of Peleus overthrew after a hard contest; but Zeus for the sake of his mother Aurora granted to him, as to his father Tithonus, the boon of immortality; and on earth was raised in his honour that colossal statue that, men say, gave forth a voice as often as it was struck by the rising sun.

Then at last dawned Achilles' day to die. Nine years past, Poseidon, friend as he was to the Greeks, had vowed vengeance against their champion, when, in one of their first onsets, he slew the god's son, Cygnus, fighting for Troy. The lord of ocean now charged Apollo with the fate of a foe his trident could not pierce. One spot in the hero's body was alone vulnerable, the heel by which his mother held him when dipped in the water of Styx. To that spot the archer-god guided a chance shaft of Paris; and thus unworthily fell the warrior that had sent so many souls down to Hades. But, if poets tell true, he himself had a nobler fate, borne away by his mother to endless life in some happy island far from the eyes of common men.

Sore was the mourning for Achilles in the Grecian camp.

> " Ten days and seven, with all their space of night,
> Both gods and mortals we bewailed thee there.
> But on the morning of the eighteenth light
> We gave thee to the fire, and victims fair
> Slew round thee, sheep and oxen; and the air

Hung sweet with smoke, thou burning in rich state
Of robes divine, sweet honey, and unguents rare,
While with a noise of arms about thee wait
Horsemen alike and footmen; and the cry was great

" At sunrise, when the fire had ceased to burn,
Thy cinders white in oil and unmixed wine
We gathered, and thy mother gave an urn
All-golden, calling it the gift divine
Of Dionysus, moulded from the mine
By work-renowned Hephæstus: there abide
The ashes of Patroclus, mixed with thine;
Antilochus lies separate at thy side,
Best loved of all thy comrades, when Patroclus died."

—Worsley: Odyssey.

As Troy had seemed ready to fall with Hector's death, so the loss of their champion for a time disheartened the host of Agamemnon. And even in death, Achilles had left among them a legacy of strife. His marvellous shield and armour, wrought by Hephæstus, were to go to the bravest of the Greeks—a gift nigh as fatal as the golden apple from which grew all that woe. For when by the voice of Trojan captives such a prize was adjudged to Odysseus, as their doughtiest foe in valour as in wisdom, great Ajax went mad for vexation, and killed himself by his own hand on a hecatomb of harmless sheep he had taken for threatening warriors. But that priceless armour Odysseus gave up to the ruddy-haired son of Achilles, who, grown to manhood beside his mother, Deidamia of Scyros, was now brought to the war in obedience to an oracle declaring that without his young arm Troy could not be overthrown.

VI. The Fall of Troy

Still Troy did not yield, for all the heroes battering ever at its gates. Achilles' son, Pyrrhus, whom the Greeks named Neoptolemus, " new in war ", showed himself a true branch of heroic stock ; but neither for him did the walls fall that had held out against his father. Then Calchas the seer, offering sacrifice, read in the entrails of the victim that Troy would not be taken without the arrows of Hercules, given in legacy to his friend Philoctetes.

This hero had indeed sailed from Aulis with the rest of the Greeks, but going on shore he had been bitten by a serpent, and the wound festered so loathsomely, seeming like to breed a pestilence, that, to be rid of his ceaseless cries, his shipmates set Philoctetes on the isle of Lemnos, and there left him to shift for himself. Ten years having passed, he might well be dead long ago ; but when Odysseus and Pyrrhus sailed to Lemnos, they found him still alive, gaunt and ragged, and full of rancour against the Greeks who had deserted him to make his solitary abode in a cave, killing game with the bow and arrows that should have been aimed at Troy. These messengers had much ado to gain his goodwill ; but by persuasion and by threats of force they brought him away to the camp in the Troad, where at last a skilled physician healed him of his grievous hurt. But no healing could help a wound made by the arrows of Hercules, poisoned in the Lernæan hydra's black blood ; and by one of them it was that Paris now met a miserable death.

Again spoke an oracle that Troy could not fall so long as it treasured its Palladium, that image of Pallas fallen from heaven. Again Odysseus showed himself bold as well as cunning. He and Diomede, in beggars' weeds, slunk by night within the walls of Troy, known to none in that disguise save only to Helen, but she, for fear or shame, did not betray her old friends, though well aware that they came on no friendly errand. Her heart was now going back to her true husband, whose feats of arms she beheld daily from the walls; and she even helped his comrades to steal from the temple of Pallas that sacred image. So unhurt they brought it at daybreak to the camp, to be hailed by the exulting Greeks as a sure sign of victory.

Yet still those oracles seemed to befool the army, against which Troy held out stoutly as ever. When the chiefs could no longer bind their followers to the weary war, Odysseus hit on the device that was at last to make an end. By his counsel they framed a huge horse of wood, moved on wheels, and hollow inside to hold twelve men, of whom he made one, along with Diomede, Pyrrhus, and other chosen warriors. Leaving this fabric full in view, charged with its baleful freight, the Greeks sailed away through the night, as if they had given up the siege in despair; but they cast anchor under the isle of Tenedos, in sight of the Trojan shore.

Those so long cooped up within Troy at first could hardly trust their eyes when in the morning they saw the enemy's camp deserted behind its smouldering watch fires. Then like bees they came swarming out of the gates to spread freely over the fields that for ten years they had trod but in hasty sallies. Eagerly they roamed from one scene to another of the quenched war, the wall raised about the Greek camp, the shore still furrowed by vanished keels, the site of Agamemnon's tent, the quarters of Achilles and of Ajax, the towering burial mound of Patroclus, the banks of the Scamander erstwhile choked by corpses. But nothing held their thankful eyes like that strange shape of a wooden horse : what could it be, and why left behind by the retreating enemy? Some were for dragging it off into the city, even if the gates had to be broken down to give it passage ; but others cried for caution, and loudest of all Laocoon, the priest of Apollo, who ran up to warn his countrymen that here must be some deceit.

> " Deem ye the foe hath passed away?   Deem ye that Danaan gifts
>   May ever lack due share of guile?   Are these Ulysses' shifts?
>   For either the Achæans lurk within this fashioned tree,
>   Or 't is an engine wrought with craft, bane of our walls to be,
>   To look into our very homes and scale the town perforce:
>   Some guile at least therein abides: Teucrians, trust not the horse!"
> —*William Morris.*[1]

" The very gifts of the Greeks are dangerous," he ended, and flung a spear piercing the hollow wood to stir a rattle of arms within ; then, were not the Trojans blinded by their fate, that trick would forthwith have been disclosed and Priam's kingdom stood firm as of old.

While some spoke of cutting the ominous gift to pieces, and some of hurling it over a rock into the sea, there went a rumour through the throng that drew all eyes away, turned on a prisoner whom certain shepherds had found lurking in the sedge by the shore, and he gave himself up to be led bound before Priam. This was Sinon, a young Greek self-devoted to play a treacherous part, sure of death if it failed. Trembling and tearful he bemoaned his lot as a victim both of friends and foes, till the Trojans, taking pity, urged him to say who he was, and how he came into such sorry plight. Feigning

---

[1] Where another translator is not named, the citations here are from Dryden's *Æneid.*

to lay aside his fear, he let himself be heartened into telling an artful tale, which seemed borne out by his unarmed nakedness. He spoke his name, and did not deny his race.

"Though plunged by Fortune's power in misery,
'T is not in Fortune's power to make me lie."

He had come to the war, he said, a boy in charge of his father's friend Palamedes, against whom Odysseus ever bore a grudge. By his wiles, it was the fate of Palamedes to be accused of treason and put to death; then Sinon, faithfully holding to the innocence of his lord, had threatened revenge on Odysseus, so as to bring on himself the ill will of such a powerful chief. Let the Trojans kill him, and they would do a pleasure to that enemy, and to the leaders of the Greeks, whose minds a hateful tongue had poisoned against him.

But Priam's people, touched by compassion, encouraged the unfortunate youth to have no fear; and he went on with his lying tale.

The Greeks, weary of the war, had designed to withdraw for a time; but contrary winds hindered them from setting sail for their native land; and celestial prodigies warned them of divine power to be appeased. An oracle declared that as Iphigenia had been doomed at Aulis, so now another victim must be offered to buy a favouring homeward wind. Calchas, won over by Odysseus, pointed out Sinon as the chosen sacrifice; and all who feared the lot might fall elsewhere, were content to let him die. Already the altar and the sacrificial array were prepared, when he broke his fetters, and fled for hiding to a swamp, from which he had the joy of seeing the Greek ships sail away, leaving him still alive on the hostile soil.

Hostile no longer, Priam bid him believe, ordering
the prisoner to be freed from his bonds; for the Trojans
made him welcome as an ally, who had so little cause
to love his own countrymen. And now they pressed
him to declare what meant that wooden horse, as he
glibly did, raising his unbound hands to heaven in protest that he spoke the truth.

The goddess Pallas, they were to know, had taken
dire offence at the Greeks for stealing her image from
Troy. Before sailing for Greece, with purpose to return
anon under better auspices, the soothsayer Calchas bid
them placate her by forming and dedicating this figure,
made so huge by cunning design, that it might not enter
the city gates, for if once it could be placed as an offering in Athene's temple, it must prove a shield for the
Trojans like that robbed Palladium, whereas if they dared
to injure it by fire or iron, their own profane hands would
bring ruin on Troy.

> "With such deceits he gained their easy hearts,
> Too prone to credit his perfidious arts.
> What Diomede, nor Thetis' greater son,
> A thousand ships, nor ten years' siege had done—
> False tears and fawning words the city won!"

Then, lo! a portent seemed to confirm Sinon's lies.
As Laocoon now stood in act to sacrifice a steer to
Poseidon, over the sea came skimming two enormous
serpents, that drew themselves on land and, with hissing
heads upreared, slid straight for the altar. They first
fell upon the priest's two young sons standing there too
scared to fly, till the scaly coils were wound about their
limbs. While the other spectators stared in speechless
amazement, Laocoon with a cry ran to plunge his knife
into those throats already gorging on his boys' flesh;

but him also the monsters involved in their loathsome embrace, twisting twice round his neck and his waist, to crush all three, laced together in helpless torment. Laocoon and his sons being thus choked to death, the serpents glided on to hide themselves in the temple of Pallas, without harming any other Trojan, so that they seemed sent as ministers of divine vengeance on the priest who had thrown a spear at that consecrated image.

The cry arose that Laocoon was justly punished, and that the Horse should forthwith be taken in, as an offering grateful to the goddess. The infatuated Trojans harnessed themselves to that fatal machine, dragging it up to the town with songs and shouts of welcome, else at every jolt they might have heard the clash of arms in its hollow womb. They even broke a breach in their wall to let it pass; and, when it was stowed in the temple, all the people gave themselves up to feast and jollity, their weapons thrown aside as no longer needed, and the gates left unguarded on what was to be the last night of Troy.

With the rest had entered that false Sinon, who, as soon as darkness fell, from the highest tower made signals with a torch to the Greek fleet at Tenedos. The ships stood back to the Trojan shore, and poured out their freight of warriors to steal up to the walls, unseen and unheard by those careless revellers. While all Troy sank to sleep, heavy-headed with wine, Sinon let out the warriors hid inside the fatal Horse. They hastened to open the gates for their friends without; but that was hardly needful, since the enemy themselves had broken down their own wall; then at dead of night a sudden din roused the Trojans, alas! too late to save their city.

Æneas, become Priam's chief defence since Hector's death, was disturbed in his sleep by the pale ghost of that hero, who, all befouled by dust and blood, seemed to bid him fly, since now it was useless to fight for Troy. He started up to hear the streets alive with a tumult of clashing arms, clanging trumpets, exulting shouts, cries of amazement, entreaty, and lamentation, all mingled with the crackle of flames. He looked out to see a glare of fire spreading through his neighbours' houses, already crashing in ruin. He ran forth to meet a priest, burdened with the sacred things of his god. "Troy is no more!" exclaimed this fugitive, and breathlessly told how the Greeks were upon them.

Such as he might think only of escaping for their lives; but Æneas made rather for where the fight raged loudest, and soon fell in with a small band of his comrades, willing like himself to make a desperate stand. So confused were the deeds of darkness, that presently they became mixed up with a band of plunderers, who hailed them as Greeks and could be cut down before they saw their mistake. Taking all advantage of such disorder, Æneas and his followers hastily stripped the fallen men, to put on their shields and helmets; and thus disguised, they slew so many of the enemy, that some straggling bands fled back towards their ships or hid themselves within the Wooden Horse. On the other hand, the Trojans might well mistake these friends for foes; and when they ran to rescue Cassandra dragged along by her hair in ruthless hands, they were overwhelmed under a hail of stones flung down from the walls of a temple held against the Greeks.

The Greeks soon rallied and came swarming back; then, one by one, Æneas saw his brave comrades fall in the medley. He himself courted death in vain; but he was borne away in the throng of fighters and flyers to where, above all, a fresh uproar broke out around

Priam's palace, hotly stormed, and as hotly defended. Intent on saving the king, he made his way inside through a secret postern, then sprang towards the highest tower, already shaking under the battering of the assailants. Soon their axes burst open the gate, and in they poured, young Pyrrhus raging like a beast of prey at their head, before whom maids and matrons fled shrieking from court to court, and from chamber to chamber, in vain seeking to escape death or slavery.

The queen Hecuba and her attendants had taken refuge with Priam at his household altar, the old king encumbered with hastily donned armour and weapons he could no longer wield. Here came flying their young son Polites, hard pressed by the raging Pyrrhus, whose spear laid him dead at his father's feet. Crying out to the gods against such cruelty, Priam, beside himself for grief, with shaking hand threw a dart that jingled harmlessly on the rabid warrior's shield, and but challenged him to savage bloodshed. He dragged down the old man, butchering him at his own altar beside the body of his son.

> "And never did the Cyclops' hammers fall
> On Mars his armours, forged for proof eterne,
> With less remorse than Pyrrhus' bleeding sword
> Now falls on Priam."
>
> —*Shakespeare.*

Æneas had come in time to witness this slaughter, which he would fain have avenged. But he stood alone; and the gruesome sight recalled to him his own helpless father in peril along with his wife and child. His comrades were dead or fled; some had even leaped into the flames in the horror of despair. There was nothing for it but to turn while escape was yet open. As he sped away, the glare of the conflagration showed him Helen crouched in a porch, her face muffled from the two peoples to whom she had wrought such woe. Æneas had a mind to slay this curse of his country and hers. But between the sword and its graceless victim came a radiant apparition of his goddess-mother, who urged him forthwith to save his family, since hostile deities were invisibly upheaving the stones of Troy and stirring the conflagration kindled by Achæan hands.

Leaving Helen to face her wronged husband as she could, the son of Venus turned away with swelling heart, and under his divine mother's protection, came safe through flames and fights to his own house. But there old Anchises refused to be a burden to him: let the doughty warrior escape, taking with him his wife Creusa and his son Iulus, for whom the grandsire foretold high destinies; he himself did not care to outlive the fall of Troy; he would stay and perish like Priam, in the tide of flames that came already raging up to their doors. But the dutiful Æneas would not leave his father behind; he took the old man on his shoulders, giving him to carry the most sacred relics of the hearth, which the hero durst not touch with his own blood-stained hands. Little Iulus he led along; and Creusa followed behind. His servants he ordered to escape separately, saving what they could, and taking each his own way, a cypress-shaded temple beyond the walls being appointed as meeting-place.

Thus Æneas left his home, picking out dark and devious passages through the burning city, for he, late so fierce in fight, was afraid of every shadow now that these helpless dear ones were in danger at his side. Silently they slunk to a broken gate, but there Anchises cried that he saw the glittering arms of Greeks close at hand; then his son hurried on to plunge into the darkness outside the walls. When he ventured to halt and

look round, he missed his wife, gone astray in their confused haste; and when he reached the temple at which
they should meet, Creusa was not there.

Distracted by anxiety, Æneas left the band of fugitives and ran back to the city. Sword in hand, he dashed
through smoke and sparks, retracing the line of his flight
in a vain search for Creusa, whose name he recklessly
kept calling into the darkness. He pushed on as far as
his house, to find it on fire and full of plundering foes.
He flew to her father Priam's palace in faint hope
she might have taken shelter there. Alas! before the
temple of Hera, he saw a flock of weeping mothers and
children standing captive beside a heap of rich spoil,
guarded by Odysseus and old Phœnix. Was this the
lot of his hapless spouse; or was hers among the bleeding corpses over which he stumbled at every step? Then
suddenly she stood before him, not indeed her living
self, but a glimmering and looming shape that struck
him dumb for dread. His hair standing on end, he
listened aghast to a voice which death inspired with
prophecy.

> " Why grieve so madly, husband mine,
>   Nought here has chanced without design:
>   Fate and the Sire of all decree
>   Creusa shall not cross the sea.
>   Long years of exile must be yours;
>   Vast seas must tire your labouring oars;
>   At length Hesperia you shall gain,
>   Where through a rich and peopled plain
>   Soft Tiber rolls his tide:
>   There a new realm, a royal wife
>   Shall build again your shattered life.
>   Weep not your dear Creusa's fate,
>   Ne'er through Mycenæ's haughty gate
>   A captive shall I ride,
>   Nor swell some Grecian matron's train—

I—born of Dardan princes' strain
    To Venus' seed allied;
Heaven's mighty mother keeps me here.
Farewell, and hold our offspring dear."
               —*Conington.*

With these words, she seemed to glide away. He would have held her, throwing his arms round the beloved neck, but they clasped empty air: Creusa had vanished like a dream.

The night passed in such scenes of agitation and amazement. Day began to break as the hero, still unhurt, made his way back to that temple outside the walls, where in his absence were gathered together a band of Trojans, men, women, and children, pale in the glare of their burning homes. Already dawn showed the walls of the city guarded by its triumphant foes. The ten years' warfare was over, the decree of fate fulfilled. There being no more hope in fight, these hapless fugitives turned their backs on the ruin of Troy, and followed Æneas to the sheltering wilds of Mount Ida.

Thence they gained the seashore, to build ships and launch forth in search of the new home foretold by Creusa's shade. Seven years were they driven here and there upon the sea, for still Juno followed them with her implacable hatred of Troy, enlisting the winds and waves to war against its wandering sons, as is told in Virgil's *Æneid.* But at last, with a choice band of heroes, Æneas landed in Italy, was betrothed to Lavinia, only child of old King Latinus, slew his rival Turnus in battle, and so came to found a second Troy on the banks of the Tiber.

And what was the end of Paris, that winsome deceiver that had brought so much misery on his kin and country? Ere this last slaughter, he had been wounded by one of the fatal arrows of Hercules. While Helen made ready to throw herself at the feet of Menelaus, praying for pardon which was not denied, her ravisher, sick at heart and tormented by pain, had crept away to Mount Ida, seeking out his long-deserted wife Œnone. Her he entreated to forget the wrong he had done her, and to heal him of his mortal hurt by herbs of which she knew the secret. And some say that she did forgive him, after all, and that their old love rekindled in the forest solitudes. But others tell how she bitterly repulsed the man who had wronged her a score of years gone: "Go back to thine adulteress and die!" He turned away miserably to die in the dark woods; and there his body was found by those herdsmen that had been foster-brethren of his happier childhood.

> "One raised the Prince, one sleek'd the squalid hair,
> One kissed his hand, another closed his eyes;
> And then, remembering the gay playmate rear'd
> Among them, and forgetful of the man,
> Whose crime had half-unpeopled Ilion, these
> All that day long labour'd, hewing the pines,
> And built their shepherd-prince a funeral pile;
> And, while the star of eve was drawing light
> From the dead sun, kindled the pyre, and all
> Stood round it, hush'd, or calling on his name."
>
> —*Tennyson.*

As the flames sank and paled in the dawn, who but Œnone came wandering that way, already half-repentant of her heart's bitterness. She asked the shepherds whose ashes were here burning; and when they spoke her husband's name, with a cry she leapt upon his funeral pyre and perished in the same flames. But Helen went back unhurt to Sparta, she who had brought destruction for her dowry to Troy.

THE HOUSE OF AGAMEMNON

I. Clytemnestra

Troy had fallen; and the princes of Greece could sail away, each with his share of its spoils borne by a train of woeful captives. But many of those heroes had no joyful home-coming after so long toils and perils. Even before leaving Asia they fell out among themselves; and when they launched forth for Greece, it was to steer different courses among the Ægean isles. Some were wrecked or driven astray by a storm on the way, for Poseidon, who had aided them against his foes, was ever fickle of favour. Some came back to find themselves forgotten, or supplanted, and to fall into unnatural strife. Some never reached home, but were fain to abide upon distant shores among barbarous folk. And darkest of all was the fate of Agamemnon, king of men, whose glory had paled on the field beside the prowess of outshining heroes. Better were it for him that he had perished before Troy, like Achilles and Hector!

> " Stabbed by a murderous hand, Atrides died,
> A foul adulterer and a faithless bride."

Never had Clytemnestra forgiven her husband for consenting to the sacrifice of Iphigenia. Sister of Helen as she was, she too played false to the brother of Menelaus, and in the long absence of Agamemnon she took for her paramour Ægisthus, his kinsman unkind, who had meanly stayed back from the war. There was ancestral hatred between these two. Their fathers, Atreus and Thyestes, were brothers, yet did one another wrong to leave a legacy of revenge among their children. Ægisthus had murdered his uncle; and now he usurped his cousin's wife and kingdom, giving out among the people that Agamemnon was dead.

But well the guilty pair knew it was not so, and in fear they looked for the day when the king should come back to his own. They had laid a train of beacons that, blazing from rocky isle to isle, and from wave-washed cape to cape, should bear to Mycenæ the news that Troy was at last taken. There came the night when an exulting watchman roused them to see those signals flashing across the sea—a cheerful sight to other Greeks, but a boding message for Ægisthus and Clytemnestra, who must now face the husband so long deceived, so terrible in his wrath.

Agamemnon's approach was announced: the joyful people poured out, hailing their triumphant king; and foremost came Clytemnestra to greet her lord with feigned gladness and treacherous smiles. While he threw himself prostrate, first of all to kiss his native earth, she looked askance at the captive woman by his side, who was indeed Priam's daughter Cassandra, bowed down by the burden of slavery, and speechless among these men of strange tongue. The queen spoke falsely of forlorn distress in her husband's long tarrying afar from home, often slain by rumour, always exposed to wounds. Now she welcomed him back, as should be a hero's meed, and bid him enter his halls, in which was preparing a feast to mark this happy day.

Thanking the gods for safe return, Agamemnon crossed

a crimson carpet spread upon his threshold. One warning cry was raised by Cassandra, whose prophetic eye saw that bright web dyed with blood. No one heeded the muttering captive, taken to be crazy for grief; but she shrank back, refusing to enter the house, through whose walls pierced her gifted sight. And soon her voice was echoed by a dreadful sound from within.

Agamemnon had asked for a bath to refresh himself before the banquet; and his wife showed herself busy to serve him. But the traitress threw a mantle of web-work round his head, and quickly twisted it about his sturdy limbs ere he could see who lurked behind the door. Standing thus hooded and caught as in a net, out upon him sprang Ægisthus with an axe, to fell that lordly man like a steer, so that he sank into the silver bath filled with his own blood. Thus unworthily died the conqueror of Troy, lamented loudest by the stranger Cassandra, till she, too, perished by the queen's jealous hatred.

The people of Mycenæ hardly dared to speak their minds, when they knew the great king murdered by a tyrant whose guards held them in dread; or he bribed the elders to silence from the rich booty brought back from Troy. Ægisthus and Clytemnestra boldly avowed their deed, which they put on the score of the crime of Atreus against Thyestes. They openly proclaimed their marriage, and Ægisthus took the kingdom for his own, making nought of secret curses as of the rightful heir-ship. Agamemnon had left a son, the boy Orestes, still too young to stand up for himself. All he and his sister Electra could do was to weep in secret at a tomb raised by the hypocritical hands of that mother and stepsire before whom these children had to hide their heartfelt horror.

For them Clytemnestra had no such love as for the

vanished Iphigenia, her eldest born. Slighted and suspected in their father's house, they were as stepchildren
to their own mother. Electra, wise beyond her years,
kept her lips shut, but her eyes and ears open, so that
she came to learn how Ægisthus had in mind to kill her
brother before he should grow old enough to avenge their
unforgotten father.

The loving sister saw but one way to save the boy,
already past his twelfth year. She charged a faithful old
servant of Agamemnon with carrying off Orestes by
stealth. They fled from Mycenæ; and the young prince
found welcome and refuge with Strophius, king of Phocis,
akin to his father by marriage, out of pity, too, willing to
protect him against Ægisthus. Electra was left alone to
watch over the hero's tomb, living in her mother's family
as a slave-girl rather than a daughter, for the stepfather
would not have her find a noble husband, who also might
take on him the inheritance of hate.

Strophius had a son named Pylades, of the same age
as Orestes. These two grew up together, sharing their
sports and tasks, and coming to love one another like
true brethren—nay, better, for they cared not to be apart,
even for an hour; and, with the keenest rivalry to excel,
they kept side by side in every exercise of virtuous youth,
both surpassing all their companions, while neither could
nor would outstrip the brother of his heart. So devoted
were they to each other, through good and ill, that the
friendship of Pylades and Orestes passed into a proverb
for Greece, as in Sicily that of Damon and Pythias.

II. Orestes

The murderer of Agamemnon might well fear Orestes, whose mind was set on avenging his father, as seemed the duty of a pious son. He had no secrets from Pylades, and all their desires were as one, so in this undertaking the friends swore to stand by each other for life and death. No sooner had they reached manhood than they set out together on the deadly errand, first seeking the oracle at Delphi, that not only encouraged their purpose but counselled artful means for carrying it out.

To Mycenæ, then, they went in disguise, bearing an urn they were to give out as filled with the ashes of Orestes, that Ægisthus might believe himself safe from his blood-foe. They spent the night in pious rites at the tomb of Agamemnon; and there in the dawn they met Electra coming out to keep fresh her father's memory, cherished by her alone in the house where another had taken his seat. Years having gone by since they parted, the brother and sister did not know each other, so when these strangers declared themselves to be from Phocis, she eagerly asked for news of Orestes.

"Alas! he is no more," answered the unknown brother, little thinking how he wrung her heart; and he went on to tell a feigned tale: how Orestes had been dragged to death through an accident in a chariot race, and how they came charged to lay his ashes beside his father's. But over the urn said to contain all that was left of him, Electra broke into such a passion of grief that now he knew his sister, and had not the heart to keep her deceived. He dried her tears by declaring himself to be no other than Orestes, in proof of which he showed Agamemnon's ring she herself had placed on his finger to keep him in mind of his filial charge. With his bosom friend Pylades to aid him, and by the counsel of Apollo, he was here to slay the slayers.

Boldly they went up to the palace, and kindly were they received by Ægisthus when he heard their story of the feigned death of Orestes, the man he had such cause to dread. No welcome could be too warm for the bearers of that urn. The guests, unarmed but for hidden daggers, sat down to eat with the king and queen, while Electra made some excuse for sending away the servants. As soon as they were alone together, these strangers started to their feet, Pylades seizing Ægisthus, Orestes his mother; and out flashed the daggers.

"Remember Agamemnon! I am his son and thine. The hour of vengeance is come!"

These were the last words Clytemnestra heard as she fell by her son's hand beside the body of the usurper. The servants, rushing in at the noise, made no stir to defend their hated master, nor were the citizens loath to be rid of a tyrant; and for the moment it appeared as if Orestes might now take his father's place unchallenged.

But soon grey heads were shaken over such a deed: however guilty, a mother's blood shed by her son must surely bring a curse on the city. And when the first flush of his exultation had passed off, Orestes himself began to be moved by remorse. A malignant fate it was that had laid on him a duty so dreadful. At his mother's grave, horror came upon him, so that by turns he raved madly with wild words and glaring eyes, or lay speechless like a dead man, tended by Electra; but neither she nor Pylades could bring him back to his right mind. No other Greek would sit with him at meat, or even sleep under the same roof. Some elders of the people were for stoning him to death, that thus might be averted the anger of the gods. But the most part voted for banishment; and so was Orestes driven forth from the city, accompanied by his faithful friend and his sister.

Bitterly now he reproached the god that had spurred him on to a crime in guise of a pious office. Thereon Apollo appeared to him in a dream, bidding him go into the wilds of Arcadia, and there dree his weird for a year till he should be called before a council of the gods, that might purge him from the stain of his mother's blood. Meanwhile, abhorred by gods and men, with every door shut against him, he was given over to the Furies, to be hunted like a beast by bloodhounds of hell. Even Strophius, the father of Pylades, turned his face from his son, as sharer in the guilt of Orestes; but the youth willingly bore banishment rather than leave his friend. Electra became his wife; and they went with her brother into a savage wilderness.

For a year Orestes wandered, mad and miserable, among desert mountains, everywhere followed by the sister Eumenides, tormenting him with their scourges and torches, and haunting his restless nights in visions of dread, till he was ready to kill himself but for the loving care of Pylades and Electra. When his punishment seemed greater than he could bear, once more he sought the shrine of Apollo, and had laid upon him a heavy task to fulfil in expiation of his sin. He must sail to Tauris in the Scythian Chersonese, and from its temple carry off the image of Artemis, so jealously guarded by a rude people and a cruel king, that even to set foot on their land was death for a stranger.

Such an errand was given in answer to the frenzied prayer of Orestes—

    "O king Apollo! God Apollo! God
    Powerful to smite and powerful to preserve!

If there is blood upon me, as there seems,
Purify that black stain (thou only canst)
With every rill that bubbles from these caves
Audibly; and come willing to the work.
No; 't is not they; 't is blood; 't is blood again
That bubbles in my ear, that shakes the shades
Of thy dark groves, and lets in hateful gleams,
Bringing me . . . what dread sight! what sounds abhorr'd!
What screams! They are my mother's: 't is her eye
That through the snakes of those three furies glares,
And makes them hold their peace that she may speak.
Has thy voice bidden them all forth? There slink
Some that would hide away, but must turn back,
And others like blue lightnings bound along
From rock to rock; and many hiss at me
As they draw nearer. Earth, fire, water, all
Abominate the deed the Gods commanded!
Alas! I come to pray, not to complain;
And lo! my speech is impious as my deed!"

—*W. S. Landor.*

Agamemnon's son asked no better than thus to risk his ruined life; and Pylades was eager to share with him that perilous adventure. In a galley manned by fifty men, they set out for the cloudy shores of the Euxine Sea, whose very name made a word of ill omen.[1]

III. Iphigenia

Orestes knew not how the priestess of that Taurian shrine was no other than his eldest sister Iphigenia, carried away in his infancy from Aulis, where the Greeks would have sacrificed her to buy a fair wind. And

---

[1] The *Pontus Euxinus* (hospitable) seems to have originally had the more fitting name of "Inhospitable" ("Αξενος), changed by some such superstitious euphemism as styled the Furies *Eumenides* to avert their anger. The Scythian Chersonese (peninsula) was the Crimea, and Tauris appears to be represented by Balaclava, that has had its hecatomb of victims in modern days.

Iphigenia, long exiled to serve Artemis among barbarous folk, had heard nought of her kin and country through a score of dark years. No word came to that remote land of the fall of Troy, of the death of Agamemnon, of his son's vengeance. Often she longed for news from her old home, even to hear its once-familiar speech; and though held in honour, even reverence, by Thoas, king of Tauris, and his people, she would have welcomed any ship that might carry her back to Greece. But no Greek came to their stormy shores, unless by luckless shipwreck, for well was known the cruel custom of this people to sacrifice strangers in the temple of their goddess.

One day as its sad priestess stood gazing across the gloomy waves that made her prison, with secret horror was she brought face to face with victims for the shrine. A band of herdsmen exultingly dragged before her two youths they had caught lurking about the temple, of foreign speech and dress, and giving themselves out for castaway mariners. Her heart thrilled within her when at their first words she knew them for countrymen.

"Unhappy ones, I cannot welcome ye!" she cried in the same speech. "Know ye not the law of Tauris, that every stranger treading its soil shall be sacrificed to Artemis, and alas! by my hands?"

"How can a people that honours the gods have such barbarous laws!" exclaimed one of the captives; but his companion stood silent, with eyes fixed on the ground, or stared wildly around him as if aware of invisible foes. "We are cast on this shore by misfortune; we claim pity, shelter, aid from pious men."

"Ye must die," spoke the priestess; and the wolfish eyes of the Taurians spoke for them. "Would, indeed, that ye spake another tongue! Your names and birth-place?"

"My name is Misery," sighed the one, and said no more; while the other threw himself at her feet, praying for mercy, like a man to whom life was dear.

"This much stands in my power," answered the priestess. "The king will consent to release one victim at my entreaty, but the blood of one is demanded as offering to the goddess. Which of you shall go back to Greece to tell the fate of his comrade?"

"Let me die, who care not to live," murmured the downcast captive.

"Nay," cried the other eagerly, "send my friend home, for I have sworn never to abandon him."

"He is worthy to live, as so am not I!"

"Hear him not! He is the last of a great race; and you know not what a stock must perish in his death."

"To me, then, death is lighter by far. None will weep for me; but this man has a new-married wife, and parents living to mourn his loss. Spare their grey hairs and the helplessness of his unborn son!"

"Strange pair, who are ye?" asked Iphigenia, moved by the warmth with which these two friends seemed to court death, each for the other's sake.

"I am Orestes, son of Agamemnon, hateful to gods and men since these hands shed my mother's blood."

"I am Pylades, who aided his friend thus to avenge the great Agamemnon."

A cry rose to the lips of the priestess, as she heard that it was her brother who stood before her, praying for death rather than life. It was all she could do to hold herself back from falling into his arms under the eyes of the Taurians, who stood by in watchful suspicion for this talk in an unknown tongue. Hastily she questioned Pylades, and from him was amazed to learn how Agamemnon died, and how Clytemnestra, and what penance had been laid on Orestes, soul-sick to madness for such a crime.

Could she bear to see slain, to slay with her own hand, the brother she had nursed as an infant, or the friend so devoted to him in his evil plight? In her heart she planned to save both those generous youths; but before her barbarian acolytes, thirsting for their blood, she would not trust herself to let Orestes know who she was. Dissembling her inward feelings for the time, she haughtily ordered the captives to be led to prison in bonds.

There they lay lamentably, looking for nothing but death together, each blaming himself for having betrayed the other by some avowal that had changed the merciful mood of that priestess. But at the dead of night their dungeon door was opened, and in stole Iphigenia, no longer with stern voice and threatening mien. Alone beside the Greeks, she told them her name and birth; and now in turn Orestes had the amazement to hear that his sister still lived, while she for the first time learned all the woes that had fallen on her father's home.

But they had to think of present danger rather than of that troubled past. The Taurians were clamouring for the sacrifice of the prisoners; and Iphigenia told with a shudder how it was her duty to officiate at this cruel rite, most hateful even were the victims not of kindred blood and speech. When she heard that they had a stout and well-manned galley waiting for them on the shore, her ready wit devised a way of escape. She went to the king with horrified looks: these captives, she declared, were outcasts so deeply stained in guilt that they would bring pollution to the temple of her chaste goddess. Before they could be rendered an acceptable offering, she must purify them with sea water that washes away all offence of man; and the image of Artemis, too, must be cleansed from the taint brought upon it by the very sight of such malefactors.

The unsuspicious king let it be so, for he had come to look up to the foreign priestess as an oracle. While he and his chiefs stayed at the temple, making ready for that sacrifice, Iphigenia went down to the shore alone, bearing the sacred image, and leading the two prisoners by a cord that bound them fast together. Then soon from the cliffs above rang out a cry of alarm, when a strange ship was seen making out to sea, carrying off victims, priestess, and image.

Men ran to tell Thoas, who wrathfully bid launch his swiftest galleys in pursuit, and from the cliffs would have hurled stones and darts on the fugitives, tugging hard at their oars, against the wind and tide that washed them back towards the shore. But lo! a dazzling light blinded the king's eyes, and from high overhead pealed out the voice of Pallas-Athene.

"Thoas, it is the will of heaven that these strangers shall go free; for my sister Artemis can no longer dwell among a barbarous people that honour her with human bloodshed! When ye have learned to think more nobly of the gods, she will return. Till then a new shrine is provided for her and her priestess in my own chosen seat, that famed city of the violet crown."

The Taurians heard with trembling, and now did not dare to stay the Grecian ship. So Iphigenia brought the image to Athens, to be there worshipped more worthily. And there, when his year's penance was up, the Areopagus was appointed as her brother's place of judgment, to which he came still led by the Furies, those stern ministers of Nemesis.

In the temple of Pallas was the court held, a solemn array of gods sitting in the likeness of old men. On his knees at the altar, as beseemed a suppliant, Orestes told his story without deceit, making his plea for mercy on the score of a father's death set against a mother's. The votes were taken by white and black stones cast into an urn. When they came to be counted, white and black, for pardon or punishment, were equal in number. Orestes covered his eyes, and the Furies made ready to throw themselves on their victim.

"Stay!" cried Pallas, appearing in her own form. "My vote is still to come."

She cast a white stone into the urn; and beneath her ægis held above his head Orestes rose a free man, while the angry Furies sank howling into the earth.

Thus absolved, the avenger of Agamemnon went home to Argos, where now the people welcomed him to his father's kingdom. They say that he married Hermione, the daughter of Menelaus and Helen, after winning her in mortal combat from the son of Achilles, to whom she had been betrothed. And so these two fought out the quarrel of their sires, a generation after so much blood began to flow for that false queen's fatal beauty.

THE ADVENTURES OF ODYSSEUS

I. His Perilous Voyage Homewards

A much-tried hero was he who had left his island home so unwillingly for the ten years' war, then, after Troy had fallen, was ten years on a wandering way back. All those years his faithful wife Penelope waited patiently for news of him, while their son Telemachus grew up to hopeful manhood without having known his father. Meantime, persecuted by Poseidon but protected by the care of Pallas, Odysseus went from one misadventure to another, brought about now by adverse fortune, now by his own fault, again by the folly of his men, who perished here and there miserably; but on their captain the gods took pity, and at last let him reach Ithaca, where he found his house given up to greedy neighbours, wasting his substance and persecuting his wife to choose one of them in place of the husband taken for dead.

> " The fate of every chief beside
> Who fought at Troy is known:
> It is the will of Jove to hide
> His untold death alone.
>
> " And how he fell can no man tell;
> We know not was he slain
> In fight on land by hostile hand,
> Or plunged beneath the main."
> —*Maginn's Homeric Ballads.*

When he set sail homewards with a small fleet of

ships, at the very outset Odysseus and his company ran
into mishap. Not content with the glory and the spoils
they had won at Troy, they must needs land on the coast
of the fierce Cicons, whose town they plundered and
held a feast on the booty. Their prudent leader was
for making off at once; but his careless crews sat gorging
and swilling, till the Cicons came back upon them
with a fresh force of warriors from the inland parts of
their country. The carousing Greeks had to stand to
arms for a battle that lasted all day, then at evening
were fain to escape on board their ships, with the loss of
several men from each crew.

Putting out to sea, they must next contend with winds
and waves, more ruthless enemies than men. They had
nothing for it but to run before a storm that drove them
out of their course and tore their sails to tatters. On the
tenth day they made an unknown land, where, going on
shore for fresh water, Odysseus sent three scouts to spy
out the people of the country. These were the Lotos-
eaters, living on a plant named lotos, which so dazed
their senses that they cared for nothing but dreamy idleness, in the languid air of that land, "where all things
always seemed the same", and no stranger had the heart
to move away from it who had once tasted its flowery
food, freely offered by those "mild-eyed melancholy
Lotos-eaters".

> " Branches they bore of that enchanted stem,
> Laden with flower and fruit, whereof they gave
> To each, but whoso did receive of them,
> And taste, to him the gushing of the wave
> Far, far away did seem to mourn and rave
> On alien shores; and if his fellow spake,
> His voice was thin, as voices from the grave;
> And deep-asleep he seem'd, yet all awake,
> And music in his ears his beating heart did make.

" They sat them down upon the yellow sand,
 Between the sun and moon upon the shore;
 And sweet it was to dream of Father-land,
 Of child, and wife, and slave; but evermore
 Most weary seemed the sea, weary the oar,
 Weary the wandering fields of barren foam.
 Then some one said, ' We will return no more';
 And all at once they sang, ' Our island home
 Is far beyond the wave; we will no longer roam '."
         —Tennyson.

The messengers sent forward had alone tasted of that entrancing food. But when Odysseus saw what a spell it worked on these men, he had them dragged away by force and tied fast on the benches of the ships, while the rest of the crews he hurried on board before they should fall under the same charm, to be bound for ever to a life of inglorious ease.

Toiling at their oars, they left the Lotos land behind, and crossed the sea to fall upon perils of another sort on a rugged shore overhung by the smoke of fiery mountain tops. Here dwelt the Cyclopes, a race of hideous and barbarous giants that neither planted nor ploughed, but lived on their half-tamed flocks and on herbs that grow wild; nor did they hold any intercourse with other peoples, having no use of sail or oar. Even in form they were strangely monstrous, each having one huge eye flaming across his forehead; and in nature they were cruelly fearsome as their looks. At an island hard by, Odysseus left his ships safely beached, all but one, with which he himself stood across to the rocky coast of the Cyclopes.

As he was coasting along, there came to view a deep cave, its dark mouth overhung by shrubs, above a yard walled in with rough stones and tree trunks as a fold for sheep and goats. Here was the home of a Cyclops named Polyphemus, so inhuman that he chose to live

apart even from his fierce fellows. Drawn ashore by
curiosity, the bold hero had a mind to explore this
gloomy haunt. His ship left hauled up on the beach
to await his return, with twelve of the bravest men
picked for companions, he climbed to the mouth of the
cave, carrying some food in a wallet, and also a goatskin full of rich wine which he had brought away from
Troy, now to serve him better than he knew.

When they reached the cave, they found it full of
lambs and kids penned up within, along with piles of
cheeses and great vessels of milk and curds. The giant
being out on the hills where he herded his flock, these
strangers made bold to feast on his stores; then the men
were for making off before he came back; but now it
was their leader's turn to be reckless, and he waited to
see the owner of such wealth, in hope to find him not
less generous than rich. Bitterly was he to repent of his
rashness.

At nightfall Polyphemus came home, shaking the
ground under his tread, and flinging down a crashing
stack of firewood from his broad back as he darkened
the mouth of the cave. The very sight of this one-eyed
monster was enough to scare his unbidden guests into
its deepest recess. When he had driven all the ewes and
she-goats inside, he closed the entrance with a rock that
would make a load for a score of wagons; then before
turning in the mothers to their young, he milked them
for his own use, setting aside part of the milk to make
cheese, and keeping part for his supper. Last, he lit a
fire, the glare of which soon disclosed those trembling
lookers-on.

"Who are ye?" he bellowed. "Pirates, or traders,
or what?"

Odysseus alone had heart to answer, and told his tale

of how they were on their way home from Troy, appealing for hospitality in the name of Zeus, the protector of helpless travellers. Polyphemus, laughing scornfully at the notion that the like of him cared for gods or men, asked where their ship was moored, which Odysseus, cunning as well as bold, knew better than to tell, but would have him believe that they had been wrecked on his coast. Without another word, the greedy giant snatched up two of the men at random, to dash them on the ground and devour their bleeding carcasses, washed down by mighty gulps of milk, after which he stretched himself out to sleep.

But there could be no sleep for his luckless prisoners, fearfully aware of the same horrible fate awaiting them in turn. Odysseus thought of falling on the heavy-headed monster with his sword; but how then could they move the stone that barred the entrance? When daylight began to peep in, the giant rolled it away with ease; but when he had driven out his flocks, he carefully put it back, shutting up those captives as if by a lid clapped to. And the first thing he had done on getting up was to grab two more of them for his breakfast.

All day the rest lay there in quaking dread, but their artful captain was scheming out a plan to get the better of that cruel host. Within the cave he had left lying a great club of olive-wood, big enough to be the mast of a ship. The end of this Odysseus cut off, and made his men sharpen it to a point and harden it in the fire; then he hid it away in the dirt that lay thick over the floor. Lots were cast for four men to help him in handling such an unwieldy weapon; and the lot fell on the very four he would have wished for strong and stout-hearted comrades.

Again the giant came back at evening; again he

milked his flock; and again he caught up two of the sailors to make a cannibal feast. Then Odysseus brought to him a bowl of dark-red wine, filled from his goat-skin, humbly offering it as a drink fit to wash down the heartiest supper. Polyphemus tasted, smacked his lips, drank down every drop, and asked for more, promising the giver something in return for a liquor which, he declared, was far better than any made in his country.

"What is thy name?" he cried, as three times the bowl was filled for him and emptied.

"My name," quoth the sly Odysseus, "is Noman. What gift hast thou for me who offer thee such noble wine?"

"Be this thy reward, then!" hiccoughed the drunken giant. "I will eat up thy fellows first, and Noman last of all."

With that he rolled over on the ground, stretching himself out to snore off the fumes of the wine. As soon as he was fast asleep, Odysseus heated in the fire the sharp stake he had made ready; then with four men bearing a hand, he suddenly drove it into the monster's eye, turning it round to be quenched in bubbling and hissing blood.

The blinded Cyclops got to his feet with such howls of rage and pain that his assailants fled out of reach, but in vain now he groped and stumbled about to catch them. The outcry he made before long brought up his neighbour giants in haste to the entrance of his cave, where they could be heard tramping and shouting through the darkness.

"What ails thee, Polyphemus, to disturb us with such a din at dead of night? Who is hurting thee in sleep? Who is driving away thy flocks?"

"Noman is robbing me! Noman is attacking me

in sleep!" bawled the furious giant; then his neighbours stalked away with surly growls, taking it that he must be unwell, and might be left to his prayers for help.

So far, so good; but for the plotters crouching at the back of the cave now came the question how they were to leave it safely. Their groaning jailer, indeed, pushed away the stone, but he sat down at the entrance, stretching his hands across it to catch them when they should try to slip out, for he thought these men as stupid as himself. But Odysseus had another trick in his bag. With osier withs he tied together the big rams by threes, a man fastened hidden among their fleecy bodies. The biggest and woolliest ram he took for himself to cling on to, face upwards, below its belly.

As soon as it was light, the rams pressed out to their pasture, their master feeling their backs as they passed, with fearful threats against that scoundrel. Noman who had worked him such a mischief. But one by one the prisoners slipped undetected through his fumbling clutches; then, once got well outside, Odysseus untied his comrades, and, driving along the pick of the flock, they hastened down to the shore, to be joyfully received by their shipmates, who had given them up for lost.

Hurriedly they put their booty on board and were launching from the beach, when Odysseus in his exultation raised a shout that brought the giant out on the cliffs, where he stood like some tall peak reared in the smoky air. Tearing up a mass of crag, and taking aim at the voice, he blindly hurled it so close to the ship as almost to crush her, and the wash of it would have swirled her back to shore, had not Odysseus sheered off with a pole, while his men needed no bidding to row their hardest. As they pulled away, in vain they begged him to be silent; he could not keep in the satisfaction of taunting that inhuman monster that had murdered his comrades.

"Cyclops, eater of men, if any ask who put out that eye of thine, to make thee uglier than ever, say it was done by no less a hand than that of Odysseus the Ithacan!"

At that Polyphemus gave a dreadful groan, for it had been prophesied to him that he should lose his sight at the hands of this very Odysseus he had so little suspected in the castaway guest. There he stood as long as they could hear him, breathing after them curses that were not lost on the wind. For this monster, barbarous as he was, had no less a father than Neptune, to whom he now prayed for calamity and destruction on those hateful strangers; and Poseidon would hear his prayer. But the last stone the giant threw, largest of all, raised a swell that carried them out of his reach; then safely they reached the isle where the other ships lay awaiting their return.

Before setting sail, Odysseus feasted his men on the Cyclops' fat sheep; and the goodliest of all he sacrificed as a thankoffering for his escape, vainly hoping to propitiate the heavenly powers that were already brewing mischief against him.

> "So till the sun fell we did drink and eat,
> And all night long beside the billows lay,
> Till blush'd the hills 'neath morning's rosy feet;
> Then did I bid my friends, with break of day,
> Loosen the hawsers, and each bark array;
> Who take the benches, and the whitening main
> Cleave with the sounding oars, and sail away.
> So from the isle we part, not void of pain,
> Right glad of our own lives, but grieving for the slain."
>   —*Worsley.*

The next land they made was the floating island of
Æolus, king of the Winds, where they found no lack
of hospitable entertainment. Æolus and his sons were
keen to hear about the siege of Troy, that filled all the
world with rumour, so they kept those welcome guests
for a whole month of eating, drinking, and talking.
When at length Odysseus grew restless to continue his
voyage, Æolus did him a rare favour by tying up all
the winds but one for him in an ox-hide bag, which
he might carry on board. Only the gentle west wind
did he leave free to waft the ships straight to Ithaca.

They sailed on, then, for nine days on a smooth sea,
and had at last come so close to their native island that
already they could see fires glowing on its shore as if
to beacon them home. All that time Odysseus had
never left the helm, so eager was he to greet his wife
and son; now he lay down to rest, believing himself
out of all peril. But while he slept, his crew put their
heads together, asking one another what treasure could
be hid in that bag on which their leader kept so close
an eye. Making sure it must be full of gold and silver,
they opened it to look, then out flew the howling winds
that in a trice drove them back from their haven, tossed
upon stormy gusts stirred from all quarters at once.

Odysseus had almost thrown himself into the sea,
when he awoke to learn what his foolish men had done;
and they too repented bitterly of their meddlesomeness,
for now the conflicting tempests carried them helplessly
back to the island of Æolus. There disembarking, their
leader explained how it had gone with him; but this
time he found the king of the Winds in no generous
mood.

"Begone, ill-starred wretch!" was his reply. "I
have no more help for him who is abhorred of heaven."

There was nothing for it but to put out to sea again, and row on at a venture, for now every wind failed them. For a week they toiled in a dead calm, and on the seventh day made the rocky harbour of the Læstrygonians, where most of the ships entered to moor themselves in a row; but Odysseus was heedful enough to tie up his own vessel to a rock outside, whence he climbed a point to spy out the land. And he did wisely, for this people, too, turned out to be cannibal giants, who flocked down in crowds to crush the ships under a shower of rocks and spear the poor sailors like fishes, so that every one of those venturing in went to feed such cruel ogres. In the nick of time, Odysseus himself cut his cable, and his men rowed off for their lives, amid the splash of rocks the Læstrygonians pelted at them till they were clear of that fatal haven.

This one crew, thus far lucky, but sad for the loss of their comrades, held on till they reached another island, so tired that on coming to shore they lay two days without being able to stir or caring to know who lived here. It was indeed the home of the fell enchantress Circe, sister of Medea, a place to which the Argonauts had found their way years before. Not till the third day did the doughty Odysseus rouse himself to mount a hill behind, coming back with a fine stag he had killed for dinner, and news that he had seen smoke rising from a thick wood to show the island inhabited.

Their misfortunes having made them prudent, they now divided themselves into two equal bands, under the captain and his lieutenant Eurylochus, the one to stay by the ship, the other to go forward in search of the natives. Lots were cast in a helmet, and it fell to

Eurylochus to take this dangerous quest, so off he set with twenty-two men, fearful of coming into the clutches of some other ogre, while their comrades were left behind lamenting over them as if never to be seen again.

And on reaching that wood to which the smoke guided them, in the middle of it the explorers saw a fine stone house, guarded, to their dismay, by a troop of lions and wolves; nor were they less troubled when these fierce beasts ran up frisking and fawning about them like dogs, wagging their tails and rubbing their noses against the sailors as if in friendly welcome. Since none of the beasts offered to bite, the men presently took heart and went forward till they could hear a woman's voice singing within as she worked at her loom. Out she came at their call, and kindly bid them enter, as they did, all but Eurylochus, who hung about outside in cautious suspicion. And well that was for him, since the enchantress entertained his mates with bewitched meat and drink on which they fell like pigs, and soon ran out scampering, grunting and squealing, every one of them turned into a bristly hog by a stroke of her wand, to join the lions and wolves that had all been men transformed by her spells. Eurylochus only waited to see them penned up in sties, fed with acorns and beechnuts; then he fled back to the ship, in too great consternation to have breath or words for at once telling what had happened.

The others having at last got the story out of him, Odysseus snatched up his sword and bow, for he was no leader to leave his men in such a plight. He bid Eurylochus go along to show the way, but as he flatly refused to risk being turned into a pig, the hero set out by himself. Then he had not gone far when he fell in

with a noble youth, whose errand was to give him friendly
warning.

> "On his bloomy face
> Youth smil'd celestial, with each opening grace.
> He seiz'd my hand and gracious thus began:
> 'Ah! whither roam'st thou, much enduring man?
> O blind to fate! What led thy steps to rove
> The horrid mazes of this magic grove?
> Each friend you seek in yon inclosure lies,
> All lost their form, and habitants of sties.
> Think'st thou by wit to model their escape?
> Sooner shalt thou, a stranger to thy shape,
> Fall prone their equal: first thy danger know:
> Then take the antidote the gods bestow.
> The plant I give, through all the direful bower
> Shall guard thee, and avert the evil hour.
> Now hear her wicked arts. Before thy eyes,
> The bowl shall sparkle and the banquet rise.
> Take this, nor from the faithless feast abstain;
> For temper'd drugs and poison shall be vain.
> Soon as she strikes her wand, and gives the word,
> Draw forth and brandish thy refulgent sword,
> And menace death: those menaces shall move
> Her alter'd mind to blandishment and love.' "[1]

This was in truth the god Hermes, sent by the guardian care of Athene; and the charm he gave to Odysseus
was the sacred herb *moly*, that has a black root but a milk-
white flower, and can be plucked only by celestial hands
—an antidote to keep men safe against all the spells of
Circe.

In spite of the god's assurance, it was with misgiving
the hero drew near that house of enchantment, and called
out its mistress. She invited him in, set him on a lordly
seat and gave him a golden goblet full of honey, meal,
and wine, mixed with her magical drugs. No sooner
had he drunk than she struck him with her wand, crying

---

[1] As in the case of the *Iliad*, translations not otherwise marked are from Pope.

"Off to the sty with your mates!" But the virtue of
the herb *moly* was stronger than her potion; and Odysseus
not only kept his feet, but, as Hermes had bid him, drew
his sword upon Circe, making as if he would kill her.
Amazed and terrified, she fell down to clasp his knees,
praying for mercy.

"Who art thou, proof to my spells?—surely no other
than the great Odysseus! Sheathe thy sword, and let
us be loving friends."

Odysseus would not trust this witch till he had made
her swear by the gods to do him no harm; nor would he
eat in her house till she agreed to undo the spell she had
laid on his men. Forthwith she anointed the pigs with
a balm that rid them in a trice of their bristles, and they
stood up taller and manlier than ever. After this proof
of goodwill, Odysseus fetched the rest of the crew to
share her hospitality, though he had to threaten Eurylochus with death before the lieutenant would again
venture himself in Circe's power.

But now she was all smiles and bounty. Bathed,
anointed, and dressed in fresh clothes, the weary sailors
were set down to a good dinner. So well did they fare,
that they were content to stay with her for days and
weeks and months, fattening like pigs in manlike form,
while they forgot all the perils and hardships gone by;
and the charms of Circe made Odysseus forget how
Penelope would be awaiting him at home.

II. From Circe's Isle to Calypso's

Thus a whole year passed by in careless ease for those
wanderers that had escaped the arms of the Cicons, and
the snare of the Lotos land, and the maw of the Cyclops,
and the giant Læstrygonians, and the cruelty of winds

and waves stirred up against them. But in the end the sailors grew tired of having nothing to do but eating and drinking and sleeping off their gluttony; then they moved Odysseus to break away from the too dear delights of this enchanted isle. It was time to be off, said they, if ever they were to see their wives and children again.

So now at last the hero roused himself as from a dream. Taking Circe in a favourable mood, he let her know how his men were longing to get home; and she did not turn a deaf ear to his prayer. Not her will but the decree of fate, she said, kept him back. So far from now refusing to let her guests go, she showed herself ready to speed them with guidance and advice. But to their dismay, she told them that they must first sail for Hades, there to seek counsel from the ghost of the blind prophet Tiresias, who even among the dead was counted wise above his fellows.

Bold as he was against earthly foes, Odysseus might well shrink from nearing the abode of the dead, and his men bemoaned themselves as already lost; but there was nothing else for it. Circe took leave of them kindly, gave them directions how to steer for that gloomy haven, and put on board a ram and a ewe for sacrifice to the powers of the under world. So with many misgivings they put to sea again, all but one, the youngest and most foolish of the crew, Elpenor, who, sleeping off a fit of drunkenness on the housetop, when roused by the bustle of departure had jumped up in such a flurry that he tumbled over to break his neck and go straight to Hades without more ado.

Away they sailed before a fair wind raised by Circe, that as darkness fell brought their ship into the deep water of Oceanus, where dwell the Cimmerians in endless night. Here drawing to land, they went on foot along the shore as far as a rock, beneath which the rivers Phlegethon, Cocytus, and Styx rush together. At this weird spot, as the enchantress had bidden, they dug a deep trench, and over it cut the throats of the sacrificed victims, so that the blood ran into it; and Odysseus poured libations of honey and milk and wine, all sprinkled with barley meal, calling on the name of Tiresias, for whom he promised his best heifer, with other worthy offerings, as soon as he got safe to Ithaca. When the pale shades sniffed the blood, they came crowding up from every nook of Hades, eager to get a taste of life.

" All the ghosts of the dead departed from the Nether Dusk 'gan fare.
  And brides there were and younglings, and burdened elders there,
  And there were tender maidens still bearing newborn woe,
  And many a man death-smitten by the brazen spear did go,
  The very prey of Ares, yet clad in blood-stained gear;
  And all the throng kept flitting round the pit from here and there
  With strange and awful crying, till pale fear fell on me.
  So therewith I bade my fellows, and urged them eagerly
  That the sheep that lay there slaughtered by the pitiless brass they
        should flay,
  And make them a burnt offering, and so to the Gods to pray;
  Unto Hades the almighty and the dread Persephone."
                                                    —*W. Morris.*

Odysseus had to draw his sword to keep back all other ghosts from the blood till Tiresias should have answered his summons. The first that pressed forward was young Elpenor, the latest come to Hades, flitting about disconsolate because his body still lay unburied at the halls of Circe; but he took cheer when his captain promised to burn it and build a tomb for him, and set up as a monument the oar at which the youngster had tugged in life. Next, to the further side of the trench came Anticleia, mother of Odysseus, whom he had left alive when he sailed for Troy, and knew not till now of her death; but though he saw her with tears, his sword held his own mother back from the trench over which she stretched her shadowy arms. At last came the blind Theban Tiresias, leaning on his golden staff; and he first was let stoop to drink that blood that gave him voice to prophesy as of old.

"Odysseus," quoth he, "thy homecoming will be no halcyon voyage, since Neptune bears a spite against the man that blinded his Cyclops son. Yet all may go well if, when ye reach the Trinacrian shore, ye harm not the herds of the Sun that pasture there. But to slay them will bring wreck on ships and men; and if thou thyself should escape in sorry plight, it will be to find thy house full of trouble. And in the end death will come to thee from the sea."

Other charges he gave for the hero to treasure in mind; then Tiresias went back to his place, and the mother of Odysseus in turn might come forward to taste the blood and in the strength of it speak to her son, eagerly asking how he came to Hades while still alive. Not less eagerly did he ask for news of home, and heard that Anticleia had died of grief for his absence, but that his father Laertes was still on earth in feeble and woeful age, and that Penelope his wife never ceased to await him with tears. Moved by the very sight of her, thrice he would have embraced the mournful ghost; but each time she melted out of his arms like a dream.

And now thronged round him many a shade, all so wild for a taste of blood, that again he had to threaten them with his sword, letting one only drink and speak at a time. Many a fair woman he beheld, and many a famous hero, among them his comrades at the siege of Troy. What was his amazement to recognize Agamemnon, so mighty of limb, now flitting among the feeble ghosts, and to hear from him how, after escaping all chances of war and weather, he had been done to death at home by his false wife! But when that king of men asked after his son Orestes, Odysseus could tell him nothing of the youth's hatching revenge against his father's foes. It was not so when Achilles came to view, for in him the living man was able to breathe a flush of pride by relating the deeds of Neoptolemus, a son worthy of his sire. That was one spark of cheer to the hero, who had so little joy in his own fate that when Odysseus saluted him as a king among the shades, the once high-souled Achilles made bitter answer—

> "Talk not of ruling in this dolorous gloom,
> Nor think vain words, he cried, can ease my doom.
> Rather I'd choose laboriously to bear
> A weight of woes, and breathe the vital air,
> A slave to some poor hind that toils for bread,
> Than reign the sceptred monarch of the dead!"

Other old friends he hailed, yea, and foes: Ajax for one frowned on him, remembering their rivalry even in death; and when Odysseus would have appeased him, the resentful ghost turned away without a word. Great ones of old he saw, Minos and Orion and Hercules; also arrant sinners, Tantalus and Sisyphus groaning in their endless torment, and Tityus stretched out upon roods of ground for a deathless vulture to prey upon his vitals. But so thick grew the crowd of doleful ghosts, and so loud their lamentation, that soon Odysseus turned away with a shudder, fearing to come face to face with the very Gorgon if he tarried longer. Back he sped to his ship, and bade the men be quick to unmoor from this dark haven of the dead.

With a will they rowed down the Ocean river, that took them into the open sea; and here again the wind

was fair to waft them back to Circe's isle. There the
first thing they did was to burn and entomb the body
of young Elpenor, that his soul might have rest among
the shades. Again the enchantress gave them friendly
entertainment; but Odysseus she drew aside to learn
how he had fared in Hades, and to ply him with warnings against the further perils of his course.

And well her warnings served him when they again
took the sea, still with a favouring wind that soon
brought them to the isle of the Sirens, those sisters of
enticing song. So sweetly they sang that all who heard
them were drawn on shore to where they sat in a field
of flowers, blooming among the bones of men thus lured
to their death. But on Circe's counsel, before they
came within earshot, Odysseus stopped the ears of his
men with wax, and made them bind himself fast to the
mast, charging them by no means to unloose him, however he might beg or command when his ears were
filled with the fatal voices.

Thus prepared, winged by their oars they flew past
the beach on which could be seen the Siren Sisters, and
over the waters came their tempting strains, heard by
the captain alone.

> " Come, pride of Achaia, Odysseus, draw nigh us!
>   Come, list to our chant, rest the oar from its rowing:
> Never yet was there any whose galley fled by us,
>   But, sweet as the drops from the honeycomb flowing,
>   Our voices enthralled him, and stayed his ongoing,
> And he passed from that rapture more wise than aforetime:
>   For we know all the toil that in Troyland befell,
> When the will of the Gods was wrought out in the war-time:
>   Yea, all that is done on the earth can we tell."
>   —*A. S. Way.*

Their song so thrilled his heart that Odysseus
struggled hard to get loose, and by cries and signs

would have bidden his men undo the cords; but they tied him up all the tighter, and deaf to him as to the Siren music, rowed their best till they were far out of hearing.   Then only they unbound him, and took the wax from their ears; and for once the Sirens had sung in vain.

But, that peril hardly passed, another arose before them where the waters boiled with a fierce roaring that made the men drop their oars, staring aghast into the smother of spray and foam.   It was all Odysseus could do to hearten them for rowing on, and he durst not tell them the worst he had learned from Circe of this fearful passage, beset by two monsters hungering for the lives of luckless mariners.   For now they must tug swiftly and steer deftly between the two rocks, no more than a bow-shot apart.   Under the lower rock was prisoned Charybdis, hateful daughter of Poseidon, that three times a day belched out a whirlpool, and three times sucked it back with all that came into its resistless gulp. Still more dreadful was the opposite den of Scylla.

" High in the air the rock its summit shrouds
  In brooding tempests and in rolling clouds.
  Loud storms around, and mists eternal, rise,
  Beat its bleak brow, and intercept the skies.
  When all the broad expansion, bright with day,
  Glows with th' autumnal or the summer ray,
  The summer and the autumn glow in vain.
  The sky for ever lowers: for ever clouds remain.
  Impervious to the step of man it stands,
  Though borne by twenty feet, though arm'd with twenty hands.
  Smooth as the polish of the mirror rise
  The slippery sides, and shoot into the skies.
  Full in the centre of this rock display'd
  A yawning cavern casts a dreadful shade:
  Nor the fleet arrow from the twanging bow,
  Sent with full force, could reach the depth below."

The ravenous creature that haunted here was, men say, a daughter of the sea-god Phorcys, on whom a jealous witch had worked woe, mixing in her bath maleficent herbs to change her into a twelve-footed and six-headed monster, greedy to prey on all that came within reach of her yelping jaws and rows of gnashing teeth. Circe had advised Odysseus to make no show of fight against such a fell foe; but he, ever too venturesome, put on his armour and took his stand at the prow as if to defy that cruel hag. Keenly scanning the rock well, at first he could see nothing of her as they shot through the gloomy strait; but when they shrank away from the yawning mouth of Charybdis to hug the opposite side, suddenly she darted out her six heads, and in a trice Odysseus saw six of his best men snatched up into the air, screaming and stretching their hands for help in vain, as she hauled them into the mouth of the cave: never in all his adventures did he see a more grisly sight!

But with that they were quit of danger, for now the scared sailors rowed clear through those jaws of death; and soon they saw loom ahead the great three-cornered island, on which they could hear the lowing and bleating of the Sun-god's herds. Mindful of warnings given him both by Tiresias and by Circe, Odysseus ordered his crew to row on without touching here; but they, weary of hard toil, would no longer obey, and Eurylochus insolently spoke for the others that, not being made of iron, they must go on shore for a night's rest. Odysseus had to give way; yet, before mooring in a harbour they found on the rocky coast, he made them all take a solemn oath not to meddle with the god's cattle; then they landed to cook their supper and to sleep away their grief for those six comrades so miserably lost.

Next morning they should have been off betimes, had not a sudden tempest risen through the night, in face of which they durst not put out to sea; and for a whole month blew contrary winds to keep them imprisoned on the island. Soon came to an end the corn and wine with which Circe had provisioned them; then the men wandered here and there, trying to catch fish or snare birds; and many a hungry eye was cast on the fat herds of the Sun-god which they had sworn not to touch.

They seemed like to starve, when Odysseus sought a solitary place in which to pray to the gods alone. While his back was turned, the mutinous Eurylochus stirred up the rest to lay hands on the sacred cattle, for, said he, no god could send them a punishment worse than dying by inches of famine. On coming back, their captain was startled by the smell of roast meat, and to his wrathful dismay he found the sailors gorging themselves on carcasses which they had butchered in guise of a sacrifice. It was too late for him to forbid, nor did his greedy men heed the prodigies that appeared to rebuke their crime, for the very hides of the dead beasts rose and walked, and the joints on the spits lowed as if still alive. For a week they kept up the impious banquet, in spite of all entreaty or warning; till at last came a blink of fine weather to tempt them to their doom.

Meanwhile, Hyperion the Sun-god had made loud complaint in heaven, threatening to forsake the sky and to shine henceforth down in Hades among the dead, unless he were granted vengeance upon those insolent men that had ravaged his beloved herds. Zeus appeased him by promising swift punishment; and Poseidon had kept an angry eye on that crew ever since the blinding of his Cyclops son. So no sooner were they out of sight of land, than the storm burst upon them afresh. The first squall blew out their mast to crush the steersman in its toppling over; and as the broken hulk tossed ungoverned upon the waves, from the dark sky shot a thunderbolt that shivered it to pieces.

Every man was swallowed up by the raging sea, save only Odysseus, who contrived to catch hold of the mast, and to tie it with other wreckage, making a raft on which he floated back towards Scylla and Charybdis. Here he was like to have been sucked down, but he caught hold of a fig tree that overhung the rock of Charybdis, and held on till the raft bobbed up below his feet, vomited out again by the black whirlpool. Once more clinging to it he drifted away; and for nine days was carried by winds and waves, whither he knew not, till the tenth night washed his raft on shore.

The hero came thus stranded on the island of Ogygia, where dwelt the divine nymph Calypso, daughter of Atlas. She, like Circe, was an enchantress, but her charms lay in lovely looks and loving eyes; and her wooded island home was as beautiful as its mistress. To a shipwrecked mariner the grotto in which she lived might well seem a blessed haven.

> " Around, thick groves their summer-dress
> Wore in luxuriant loveliness—
> Alder and poplar quiver'd there,
> And fragrant cypress tower'd in air.
> And there broad-pinion'd birds were seen,
> Nesting amid the foliage green;
> Birds, which the marge of ocean haunt—
> Gull, prating daw, and cormorant;
> And there, the deep mouth of the cave
> Fringing, the cluster'd vine-boughs wave.

Sprung from near sources, bright and gay
Four limpid fountains urge their way
Divergent, o'er the parsley'd mead,
Where the sweet violet droops its head—
A scene, should gods survey the sight,
E'en gods might gaze on with delight!"
                                    —*Wrangham.*

To this solitary abode Calypso welcomed Odysseus with kindness, soon warming into love for the guest who, time‑worn and toil‑scarred, was still a goodly man in her soft eyes. So well she loved him that she would have him never leave the island; and at first the hero was content to rest here from his weary wanderings. So months sped by, and years, as in a dream. A spell of immortal beauty seemed laid upon Penelope's husband, so that he forgot all but the passing hours of happiness. Yet as time went by, he remembered his own rough island; and often, stealing apart from his charmer, would sit by the shore alone, to gaze over the waves with wistful thoughts of home.

Meanwhile at Ithaca his sire Laertes and his wife Penelope had heavy hearts, vainly hoping his return. The suitors of the faithful queen grew more and more urgent, living insolently in the house of Odysseus, and wasting his substance, since now they had no fear to see him back. The lad Telemachus had been growing up to be like his father; but for long he was too modest to withstand the riotous crew making themselves at home, as if already his inheritance had passed to a stepfather. Then there came a day when Pallas-Athene breathed into him the spirit to rebuke those self-invited guests, and to declare that he meant being master in his own house. And when they jeered at the youth, with threats and complaints of Penelope's obduracy, he suddenly announced his intention of taking ship for the mainland, there to

seek out news of his father. If he could hear of him
as still alive, he would put up with the suitors for one
year more; but if Odysseus were certainly dead, he himself would insist on his mother making her choice among
them, as at liberty to marry again.

She herself had practised craft against the importunity
of the suitors. Some god inspired her, as she thought,
to set up a loom for weaving a great and splendid web
to be seemly shroud for old Laertes; and not till it was
ended, she told them, would she be free to wed. Cease-
lessly her fingers worked at it, but every night she sat
up by torchlight, privily undoing the labour of the day.
The tale came to be told in Hades by one of those long-
deceived suitors, at last sent to his doom.

"We wooed the wife of Odysseus, the lord so long away,
And unto that loathly wedding said she neither yea nor nay,
But the black doom and the deathday devised for us the while;
Yea in our heart she devised us moreover this same guile;
With a web that was great and mighty her loom in the house did she
    gear,
A fine web, full of measure, and thus bespake us there.

"'O younglings, ye my Wooers, since the godlike Odysseus is dead,
Await ye abiding the wedding till I to an end have sped
This cloth, for fear the warp-threads should waste and come to
    nought.
'Tis a shroud for the lord Laertes 'gainst the day when he shall be
    caught
At the last by the baleful doom of Death, the Outstretcher of men:
Lest the women of Achæans through the folk should blame me then,
—Lo the man of many possessions he lieth lacking a shroud!'

"So she spoke, for the while prevailing o'er our hearts the high and
    proud,
And thenceforth o'er that web the mighty by daylight still she
    wrought;
But ever by night undid it when the candles thereto she had brought.

Three years she beguiled the Achæans, and the thing by guile did hide,
But when came on the fourth year and the seasons came in their tide,
By all the waning of moons and the many days fulfilled,
Then one of the women told us, who in the guile was skilled,
And we found her there unweaving the noble web of cloth;
And so to an end must she bring it perforce and exceeding loth."

—*W. Morris.*

That device being treacherously disclosed, she had no further excuse for putting off the choice pressed upon her. If her true-loved husband came home, it must be soon or never. So she waited in prayers and tears, while young Telemachus secretly sailed away to Greece, inspired and accompanied by Pallas in disguise of his honest guardian Mentor.

Landing at Pylos, he sought out old Nestor, who had much to tell of the Trojan war, but could not tell what had become of Odysseus. Nestor's son, Pisistratus, drove him on to Sparta, to be there courteously received by Menelaus and Helen, now reconciled after their long divorce. Menelaus was not without tidings of his famous comrade. He himself had made a wandering voyage home, in the course of which it was his fortune to come upon Proteus, the wise old man of the sea, whose knowledge had to be wrung from him by force. When Menelaus and his companions, disguised in seal skins, caught that keeper of Poseidon's herds, basking on the shore, he changed in their hands to a lion, a leopard, a boar, and a serpent in turn, now melting into a fountain, now springing up as a tree; but to those bold enough to hold him fast under all his transformations, he was bound to tell truth at the end. Thus constrained, he had let Menelaus know how Odysseus was a prisoner in Calypso's cave, vainly longing to go free from her flowery charms. Having heard of his father as still alive, Telemachus

made haste back to Ithaca, where the suspicious suitors.
on learning his absence, were now plotting an ambush to
fall upon him as he reached home.

Mentor had abandoned him on the journey, resuming
the divine form of Pallas, who went about a greater service to this house which she had taken under her charge.
When now for seven years Odysseus had lain in Calypso's
isle, half-entranced, half-yearning to escape, the maiden
goddess pled his cause in a council of Olympus, from
which only Poseidon was absent. That insatiable per-
secutor of the much-enduring man having gone off to
enjoy a hecatomb offered him by the Ethiopians, the
other gods were easily moved to pity for such a hero,
and Zeus himself now remembered how dutiful in prayers
and offerings Odysseus had been during the days of his
prosperity. So while Pallas went back to earth as counsellor of Telemachus, Hermes was sent to Calypso, bearing a supreme command that her guest should be let go
and furthered on his voyage homewards.

Ill-pleased was Calypso with this injunction, which she
durst not disregard. Yet when she sought out Odysseus
sitting homesick on the shore, to tell him how his heart's
wish might now be gratified, she still would have tempted
him to stay, reminding him of the trials and perils of the
sea, promising to share with him her own immortality, if he
could forget that mere woman Penelope, who surely did
not rival herself in beauty. His first idea of her tidings
had been that they were too good to be true, and that
there must be some trick under her offer to let him build
a boat for leaving the island; but she swore by the Styx,
mightiest oath of the gods, that no harm was intended
him: he was verily free to go, if he could bear to leave
her. Then it wrung her heart to hear him answer with
kindling eye—

"Goddess and mistress, be not wroth with me
　　Herein: for very well myself I know
　　That, set beside you, wise Penelope

"Were far less stately and less fair to view,
　　Being but mortal woman, nor like you
　　Ageless and deathless: but yet even so
　　I long and yearn to see my home anew;

"And through all days I see that one day shine:
　　But if amid the ocean bright as wine
　　Once more some God shall break me, then once more
　　With steadfast purpose would my heart incline

"Still to endurance, and would suffer still,
　　As ofttimes I have suffered, many an ill
　　And many a woe in wave or war; and now
　　Let this too follow after, if it will."

　　　　　　　　　　　　　　　—*Mackail.*

Much as it went against her heart, Calypso did all she could to speed his departure. She gave him tools to cut down trees, with which he built a raft, and her own garments she brought to make sails for it, and stored his little craft with victuals and skins of wine and water; and she raised for him a softly favouring breeze, when on the fifth day he launched forth, too ready to see the last of that charming hostess.

III. New Friends in Need

Once out at sea, his sailor-craft came back to Odysseus, long as he had lain idle on land. Steering heedfully by the Pleiades and the North Star, for seventeen days he never shut his eyes nor took his hand from the helm, till the eighteenth dawn showed him welcome land ahead. But now Poseidon, returning from his banquet among the Ethiopians, spied out that lonely voyager, and made haste to work him ill. The wrathful god lashed up the sea with his trident, calling forth storm winds from every quarter to wrestle round the little raft and whirl it about like thistledown.

"Would that I had died illustriously among the heroes of Troy!" was Odysseus' thought, as he felt his frail craft breaking up beneath him.

A kindly sea nymph, perching on the wreck in form of a gull, advised him to take to swimming; but though already half-drowned, the poor sailor tried to stick to his raft as long as she would hold together, for he feared some new trick being played upon him by mischievous gods. Before long, however, he saw nothing else for it but to throw off his garments and plunge among the waves; and that sea nymph Leucothea, who, in mortal form, had been Ino, daughter of Cadmus, cast over him a magic scarf that bare up his stalwart body. When Poseidon saw him beaten about from billow to billow, he made no more ado, but drove home in his chariot, chuckling over the perilous plight of one to whom he owed such a grudge.

And now indeed the hero had been lost but for the aid of Pallas, who laid all the winds but one, and let that carry him steadily towards the land. Two days and two nights he kept himself afloat on the swell; and when the third morning broke, a joyful sight of wooded hills close by gave him strength to strike out for dry ground. But it was no easy matter to get on shore, for before him stretched a sheer wall of surf-beaten rocks, rising suddenly from deep water. Dashed against the sharp edges, to which he would have clung with his bleeding hands, he found himself sucked back by the waves before he could get firm hold or footing to climb beyond their reach. There was nothing for it but to swim a little

way out, and keep on along the coast till he came off
the mouth of a river. Praying the god of this stream
to receive him as a suppliant, he turned into its quiet
channel, where at last he was able to drag himself ashore,
so battered out of breath and strength that he lay in a
swoon, and only after a little was able to kiss the ground
in token of thankfulness.

But not yet did he seem safe. Night was drawing
on, and the chill wind numbed his weary nakedness. He
crawled into a wood for shelter, and made himself a bed
of dry leaves, to forget his troubles in such sleep as falls
on men who for long have not dared close an eye.

> " As some poor peasant, fated to reside
> Remote from neighbours, in a forest wide,
> Studious to save what human wants require,
> In embers heaped preserves the seeds of fire:
> Hid in dry foliage thus Ulysses lies
> Till Pallas poured soft slumbers on his eyes."

Now the island where he had this time come on shore
was Scheria, inhabited by the rich Phæacians, a people
better known as traders than as warriors, whose city and
the palace of their king Alcinous stood not far from that
river mouth that gave the hero refuge. Softly and sump-
tuously they lived, yet their women folk, high and low,
were not too proud for housewifely cares. That night,
as Nausicaa the king's daughter lay asleep, a dream sent
by Pallas put into her head to see after a great washing
of linen, that all things might be ready for her marriage
feast, now that she had no lack of suitors. So in the
morning she asked her father to let her have a mule
wagon, which she loaded with the foul clothes of the
family, and drove off with her maids to the river bank
for a long day's work.

Turning out the mules to graze, this bevy of girls

set the garments soaking in cisterns of fresh water, and vied with each other in the trampling them under their white feet, as seemed task fit for a king's daughter who hoped to be mistress of a lordly home. When the cleansed apparel had all been wrung out and spread to dry on the sunny beach, they bathed and anointed themselves; then, after taking their dinner in the open air, began to play at ball by way of pastime, Nausicaa singing to them while they waited for the sun to finish their work. None of these sportive maidens guessed how a shipwrecked man was sleeping in the wood close by; nor did their merry noise disturb the tired Odysseus till late in the day, when, on a ball thrown amiss falling into the river, they all raised such a shrill clamour that he woke up with a start.

Peering out of his covert, at first he was ashamed to show himself near this troop of girls, without a rag on him as he stood. But he must not lose such a chance of succour in such hard plight, so he plucked a leafy branch to make a screen for his body, and thus strangely arrayed came forth to view. At the sight of a naked man, all bruised and brine-stained, with famine in his eye, these handmaidens might well shriek and run for it, as from a savage lion, Nausicaa alone standing fast, for she had a princely nature, and could guess that the destitute stranger meant her no harm.

Slenderly graceful like a palm tree, she stood, then, to listen while, accosting her with as much reverence as if she were a goddess—and so indeed she seemed to him by her pitiful looks—Odysseus told his tale of twenty days spent on the sea that had flung him at last to shore, and besought her for any scrap or wrap of clothing she had to spare, and for guidance to the nearest town, if she wished heaven to grant her a good husband and a happy home.

Soon made sure that this was no fierce ruffian, but an honest man in distress, Nausicaa answered him kindly, calling back her maids, with orders to bring him a shirt and a cloak and a cruse of oil. With these, going a little apart, he washed off the ooze and slime from his limbs; and when he had anointed and dressed himself he looked another man, of whom Nausicaa thought she would wish no goodlier for her spouse. But now modesty and the fear of scandalous tongues prompted her not to be seen in company with so handsome a foreigner. The clean clothes having been packed up, while Odysseus was refreshed with meat and drink from her store, she bid him then follow the wagon that would show him the way to her father's house.

Thus guided, he entered the walled city of the Phæacians, wondering at its greatness and its busy harbour; still more, when Pallas, in the shape of a little girl, led him to the palace gate of the king. Never in all his wanderings had he seen such magnificence!

> " Resplendent as the moon, or solar light,
> Alcinous' palace awed the o'erdazzled sight.
> On to its last recess, a brazen wall
> That from the threshold stretch'd, illumined all;
> Round it of azure steel a cornice roll'd,
> And every gate, that closed the palace, gold.
> The brazen threshold golden pillars bore,
> A golden ringlet glitter'd on the door,
> The lintel silver, and to guard his gate,
> Dogs in a row, each side, were seen to wait,
> In gold and silver wrought, by Vulcan made,
> Immortal as the god, and undecay'd.
> From the far threshold, to its last retreat,
> Ranged round the wall, rose many a lofty seat,
> With fine-spun carpets strew'd, by virgins wrought,
> Where, as each newborn day new pleasures brought,
> Phæacia's chiefs, from thought and care released,
> Sat throned, and lengthen'd the perpetual feast.

Stood on bright altars golden youths, whose hands
Lit through the night the guests with flaming brands:
And fifty maids administering around,
Some, the ripe grain beneath the millstone ground,
Some whirl'd the distaff, and the fleeces wove
Swift as the leaves that shake the poplar grove:
And ever as they plied their radiant toil,
The glossy web shone like transparent oil.
Nor less expert their course the seamen kept,
Than through the loom the female shuttle swept,
The gift of Pallas, who had there combined
The skilful hand with the inventive mind.
Without the court, yet nigh the city's bound,
A garden bloom'd, four-acred, wall'd around;
Tall trees there grew, the red pomegranate there,
Each glossy apple, and each juicy pear,
Sweet figs, and living olives: none decay'd
Or in the summer blaze, or winter shade;
While western winds unfolding every flower,
Here gemm'd with buds the branch, there fill'd with fruits the
    bower."   *—Sotheby.*

For a little, Odysseus stood abashed on the brazen threshold, hardly venturing to enter so sumptuous an abode, for Nausicaa, driving on ahead, had taken herself off to the women's chambers. But, encouraged by the advice she had given him, he passed in, then on to the hall where Alcinous was banqueting with his lords. For the queen Arete he made, and bowing before her, clasped her knees with a humble entreaty for succour to a man in sore need. This done, he sat down in the ashes by the hearth, as became a suppliant.

Astonished by his sudden appearance among them, the guests stared upon him in silence, till one of the oldest spoke to remind the king what was due to misfortune. Thus prompted, Alcinous rose to give the stranger his hand and lead him to a seat of honour, where food and wine were quickly set before him, and a silver bowl into which from a golden ewer one of the serving maids poured clear water to lave his fingers.

This king and his people were so hospitable to a guest, as remembering how they might entertain some god unawares. They did not much trouble the castaway with questions while he ate and drank heartily after his long fast; yet before being shown to a snug bed outside the hall, he told the king and queen of his shipwreck, and how he had been found destitute on the shore by Nausicaa. Arete had guessed something of this when she recognized the clothes he wore as the work of her own looms. All he begged now was to be sent home across the sea, to which Alcinous readily agreed without even asking his name or country, for the Phæacians were so skilled mariners that it would be easy for them to steer to any point.

Next day, while a ship was being fitted out for him, Alcinous and his lords did their best to entertain the stranger. The more he saw of him the more the king liked his guest's looks; now that he was rested and refreshed, Odysseus had such a stately mien that he might well be taken for a king, if not for a disguised god. When, still keeping his name secret, he declared himself only a mortal man, Alcinous pressed him to stay in Scheria, as his son-in-law, if he chose; nor was the modest Nausicaa loath to have him for a husband; but all the hero's mind was set on home, and the Phæacians had too much courtesy to keep him against his will.

At the games held in his honour, the stranger would have been content to look on; but when rudely challenged by the best Phæacian athlete, he caught up a quoit of extraordinary size and hurled it far beyond the mark of any other competitor. Warmed by such easy victory, he even began to boast, offering to box or wrestle or shoot with any of them, except the king's son, with whom, as his host, he did not care to contend; only, he granted, they could beat him at running, since his legs were still weak and stiff from the sea. Wondering what champion this might be, the Phæacians spoke no more of matching themselves against him. Indeed they were not so good at feats of strength as at singing and dancing and the like diversion, fonder of feasting, too, than of rough frays.

After the games came a banquet, when the blind bard Demodocus was fetched to spice the fare with songs of love, such as the idle Phæacians heard gladly; but their unknown guest, sending him a mess of meat from his place, bespoke in turn the tale of Troy's fall. That, then, the bard sang so stirringly, and so loudly extolled the son of Laertes, as first among heroes of fame, that Odysseus could not keep back his tears. Alcinous, sitting beside him, noted how he turned his head to weep; then this kindly host cut short the song that moved in his guest such painful memories.

"Who and whence art thou, to grieve for the fate of Troy?" he asked; and the answer was—

"I am Odysseus."

Amazed were the king and his lords to hear how this needy stranger, who had sat silent among them, was no other than that illustrious hero vanished for years from the knowledge of men. Eagerly they sought to learn all that had befallen him through those weary years; and half the night he kept them listening to a tale of adventures that would make matter for many minstrels.

But now it seemed as if his troubles were indeed near an end. For if the Phæacians had been friendly and serviceable to the nameless castaway, they had nothing too good for the renowned warrior. Already they had given him bounteous gifts; and furthermore at the king's

bidding they heaped up for him a treasure of gold and
bronze vessels and goodly raiment, to be loaded upon
the ship that should bear him home without delay.
Alcinous himself visited it to see everything made taut
and trim.   Once more the guest was royally entertained
with feast and song; but all day his eyes turned to the
sun, as if to speed its setting, for no tired ploughman
ever longed so much to come to an end of his furrows.
And when darkness gave signal for departure, over a
farewell cup he invoked blessings on Alcinous and his
people, then joyfully went down to the harbour to get
on board.   The sailors spread a soft couch for him in
the stern that he might sleep out the short voyage to
Ithaca.   No sooner had they loosed their hawser and
dipped their oars in the gleaming surf, than the island-
born chief was rocked into a deep slumber, and knew
not how

> " As all together dash four stallions over the plains
>   At the touch of the whistling lash, at the toss of the glancing reins,
>   And they bound through the air, and they fly, as upborne on the
>   wings of the wind,—
>   So was the stern tossed high as the good ship leapt, and behind
>   Rushing the dark wave sped of the manifold-roaring sea;
>   And unswervingly onward she fled: so swiftly, so surely went she,
>   Not the falcon could match her, whose flight is the fleetest of all
>   things that fly,
>   So fast did she cleave and so light she rode over the waves tossing high,
>   As onward the hero she bore who in wisdom was like to a god,
>   Who had suffered affliction before, heart-troubles, a weariful load,
>   In battles of warring men, and on waves of the troublesome sea:
>   Yet peaceful slept he then, from their very remembrance free."
>   —A. S. Way.

Odysseus had not yet awoke when at dawn the ship
sighted Ithaca, its shores well known to the Phæacian
mariners.   The crew ran their prow ashore in a sheltered

cove, marked by a sea-hollowed rock that made a sacred haunt of the Naiads. Quietly they lifted his couch to lay him on the sand; and hard by, about the roots of an overshadowing olive tree, they piled up the gifts bestowed upon him by their countrymen. There they left him still sleeping, while they rowed back to Scheria.

But Poseidon frowned to see his foe thus brought safely home, whom he had meant to afflict a while longer, though it was the will of Zeus that in the end he should reach Ithaca. The sea-god went off to complain to his brother how those presumptuous Phæacians had crossed his purpose; and the careless king of Olympus gave him full leave to punish them. So he did by turning the ship into a rock just as it was steering back into port; and there it stood rooted in the sea, like a mountain overhanging the city of Alcinous, who for doing such friendly service to a stranger was fain to make a sacrifice of twelve choice bulls that might appease the offended deity.

IV. The Return to Ithaca

When Odysseus woke up to find himself alone, the air was dark with mist hiding all the landmarks of his native island, so that he feared the sailors must have treacherously set him on shore in some strange country. Even when he saw and counted his rich presents laid out safe under the olive tree, he could not believe but that a trick had been put on him. As sorrowfully he paced the beach, crying out upon his hard fate, and upon himself for having trusted the glib-tongued Phæacians, there approached him through the mist what seemed a young and comely shepherd, whom he hastened to meet.

It was in truth his divine protectress, Pallas, who in playful mood took this shape to guide him; and she too had sent the mist to conceal his arrival from the enemies that filled his home. So pleased was he to see anyone, that he saluted the seeming shepherd with the regard due to a god, begging him to say what country this might be.

"He must be a stranger indeed," was the reply, "not to know Ithaca, a small and rugged island, yet famed as far away as Troy!"

Glad as he was to hear himself at home after all, the crafty Odysseus had not wholly shaken off his distrust; so he thought well to tell a lame and lying tale of how he came to be here, deserted by dishonest shipmates, who yet had not robbed him of his treasure.

The young shepherd listened with a smile, all at once vanishing from his sight, where the goddess now stood before him in her own majestic form, and laughingly reproached him for his crafty shifts, of which forsooth he would soon have much need.

In reply, the hero might well complain of her fickle guardianship: now she came to his aid in one or another shape; then again she left him suffering under the worst strokes of fate; and even now, for all he could be sure, she might be cheating him with some false hope. The astute Pallas explained that she had to beware of offending her uncle Poseidon, whose heart was still hot against Odysseus for blinding that one-eyed son of his. But to show herself truly his friend, she blew away the mist, then at once he could recognize the familiar scenes of his own island, falling on his knees to salute this native earth, with thanks to the sea nymphs that had wafted him home at last.

First helping him, like the prudent goddess she was, to hide away his treasure in the Naiads' cave, she sat down with him below the olive tree to let him know how matters stood in his house, taken possession of by a greedy crowd of suitors for his wife's hand, who would give her true husband no kindly welcome. Penelope, he heard with joy, was still faithful to him, though she had always much ado to put off their importunity. Telemachus had left home in search of his father, and the suitors were plotting to rid themselves of the heir on his return; but the goddess undertook to bring him quickly and safely back. Meanwhile, she advised Odysseus to take refuge with Eumæus, the keeper of his swine, and thence to spy out the state of his enemies before revealing himself. The better to escape their malice, he must be transformed as a lowly beggar.

> " She spake, then touch'd him with her powerful wand.
> The skin shrunk up, and wither'd at her hand.
> A swift old age o'er all his members spread.
> A sudden frost was sprinkled on his head.
> Nor longer in the heavy eye-ball shin'd
> The glance divine, forth beaming from the mind.
> His robe, which spots indelible besmear,
> In rags dishonest, flutters with the air.
> A stag's torn hide is lapp'd around his reins.
> A rugged staff his trembling hand sustains;
> And at his side a wretched scrip was hung,
> Wide-patch'd, and knotted to a twisted thong.
> So look'd the chief, so mov'd, to mortal eyes
> Object uncouth, a man of miseries;
> While Pallas, cleaving the wild fields of air,
> To Sparta flies, Telemachus her care."

Thus disguised, Odysseus took a rough mountain track that led him to the spacious pens in which hundreds of swine were kept under charge of old Eumæus, a servant ever true to the memory of his master, and full of grudge against the usurping guests who daily devoured his fattest boars. As this honest swineherd sat cutting himself sandals out of a hide, a loud barking hailed the approach of a stranger, on whom four dogs, wild as wolves, flew out so fiercely that he might have been torn in pieces had crafty Odysseus not at once sat down to disconcert their onset; then Eumæus rushed out to drive them away with stones.

He for his part showed no want of kindness to one he took for a beggar. He led the unknown man into his hut, strewed for him a couch of rushes with a hide laid on the top, and made haste to kill and cook two young sucking-pigs to set before him with barley meal and wine. While Odysseus ate hungrily, Eumæus went on lamenting over his master, whose absence kept him poor, and abusing the suitors that consumed the pick of his herd, so that he could do no better for a guest. Odysseus asked that much-missed master's name, of whom a wanderer like himself might have heard some news. Nay, growled the swineherd, he had heard enough of lying tales brought by beggars from all quarters, seeking Penelope's bounty on pretence of having known her husband. Let who will believe them: the great Odysseus, the best master that ever was, must long ago have made food for fishes or vultures; else why did he not come back to set things right at home?

"Not so!" cried the beggar. "Poor as I am, I hate lying; and I make bold to swear that this year—nay, before another month be out—Odysseus shall come back to his own!"

The swineherd shook his head, like one who had too often heard such promises; and would talk no more on a painful theme. Now that the guest had supped, he asked his name and how he came to Ithaca. For all his professed hatred of lying, Odysseus was a good hand at a fable: hereupon he told a long one, making himself out a Cretan, and inventing a string of mishaps that had brought him into slavery and cast him naked on this unknown island.   In the course of his adventures, he declared, he had heard of Odysseus as bound for home with great wealth.   Did Eumæus still not believe?   Let them make a bargain, then.   If Odysseus came back, the swineherd should give him a cloak and shirt and send him on to his own home; if not, he was willing to be pitched over a cliff as example to other lying beggars.

Heaven forbid! exclaimed the host, that he should so use a man who had eaten under his roof-tree.   And soon again he showed himself as hospitable as rough of speech.   For at evening the under-herdsmen came home driving in the grunting and squealing swine to be shut up for the night; then their master bid them pick out the fattest boar to make a fit feast for this stranger.   Before they all sat down together to meat, Eumæus piously burned the bristles of the beast as a sacrifice, praying the gods for his lord's safe return; and when he cut the flesh into portions, one was set apart for Hermes, the conductor of souls.   The guest was honoured with the juiciest slices, and made a second hearty meal with the rest, before they all lay down to rest.

Then crafty Odysseus again bethought him of a trick for putting his host's kindness to further proof. He told another tale of how, lying before the walls of Troy one cold night, he got Odysseus to send one of the soldiers running off on a message to the fleet, that he himself might borrow this man's cloak.   Eumæus took the hint to lend the half-naked beggar a warm covering for his bed of skins in front of the fire.   Outside, it was blowing and raining, dark as pitch; but, while his underlings slept under cover, the keeper, wrapped in a weather-proof mantle, and armed with sword and javelin, spent all night in the open air, to keep good watch over his absent master's flock. This trusty fellow was a slave stolen in childhood by Phœnician traders, and sold to Laertes of Ithaca, to whom and to his son he showed by careful service his gratitude for kind usage. So he told Odysseus next day, when the disguised stranger heard of his old father as still alive, though sorely grieving for the son whose disappearance had been the death of his mother.

Still playing on the swineherd's goodwill, Odysseus talked of going up to the town, presenting himself in Penelope's halls, appealing to her bounty, or offering himself as servant to those suitors that were said to be eating her out of house and home. As if such proud lords would care to have a ragged beggar about them! blurted out Eumæus. No, no, the stranger could do no better than stay where he was for a while; times were not so bad but that there was something going for an honest guest: he could pay his welcome by telling stories of his wandering life, till Telemachus came home, who would be sure to prove openhanded to a man in need.

And Telemachus was not long in coming, having been speedily brought back from Sparta by Pallas, who also warned him how the suitors had laid an ambush for him; so that instead of sailing straight to the town harbour, he landed on a lonely shore of Ithaca, and on foot made first for the swineherd's hut. Eumæus and his new friend were cooking their morning meal when they heard steps without that did not set the dogs barking as for a stranger; then at the open door stood the form of a noble youth to bring the swineherd to his feet with cries of hearty welcome. He kissed his young master as one from the dead, weeping tears of joy; and the first question of Telemachus was whether Penelope had yet been forced into a marriage with one of the suitors. No, Eumæus could assure him; she still remained shut up in her chamber, mourning ever her absent lord.

Glad of that news, Telemachus entered the hut, and let the swineherd take his spear. The ragged vagrant would have risen to give him place; but the young master courteously bid him keep his seat. When he sat down to eat, waited on by Eumæus, he asked who this stranger might be; and the swineherd repeated the tale told him by Odysseus. Telemachus looked grave to hear that a needy beggar had waited his return in hope of relief. What could he do for the poor, forsooth, who was hardly master at his own house? He also advised the man not to go near those insolent intruders: let him stay where he was, and Telemachus would send down some food and clothes for him.

Eumæus presently went off to tell Penelope of her son's safe return. Father and son were left together, yet not alone, for Pallas stood at the door, visible only to Odysseus and to the dogs that shrunk cowering and whining away. She beckoned him forth; she whispered to him that the time was come to reveal himself to his son; she touched him with her wand to undo that lowly disguise. So the grey, hobbling, toothless beggar strode back into the hut a well-clad stalwart form, erect and black-bearded, in the prime of life, at sight of whom Telemachus cast down his eyes in amazement, uttering a prayer as to one of the gods.

"No god am I, but thy father so long lamented!"

So spoke the hero, embracing his son with tears of joy; but to Telemachus it seemed too good to be true, and he cried:

> " ' My father,' saidst thou? ' No, thou art not he,
> But some Divinity beguiles my soul
> With mock'ries, to afflict me still the more;
> For never mortal man could so have wrought
> By his own pow'r; some interposing God
> Alone could render thee both young and old;
> For old thou wast of late, and foully clad,
> But wear'st the semblance, now, of those in heav'n!'
>   To whom Ulysses, ever wise, replied,
> ' Telemachus! it is not well, my son!
> That thou should'st greet thy father with a face
> Of wild astonishment and stand aghast.
> Ulysses, save myself, none comes, be sure.
> Such as thou see'st me, num'rous toils achieved
> And woes sustain'd, I visit once again
> My native country in the twentieth year.
> This wonder Athenæan Pallas wrought,
> She cloth'd me even with what form she would,
> For so she can.   Now poor I seem and old.
> Now young again, and clad in fresh attire.
> So easy is it to the Pow'rs above
> T' exalt or to debase a mortal man.' "

—Cowper.

At last made to understand that his long-lost sire stood before him in flesh and blood, Telemachus was so overcome with joy that they might have sat weeping in one another's arms all day. But the wary Odysseus knew that it was a time for deeds rather than words. Hastily telling how he had come to be landed on Ithaca, he questioned the youth as to the number of the suitors who were vexing his wife and eating up his substance. Alas! Telemachus told him, they were too many and too bold to be driven away. Leave that to him and to the help of the gods, quoth Odysseus: let his son do as now directed. He must go home without a word of his father's return, even to Penelope. Later, Eumæus would bring the disguised beggar to his own house; then, however he might be insulted or ill-used by the suitors, Telemachus should bridle his feelings till the hour of reckoning came.

> " And though they deal upon me sore despite,
> Even in mine own house, let thy soul forbear!
> Ay, though with missiles they would wound outright,
> And drag me from the doors by feet and hair,
> Calmly look on, and let thy soul forbear!
> Yet from their folly bid them still relent,
> And strive to turn them with a gentle prayer,
> Albeit I know that they will not repent,
> So surely their dark hour of doom stands imminent."
>
> —*Worsley.*

By and by, Eumæus came back from the house, where Penelope had heard with joy of her son's return; but that made ill hearing for the suitors when they knew how he had slipped through their snares. The swineherd was not yet to be trusted with the secret, so Pallas had once more transformed his master into an old cripple in rags. Telemachus spent the night with them; and next morning, when he went to his mother, he bid Eumæus bring the man to the town to try his luck at begging: he himself had too much trouble of his own to look after poor people. So he said, exchanging secret smiles with his father, whom he feigned to treat so lightly.

Soon afterwards, Eumæus followed with the stranger, leaning on a staff, bearing a wallet on his bent back, and to all appearance a right mendicant. As they drew near the town, over which rose the high walls of its lord's abode, they fell in with Melanthius the goatherd, driving the best of his flock to feast the suitors, whose favour he cared for more than his true master's weal. This rude fellow had nothing to give the old beggar but contemptuous words, even fetching Odysseus a kick as he passed, which the hero endured meekly, though he had half a mind to fell the churl with his staff. Eumæus cried shame on the insolent fellow, who would have to mend such manners if ever their master came to his own again. Melanthius answered with coarse abuse, declaring that they would see no more of Odysseus, as sure as that Telemachus would soon be killed by the suitors. He hastened on to join the revels of those new friends; while the other two more slowly approached the great house, where a sound of music and a savoury smell of cooking showed what was going on within.

But here the master of this house did not pass unmarked by one old friend. Near the gate lay a worn-out dog that pricked up its ears and raised its head at his voice, only to fall dead in the effort of crawling forward to lick his hand.

" It was Argus, Odysseus' hound; himself had reared him of yore;
   Yet or ever his pleasure he found in the chase, unto Ilium's shore
   Was he gone; yet the dog long ago with the young men wont to fare
   Through the woodland pursuing the roe and the mountain-goat and
      the hare.
   But he lieth a cast-off thing,—for far away now is the king,—
   Where in front of the doors the dung of the mules and the kine from
      the stalls
   Had been swept in heaps and flung, till the time should come for the
      thralls
   To spread it forth on the tilth-lands broad of Odysseus the king.
   There lieth Argus in filth, all vermin-festering.
   Yet now, as his dying eyes behold Odysseus appear,
   He is moving his tail as he lies for joy; he is drooping the ear:
   But his strength is utterly gone, and he cannot crawl more near.
   And Odysseus looking thereon must turn him away; for the tear

Sprang to his eye, but he wiped it unmarked of the swineherd, and said:
'Eumæus, 'tis passing strange, this hound in the litter laid.
Grand is his frame, yet what he hath been I do not know,
Whether fleetness in running he had to match this goodly show,
Or was but as the dogs that be pampered with dainties from feastful
      boards,
And are nurtured for vain fair-seeming by pride-uplifted lords.'
And Eumæus the swineherd spake to the beggar-king and replied:
'Of a surety this is the hound of a king that afar hath died.
If his frame were but now as of old, and his deeds as the deeds of
      yore,
When Odysseus left him, passing away unto Troy-land shore,
Thou wouldst marvel beholding the fleetness and strength this dog
      showed then.
There was never a beast that escaped through the depth of the
      forest-glen,
Whatsoever he chased; for he followed with scent unerring the track.
But evil hath compassed him now; for the lost will never come back,
And the heedless women folk tend him not, but they leave him to lack.
Yea, thralls, when they feel no longer the hand of their lord and the
      might,
Have no more will to render him honest service aright.
For the half of the manhood of man Zeus Thunderer taketh away
When his feet are caught in the net of the bondage-bringing day."
                                                            —*Way.*

When they entered the hall, Eumæus was beckoned
by Telemachus to a seat at the banquet, while Odysseus
held himself back near the door, as beseemed the humble
part he was playing. There his son sent him a portion of
bread and meat, which he ate sitting apart, and at first
passed without notice, the eyes of all being fixed on a
bard who was cheering their feast with song. When his
strains came to an end, the old beggar rose to go round
the table with bent head and outstretched hands, not so
much for what he should get, as to test the disposition
of these usurpers of his home. Most of them gave him
something, as well they might be liberal with what was
another's, so that soon he had his wallet stuffed with

bread and meat. But Melanthius the goatherd again reviled him and the swineherd who had brought him; and Antinous, the most insolent of the suitors, called for him to be turned out of the house, where this man behaved as if already its master. In vain, with a suppliant whine, Odysseus stooped to flatter the haughty lord, canting forth one of those false tales of which he had so many in his scrip, making himself out a once-rich man, who would never in his own prosperity have turned the poor from his door; then, taking another tone, he went on to upbraid the selfish churl who grudged him a morsel of bread not his own. This so enraged Antinous that he flung his footstool at the beggar, who bore the blow without moving, and went back to his place at the threshold audibly praying to whatever gods cared for the poor, that Antinous might come to the bad end of one who despised misfortune.

Antinous still fumed and threatened, heedless of Telemachus, sitting in silent fury to see his father thus used in his own house. But other suitors took shame for their comrade's rudeness; and one of them openly rebuked him for so serving a poverty-stricken man, who for all they knew might be a god in disguise. And when word was brought to Penelope in her chamber how Antinous had insulted a suppliant under her roof, she too was indignant at such a breach of hospitality. Through Eumæus she sent for the beggar to partake her bounty, the more readily as she heard that he professed to have known Odysseus. And, just then, Telemachus happened to sneeze so loudly that it resounded through the whole house, which his mother took for an omen of good news; and was still more eager to hear what the stranger might have to tell.

Odysseus, for his part, showed no haste to meet his

wife, perhaps as remembering a warning given him in Hades by the ghost of Agamemnon, that had some cause not to trust woman's faith. He excused himself for not at once obeying Penelope's summons, promising to come to her at sunset, when he might be able to slink unnoticed through the crowd of revellers, and then their talk would stand in less danger of interruption. For the present, while Eumæus went back to his pigs, he himself remained in the hall, keenly watching those enemies of his home, all unaware who was among them.

Now there came up a real beggar, Irus by name, a greedy drunken braggart, well known as doing odd jobs about the place. He was ill-pleased to see another of the same trade here before him, and at once began to abuse this stranger, and talk of turning him out. Odysseus answered that there was room for both of them, and that the other might not find it so easy to turn him out. Deceived by his modest speech, Irus grew louder and more abusive; and the mischievous suitors egged him on, taking it for fine sport to set these two by the ears. Antinous laughingly proposed a fight between them, the prize to be a goat's paunch full of blood and fat, which was already put down at the fire for supper. The jovial crew would not listen to Odysseus' protest that he was a broken-down old man, unable to stand against a sturdy young fellow. Well then, since they would have it, he was ready to fight Irus, if he could be sure of getting fair play. That Telemachus promised him, and so did the rest.

Irus had been willing enough to try for an easy victory, but the stranger, stripping off his rags, disclosed such sturdy limbs that everyone saw he could make a better fight of it than had been expected. The more the boaster looked at this stalwart form the less he liked it;

and now he was for backing out, even had to be dragged by force into the ring made for them in the courtyard. Trembling, he stood before the opponent who knew that he could kill him with a single blow of his fist. But, not to unmask himself by putting forth all his strength, Odysseus merely knocked the fellow down so that blood ran out of his mouth, and he lay spluttering and sprawling on the ground amid the brutal laughter of his backers. He durst not again stand up to the old man, who dragged him out by the foot, propped him up against the wall, with his staff in his hands and his torn cloak hung about him like a scarecrow, contemptuously bidding him stay there to keep off dogs and pigs.

When he himself came to sit meekly down in his former place at the door, as if he had done nothing out of the way, the suitors were inclined to treat such a doughty beggar with more consideration. Antinous brought him the promised prize; and Amphinomus, of nobler nature than the rest, gave him some bread into the bargain, and pledged him in a cup of wine, wishing him better fortune. That kindness moved Odysseus to tell the young lord that he knew his father, a worthy man, for whose sake he would drink to him with some good counsel.

> " Then hear my words, and grave them in thy mind!
> Of all that breathes, or grov'lling creeps on earth
> Most man is vain, calamitous by birth.
> To-day, with power elate, in strength he blooms.
> The haughty creature on that power presumes.
> Anon from Heaven a sad reverse he feels.
> Untaught to bear, 'gainst Heaven the wretch rebels,
> For man is changeful, as his bliss or woe;
> Too high when prosperous, when distress'd too low.
> There was a day when, with the scornful great,
> I swell'd in pomp and arrogance of state,

Proud of the power that to high birth belongs,
And us'd that power to justify my wrongs.
Then let not man be proud; but firm of mind,
Bear the best humbly, and the worst resign'd.
Be dumb when Heaven afflicts; unlike yon train
Of haughty spoilers, insolently vain,
Who make their queen and all her wealth a prey;
But vengeance and Ulysses wing their way.
Oh! may'st thou, favour'd by some guardian power,
Far, far be distant in that deathful hour;
For sure I am, if stern Ulysses breathe,
These lawless riots end in blood and death."

Now attention was withdrawn from the old beggar by the appearance of Penelope in the hall, who came to rebuke her son for allowing such a disturbance and letting a stranger be ill-treated in his house. Bitterly Telemachus answered that it was no fault of his: what could he do against all those masterful wooers of hers who made themselves so much at home? Willingly would he see every one of them served as Irus had been. As he spoke, the self-invited guests came flocking around her, each pressing his suit with flattering compliments. Indeed Pallas had for the nonce made Penelope look more beautiful than ever in their eyes; and Antinous spoke out for the rest that they would by no means take themselves off till she had chosen one of them as a husband.

"Alas!" sighed the queen, "care and affliction may well have marred my charms; yet how can I hold out against you longer? My dear lord, setting forth for Troy, charged me, if he came not back, to keep myself unwed till Telemachus' beard was grown. The time has come; and soon I must choose among you, though never again can I be happy in a husband. But yours makes strange manner of wooing. A suitor is bound to

offer presents, rather than to live riotously at the expense
of her he loves."

At this reproach the aspirants to her hand were eager
to vie with one another in generosity. Each sent his
servant for some precious gift to lay before her, one
offering a richly embroidered garment, one a string of
amber beads, one a pair of glittering ear-rings, another
a costly necklace, and so forth. Penelope had all their
presents taken up to her chamber, to which she presently
retired without noticing the beggar, who chuckled to see
how his prudent wife had the art to spoil those spoilers.

When she was gone, the suitors fell to singing and
dancing by torchlight; and Odysseus was content to hold
the torches for them in his own hall, still mocked and
insulted by the lusty revellers. One of them, Eurymachus, scornfully asked what work he could do, and
if he were too lazy to take a servant's place, instead of
strolling about the country as a useless beggar. To this
the hero boldly replied—

> " I wish, at any work we two were tried,
>   In height of spring-time, when heaven's lights are long,
>   I a good crook'd scythe that were sharp and strong,
>   You such another, where the grass grew deep,
>   Up by day-break, and both our labours keep
>   Up till slow darkness eased the labouring light,
>   Fasting all day, and not a crumb till night;
>   We then should prove our either workmanship.
>   Or if, again, beeves, that the goad or whip
>   Were apt t' obey before a tearing plow,
>   Big lusty beasts, alike in bulk and brow,
>   Alike in labour, and alike in strength,
>   Our task four acres, to be till'd in length
>   Of one sole day; again then you should try
>   If the dull glebe before the plow should fly,
>   Or I a long stitch could bear clean and even.
>   Or lastly, if the Guide of earth and heaven

Should stir stern war up, either here or there,
And that at this day I had double spear,
And shield, and steel casque fitting for my brows;
At this work likewise, 'midst the foremost blows,
Your eyes should note me, and get little cause
To twit me with my belly's sole applause."

—*Chapman.*

The man who was so ready to rail at other idlers, he ended, might talk big among those that knew no better; but if Odysseus came to the house, its wide gates would be too narrow for this vaunter's haste to be off.

Eurymachus was so angry on being thus spoken back to, that he flung a stool at the impudent beggar, but only hit the cup-bearer and spilt a jug of wine, while Odysseus took refuge beside Amphinomus. The uproar was now past bearing, and Telemachus begged the drunken crew to have done with it. Amphinomus backed him up in declaring it time for bed. So after a parting cup of wine and water, and a drink offering to the gods, they all went off, each to his own quarters, leaving father and son alone together.

No sooner were they unwatched than Odysseus bade Telemachus help him in hiding away the arms and armour that hung round the hall. If the suitors missed them, excuse might be made that the bright metal was begrimed by smoke, or that weapons were as well out of the way of men like to fall quarrelling over their wine. Only a couple of swords, spears, and shields were left at hand, ready for their own use when the time came. This done, his father sent the youth to bed, he himself sitting up to talk to Penelope.

All being at last quiet, Penelope came down into the hall with her maids, who cleared the disordered banquet-board, and made up the fire, beside which their mistress sat on her chair of ivory inlaid with silver. One of the maids spoke sharply to Odysseus, and would have turned him out; but Penelope rebuked her, ordering a seat to be set for the old beggar, that she might hear what he had to tell of the husband ever in her mind.

Strange to say, sitting with him in the firelight, she did not know that long-parted spouse, nor did she recognize his voice when she began by asking who and whence he was, and he put the question off by declaring himself a man of sorrows, who would fain not recall his past. Yet she took him at once into her confidence, explaining her woeful plight, and the device by which she had so long warded off the importunity of her suitors, weaving diligently at that costly web but by night secretly undoing the labour of the day.

Glad as he was to learn her faithfulness, not yet would Odysseus reveal to this patient wife that her widowhood was at an end. With his wonted craft, he spun a story of how he came from Crete, and how he had there made acquaintance with Odysseus, nor did her emotion stir him to betray himself.

> " She listened, melting into tears
> That flowed as when on mountain height the snow,
> Shed by the west-wind, feels the east-wind's breath,[1]
> And flows in water, and the hurrying streams
> Are filled, so did Penelope's fair cheeks
> Seem to dissolve in tears,—tears shed for him
> Who sat beside her even then. He saw
> His weeping wife, and pitied her at heart;
> Yet were his eyes like iron or like horn,
> And moved not in their lids; for artfully
> He kept his tears from falling."
> —*W. C. Bryant.*

Twenty years had passed, ran his tale, since he thus

[1] It is hardly needful to point out that the poet has not our insular climate in view.

saw Odysseus; and in proof he described the very mantle
that chief wore and the gold brooch fastening it, which
with fresh tears she could remember as her parting gifts.
But quite lately he had heard of her husband as on his
way home, well and wealthy; and he called the gods to
witness his firm belief that ere long she would see the
long-lost one restored to her.

"So may it be!" sighed Penelope; "and if thy good
news come true, it shall not go without reward."

With that she would have bidden her maids spread
a soft bed for the stranger; but he laughed off all such
luxury as unfit for a hardy sailor. No maids to wait on
him, unless some elderly woman to wash his feet! Penelope gave him to the charge of Eurycleia, the head of her
household, who put him to confusion by remarking how
like he was to Odysseus in figure and in voice. This
old servant had been his own nurse, and he had to hide
his face from the firelight lest she should know him. But
as she was bathing his legs in warm water, she found on
his knee the scar given him in youth by a wild boar, a
wound she herself had dressed and could not now mistake it. In her surprise she let his foot fall, upsetting
the bath. For a moment amazement tied her tongue,
then she would have cried out her master's name, had
he not caught her by the throat, drawing her close to
whisper a command of silence. He was indeed Odysseus,
come to cleanse his house of its foes, but on pain of her
life she must not disclose him yet. The joyful old crone
promised secrecy, and without a word fetched more hot
water to finish her task; after which he went to warm
himself at the fire, taking care to hide that scar beneath
his rags.

There, before she left the hall, Penelope again addressed him. She told how, lying in bed, turning over

in her sad mind whether to remain true to the memory of Odysseus, or to rid her son's heritage of this locust swarm of suitors, if she let herself be led off by one of them as his wife, she had fallen into a dream in which she saw her flock of fat geese scattered and slain by an eagle swooping from the skies. Her guest readily interpreted that dream as a presage of Odysseus being at hand to harry the greedy suitors. But she shook her head, saying how false dreams came through the gate of ivory, as well as true ones through the gate of horn. Another device, she let him know, had come into her mind. One of her husband's feats had been to send an arrow straight through twelve axe-heads set up in a row. To this test she proposed to invite the suitors before another sun set; then whichever of them could bend the great bow of Odysseus and rival his unerring aim, him she would take for her new lord.

Let her so do without delay, replied the stranger, for he took on himself to say that before any one of that crew could bend his bow, Odysseus himself would be among them.

Penelope declared herself so pleased by his counsels that she could have stayed up all night to listen to him; but sleep was needful to mortals. Leaving her guest, then, to the care of the servants, she went to the chamber in which night by night she had bedewed her lonely couch with tears ever since Odysseus left her for that woeful war.

It was long before Odysseus could sleep on the bull's hide and heap of sheepskins where old Eurycleia wrapped him up with a warm coverlet. Lying in the silent hall, he heard outside the wanton laughter of the maidservants, debauched by those insolent interlopers; and his heart burned to understand into what disorder they had brought his house. He could hardly restrain himself from springing up to make an end to such unseemly riot; but he tried to keep patient for one more night.

> " Bear up, my soul, a little longer yet;
> A little longer to thy purpose cling!
> For, in the day when the dire Cyclops ate
> Thy valiant friends, a far more horrible thing
> Thou didst endure, till wit had power to bring
> Thee from that den where thou did'st think to die."
> —*Worsley*.

And as he tossed from side to side, scheming how he, one against so many, should avenge himself on the spoilers of his wife and son, Pallas stood over him, assuring him of her aidance, and shedding the balm of forgetfulness upon his fevered eyes. So he slept that night in his own home.

V. The Day of Doom

That night Penelope awoke from a dream of her husband; then grief to think that soon she must take a less worthy spouse made the house resound with her weeping. Thus roused, at daybreak, Odysseus stepped forth into the open air, and lifting his hands to heaven, prayed Zeus for some sign of favour. The response was a peal of thunder that cheered not his heart alone. In the outer court, where the suitors had been wont to take pastime by casting quoits or hurling spears at a mark, he stood beside the mill at which twelve women were kept hard at work grinding corn for that insatiate company: one of them, weaker than the rest, had been up all night at her task, but now she paused in it to exclaim—

"Thunder from a clear sky is a lucky omen: would it might mean the last time those tyrants of mine are to feast in the house of Odysseus!"

The hero overheard her, and took her words too for a good omen. Now sunrise set all the household astir. The maids lit the fires, swept and sprinkled the floors, wiped the tables, and cleaned the vessels under the eye of old Eurycleia. Some of them came out to fetch water from the fountain, while menservants fell to chopping firewood. To-day was to be a feast in honour of Apollo, when it behoved to have everything of the best.

Up came Eumæus driving in three fat pigs for the banquet; he greeted Odysseus kindly, and asked how it fared with him among the rude suitors. Next came Melanthius with his goats, who still growled at the beggar, promising him a taste of his fist, if he did not go off to beg elsewhere. Odysseus bowed his head without a word. More friendly was a third cattle-herd, Philœtius, who, after saluting the stranger, guessed him to be one that had seen better days.

"Nay, he reminds me of our good master, who perhaps is wandering about in like rags, if he be yet in the land of the living. So must I go on rearing his cattle to be devoured by a crew that care neither for gods nor men! I have often thought of running away; but the hope holds me that Odysseus may yet come back to send them packing."

"Friend," murmured the hero, "I vow by Zeus that you shall see Odysseus slaying these usurpers."

"Gladly would I lend a hand," answered the faithful herdsman; and Eumæus, too, prayed that he might see that day.

Telemachus, having risen and dressed, still feigned

not to notice his father, though he carefully enquired from Eurycleia as to the guest's entertainment. And soon arrived the suitors who had been laying their heads together to kill the young master forthwith. But, as they hatched their plot, an eagle with a dove in its claws flew by on the left, and this Amphinomus took for an unfavourable omen; so they agreed to spare Telemachus for the present, giving themselves up to another day of revelry.

After due sacrifices they sat down to dinner, waited on by the herdsmen. Telemachus had put his father at a table apart, where he got his portion of meat and wine served him like the rest; and to-day the young master plainly bid the suitors know that this was his house, in which he would not have a guest insulted. In spite of such warning, one ribald fellow named Ctesippus jestingly flung an ox foot at the old beggar, who ducked his head with a bitter smile, and it hit the wall. Had it not missed, exclaimed Telemachus, he would have run Ctesippus through with his spear: let them kill him at once, if they pleased; but he could no longer bear to see his house turned upside down.

So bold was his tone, that for a little the suitors sat rebuked, till one of them, Agelaus, spoke up for the rest. If Telemachus were so anxious to get rid of them, why did he not persuade his mother to choose a new husband, now that there was no chance of her seeing Odysseus again? To this the young man protested that he did not hinder his mother from making a choice, but neither would he press her to leave his own house.

That quarrel passed off, for the suitors now grew warm with wine; and Pallas was at work stealing their wits. They took to mad laughter till they cried, then

in their bleared eyes the meat before them seemed gory,
as some dark shade of coming ill fell on their heedless
hearts. One of those who sat at table was the seer
Theoclymenus, who had come with Telemachus from
Sparta, and he suddenly started up with a cry.

> " ' What is the fate of evil doom
>   Now threatening you, unhappy race?
> I see that night in thickest gloom
>   Wraps every limb, and form, and face.
>
> " ' Out bursts like fire the voice of moan,
>   Drowned are your cheeks with sorrow's flood;
> And every wall and pillared stone
>   Is soaked and dabbled in your blood.
>
> " ' Through hall and porch, full many a ghost
>   Crowds towards the mansion of the dead;
> The sun from out the heavens is lost,
>   And clouds of darkness rushing spread.'
>
> " He ceased, and they with jocund cheer
>   Into glad peals of laughter broke.
> Eurymachus addressed the seer,
>   And thus in taunting accents spoke.
>
> " ' Mad is the new-come guest. 'T is meet
>   Instant to take him from our sight,
> And lead him to the public street
>   Since he mistakes the day for night.'
>
> " Then thus replied the seer divine:
>   ' From thee no guide shall I request,
> For eyes, and ears, and feet, are mine,
>   And no weak soul inspires my breast.
>
> " ' Then from this fated house I go;
>   Swift comes the destined vengeance on;
> None shall escape the deadly blow
>   Of all the suitors—no, not one.' "
>
>   —*Maginn.*

He burst out, foreseeing the tragedy at hand; while
one of the youngest suitors sneered at Telemachus:

"Strange guests has this house! First we sit down with an idle beggar, then with a fellow who sets up for a diviner. Let us ship off the pair of them to sell as slaves for what they will fetch!"

Telemachus said not a word, but kept an eye on his father, awaiting the signal for action. And the suitors, little aware what a supper was in store for them, went on with their day-long banquet, till it was broken up by Penelope's appearance in the hall. She bore the huge bow and quiver, stored away for years, that had been given her husband by a hero of old; and behind her the handmaids carried in a chest full of steel and bronze axes. All eyes turned upon the lady, who, standing by a pillar of the hall, her face hidden by a veil, gave forth mistressfully—

"Hearken to me, ye arrogant suitors, who day by day
Afflict mine house with devouring and drinking its wealth alway,
While my lord hath been long time gone: and through all this weary
 tide
Could your false hearts find for your lips no word-pretence beside,
Save this, that each of you sorely desired to win me his bride.
Come, suitors—for this is the contest appointed your wooing to end—
I will set you the mighty bow of Odysseus the hero divine:
Whosoe'er of you all with his hands shall the bow most easily bend,
And shoot through the rings of the axes twelve ranged all in line,
Him will I follow, forsaking this beautiful home of mine,—
Dear home, that knew me a bride, with its wealth of abundant store!
I shall never forget it; in dreams I shall see it for evermore."

A. S. Way.

With this she bade Eumæus set up the axe-heads in a row, as he began to do in spite of such tears as the very sight of his master's bow brought to his eyes. Antinous jeered at the swineherd's soft-heartedness; but Telemachus carried out that charge for him, proudly then declaring that he himself must be first to make the trial.

"And if I can accomplish it," quoth he, "with none of you shall my mother go away from this house."

Twice, thrice he strove to string the stiff bow, but could not bend it. A fourth effort might have hitched the cord into its notch, had he not been checked by a sign from Odysseus, and gave it up for the others to show their more manly strength.

It was agreed that they should try in turn, going from left to right in the order of their seats at table. And the first to take the bow in hand was Leiodes, a priest, the gentlest and most modest of the suitors, but no man of muscle, and his weak arms soon threw it down in despair. Antinous laughed at so feeble an attempt, yet, seeing that this would be no easy task for the sturdiest of them, he called on Melanthius to light a fire in the court and to bring a ball of lard, to warm and grease the tough wood. But for all they could do to make it supple, one after another tried in vain to bend the bow of Odysseus.

Unable to look on unmoved, Eumæus had gone outside with his fellow herd Philœtius. Odysseus followed them to ask—

"Were some god to bring back Odysseus, are you the men to stand by him against those spoilers of his house?"

"Would the gods gave us to prove our fidelity!" was their answer; but they stared when now he told them that he himself was Odysseus.

Not till he pulled aside his rags to show them that well-remembered scar of the boar's tusk, did they recognize their travel-worn master; and they fell upon him with tears and kisses. But this was no time for idle joy. He charged Eumæus to see that the bow came lastly into his own hands, then to shut the doors of the women's apartments and keep them out of the way, while Philœtius was at once to bar the outer gates that none should escape.

Followed by those faithful servants, he went back into the house, where Antinous and Eurymachus, the most arrogant of the suitors, were now trying in turn the ordeal that baffled them like the others. Eurymachus showed himself overcome by shame at his failure, but Antinous was for putting off the trial till next day. This feast day of Apollo, he weened, were better spent in drinking and making offerings to that heavenly archer, who to-morrow might grant them more strength and skill.

As the wine again went round, out stepped that ragged beggar, demanding the bow that he might try whether adversity had unstrung his sinews.

"Is the fellow drunk!" cried scornful Antinous, rebuked by Penelope, whose will was that this stranger too should have his chance. Thereupon Telemachus stood up to announce that he only had the right to say who should handle his father's bow. He asked his mother to leave the hall and keep to her own apartments with the women: such disputes were for a man to settle.

When Penelope had retired, Eumæus was for bringing the bow to Odysseus, but the suitors raised so high an outcry that he would have put it down, had not Telemachus hotly ordered him not to mind them. The bow, then, was given to the beggar, who at once began handling it carefully and lovingly, turning it over to make sure the horns had not been worm-eaten in all those years. The suitors took for certain he could make nothing of it; but to their consternation he strung it as lightly as a bard tunes his lyre, and twanged the tight cord so that it twittered like a swallow at his touch. At that moment there came a peal of thunder overhead to stir up his heart; but the suitors turned pale, as the seeming beggar fixed an arrow on the bowstring, and without rising from his seat, he shot it straight through the heads of the twelve axes, not one missed.[1]

"Your guest, Telemachus, has not put you to shame!" he cried exultingly.

With proud glance he gave a signal that brought the eager youth to his side, sword and spear in hand, while, as if by magic, the beggar stood up in appalling might.

> "Then fierce the hero o'er the threshold strode;
> Stripped of his rags, he blazed out like a god.
> Full in their face the lifted bow he bore
> And quivered deaths, a formidable store.
> Before his feet the rattling shower he threw,
> And thus terrific to the suitor-crew:
> 'One venturous game this hand has won to-day,
> Another, princes, yet remains to play!'"

Therewith he let fly the first deadly shaft. Antinous had raised a cup of wine to quench his dismay, when it struck him on the throat, and he rolled over, dragging the table and the meats on it to the floor, where the wine mingled with his blood, such a slip was there between the cup and the lip. The other suitors started to their feet, still not fully aware what a fate was upon them all, and they angrily cried out at the man who had killed their comrade, by mischance as they thought, till they heard his voice above the uproar.

---

[1] Commentators have puzzled themselves over the shape of the axe-heads through which this shot had to be made, whether rings, curved notches, the gap between two-headed axes, or what.   There is also controversy as to the arrangement of the house: we may best conceive of the banqueting hall as a roofed space or cloister opening at one side upon an inner courtyard in which the axes were set up, beyond which again came an outer enclosure. As to the geography of the poem, *savants* who have variously mapped the hero's course, seem to forget that poets hold masters' certificates to navigate seas of fancy

"Dogs, did ye deem Odysseus dead? Ye have wasted my substance, ye have debauched my servants, ye have sought to take my wife. Now shall ye die, as enemies of gods and men!"

At the very name of Odysseus that trembling band shrank before him; and Eurymachus, speaking for the rest, would have softened the hero's rage.

"We have indeed done thee wrong," he confessed. "But Antinous was foremost in the trespass that has cost him his life. Spare us, and we will make amends, paying for our misdeeds in gold and bronze and oxen."

"All that ye own is too little to make amends for what ye owe me," was the fierce answer. "But I shall take payment in full. Ye must fight for your lives, forfeit to my vengeance."

When they saw no hope of mercy, the terrified suitors had to stand on their defence. They looked vainly for the arms hung round the hall, which through the night had been hidden out of their reach. Drawing their swords, they caught up the overturned tables to serve as shields, and rushed in a body upon Odysseus. But their leader Eurymachus fell with an arrow in his heart; and when Amphinomus took his place, Telemachus brought him too to the ground, transfixed by a spear; then the rest drew back to take hurried counsel and to look about for some way of escape.

While Odysseus held them in check with his arrows, Telemachus hastened to bring from the storeroom arms for Eumæus and Philœtius. The traitor Melanthius, having stolen along back ways, was doing the same for the enemy; but his fellow herds caught him in the storeroom, and hung him helplessly to the rafters to await further punishment. Odysseus had kept on shooting down the suitors one by one, so long as his arrows lasted.

They fled back in the courtyard as far as might be out of reach of his deadly aim; and he took his stand at a postern, their only way of escape, soon with three well-armed men at his side, yea four, for Pallas appeared by him in the likeness of his old friend Mentor. Before long, indeed, she took a more shadowy form, soaring up to hover above the fight, warding off the spears of the foemen from Odysseus, or flashing dismay into their eyes with her terrible ægis.

Still outnumbering that little band, they huddled together at the farther end of the court, like cattle tormented by flies, and let themselves be slain helplessly, as doves by vultures. Leiodes the priest fell at the knees of Odysseus praying for mercy, as aforetime he had prayed that the hero might never return; but his prayers did not avail him. More fortunate was Phemius the bard, who pleaded, nor in vain, that he had been forced into singing for the godless crew. Medon the herald also was spared at the request of Telemachus, to whom in his boyhood this man had been kind, and he had warned Penelope of the suitors' plot against her son. These two fearfully clung to the altar of Zeus, but the rest lay gasping in their blood, like a net full of fish drawn on the beach; and Odysseus went from one quivering corpse to another to make sure that they would trouble him no more.

When all was over, he sent Telemachus to call Eurycleia. She found her master ranging up and down like a lion over the prey; and when she saw the ground strewn with the enemies of his house, the old nurse raised an exultant cry, at once silenced by Odysseus—

"Woman, experienced as thou art, control
Indecent joy, and feast thy secret soul.

To insult the dead is cruel and unjust,
Fate and their crime have sunk them to the dust."

What he sought from her was to know which of the
servants had been misled by the suitors. Of fifty maids
that made the household, she pointed out twelve as
unfaithful to their duty and their mistress. These he
ordered to be hanged; and Melanthius, too, was now
put to a cruel death for taking the part of his master's
foes. Lastly, the executioners washed their hands and
feet; then Odysseus had fire lit and sulphur burnt on it
to purify his house from the reek of blood.

This done, the doors were unlocked, behind which
Penelope and her maids had been shut up safe from harm.
They came forth astonished to find the house cleansed
from its plague; but not even yet could Penelope believe that the ragged and gore-grimed beggar was no
other than her husband: only some god, she thought,
could have so dealt with that throng of oppressors. In
vain Telemachus besought her to speak to his father. She
turned away her eyes and stood dumb for amazement.

Odysseus bid the bard Phemius strike his lyre to set
the servants dancing, sounds of revelry that brought a
crowd about the house outside, little aware what had
gone on within, but taking it that Penelope's wedding
was come at last. Meanwhile, the hero retired with old
Eurycleia to the bath, from which he came forth washed
and anointed, in goodly clothes, looking like a god indeed, for Pallas had breathed over him an air of more
than manly beauty.

Still Penelope was hard of belief that it could be her
own husband who sat down before her. To try him, she
bade Eurycleia bring out the bed of Odysseus from his
chamber.

"Nay," quoth he, "there is no man living can move that bed, unless some god aid him. For I built this house round an olive tree, and the stump I dressed to be the post of my bridal bed, as is known only to me and to thee."

That proof broke down Penelope's lingering disbelief. She threw her arms round her husband's neck, with tears, kisses, and excuses for having been so slow to own him.

> "'Frown not, Odysseus; thou art wise and true!
> But God gave sorrow, and hath grudged to make
> Our path to old age sweet, nor willed us to partake
>
> "'Youth's joys together. Yet forgive me this,
> Nor hate me that when first I saw thy brow
> I fell not on thy neck, and gave no kiss,
> Nor wept in thy dear arms as I weep now.
> For in my breast a bitter fear did bow
> My soul, and I lived shuddering day by day,
> Lest a strange man come hither, and avow
> False things, and steal my spirit, and bewray
> My love; such guile men scheme, to lead the pure astray.'
>
> . . . .
>
> "Sweet as to swimmers the dry land appears,
> Whose bark Poseidon in the angry sea
> Strikes with a tempest, and in pieces tears,
> And a few swimmers from the white deep flee,
> Crested with salt foam, and with tremulous knee
> Spring to the shore exulting; even so
> Sweet was her husband to Penelope,
> Nor from his neck could she at all let go
> Her white arms, nor forbid her thickening tears to flow."
>
> —*Worsley.*

Much had the so-long-sundered pair to hear and to tell between them. The whole night would not have been enough for the story of twenty years, had not Pallas drawn out their rapturous hours by her guardian care, holding back the fleet steeds of Aurora beneath the ocean.

to lengthen the night after that day when Odysseus came
to his own.

VI. The End of the Odyssey

But not yet were the hero's trials at an end. Next
day he went to visit his aged father Laertes, who lived at
a farm some way from the town. Odysseus found him
working alone in his vineyard, sorrily dressed and bowed
down by years of grief for his lost son. Tears filled the
wanderer's eyes to see him so woebegone; yet this crafty
man, after his wont, must needs play on broken heart-
strings by a freshly feigned tale. He went up to the half-
blind greybeard with a story of his having met with his
son in distant lands; but when Laertes piteously lamented
him as one dead and gone, he could not bear to keep up
that deceit.

"Know'st thou me not?" he cried, throwing his arms
round the old man's neck. "I am Odysseus himself!"

But now Laertes was slow to trust the good fortune
despaired of so long. Not till his son had let him see
that scar of the boar's tusk would he believe; and all
doubt left him, when Odysseus pointed out in the orchard
the trees his father had given him in childhood to be his
very own. Then Laertes thanked heaven that the gods
still lived to do justice on earth; and joy so worked on
his withered heart, that after changing those mean clothes,
as sign of mourning laid aside, he seemed to have grown
years younger in an hour.

With his household he sat down to feast in honour
of his son's return; but soon the merrymaking was disturbed. News having spread of the suitors' fate, their
kinsmen and friends had gathered at the house of Odysseus to bear away the dead bodies to their homes in

Ithaca and the adjacent isles. Amid their lamentations, they cried loudly for revenge, and the father of Antinous stirred them up against the returned hero who had worked such woe to them and theirs. Others spoke for peace, saying that the dead men had brought their doom upon themselves; but, while half of the crowd dispersed to their own homes, the rest hurried off to fall upon Odysseus in his father's house.

At the noise of their approach, the servants of Laertes flew to arms, the old man himself donning armour he could hardly bear. They sallied forth to meet the foe, with Odysseus at their head, and by his side Telemachus eager to show himself worthy son of so brave a sire. Already the spears had begun to whiz and to clang upon helmet and shield, when Zeus sent a thunderbolt to stay their hands, and an awful voice forbade further slaughter. Thereupon Pallas herself appeared in the form of Mentor between the hostile bands, who at her command dropped their arms to make a covenant of atonement and goodwill.

So ends the story of Homer's *Odyssey*; but other legends tell of further adventures in which the hero vanished from the sight of men. His death, it had been prophesied, should come out of the sea; and after so many wanderings he may well have found it hard to live on land at ease. In Hades, Tiresias had enjoined on him a penance whereby he might appease the anger of Poseidon: he must seek out a people that never saw the sea, nor knew of ships, nor tasted salt; he should go among them bearing an oar which the simple folk would mistake for a winnowing fan; and upon this sign he was to sacrifice a ram, a boar, and a bull to that offended deity, with due offerings to the other gods: thus he might end his days in peace and honour.

We hear nothing of how this penance was performed, but only that, once more deserting Penelope and giving up his kingdom to Telemachus, the bold Odysseus again sailed to tempt fortune on unknown seas. Later bards had glimpses, as in a vision, of how it may have fared with him in some new world of waters and enchanted islands. Tennyson imagines for us what must have been the dauntless and restless mind of such a hero in his shortening days.

> " My mariners,
> Souls that have toil'd, and wrought, and thought with me—
> That ever with a frolic welcome took
> The thunder and the sunshine, and opposed
> Free hearts, free foreheads—you and I are old;
> Old age hath yet his honour and his toil;
> Death closes all: but something ere the end,
> Some work of noble note, may yet be done,
> Not unbecoming men that strove with Gods.
> The lights begin to twinkle from the rocks:
> The long day wanes: the slow moon climbs: the deep
> Moans round with many voices. Come, my friends,
> 'T is not too late to seek a newer world.
> Push off, and sitting well in order smite
> The sounding furrows; for my purpose holds
> To sail beyond the sunset, and the baths
> Of all the western stars, until I die.
> It may be that the gulfs will wash us down:
> It may be we shall touch the Happy Isles,
> And see the great Achilles, whom we knew.
> Tho' much is taken, much abides; and tho'
> We are not now that strength which in old days
> Moved earth and heaven; that which we are, we are;
> One equal temper of heroic hearts,
> Made weak by time and fate, but strong in will
> To strive, to seek, to find, and not to yield."

But a poet strained his eyes further into Odysseus' fate, when from the much-enduring man's soul in *Inferno*, Dante took the tale how that venturesome crew had

safely passed the Pillars of Hercules, on unknown seas
to come in view of the highest mountain they ever
beheld.

> " Joy seized us straight
> But soon to mourning changed. From the new land
> A whirlwind sprung, and at her foremost side
> Did strike the vessel. Thrice it whirled her round
> With all the waves, the fourth time lifted up
> The poop, and sank the prow: so fate decreed·
> And over us the booming billow closed.'

HERO AND LEANDER

The Trojan land had tales of love as well as of war. Who has not heard of Leander, bold youth of Abydos, he that wooed fair Hero, Aphrodite's priestess at her shrine on the Thracian shore? Many lovers sighed for a maid fit to rank among the Graces; yet she smiled upon none but Leander, who lived at once so near and so far from her temple-dwelling at Sestos. For the strong tide of the Hellespont rolled between them night and day; and their eyes strained across it to catch each other's smiles thrown in vain from Europe to Asia.

But all-powerful love can find a way over the wildest water. At the close of each day, as Hesperus led in the stars, Leander stole down beside the Mysian strand, his eager eyes watching for the light of a torch with which Hero nightly beckoned him through the darkness to her sea-washed tower. That was signal for him to plunge into the waves, swimming swift and strong athwart the sundering current till, guided by that friendly gleam, he came safe across to rest in the arms of his Thracian bride. When dawn spread in the eastern sky, he anointed his limbs afresh with oil, and, all aglow from a parting kiss, swam back to Abydos, "himself the pilot, passenger and bark".

So he did throughout the summer weather, night by night, and all went well. Then came rough winter, bringing clouds and chills and tempests, and alas!

> "That night of stormy water
> When Love, who sent, forgot to save

The young, the beautiful, the brave,
The lonely hope of Sestos' daughter.
Oh! when alone along the sky
Her turret torch was blazing high,
Though rising gale and breaking foam
And shrieking sea-birds warned him home,
And clouds aloft and tides below,
With signs and sounds forbade to go—
He could not see, he would not hear,
Or sound or sign foreboding fear;
His eye but saw that light of love,
The only star it hailed above;
His ear but rang with Hero's song,
'Ye waves, divide not lovers long!'"

—Byron.

That stout swimmer had not shrunk from the roaring billows, on which for once he was tossed astray, now dragged down below the black water, now heaved up to catch a glimpse of the beacon that should be his guiding star. His breath failed him; his strokes grew feebler; chill spray and blinding foam hooded his eyes bent longingly towards the flickering torch. Suddenly it went out, when, through the howl of the storm, he might wellnigh have heard Hero's exclamation where she stood vainly trying to shield the light with her robe.

Anxiously she watched out the dark night, at once hoping and fearing that Leander had not ventured his perilous passage. But when, by the first gleam of day, she looked forth from her tower, it was to see his white body washed upon the rocks below, and the sullen foam stained by his blood. With one miserable cry, tearing off her priestly vestments, she leaped into the waves, to die beside her lover and be united to him in fame.

CUPID AND PSYCHE

I. Aphrodite's Rival

Once upon a time a king and queen had three fair daughters, of whom the two eldest at fit time came to wed princely suitors. But the youngest, Psyche, was so wondrously beautiful that no one durst woo her, who seemed worthy rather of adoration. Men gazed at her from afar as at a goddess, and the rumour went that this was no mortal maiden, but Aphrodite herself revealed on earth to show her matchless charms in flesh and blood.

So eager was all the world to behold this prodigy, that far and wide the altars of the true goddess stood cold and silent, her chief shrines at Cnidus, Paphos, and Cythera deserted by the crowds flocking to strew flowers under the feet of Psyche. The jealous Aphrodite, seeing herself neglected for such a rival, called on her son to avenge her with his mischievous arrows.

"Inflame her heart with love, but with hottest love for the meanest wretch alive, so that together they may come to poverty and sorrow!"

Young Cupid needed not the kisses and caresses with which she would have coaxed him to such an errand. Ever too ready to play his cruel tricks, he promised to do his mother's bidding, and flew off to work harm for Psyche. But at the first sight of her beauty he was so amazed that he dropped on his foot the shaft he had made ready for her, and so became wounded by the enchantment of his own weapon. Himself unseen, he loved this mortal as hotly as he thought to make her love some unworthy man.

> " From place to place Love followed her that day,
> And ever fairer to his eyes she grew,
> So that at last when from her bower he flew,
> And underneath his feet the moonlit sea
> Went shepherding his waves disorderly,
> He swore that of all gods and men no one
> Should hold her in his arms but he alone;
> That she should dwell with him in glorious wise
> Like to a goddess in some paradise;
> Yea, he would get from Father Jove this grace
> That she should never die, but her sweet face
> And wonderful fair body should endure
> Till the foundations of the mountains sure
> Were molten in the sea; so utterly
> Did he forget his mother's cruelty."
>
> *—W. Morris.*

Meanwhile it grieved Psyche's parents that so many came to wonder at but none to wed their youngest daughter, left at home like a virgin-widow, lamenting her too renowned charms. The anxious father sought an oracle of Apollo to know how she should find a husband; and the answer filled him with dread. On the top of a high rocky mountain, he was told, he must leave his daughter alone in bridal array. There should she be wooed by one of whom the very gods stood in fear: she whom men likened to Aphrodite was worthy of no common mate.

Hard was it to part with their daughter thus; but her parents durst not disobey the oracle. At nightfall they led her up the mountain, with a wedding train that seemed rather a funeral, for the light of the torches burned dim, and the songs of the bridesmaids turned to dirges, and poor Psyche was fain to dry her tears with her bridal veil. But having resigned herself to this strange fate as the will of the gods, she strove to comfort her weeping friends. The top of the mountain reached, they quenched the torches, and with tearful farewells left the maiden alone at dead of night as if borne here to her tomb.

When all were gone, Psyche stood shuddering in the chill darkness, so full of fear that she had almost called them to stay, or hurried after their footsteps while still heard on the mountain side. But soon came a gentle Zephyr that softly wrapped her about and carried her away to lay her on a bed of scented flowers, where all the rest of the night she slept off her sadness and weariness.

Daylight awoke her to look round in wonder. Close at hand, she saw a grove of tall trees, through which flowed a crystal stream, and on its banks stood a house so noble that it appeared the home of a god. The roof of costly woods was borne up by golden and ivory pillars; the floor was paved with coloured marbles, and the walls glowed with pictures inlaid in gems and precious metals. When Psyche ventured to enter, she found vast inner halls more and more splendid the farther she stole on tiptoe, filled with treasures from every part of the earth, and everywhere lit by a gleam of gold shining like the sun. And what seemed most marvellous, all these riches were unguarded, every door stood open, and no living form came to view, as she passed from chamber to chamber, lost in astonishment at the wealth of their unknown lord.

"Who can it be that owns so many rich and beautiful things!" she cried out at length; and soft voices answered in her ear, though as yet she saw no human form.

"All are thine, Psyche! And we are thy servants, appointed to wait on thee. Command us as thou wilt, and it shall be done."

When she was tired of wandering through the palace, and feasting her eyes on its beauty, Psyche took courage to try what such invisible attendants could do for her. Having refreshed herself by bathing in a bath of silver, she took her place at a golden table that was at once spread with the finest fare; then as she ate and drank, soft music arose and a choir of sweet voices filled the room where she sat alone.

So the day passed by as in a dream; and when night fell, she would have lain down on a soft couch spread for her by those unseen hands. Now was she aware of a shadow by her side, and had almost cried out for terror. But her fears were kissed away as she found herself warmly embraced in the darkness, and heard a voice murmuring in kindest tones—

"Dear Psyche, I am the husband chosen for thee by destiny. Ask not my name, seek not to see my face; only believe in my love, and all will be well with us!"

The very sound of his voice and the very touch of his hand won Psyche's heart to this unseen bridegroom. All night he told her of his love, and before daylight dawned, he was gone, since so it must be, promising with a kiss to return as soon as darkness fell.

Thus it was, night after night, that went by in tender speeches and endearments; yet never could she see her lover's face.

II. The Jealous Sisters

Psyche rejoiced in the love of this husband who came to her only by night; but sad were the long days through which she had to live alone. She soon wearied of wandering about her splendid house that seemed like a gilded cage; the daintiest food did not please her so long as no one shared it; the sunlit hours went too slowly by in sighing for the darkness that should bring back the joy of her life. In vain she begged him not to leave her by day, when she might see his face.

"It may not be," he whispered, and sealed her lips with kisses. "A dire danger threatens thee, if thou shouldst know who or what I am. Be content to trust in my love, that is ever thine."

Strive as she might to be content, still poor Psyche pined in that daily solitude; and she besought her unseen husband to let her have at least a visit from her sisters to cheer her in his absence.

"Dearest Psyche!" cried he, "I fear they will come to do thee harm. Already they seek thee on the rocky crest where thou wert last seen of men; but they bring hate and peril for our love."

Yet she wept and entreated, till in the end he gave her leave to see her sisters, making her promise to tell them nothing about himself. So next morning, when he vanished with daylight, the same Zephyr that had wafted Psyche to this beautiful valley, was charged to catch up her two sisters and bring them to the house in which she lived alone with invisible attendants.

Glad was she to see them again, and not less amazed were they by the riches and adornments of her new home. But when eagerly they questioned her as to the master of all this wealth, she put them off with short answers. Her husband, she said, was a handsome young prince who stayed out all day hunting in the woods. And lest she should be tempted by their curiosity to say more, she made haste to dismiss the sisters with costly presents before the hour that should bring him to her arms.

But they, filled with envy of her good fortune, came back next day set on knowing who could be that great lord so much richer than their own husbands. With caresses they again sought to worm the secret out of her; and this time, forgetting what she had said of him before, she gave out her husband as a grey-bearded merchant, whose affairs called him often away from home. Nor did the sisters fail to note how she contradicted herself, so letting them understand she had something to hide.

Again dismissed with rich presents, the jealous elders were hotter than ever to know the secret of Psyche's marriage. They guessed that this husband of hers must be no mere man, and enviously railed at her for making a mystery of his real name. So they hatched a plot, of which he was well aware, for that night he murmured in her ear—

"Dearest one, beware of thy sisters. To-morrow they will tempt thee to look on me; but that would be the end of our happiness."

With tears and kisses Psyche vowed she would rather die a hundred times than disobey his least wish; and when left alone in the morning, she was determined to keep her secret. But soon came the sisters, who now coaxed and threatened her by turns, till in her confusion she owned to not having told them the truth. At last they pressed her to a confession that she had never seen this bridegroom who visited her only by dark night, and that she knew not even his name.

"Dear sister," said they, "it is as we feared. Believe us, who are older and wiser, and mean thy welfare. That false bridegroom is in truth a loathly monster that durst not meet the eye, lest love should be changed to horror. For all his fair words, his purpose is to devour thee secretly; and such will soon be Psyche's fate unless she act by our counsel."

"What shall I do?" cried Psyche, wringing her hands, for she believed their false words, knowing not why else her husband should remain ever unseen.

"Have ready a lamp and a sharp knife," they bid her. "As soon as he is asleep, light the lamp, then the sight of the monster's hateful form will steel thy hand to drive the knife to his cruel heart. Thus only canst thou save thine own life."

Earnestly urging her to follow their counsel without delay, her sisters left Psyche tossed in mind like the waves of the sea. She doubted whether to obey them or her own heart. She at once loved her unseen husband and hated the monster they pictured him to be. But as night drew near, she made ready the lamp and the knife, with which she hoped to find courage to save herself from the threatened destruction.

As always, her husband came home with the darkness, and after embracing Psyche, lay down in bed. Curiosity now aiding dread, she made up her mind at least to see what shape he bore. When his breathing told that he was asleep, she rose to light the lamp; then holding it up in one hand and the sharp knife in the other, she stole softly to his side.

A cry had almost burst from her lips, as the lamp-gleam showed the sweetest and loveliest of monsters,

Cupid himself in the bloom of youthful beauty, with ambrosial locks curling about his rosy cheeks, and snow-white shoulders on which his wings were softly folded like flowers. At such a sight the knife dropped from Psyche's trembling hand. Beside him lay his bow and quiver, whence she drew out one of the golden-tipped arrows, and in examining it pricked her finger, instantly inflaming her blood with new love for a husband no longer unseen.

Bending over this sleeping form, she would have hastily stooped to kiss him, when in her agitation she let a drop of hot oil fall from the lamp upon his shoulder. Roused by the smart, Cupid sprang up, and at a glance understood all.

"Ah, Psyche!" he exclaimed, "thou hast ruined our love. Why listen to thy treacherous sisters rather than to my warning? Now we must part for ever!"

In tearful entreaties she sank before him, and sought to clasp his knees; but he spread his wings and flew into the air without a look of forgiveness. At the same moment, the enchanted palace vanished about her like a dream, then Psyche stood alone in the cold darkness, calling vainly for the love she had lost, with his last words ringing in her ears.

> "Farewell! though I, a god, can never know
>   How thou canst lose thy pain, yet time will go
>   Over thine head, and thou mayst mingle yet
>   The bitter and the sweet, nor quite forget,
>   Nor quite remember, till these things shall seem
>   The wavering memory of a lovely dream."
>   —*W. Morris.*

III. Penance and Pardon

Psyche's first thought, as she turned away from the scene of her lost happiness, was to die in despair. Coming to a river bank, she threw herself into its black water; but the pitiful stream washed her ashore on the further side, and she wandered on, hardly knowing where she went. She passed through the cities where lived her sisters; and these jealous women would have persuaded her that she had done well to follow their advice, since love was a cruel monster, for all the fair shapes he could take. Yet, on hearing truly how it had gone with her, the sisters in turn stole away to the top of that high mountain, each hoping that she herself might be chosen for the bride of a god. Far otherwise it fared with them, when, one after the other, they were caught up by a strong wind and dashed to destruction over the misty cliffs.

Meanwhile Psyche went her way alone through the world, everywhere seeking in vain for her vanished love. He, fevered by the pain of his burnt shoulder, or rather by the same grief as gave Psyche no rest by night and day, had taken refuge in his mother's chamber, and lay sick of a wound he durst not own. But a telltale bird whispered in Aphrodite's ear how Cupid had deigned to love a mortal, and hot was her anger to learn this no other than the very maid boasted on earth as her rival.

In sore dudgeon the resentful goddess tended her son with rating and upbraiding. She threatened to take away his arrows, to unstring his bow, to quench his torch and to clip his wings, that he might no more fly about playing mischievous pranks on gods and men. And though she could not bring herself to punish him as he deserved, all the more eagerly she sought out Psyche for her vengeance. In vain her sister goddesses strove to appease her, making excuses for that wilful boy, reminding her that he must not be treated always as a child, asking who might choose a bride if not the god of love, and why marriage should be hateful in her family of all others.

Their jests but stirred the mother of Cupid to direr wrath. By leave of Zeus, she sent down Hermes to proclaim through the world that whoever sheltered Psyche should be punished as an enemy to the gods, but seven kisses from Aphrodite herself were offered as reward to whoever gave her up. This proclamation reached poor Psyche's own ears, when, tired of the bootless search for her husband, she was ready to throw herself on his mother's mercy; and, going from one temple to another, some kinder goddess gave her counsel to seek forgiveness at the queen of Love's. Having none other refuge in her hapless plight, as a humble suppliant she approached the halls of Aphrodite, where she had no sooner told her name than one of the servants dragged her by the hair into her mistress's presence.

"At last!" the goddess greeted her with mocking laughter. "At last, thou comest to greet thy mother-in-law! Or is it to visit that husband of thine, that lies sick through thy hurting? I have had trouble enough to catch thee; but now thou shalt not go without learning what it is to rival Aphrodite."

Tearing her clothes for rage, she gave over Psyche to be scourged by sore tormentors who stood ready to obey her will. All day, the offended goddess cast about for means of wreaking her spite against the unwelcome daughter-in-law, who next morning was called to where Aphrodite had mixed up together a heap of wheat, barley, millet, peas, beans, and other seeds.

"Behold!" was her scornful greeting. "An ill-favoured face like thine can earn a husband only by industry; so I will try thee at work. Sift me all these seeds, laying each kind apart; and let me see it done by evening."

With this the goddess went off in richest array to a wedding feast, leaving her daughter-in-law a task which she soon gave up as hopeless, and sat down to await fresh chastisement, since so it must be. But a little ant took pity on her despair, and called out a troop of his kind to help Cupid's bride. Diligently they ran and carried all day, separating and sorting the different seeds, then vanished when the work was done.

At nightfall Aphrodite came back from the feast, wreathed with roses, scented with odours, and flushed with wine. Darkly she frowned to see how the task had been accomplished.

"This is no work of thine!" she cried, flinging to Psyche a crust of bread, and leaving her to sleep on the bare earth, while the goddess retired to her own luxurious couch. She had taken care to have her son locked up in an inner chamber, lest he and his bride should come to know how near they were to each other.

Next morning Psyche was roused betimes by her tyrant, who led her in sight of a rocky hill, and showed her a thicket at the top, about which fed a flock of wild sheep with fleeces shining like gold.

"They are untamed as lions," Aphrodite told her, "but I must needs have a handful of their golden fleece. Fetch it for me before the sun sets."

In silence Psyche set out on this errand; but soon she thought of throwing herself from the rocks rather than venture to handle such wild beasts, that could hence be seen butting at each other fiercely with their great horns. Then as she looked down upon a deep pool which seemed fit for a grave, the Nymph of that fountain spoke from its depths.

"Psyche, defile not with thy death my sacred water! I know what troubles thee, and can give helpful counsel. Now, in the heat of the sun, the wild creatures play and fight, and it would be dangerous to come near their sharp horns, yea, their venomous teeth. But when they are tired, they will lie down to sleep in the shade; then thou mayst safely steal up to where they have left their fleecy gold, torn by thorns or hanging to the branches."

She took this good advice, and when the sheep lay down to rest, she was able to gather off the thorns a whole lapful of their golden wool, which she brought back long before evening. But obedience still gained her no favour.

"I will try thy courage and strength where there will be none to help," said Aphrodite. "Behold that cloudy mountain, from whose crest flows a black stream that waters the Stygian marsh and falls into the fiery river of Cocytus. Haste to fill this crystal urn from its icy source, then bring it back to me before sunset."

Psyche took the urn, and patiently set out on her errand, from which soon she never thought to come back alive. For as she toiled upwards, she saw how the way was guarded by fearsome dragons that from afar glared at her with burning eyes and hissed out of their swelling throats. And the cold stream was its own guard, falling over the slippery cliffs in cataracts that, as they dashed into a dark abyss, warned her back with angry voices.

"What doest thou here? Away, or be swept from our path!"

Long before she got near the top, Psyche sank down like a stone, too much dismayed even for tears.

But a friend was at hand.   Overhead hovered the eagle
of Zeus, that, mindful how Cupid had guided its course
when sent to fly away with Ganymede from Mount Ida,
was now willing to serve his hapless bride.

"Weak and unknowing one," screamed the royal bird,
as it swooped down upon the mountain side, "canst
thou hope to steal a drop from that sacred spring, or
even to approach it?   The very gods, yea Zeus himself,
hold its black water in dread.   But give the task to me."

She let the urn be snatched away in the eagle's claws,
and swiftly it soared over the heads of the spitting
dragons, and above the boiling cataracts, into clouds that
darkly wrapped the summit; then soon it came back
with the urn filled from Stygian springs.   Psyche thankfully took it, to carry it carefully down without spilling
a drop.   Yet not a whit was her mistress appeased.

"Art thou, then, a witch, or wicked enchantress, so
lightly to finish such perilous tasks?" said Aphrodite
mockingly.   "But thou shalt be tried still further, my
darling, and learn what it is to have the goddess of love
for a foe!"

Too tearful were it to tell of all her spite made the
hated daughter-in-law do and suffer.[1]   But those trials had
an end when Cupid got to hear of his mother's cruelty,
that made him love Psyche all the more.   Escaping secretly
from his sick-chamber, he flew up to Olympus, and
besought Zeus to favour his wedding with a daughter
of men.

"Art thou one to ask indulgence at my hands!"

---

[1] In Apuleius, Psyche's last ordeal is being sent to Hades to seek for Aphrodite a
blush of Persephone's beauty.   This episode may be here omitted, as repeating the
experiences of Orpheus and other adventurers in the nether-world, while the heroine
also repeats her fault of curiosity, for, like Pandora, she opens the casket containing
the charm, that would have been lost but for Cupid's interference as she lay overcome
by a swoon.

quoth that father of the gods, stroking the lad's smooth face. "On which of us, pray, hast thou not played those tricks of thine? I myself have been turned into a bull, a swan, or what not, through thy frolicsome roguery. But we cherish thee kindly as the spoilt child of Olympus, for all thy faults; and if I grant thy prayer, be mindful of the grace thou hast ill deserved."

Forthwith Zeus sent out Hermes to summon a meeting of the gods, to which Aphrodite must come among the rest on pain of high displeasure; and Psyche, too, was brought in with downcast eyes that lit up at the sight of her lost lover among the radiant band. When all were assembled, the father of heaven thus addressed them—

"Gods and goddesses, ye all know this tricky boy, who has grown up among us, and whose wild pranks I have often had to chastise. Now he is of an age to settle down, with his wanton restlessness fettered in chains of marriage. He has chosen a bride among the daughters of men, to whom he has plighted his troth for weal or woe. What is done, is done; and so·be it! Thou, mother of love," he turned to Aphrodite, "do not grudge this alliance with a mortal. To make her the equal of her spouse, I raise her among the gods: henceforth let none despise a child of heaven; and thou, Psyche, take from me the gift of immortality in reward of thy faithful love."

With this he held a goblet of nectar to her trembling lips. Psyche drank the wine of the gods; but the charm of deathlessness that ran through her veins was not such a strong cordial as to find Cupid's arms once more thrown round her, in full light of day. All the gods hailed their union; for even Aphrodite ceased to frown when she saw her son's pouting face now bright with smiles, nor could she scorn a daughter-in-law welcomed to Olympus.

So now their wedding feast was held in the home of the gods. Hephæstus cooked the dishes; Dionysus and Ganymede filled the wine cups. The Seasons wreathed the guests with blooming flowers; the Graces scattered perfumes; the Muses sang sweetly to Apollo's lyre; and who but proud Aphrodite herself led the dance! After all their troubles, Cupid and Psyche were made happy; and their first child was a daughter named Joy. Nor was this last of the immortals the least among them in the eyes of generations to come, and in the honour of poets for her that had no priest.

> "O brightest! though too late for antique vows,
>   Too, too late for the fond believing lyre,
> When holy were the haunted forest boughs,
>   Holy the air, the water, and the fire;
> Yet even in these days so far retired
>   From happy pieties, thy lucent fans,
>   Fluttering among the faint Olympians,
> I see, and sing, by my own eyes inspired.
> So let me be thy choir, and make a moan
>   Upon the midnight hours;
> Thy voice, thy lute, thy pipe, thy incense sweet
>   From swinged censer teeming;
> Thy shrine, thy grove, thy oracle, thy heat
>   Of pale-mouthed prophet dreaming."
>
> —*Keats.*

THE RING OF POLYCRATES

Of all men in the world none seemed to be more fortunate than Polycrates, tyrant of Samos. That rich island he had mastered by force; and there for a time he reigned along with his two brothers, till having slain one of them and banished the other, he made himself its sole ruler. For long all prospered with him. No day passed but brought news of some victory to his fleet, or some ship came sailing back to the harbour laden with slaves and booty. So mighty grew his power that he hoped to make himself lord of the sea, and of all Ionia, where no city had so many galleys or so well-armed soldiers as Samos.

In the flush of his triumphs, Polycrates offered himself as an ally to Amasis, the great king of Egypt, who at first welcomed his friendship, but soon sent him this message.

"A man ever fortunate has much to fear. None rise to such power as thine without making enemies, and so long as one of them lives, he cannot be secure. Nay, the gods themselves are jealous of men with whom all goes too well; good and ill by turns make the common lot of mortals. I never heard of any so great as to have no cares, who yet came to a happy end. It were well for thee, then, to choose out thy richest treasure and offer it as a sacrifice to the gods, that still they may forbear to lay on thee tribute of adversity."

Pondering on this counsel, the tyrant judged it wise. After surveying his treasures, he chose out from them an emerald seal-ring of great price, as what he would least like to lose; and this it seemed best to sacrifice. He put out to sea in a sumptuous galley, whence, in the eyes of his courtiers and guards, he solemnly threw the ring into deep water, trusting it might buy him the favour of the gods.

Before reaching home, he grudged that costly gem, and for days he sat reproaching himself for having thrown it away. A week had not passed when a poor fisherman brought to the palace a large fish which he thought worthy to be a present for the lord of Samos, who accepted it as his due. Then soon his servants came running to him with his sparkling ring, found inside the fish when it came to be cut up.

Polycrates took this for a sign his luck would ever be unbroken. He wrote joyfully to Amasis how he had followed his counsel, but how the gods had given back the precious offering. In answer, to his astonishment, the wise king sent a herald renouncing alliance with him as one who seemed destined to some signal calamity.

Yet the tyrant in his pride would take no warning. It is told of him that, gathering together all who murmured against his rule in Samos, he sent them in a fleet to help Cambyses, king of Persia, in his war on Egypt, since its king shrunk from his friendship. But these exiles, instead of fighting for one they hated, sailed over to Greece, and at Sparta sought aid against their tyrant. Then the Spartans, whose way was to be short in speech as strong in deeds, mocked at the long oration with which the eloquent strangers appealed to them.

"We have forgotten the beginning of it, and do not understand the end," was their answer to the Samian speech.

The men of Asia, then, bethinking themselves how to address these Laconians in their own manner, came back with an empty sack, and this time said no more than "The sack wants meal!" But still the laconic Spartans found fault with this speech as too long: to say "meal" would be enough for them, when the sack was shown empty.

In the end, however, they agreed to send an expedition against Polycrates, whose rich spoils the men of Sparta did not despise, for all that they professed to value no money but what was of iron. But they failed to conquer Samos; or, as some say, Polycrates bought them off with a cheat of lead money cunningly gilded.

Now the tyrant's pride and confidence were unbounded. He thought himself invincible, yet after all he was to come to ruin through his covetousness. The Persian satrap Orœtes, jealous of his wealth and power, wrote from Magnesia, proposing alliance and offering Polycrates a great treasure to help him in his conquests. The greedy lord of Samos sent a servant to see this treasure, to whom were shown eight chests filled with stones, but covered at the top with gold, ready for Polycrates to take away. He, on this report, could not be hindered from visiting the false Orœtes, though oracles and omens were adverse, and though his daughter begged him to stay at home, since in a dream she had seen him raised in the air, washed by Jove, and anointed by the sun.

But Polycrates took this dream to presage an exaltation, of which he made sure. He went to Orœtes, who, having got him into his hands, ordered him to be straightway crucified. So came to be washed by the sky and anointed by the sun a man who thought he had nothing to fear from heaven or earth.

CRŒSUS

The Lydians are said to have been the first people who coined money; and their king Crœsus had gathered so much gold that his name became a proverb for wealth. It is told that when Solon visited him at Sardis, the king showed this wise Greek over his treasure chambers, expecting to be admired as the most fortunate of men. But Solon looked coldly on all his display of riches, and bid him know that no man could be called happy till his death. Crœsus had cause thereafter to remember another saying of Solon, that his gold might be taken away by one who had more iron. Having in mind to make war on Cyrus, the king of Persia, he sent rich gifts to the oracle of Delphi, seeking to learn if this undertaking would turn out prosperously for him. The oracle gave answer that his war against Persia would overthrow a great empire. So it was when he himself came to be overthrown, and passed under the power of Cyrus with all his kingdom.

But even before the conquest of Lydia by the Persians, Crœsus was to learn how gold is no sure shield against calamity. He had two sons, one of whom was deaf and dumb, but the other, named Atys, such a youth as made his father's pride and joy. One night Crœsus dreamt that Atys would be wounded to death by an iron weapon. This dream so much troubled him, that he would no longer allow his favourite son to lead the Lydian army; he found him a wife to keep him at home; and all kinds of swords, spears, and other arms hung up in the palace he had stored away in a secret place, lest by accident any deadly point or edge might hurt the beloved Atys, who for his part, like a young man of courage and spirit as he was, took it ill that he should be so carefully guarded against harm.

Soon after his marriage, there came tidings of a huge wild boar ravaging the mountain region of Mysia. The Mysians sought help from the king against this terrible monster; and he sent them a band of picked hunters and hounds. Atys was eager to make one of this party, protesting that else he should pass for a coward with the people, with his old comrades in war and the chase, even with his new-wed wife. So hard he pressed for leave, that Crœsus had to explain his refusal by relating the dream in which he had seen his son slain by iron.

"A boar's tusks are not of iron!" cried the young man lightly; and gave his father no peace till he unwillingly agreed to let Atys go on that hunt.

To guard him the more surely, he gave Atys in special charge of a brave warrior named Adrastus, grandson of Midas, who had taken refuge at the court of Crœsus, banished from home on account of having accidentally killed his own brother. Grateful to the Lydian king for having harboured him in distress, Adrastus promised faithfully to watch over Atys and to answer for his safety with his own life.

The hunters set out in high spirits; they tracked the boar to its haunt; they closed round it in a circle, each keen to be foremost in striking it with spear or javelin. The boar fell under a shower of darts, but one went amiss. As Atys pressed in before the rest, he was pierced by the spear of Adrastus, and died according to his father's dream.

Miserable was the grief of Crœsus when he heard how his dream had come true; and most wretched was this rich king as he met the mournful train that brought the body of his son. With it came Adrastus, who fell on his knees and stretched out his hands, supplicating the bereaved father to take his life in atonement. For all Crœsus' affliction, he pitied and pardoned the remorseful man who unwittingly had worked the will of fate. But the remorseful Adrastus could not forgive himself, and he offered up his own life as a sacrifice upon the tomb of Atys, thus untimely taken before the Persian conqueror taught Crœsus how truly Solon had spoken: *Call no man happy till his death.*

THE TREASURY OF RHAMPSINITUS

Rhampsinitus of Egypt was another king of such great riches as might well put him in fear of robbery. To guard them safely he had built a strong treasure-house, of which he kept the key, and believed that no man could enter but himself. But the mason who built it had left one stone loose, which might easily be moved from the outside to let him in by stealth whenever he pleased: so are tyrants served.

When this man came to die, he told his two sons the secret of the stone, that they might rob the covetous king at will, by such an inheritance to live at ease and support their mother. Night after night, then, they stole into the treasury, and brought out as much gold as they could carry away. For a time their thieving went unnoticed, till at last Rhampsinitus began to suspect that some furtive hand must be at the heaps of money he found dwindling day by day; and to catch the thief he had man-traps set within the walls.

All unaware, the brothers came next night to turn the stone as before; then the first of them that pushed in, found himself held fast in a trap, from which no struggling could break him loose. Having nothing else for it, and expecting no mercy from the king, he bid his brother cut off his head, that it should never be known who the robbers were, nor need he, the living man, be brought into suspicion. The brother, unwilling as he was, did so, since so he must: he killed the unlucky companion of his adventure, and hastened away, carrying away the head that might have told a tale against them both.

Great was the king's astonishment to find a headless body in his trap; but the stone having been carefully replaced, he could not guess how the man had got in, nor even who he was, still less who had taken away the head. In this quandary, Rhampsinitus ordered the corpse to be hung up to a wall in public view, and sentinels set beside it, charged to seize and bring before him anyone that showed signs of grief over this dead man, whose friends or kindred might thus betray themselves.

But the robber's mother already knew his fate, and could not bear to let his body hang unburied, a gazing-stock for the people. She bid her surviving son fetch it away at all risks, else she would inform the king how he had broken into the treasury. Since the tearful woman would have it, he set his wits to work on some plan of cheating the sentinels, and hit upon this. With the money he had stolen, he bought a string of asses and loaded on them skins full of wine, to drive them by the wall on which his brother's body hung; then as he came past the watchful guard, he contrived to let the wine run out at the necks of the skins.

At the sight of wine flowing freely, the soldiers pressed forward to catch it in their drinking-vessels. At first the owner pretended to be angry, and all at a loss what to do with his leaky skins; but soon he made friends with the thirsty sentinels, desiring them to drink at will, rather than let the wine go to waste. So they did, drinking cup after cup till man by man they reeled over in drunken slumber. It being now dark, there was no one to hinder him taking his brother's body down; but before carrying it home, he shaved half the beards and the right cheeks of the heavily sleeping sentinels, leaving them thus marked for derision.

So bold grew this man that he came making love to the king's own daughter, who coaxed him into boasting that it was he who had robbed the treasury and cheated the guards. Hearing this in the dark, she would have seized him by the arm to give him up to her father; but the cunning fellow under his cloak had hidden one of the dead man's arms, which she now grasped to find it come away in her hand, while the thief slipped away without letting her see his face.

Rhampsinitus was so set on finding out who this bold and clever man could be that, all other efforts being in vain, he at last proclaimed full pardon and reward for him on disclosing himself. Trusting this promise, the man confessed himself to the king, who was so taken by his shrewdness as to give him his daughter in marriage and make him guardian of the treasury he had robbed.

THE LOVER'S LEAP

Sappho, famed as a poetess through the old Greek world, was a daughter of Lesbos, famous also for its wine. Her brother Charaxus, carrying wine to Egypt, is said to have ransomed from slavery and married Rhodopis, "the rosy cheeked", whom Sappho celebrated in an ode; and this woman, slave as she was, grew so rich that one of the pyramids passed for her monument. But another tale is told of Rhodopis and her fortune: that, as she was bathing in the Nile, an eagle caught up one of her sandals and carried it away over the fields of Egypt, to drop it into the lap of the king as he sat on his throne at Memphis; then the beauty of that sandal so took his heart that he sent out far and wide till he found the owner to make her his queen, after whose death he built a pyramid in memory of her.

Sappho had many lovers; but the one she loved best of all, she loved in vain. Between the islands of Lesbos and Chios plied a ferryman named Phaon, who was one day loosing his boat to set forth, when up came a hobbling old crone begging a passage, for love not for money, as she had not an obol to pay him.

"In with thee and welcome!" quoth Phaon, giving no more heed to this bundle of rags, as it seemed, huddled up among his other passengers.

The sun shone on a smooth sea, and a gentle wind filled the sail to carry the boat over without stroke of oar, as if some heavenly power wafted it on its way.

Then as the rest stepped on land, that old woman turned to thank Phaon for his kindness. But lo! she was old and bent no more; she showed fair and proud and richly clad, manifest now to the amazed ferryman as no other than Aphrodite, queen of love, who addressed him with a radiant smile.

"For the service thou hast lightly done me, I give thee a boon not to be bought by all the gold in the world: be for ever young and beautiful, as beseems one whose life is lit by my favour."

She breathed upon him, and in a trice Phaon felt himself another man. Fresh young blood throbbed from his heart; his wrinkled and sun-tanned cheeks grew smooth; the burden of years fell away from him; and he stood up the loveliest youth in Lesbos. They tell, too, how the goddess gave him an alabaster box of ointment, which was a charm to work on every woman that saw him, so that all the island's daughters could not but love him. But some say that the spell bestowed upon him lay in the root of a certain plant.

Too soon the eyes of Sappho were drawn to the transformed ferryman; and too surely her heart was caught in the spell of his blooming face. Forgetting her earlier sweethearts, she loved none but Phaon; and none like him. But alas! he loved her not again, for Aphrodite in making his face young and beautiful, had left his heart untouched. Friendly to man and woman, he would have no maid's devotion; and he turned away with a laugh from the passionate sighs which Sappho was skilled to put into song. When to songs and sighs his ears proved deaf, neither words nor tasks could soothe her longing.

> "As o'er her loom the Lesbian maid
> In love-sick languor hung her head,

Unknowing where her fingers strayed
She weeping turned away and said—

    " ' Oh, my sweet mother, 't is in vain,
    I cannot weave as once I wove,
    So wildered is my heart and brain
    With thinking of that youth I love.' "
               —*T. Moore.*

In vain, striking her lyre to the verses we still call
Sapphics, she invoked the goddess who had wasted on
Phaon that boon of beauty—

" Splendour-throned Queen, immortal Aphrodite,
Daughter of Jove, Enchantress, I implore thee
Vex not my soul with agonies and anguish;
    Slay me not, Goddess!
Come in thy pity—come, if I have prayed thee;
Come at the cry of my sorrow; in the old times
Oft thou hast heard, and left thy father's heaven,
    Left the gold houses,
Yoking thy chariot. Swiftly did the doves fly,
Swiftly they brought thee, waving plumes of wonder—
Waving their dark plumes all across the æther,
    All down the azure.

    .   .   .   .   .

So once again come, Mistress; and, releasing
Me from my sadness, give me what I sue for,
Grant me my prayer, and be as heretofore now
    Friend and protectress."
               —*Edwin Arnold.*

In vain she would have lured Phaon with her
sweetest songs; she had to sing of him to the winds.

" Peer of gods he seemeth to me, the blissful
Man who sits and gazes at thee before him,
Close beside thee sits, and in silence hears thee
    Silverly speaking,
Laughing love's low laughter. Oh this, this only
Stirs the troubled heart in my breast to tremble!
For should I but see thee a little moment,
    Straight is my voice hushed;

Yea, my tongue is broken, and through and through me
'Neath the flesh impalpable fire runs tingling;
Nothing see mine eyes, and a noise of roaring
    Waves in my ear sounds;
Sweat runs down in rivers, a tremor seizes
All my limbs, and paler than grass in autumn,
Caught by pains of menacing death, I falter,
    Lost in the love-trance."
                      —J. A. Symonds.

In vain for her came the shades of evening, so kindly to man and cattle.

" Oh Hesperus! thou bringest all good things—
Home to the weary, to the hungry cheer,
To the young bird the parent's brooding wings,
The welcome stall to the o'erlaboured steer;
Whate'er of peace about our hearthstone clings,
Whate'er our household gods protect of dear,
Are gathered round us by thy look of rest;
Thou bring'st the child, too, to the mother's breast."
                      —Byron.

In vain, when the unresponsive loved one went far out of reach of her endearments, she wrote to call him back to Lesbos.

" Gods, can no prayers, no sighs, no numbers move
One savage heart, or teach it how to love?
The winds my prayers, my sighs, my numbers bear;
The flying winds have lost them all in air.
Or when, alas, shall more auspicious gales
To these fond eyes restore thy welcome sails?
If you return, ah, why these long delays?
Poor Sappho dies while careless Phaon stays.
O launch the bark, nor fear the watery plain:
Venus for thee shall smooth her native main.
O launch thy bark, secure of prosperous gales:
Cupid for thee shall spread the swelling sails.
If you will fly—(yet ah, what cause can be,
Too cruel youth, that you should fly from me?)

If not from Phaon I must hope for ease,
Ah, let me seek it from the raging seas:
To raging seas unpitied I 'll remove;
And either cease to live or cease to love."

—Ovid, translated by Pope.

At last, growing old in despair, she could no longer endure the pangs of her despised love. Then as now, the sea broke upon a tall white cliff, crowned by a temple of Apollo, from which love-lorn maidens were wont to hurl themselves, to cure this and all other ills. Here, dressed in virgin white, she came to end her life, yet hoping against hope maybe that the waves might bear her to Phaon's side. Singing her last song, Sappho took the fatal leap, to be seen no more of men, among whom will never be forgotten the name and fate of one celebrated as the Tenth Muse.

ER AMONG THE DEAD[1]

Plato relates this tale of Er, a brave warrior of Pamphylia, who falling in battle had been laid on the pile to be burned, since he showed no sign of life. But there his body remained uncorrupted till the twelfth day, when, to the amazement of his friends, he rose as from the dead and told them how it had gone with him in the world of the Shades.

His soul, passing out of the body, had found itself among a crowd of others in a wonderful scene, where two chasms opened down through the earth, and two other passages led upwards to heaven. Here sat the judges who pronounced every man's sentence. The souls of the just were bidden take the heavenly way, each bearing in front a scroll that was his title to blessedness; while on the backs of the rest were hung records of their evil deeds; and they had to descend underground. But when it came to Er's turn, the judges decided that he should bear back to our world a report of what he saw and heard among the dead.

He saw, then, how the newly dead went their separate ways by one of the two openings upwards and downwards, while through the other two kept rising back to earth hapless shades, covered with filth and dust, and to meet them came from heaven a shining stream of

[1] This seems an artificial myth, composed for Plato's *Republic* by way of moral; but it may be based on some old story, and in the name of the hero has been found a hint of *Zoroaster*.

pure souls. On the plain between they mingled, recognizing those whom they had known during life, and eagerly exchanging news, the just full of joy, but the evildoers tearfully lamenting what they had borne for a thousand years. Er learned that each crime done in the flesh must be expiated during a tenfold term of shadowy life; that the most dreadful chastisements were for the impious and for parricides, and the richest rewards for those who had benefited their fellow men. He heard asked and told the fate of Ardiæus, a tyrant of his own country, who a thousand years before had killed his father and his elder brother among other crimes. As the souls that so long ago came down with this malefactor were at last released from their penance, they had shuddered to see how the chasm closed before him, and how he, along with others of like guilt, was dragged back by hideous fiery forms to be bound head and foot, flayed with scourges, and torn through blood-dripping thorns before being again cast back into the depths of Tartarus.

The souls now destined to return to earth remained for a week in this place; then on the eighth day they set out for a pillar of light that after four days' march came into view glowing like a rainbow, but more brilliant and more ethereal. This light is the axis of heaven and earth; and in the midst of it hangs by chains the adamantine spindle of Necessity, which she turns on her knees to keep whirling eight variously coloured circles that are the courses of the sun, the moon, the planets, and the fixed stars. With each circle whirls a Siren, chanting on a single note, so that their eight voices mingle in harmony to make the music of the Spheres.

Around the throne of Necessity, at equal distances sat her three daughters, the Fates—Lachesis, Clotho, and

Atropos—robed in white and wearing fillets on their heads. Their voices kept time with the Sirens: Lachesis sang the past, Clotho the present, Atropos the future; while from time to time all three touched the spindle to keep it turning. The souls had first to present themselves before Lachesis, ranged in order by a herald or minister who, placing on her knees the lots to be drawn for each, made proclamation to them all.

"Thus says the virgin Fate, daughter of Necessity: wandering souls, ye are about to enter a new body of life. Each may choose his own lot in turn; but the choice will be irrevocable. Virtue has no respect of persons; it cleaves to who honours it, and flies from the despiser. On your own heads be your fortune: the gods take for it no blame."

First they had to draw lots for the order which they should choose, except only Er, bidden to stand by and watch. The same hierophant then strewed on earth before them all the conditions of human life, from tyranny to beggary, fame, beauty, riches, poverty, health, sickness, these fates either unmingled or a blending of good or evil. There were animal lives, too, mixed up with men's and women's. That minister of the fates now urged the souls not to choose hastily, since the last had as good a chance as the first.

But he who came foremost eagerly seized on the greatest sovereignty that offered itself; then, having looked closer into this lot, found that he was destined to devour his own children, among other enormities, whereon he cried out bitterly, accusing for such a choice fortune, the gods, everything but his own folly. This soul had come from Elysium, and had formerly lived in a well-ordered state, where he owed his virtue rather to custom and disposition than to wisdom. So indeed not a few of the souls from Elysium went wrong in their choice, for want of experience in the evils of life. On the other hand, those released from the world below had often been schooled by their own sufferings and those of others to be more considerate. Thus it happened that most of the souls now exchanged a good for an evil lot, or the contrary.

Er was struck both by pity and amusement to note how strangely the souls made their choice, guided apparently by some recollection of their former life. He saw Orpheus pick out the body of a swan, as if in hatred of the women who had torn him to pieces, not caring to owe his birth to such a one. He saw a swan choose the human figure, and other birds become musicians, while Thamyris took for himself the form of a nightingale. One soul chose to be a lion: this was Ajax, son of Telamon, who had never got over his rage when the arms of Achilles were awarded to another; and he would not be a man again. Him followed Agamemnon, whose former fate also had soured him against mankind, so now he selected the life of an eagle. Atalanta, admiring the honour in which strength of body was held, chose to become an athlete outright. The soul of Epeus, maker of the Trojan Horse, preferred the lot of a woman clever with her fingers; and the buffoon Thersites, who came up among the rest, was turned into a monkey. Ulysses came last of all; and he, remembering the past mishaps that had sickened his soul of adventurousness, carefully searched out and at last found, in an out-of-the-way corner, a quiet simple life which all the other souls had despised; then he exclaimed that had he had the first choice, he would have asked no better.

When all the souls had made their choice, in the

same order they passed before Lachesis, who gave to each the guardian genius that should accompany him through life and carry out the destiny bound up with his chosen lot. This genius led them to Clotho, that with a turn of the spindle she should confirm their choice. Each soul had to touch the spindle, and next was brought up to Atropos, twisting the thread between her fingers to make unbreakable what had been spun by Clotho. Lastly they defiled before the throne of Necessity, the soul and its genius side by side.

Thence they passed on to the bare plain of Lethe, where no tree shaded them from a scorching heat. The night was spent by the river of Forgetfulness, whose waters can be borne away in no vessel. From its stream each must drink, and some rashly drank too deep, so as to lose all memory of what had gone before. Thereupon they fell asleep, but towards midnight burst out a din of thunder and earthquake, by which the souls were roused to be scattered here and there like shooting stars to the different spots where they should be reborn. As for Er, he had not been suffered to drink of Lethe, yet he knew not how his soul came back to his body; but all at once, opening his eyes next morning, he found himself alive stretched out on his funeral pyre.

DAMON AND PYTHIAS[1]

(AFTER SCHILLER.)

The halls of Dionysius
Had Damon sought with hidden steel,
But, seized and bound by watchful guards,
Must needs his stealthy aim reveal.
Bold was the desperate man's reply:
"I would have freed the commonweal!"
Then short the tyrant's sentence—"Die!"

"Behold me ready for my fate,
Nor would I crave my life from thee;
Yet wert thou pleased to grant respite,
My sister's wedding day to see,
Pythias, my friend, will lie in bail—
Three days I ask, and only three—
He braves thy vengeance, should I fail."

Sour smiled the lord of Syracuse,
And answered after hasty thought:
"The boon I grant—so let it be,
Yet by thy surety's peril bought:
Beyond the term if thou delay,
He to the shameful cross is brought,
And thus thy guilt is done away."

[1] In Schiller's ballad, which a little expands the classical story, the names of the heroes stood originally *Mœrus* and *Selinuntius*; and by Cicero Pythias is named *Phintias*; but this translation presents them in the nomenclature that has become most famous.

His friend he seeks and tells his need:
" So thou wilt pledge thy life for mine,
Three days of grace have I to pay
The forfeit of my rash design.
Thou know'st the cause; thou know'st my faith—
Ere the third sun hath ceased to shine,
I win thee back from bonds and scaith."

His friend embraced him silently,
And to the tyrant's dungeon sped.
Then Damon to his sister's home
Hath ta'en his way, and seen her wed;
But the third morning's early dawn
Rouses him from his restless bed,
While a dear life still lies in pawn.

All through that night, the mountain tops
Had been beset with storms of rain.
The springs welled up, the brooks rushed down,
The anxious traveller toiled in vain;
Hourly he saw the river swell,
And, ere the bridge his haste could gain,
Its arch in crashing ruin fell.

Dismayed he wandered by the brink,
And gazed upon the further shore:
He cried aloud, no answer came,
Only the torrent's echoing roar;
He looked around, no help saw he,
No bridge, no boat to bear him o'er
That stream fast growing to a sea.

Kneeling, with tears and lifted hands
To heaven he raised his piteous cry.

" Oh, stem, ye gods, the sundering flood!
Let me but pass!—the moments fly;
And, when the clouded sun goes down,
For me my trustful friend must die,
Should I have failed to reach yon town!"

But still the waters rush and roar,
Still mounts the sun with watery beam,
Then Damon, fearless in despair,
Plunges into the swollen stream,
And struggles through its whirling tide,
Till, favoured by the will supreme,
He wins across to grasp the side.

He gained firm ground, and hurried on;
But while his thanks to Jove he spoke,
From shelter of a gloomy wood
What crew of savage outlaws broke!
They barred his path, that robber band,
And, menacing with murderous stroke,
Bade the belated traveller stand.

" What would ye?   Forfeit to the king
My life; nought else have I to take!"
Suddenly from the nearest hand
He snatched a heavy knotted stake,
To fall on them with maddened cry:
" No pity, then, for Pythias' sake!"
Three he strikes down, the others fly.

Soon, as the sun shines hotly forth,
He flags beneath its scorching ray;
Fainting he strives to stagger on,
But sinks upon his knees to pray:

"Twice aided thus in desperate strait,
Shall I now perish by the way,
And leave my friend to such a fate!"

And hark! there gathers, hard at hand,
A purling murmur on his ear.
And see! from out the barren rock
A fountain's silvery spray appear,
Trickling into a green-set pool.
The grateful waters, crystal clear,
His fevered limbs refresh and cool.

When now the sunset gleams aslant
Through leafy screens, and on the meads
Each tree draws out a lengthening shade,
Two travellers from the town he heeds,
For words that chill his heart with dread
He hears them say as past he speeds,
"Soon Pythias to the cross is led!"

What inward goadings urge him on!
What anxious tremblings wing his feet!
At length, the towers of Syracuse,
Gilt with the evening's glory, greet
His eager eyes; but at the gate,
Comes hurrying forth his lord to meet,
The faithful servant, Philostrate.

"Back! Back! Thy life thou still mayst save,
But for thy friend thou com'st too late.
By now he hangs in writhing throes;
From hour to hour did hope await
Thy coming, and his steadfast faith
The tyrant's scoff could not abate:
Now hope and trust are lost in death."

" Is it too late?   Can I not save?
In vain did Pythias hold me true?
Yet shall no tyrant mock at love,
If doom our comradeship renew!
Boast not that friendly faith hath failed,
Thou cruel king!   For one, let two
Victims upon the cross be nailed."

The dusk draws on.   Lo! by the gate
That fearsome engine raised on high,
Whereto rough ropes and brutal hands
Are binding Pythias to die.
The guards, the gaping crowd give way—
" Hold, butchers, hold!   See, here am I,
The man for whom in plight he lay!"

The friends fell in each other's arms;
Wondered the people all to see.
They wept for mingled joy and grief,
Nor any eye from tears was free.
This tale men carried to the king,
And some touch of humanity
Stirred him before his throne to bring

Damon and Pythias.   Long he gazed,
Astounded, on them: " Ye the art
Have found to teach me trust is true,
And unto mercy move my heart.
If such the love of friends, let me
With your fair fellowship have part,
And in so strong a bond join Three!"

RHŒCUS

(James Russell Lowell.)

Hear now this fairy legend of old Greece,
As full of freedom, youth, and beauty still
As the immortal freshness of that grace
Carved for all ages on some Attic frieze.

  A youth named Rhœcus, wandering in the wood
Saw an old oak just trembling to its fall,
And, feeling pity of so fair a tree,
He propped its gray trunk with admiring care,
And with a thoughtless footstep loitered on.
But, as he turned, he heard a voice behind
That murmured "Rhœcus!" 'T was as if the leaves
Stirred by a passing breath, had murmured it,
And, while he paused bewildered, yet again
It murmured "Rhœcus!" softer than a breeze.
He started, and beheld with dizzy eyes
What seemed the substance of a happy dream
Stand there before him, spreading a warm glow
Within the green glooms of the shadowy oak.
It seemed a woman's shape, yet all too fair
To be a woman, and with eyes too meek
For any that were wont to mate with gods.
All naked like a goddess stood she there,
And like a goddess all too beautiful
To feel the guilt-born earthliness of shame.

" Rhœcus, I am the Dryad of this tree,"
Thus she began, dropping her low-toned words
Serene, and full, and clear, as drops of dew;
" And with it I am doomed to live and die;
The rain and sunshine are my caterers,
Nor have I other bliss than simple life;
Now ask me what thou wilt, that I can give,
And with a thankful joy it shall be thine."

Then Rhœcus, with a flutter at the heart,
Yet, by the prompting of such beauty, bold,
Answered: " What is there that can satisfy
The endless craving of the soul but love?
Give me thy love, or but the hope of that
Which must be evermore my spirit's goal."
After a little pause she said again,
But with a glimpse of sadness in her tone,
" I give it, Rhœcus, though a perilous gift;
An hour before the sunset meet me here."
And straightway there was nothing he could see
But the green glooms beneath the shadowy oak,
And not a sound came to his straining ears
But the low trickling rustle of the leaves,
And far away upon an emerald slope
The falter of an idle shepherd's pipe.

Now, in those days of simpleness and faith,
Men did not think that happy things were dreams
Because they overstepped the narrow bourn
Of likelihood, but reverently deemed
Nothing too wondrous or too beautiful
To be the guerdon of a daring heart.
So Rhœcus made no doubt that he was blest,
And all along unto the city's gate

Earth seemed to spring beneath him as he walked,
The clear, broad sky looked bluer than its wont,
And he could scarce believe he had not wings,
Such sunshine seemed to glitter through his veins
Instead of blood, so light he felt and strange.

Young Rhœcus had a faithful heart enough,
But one that in the present dwelt too much
And, taking with blithe welcome whatsoe'er
Chance gave of joy, was wholly bound in that,
Like the contented peasant of a vale,
Deemed it the world, and never looked beyond.
So, haply meeting in the afternoon
Some comrades who were playing at the dice,
He joined them and forgot all else beside.

The dice was rattling at the merriest,
And Rhœcus, who had met but sorry luck,
Just laughed in triumph at a happy throw,
When through the room there hummed a yellow bee
That buzzed about his ear with down-dropped legs
As if to light.   And Rhœcus laughed and said,
Feeling how red and flushed he was with loss,
" By Venus! does he take me for a rose?"
And brushed him off with rough, impatient hand.
But still the bee came back, and thrice again
Rhœcus did beat him off with growing wrath.
Then through the window flew the wounded bee,
And Rhœcus tracking him with angry eyes,
Saw a sharp mountain-peak of Thessaly
Against the red disc of the setting sun,—
And instantly the blood sank from his heart,
As if its very walls had caved away.
Without a word he turned, and, rushing forth,

Ran madly through the city and the gate,
And o'er the plain, which now the wood's long shade,
By the low sun thrown forward broad and dim,
Darkened wellnigh unto the city's wall.

Quite spent and out of breath he reached the tree,
And, listening fearfully, he heard once more
The low voice murmur " Rhœcus! " close at hand:
Whereat he looked around him, but could see
Nought but the deepening glooms beneath the oak.
Then sighed the voice, " Oh, Rhœcus! nevermore
Shalt thou behold me or by day or night,
Me, who would fain have blessed thee with a love
More ripe and bounteous than ever yet
Filled up with nectar any mortal heart:
But thou didst scorn my humble messenger,
And sent'st him back to me with bruised wings.
We spirits only show to gentle eyes.
We ever ask an undivided love;
And he who scorns the least of Nature's works
Is thenceforth exiled and shut out from all.
Farewell! for thou canst never see me more."

Then Rhœcus beat his breast, and groaned aloud,
And cried, " Be pitiful! forgive me yet
This once, and I shall never need it more!"
" Alas!" the voice returned, " 't is thou art blind,
Not I unmerciful; I can forgive,
But have no skill to heal thy spirit's eyes;
Only the soul hath power o'er itself."
With that again there murmured " Nevermore!"
And Rhœcus after heard no other sound,
Except the rattling of the oak's crisp leaves,
Like the long surf upon a distant shore,

Raking the sea-worn pebbles up and down.
The night had gathered round him: o'er the plain
The city sparkled with its thousand lights,
And sounds of revel fell upon his ear
Harshly and like a curse; above, the sky,
With all its bright sublimity of stars,
Deepened, and on his forehead smote the breeze:
Beauty was all around him and delight,
But from that eve he was alone on earth.

CEPHALUS AND PROCRIS

(Thomas Moore.)

A Hunter once in that grove reclined
  To shun the noon's bright eye,
And oft he wooed the wandering wind
  To cool his brow with its sigh.
While mute lay even the wild bee's hum,
Nor breath could stir the aspen's hair,
His song was still "Sweet air, oh come!"
While Echo answered "Come, sweet air!"

But, hark, what sounds from the thicket rise!
  What meaneth that rustling spray?
"'T is the white-horned doe," the Hunter cries,
  "I have sought since break of day!"
Quick o'er the sunny glade he springs,
The arrow flies from his sounding bow;
"Hilliho—hilliho!" he gaily sings,
While Echo sighs forth "Hilliho!"

Alas, 't was not the white-horned doe
  He saw in the rustling grove,
But the bridal veil, as pure as snow,
  Of his own young wedded love.
And, ah, too sure that arrow sped,
For pale at his feet he sees her lie;—
"I die, I die," was all she said,
While Echo murmured, "I die, I die!"[1]

---

[1] Our poet hardly brings out all the points of this story, as that poor Procris was spying on her husband, believing herself to have some cause for jealousy in his invocation of an invisible being, and that she herself had given him the fatal dart by which she fell, a charm bestowed on her by Artemis.

TITHONUS[1]

(Tennyson.)

The woods decay, the woods decay and fall,
The vapours weep their burthen to the ground,
Man comes and tills the field and lies beneath,
And after many a summer dies the swan.
Me only cruel immortality
Consumes: I wither slowly in thine arms,
Here at the quiet limit of the world,
A white-hair'd shadow roaming like a dream
The ever silent spaces of the East,
Far-folded mists, and gleaming halls of morn.

Alas! for this gray shadow, once a man—
So glorious in his beauty and thy choice,
Who madest him thy chosen, that he seem'd
To his great heart none other than a God!
I ask'd thee, " Give me immortality ".
Then didst thou grant mine asking with a smile,
Like wealthy men who care not how they give.
But thy strong Hours indignant work'd their wills,
And beat me down and marr'd and wasted me,
And tho' they could not end me, left me maim'd
To dwell in presence of immortal youth,
Immortal age beside immortal youth,

[1] Tithonus was Priam's brother, beloved by Eos (the Dawn), who procured for him the gift of immortality, but without enduring youth, so that he became a prototype of Swift's *Struldbrugs*.

And all I was, in ashes.   Can thy love,
Thy beauty, make amends, tho' even now,
Close over us, the silver star, thy guide,
Shines in those tremulous eyes that fill with tears
To hear me?   Let me go: take back thy gift.
Why should a man desire in any way
To vary from the kindly race of men,
Or pass beyond the goal of ordinance
Where all should pause, as is most meet for all?

A soft air fans the cloud apart; there comes
A glimpse of that dark world where I was born.
Once more the old mysterious glimmer steals
From thy pure brows, and from thy shoulders pure,
And bosom beating with a heart renew'd.
Thy cheek begins to redden thro' the gloom,
Thy sweet eyes brighten slowly close to mine,
Ere yet they blind the stars, and the wild team
Which love thee, yearning for thy yoke, arise,
And shake the darkness from their loosen'd manes,
And beat the twilight into flakes of fire.

Lo! ever thus thou growest beautiful
In silence, then before thine answer given
Departest, and thy tears are on my cheek.

Why wilt thou ever scare me with thy tears,
And make me tremble lest a saying learnt,
In days far-off, on that dark earth, be true?
"The Gods themselves cannot recall their gifts."

Ay me! ay me! with what another heart
In days far-off, and with what other eyes
I used to watch—if I be he that watch'd—
The lucid outline forming round thee; saw

The dim curls kindle into sunny rings;
Changed with thy mystic change, and felt my blood
Glow with the glow that slowly crimson'd all
Thy presence and thy portals, while I lay,
Mouth, forehead, eyelids, growing dewy-warm
With kisses balmier than half-opening buds
Of April, and could hear the lips that kiss'd
Whispering I knew not what of wild and sweet,
Like that strange song I heard Apollo sing,
While Ilion like a mist rose into towers.

Yet hold me not for ever in thine East:
How can my nature longer mix with thine?
Coldly thy rosy shadows bathe me, cold
Are all thy lights, and cold my wrinkled feet
Upon thy glimmering thresholds, when the steam
Floats up from those dim fields about the homes
Of happy men that have the power to die,
And grassy barrows of the happier dead.
Release me, and restore me to the ground;
Thou seest all things, thou wilt see my grave:
Thou wilt renew thy beauty morn by morn;
I earth in earth forget these empty courts,
And thee returning on thy silver wheels.

LAODAMIA[1]

(WORDSWORTH.)

" With sacrifice before the rising morn
Vows have I made, by fruitless hope inspired;
And from the infernal gods, mid shades forlorn,
Of night, my slaughtered lord have I required:
Celestial pity I again implore;
Restore him to my sight—great Jove, restore!"

So speaking, and by fervent love endowed
With faith, the suppliant heavenward lifts her hands;
While, like the sun emerging from a cloud,
Her countenance brightens, and her eye expands;
Her bosom heaves and spreads, her stature grows;
And she expects the issue in repose.

O terror! what hath she perceived?   O joy!
What doth she look on? whom doth she behold?
Her hero slain upon the beach of Troy?
His vital presence—his corporeal mould?
It is—if sense deceive her not—'t is he!
And a god leads him—wingèd Mercury!

Mild Hermes spake—and touched her with his wand
That calms all fear: " Such grace hath crowned thy
    prayer,

[1] See page 237.

Laodamìa! that at Jove's command
Thy husband walks the paths of upper air:
He comes to tarry with thee three hours' space;
Accept the gift—behold him face to face!"

Forth sprang the impassioned queen her lord to clasp,
Again that consummation she essayed;
But unsubstantial form eludes her grasp
As often as that eager grasp was made.
The phantom parts—but parts to re-unite,
And re-assume his place before her sight.

" Protesilàus, lo! thy guide is gone!
Confirm, I pray, the vision with thy voice:
This is our palace—yonder is thy throne:
Speak, and the floor thou tread'st on will rejoice.
Not to appal me have the gods bestowed
This precious boon—and blessed a sad abode."

" Great Jove, Laodamìa, doth not leave
His gifts imperfect: spectre though I be,
I am not sent to scare thee or deceive;
But in reward of thy fidelity.
And something also did my worth obtain;
For fearless virtue bringeth boundless gain.

" Thou know'st, the Delphic oracle foretold
That the first Greek that touched the Trojan strand
Should die; but me the threat could not withhold:
A generous cause a victim did demand;
And forth I leapt upon the sandy plain;
A self-devoted chief—by Hector slain."

" Supreme of heroes—bravest, noblest, best!
Thy matchless courage I bewail no more,
Which then, when tens of thousands were depressed
By doubt, propelled thee to the fatal shore;
Thou found'st—and I forgive thee—here thou art—
A nobler counsellor than my poor heart.

" But thou, though capable of sternest deed,
Wert kind as resolute, and good as brave;
And he, whose power restores thee, hath decreed
That thou should'st cheat the malice of the grave;
Redundant are thy locks, thy lips as fair
As when their breath enriched Thessalian air.

" No spectre greets me, no vain shadow this:
Come, blooming hero, place thee by my side!
Give, on this well-known couch, one nuptial kiss
To me, this day a second time thy bride!"
Jove frowned in heaven; the conscious Parcæ threw
Upon those roseate lips a Stygian hue.

" This visage tells thee that my doom is past:
Know, virtue were not virtue if the joys
Of sense were able to return as fast
And surely as they vanish.   Earth destroys
Those raptures duly—Erebus disdains:
Calm pleasures there abide—majestic pains.

" Be taught, O faithful consort, to control
Rebellious passion; for the gods approve
The depth, and not the tumult, of the soul;
A fervent, not ungovernable love.
Thy transports moderate; and meekly mourn
When I depart, for brief is my sojourn."

" Ah, wherefore?   Did not Hercules by force
Wrest from the guardian monster of the tomb
Alcestis, a re-animated corse,
Given back to dwell on earth in vernal bloom?
Medea's spells dispersed the weight of years,
And Æson stood a youth mid youthful peers.

" The gods to us are merciful—and they
Yet further may relent: for mightier far
Than strength of nerve and sinew, or the sway
Of magic potent over sun and star,
Is love, though oft to agony distressed,
And though his favourite seat be feeble woman's breast.

" But if thou goest I follow—" "Peace!" he said—
She looked upon him and was calmed and cheered;
The ghastly colour from his lips had fled;
In his deportment, shape, and mien, appeared
Elysian beauty, melancholy grace,
Brought from a pensive, though a happy place.

He spake of love, such love as spirits feel
In worlds whose course is equable and pure;
No fears to beat away—no strife to heal—
The past unsighed for, and the future sure:
Spake of heroic arts in graver mood
Revived, with finer harmony pursued:

Of all that is most beauteous—imaged there
In happier beauty; more pellucid streams,
An ampler ether, a diviner air,
And fields invested with purpureal gleams;
Climes which the sun, who sheds the brightest day
Earth knows, is all unworthy to survey.

Yet there the soul shall enter which hath earned
That privilege by virtue. " Ill," said he,
" The end of man's existence I discerned,
Who from ignoble games and revelry
Could draw, when we had parted, vain delight
While tears were thy best pastime, day and night:

" And while my youthful peers, before my eyes,
(Each hero following his peculiar bent)
Prepared themselves for glorious enterprise
By martial sports, or, seated in the tent,
Chieftains and kings in council were detained;
What time the fleet at Aulis lay enchained.

" The wished-for wind was given; I then revolved
The oracle, upon the silent sea;
And, if no worthier led the way, resolved
That, of a thousand vessels, mine should be
The foremost prow in pressing to the strand,
Mine the first blood that tinged the Trojan sand.

" Yet bitter, ofttimes bitter, was the pang
When of thy loss I thought, beloved wife!
On thee too fondly did my memory hang,
And on the joys we shared in mortal life,
The paths which we had trod—these fountains—
    flowers;
My new-planned cities, and unfinished towers.

" But should suspense permit the foe to cry,
'Behold, they tremble! haughty their array,
Yet of their number no one dares to die!'
In soul I swept the indignity away:
Old frailties then recurred: but lofty thought,
In act embodied, my deliverance wrought.

"And thou, though strong in love, art all too weak
In reason, in self-government too slow;
I counsel thee by fortitude to seek
Our blest re-union in the shades below.
The invisible world with thee hath sympathized;
Be thy affections raised and solemnized.

"Learn by a mortal yearning to ascend
Towards a higher object.　Love was given,
Encouraged, sanctioned, chiefly for that end:
For this the passion to excess was driven—
That self might be annulled: her bondage prove
The fetters of a dream, opposed to love."

Aloud she shrieked! for Hermes reappears!
Round the dear shade she would have clung—'t is vain.
The hours are past—too brief had they been years;
And him no mortal effort can detain:
Swift, toward the realms that know not earthly day,
He through the portal takes his silent way,
And on the palace floor a lifeless corse she lay.

By no weak pity might the gods be moved;
She who thus perished, not without the crime
Of lovers that in reason's spite have loved,
Was doomed to wander in a grosser clime,
Apart from happy ghosts—that gather flowers
Of blissful quiet mid unfading bowers.

Yet tears to human suffering are due;
And mortal hopes defeated and o'erthrown
Are mourned by man, and not by man alone,
As fondly he believes.　Upon the side
Of Hellespont (such faith was entertained)
A knot of spiry trees for ages grew

From out the tomb of him for whom she died:
And ever, when such stature they had gained
That Ilium's walls were subject to their view,
The trees' tall summits withered at the sight;
A constant interchange of growth and blight!

ARETHUSA[1]

(Shelley.)

Arethusa arose
From her couch of snows
In the Acroceraunian mountains,—
From cloud and from crag,
With many a jag,
Shepherding her bright fountains.
She leapt down the rocks
With her rainbow locks
Streaming among the streams:—
Her steps paved with green
The downward ravine
Which slopes to the western gleams:
And gliding and springing,
She went, ever singing,
In murmurs as soft as sleep;
The Earth seemed to love her,
And Heaven smiled above her,
As she lingered towards the deep.

Then Alpheus bold,
On his glacier cold,
With his trident the mountains strook;
And opened a chasm
In the rocks;—with the spasm
All Erymanthus shook.
And the black south wind
It concealed behind

[1] Arethusa is the fountain nymph alluded to in the story of Persephone (p. 124).

The urns of the silent snow,
    And earthquake and thunder
    Did rend in sunder
The bars of the springs below:
    The beard and the hair
    Of the river God were
Seen through the torrent's sweep,
    As he followed the light
    Of the fleet nymph's flight
To the brink of the Dorian deep.

    " Oh, save me!   Oh, guide me!
    And bid the deep hide me,
For he grasps me now by the hair!"
    The loud Ocean heard,
    To its blue depths stirred,
And divided at her prayer;
    And under the water
    The Earth's white daughter
Fled like a sunny beam;
    Behind her descended,
    Her billows, unblended
With the brackish Dorian stream:—
    Like a gloomy stain
    On the emerald main
Alpheus rushed behind,—
    As an eagle pursuing
    A dove to its ruin
Down the stream of the cloudy wind.

    Under the bowers
    Where the Ocean Powers
Sit on their pearled thrones:

Through the coral woods
Of the weltering floods,
Over heaps of unvalued stones:
Through the dim beams
Which amid the streams
Weave a net-work of coloured light;
And under the caves,
Where the shadowy waves
Are as green as the forest's night:—
Outspeeding the shark,
And the sword-fish dark,
Under the ocean foam,
And up through the rifts
Of the mountain clifts
They passed to their Dorian home.

And now on their fountains
In Enna's mountains,
Down one vale where the morning basks
Like friends once parted
Grown single-hearted,
They ply their watery tasks.
At sun-rise they leap
From their cradle steep
In caves of the shelving hill;
At noon-tide they flow
Through the woods below
And the meadows of Asphodel;
And at night they sleep
In the rocking deep
Beneath the Ortygian shore;—
Like spirits that lie
In the azure sky
When they love but live no more.

CUPID'S TRICK

(Anacreon—*translated by* T. Moore.)

'T was noon of night, when round the pole
The sullen Bear is seen to roll;
And mortals, wearied with the day,
Are slumbering all their cares away:
An infant, at that dreary hour,
Came weeping to my silent bower,
And wak'd me with a piteous prayer,
To shield him from the midnight air.
" And who art thou," I waking cry,
" That bid'st my blissful visions fly?"
" Ah, gentle sire!" the infant said,
" In pity take me to thy shed;
Nor fear deceit: a lonely child
I wander o'er the gloomy wild.
Chill drops the rain, and not a ray
Illumes the drear and misty way!"

I heard the baby's tale of woe;
I heard the bitter night-winds blow,
And sighing for his piteous fate,
I trimm'd my lamp and op'd the gate.
'T was Love! the little wandering sprite,
His pinion sparkled through the night.
I knew him by his bow and dart;
I knew him by my fluttering heart.

Fondly I take him in, and raise
The dying embers' cheering blaze;
Press from his dank and clinging hair
The crystals of the freezing air,
And in my hand and bosom hold
His little fingers thrilling cold.

And now the embers' genial ray
Had warm'd his anxious fears away;
" I pray thee," said the wanton child,
(My bosom trembled as he smil'd,)
" I pray thee let me try my bow,
For through the rain I 've wander'd so,
That much I fear, the midnight shower
Has injur'd its elastic power."
The fatal bow the urchin drew:
Swift from the string the arrow flew;
As swiftly flew as glancing flame,
And to my inmost spirit came!
" Fare thee well," I heard him say,
As laughing wild he wing'd away;
" Fare thee well, for now I know
The rain has not relax'd my bow;
It still can send a thrilling dart,
As thou shalt own with all thy heart!"

INDEX

WITH PRONUNCIATION OF NAMES ACCORDING TO ENGLISH USAGE

[The method of transliteration here used is based on that adopted in *The Imperial Dictionary of the English Language*, as follows:—*a* as in *man*, except often when followed by *r* in same syllable, when it is as *a* in *far*; *ā* long, or as in *mane*; *au* as in *cause*; *e* as in *met*; *ē* as in *mete*; *i* as in *in*; *ī* as in *mine*; *o* short, or as in *on*; *ō* long, or as in *go*; *u* as in *us*; *ū* as in *use*.]

Abderus (ab-dē′rus), companion of Hercules, 106.

Absyrtus (ab-sir′tus), brother of Medea, 158, 166.

Abydos (a-bī′dos), town on the Hellespont, 367.

Acarnan (a-kar′nan), son of Alcmæon, 216.

Acarnania (a-kar-nā′ni-a), 217.

Acastus (a-kas′tus), son of Pelias, 153.

Achæans (a-kē′anz), the, 6.

Achelous (a-ke-lō′us), river, 215.

— river god, 47, 115, 216.

Acheron (a′ker-on), river of Hades, 25.

— river of the Euxine, 157.

Achilles (a-kil′lēz), son of Peleus and Thetis, 26, 232, 238, 269, 312.

Acis (ā′sis), lover of Galatea, 66.

Acrisius (a-kris′i-us), king of Argos, 75.

Acropolis (a-krop′o-lis) of Athens, the, 88.

Actæon (ak-tē′on), 36.

Admetus (ad-mē′tus), king in Thessaly, 118, 153.

Adonis (a-dō′nis), 39.

Adrastus (a-dras′tus), king of Argos, 206.

— refugee at Sardis, 288.

Æacus (ē′a-kus), judge in Hades, 27.

Aedon (a-ē′don), wife of Zethus, 66.

Æetes (ē-ēt′ēz), king of Colchis, 152, 158.

Ægean (ē-jē′an) Sea, or Archipelago, the, 75, 186, 283.

Ægeus (ē′jūs), king of Athens, 177.

Ægis (ē′jis) of Athene, the, 85.

Ægisthus (ē-jis′thus), paramour of Clytemnestra, 284.

Æneas (ē-nē′as), son-in-law of Priam, 234, 248, 263, 276, 281.

Æneid (ē′ne-id or ē-nē′id), *the*, 61, 281.

Æolus (ē′o-lus), king of the Winds, 53, 304.

Æsculapius (es-kū-lā′pi-us), 33.

Æson (ē′son), king of Iolcos, 148.

Æthra (ēth′ra), mother of Theseus, 177.

Ætolia (ē-tōl′i-a), 90.

Africa (af′ri-ka), 21, 110, 167.

Agamemnon (a-ga-mem′non), king of Argos, 231, 240, 283, 311, 401.

Agelaus (a-je-lā′us), suitor of Penelope, 353.

Agenor (a-jē′nor), king of Tyre, 192.

Ages of Man, the, 18.

Aglaia (a-glai′a), one of the Graces, 40

429

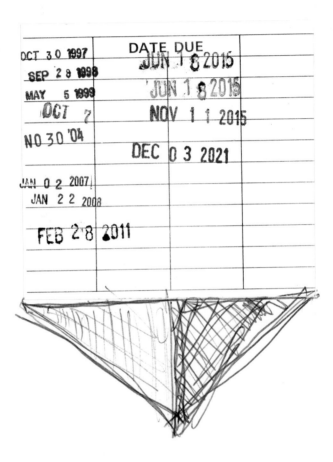